Nineteenth and Twentieth Century Drama: A Selective Bibliography of English Language Works

Numbers 1-3029

Lawrence S. Thompson

G. K. HALL & CO., 70 LINCOLN STREET, BOSTON, MASS.

Library of Congress Cataloging in Publication Data

Thompson, Lawrence Sidney, 1916-
    Nineteenth and twentieth century drama.

    Includes indexes.
    1. English drama--19th century--Bibliography.
2. American drama--19th century--Bibliography.
3. English drama--20th century--Bibliography.
4. American drama--20th century--Bibliography.
I. Title.
Z2014.D7T5 [PR721]   016.822'008   75-29255
ISBN 0-8161-7842-9

This publication is printed on permanent/durable acid-free paper.

Manufactured in the United States of America

To Haven and Ann

Contents

Introduction

The present catalog is the first part of what will ultimately be a bibliography of the dramatic literature of the English-speaking peoples of the nineteenth century, as comprehensive as possible, and of the twentieth century selectively. While each volume will be in a separate alphabet, the numbers of the items will be consecutive, and the indexes cumulative.

All types of dramatic literature are included. Classical and traditional drama, as well as monologues, children's plays, puppet plays, vaudeville, school drama, tendentious drama (e.g., temperance plays), and other genres not in the formal tradition of classical tragedy or comedy are within the scope of the bibliography. Indeed, some of the material is from what may be unique originals (e.g., at least one from the compiler's collection of Kentucky imprints). Some of the material is quasi-dramatic.

All of the material is in print in the sense that microfiches and eye-legible copy are available immediately from the master negatives in the General Microfilm Company's vaults in Cambridge, Massachusetts. Each year over 500 new titles are added, and handlists are available to supplement this bibliography until they are cumulated in a second volume. Thus, by the very nature of the genesis of this bibliography, the present portion is uneven.

Originally it was planned to follow standard bibliographies, and this policy will continue, but with interruptions. For nineteenth-century British drama it is easy enough to identify the dramatic literature through the Cambridge Bibliography of English Literature and the sixth volume of Allerdyce Nicoll's A History of English Drama which contains the catalog of plays for 1680-1900. For the early twentieth century, his English Drama, 1900-1930, is the best available guide. Yet even for British plays this is insufficient, for there are many important manuscripts in the Lord Chamberlain's Collection in the British Library. American dramatic literature must be pieced together, for the Bibliography of American Literature includes relatively few plays due to the necessarily selective policy of the editors in choosing authors for inclusion. A list of American playwrights was compiled, and titles of works by them were

recorded from such sources as G. K. Hall's catalog of the Harris
Collection at Brown, the Library of Congress catalog, and, as far as
it has gone, the National Union Catalog of pre-1956 imprints.

Above all, the collection is intended to be a source of immediate
assistance to students of dramatic literature, and many specific
titles, often not in the bibliographies mentioned, are made available
in photographic reprints to assist scholars who need them at once.
Thus we have many variant editions or even second or third copies of
the same edition with stage directions for a specific production.
Not only are classic translations of foreign authors (e.g., Sir
Walter Scott's Götz von Berlichingen) in the collection but also
other translations of importance for the literature of the English-
speaking peoples. There are titles from all geographical areas due
to the proliferation of English as a literary medium, thus not simply
the work of Tagore but also that of less important Indian dramatists
who write in English. In general, however, works in foreign languages such as the plays written for the once flourishing German
stage of St. Louis or French stage of New Orleans have been included
in corresponding collections of the dramatic literatures of those
languages. A minor exception is the occasional parallel text,
generally of the English original and the translation (mainly German
but also a few others as in the case of grand opera) when the intro-
ductions or critical apparatus may be of importance. Whenever certain unusual groups such as nineteenth-century American temperance
plays or "Ethiopian" drama (basic for the study of the Black in
American tradition) are available, they were included for fear of
losing the opportunity to include something that might not exist
elsewhere in individual titles or a corpus. Thus there are some
"Ethiopian" plays found by the compiler in a hole-in-the-wall Chicago bookshop some years ago. A few non-dramatic titles appear,
since they were bound with dramatic titles and are pertinent to them
for the readers of the microfiche edition.

A large proportion of the collection has been copied from
originals in the Library of Congress, and for the sake of convenience
Library of Congress catalog cards were used both for descriptive and
indexing purposes. Certain inconsistencies reflect the varying
Library of Congress practices over the last three-quarters of a
century. In the case of other titles not copied from the Library
of Congress the general style of the printed cards has been followed.
Supplementary information and corrections will be welcomed by the
compiler for use as corrigenda and addenda to be printed in future
volumes.

Like other massive collections, this one will never be complete.
Hopefully it will ultimately include the corpus of published British
and American drama of the nineteenth and early twentieth centuries
as recorded in the bibliographies as well as other representative
pieces not found in these sources. Deus sit propitius huic biblio-
grafico!

Drama File

1   ABARBANELL, JACOB RALPH. A model pair, a comedy in one act.
    By Jacob Abarbanell (Ralph Royal [pseud.]). Chicago, The
    dramatic publishing co., 1882. 11p.

2   ABBOTT, GEORGE, 1889-   . Coquette; a play in three acts,
    by George Abbott and Ann Preston Bridgers. New York,
    London [etc.] Longmans, Green and co., 1928. x, 137p.

3   ACKERMAN, IRENE. The gold mine. A play. In five acts. By
    Irene Ackerman. New York, J. Polhemus, 1881. 52p.

4   _____. Inez, a drama in three acts. By Irene Ackerman. New
    York, C. H. Bauer [1882]. 62p.

5   Actus Fatis, a play written in honor of Vergil's birthday by
    the members of the Vergil Class, Hockaday School, Dallas,
    Texas, Marguerite Grow, Teacher. [n.p., n.d.]. 6p.
    (American Classical League Service Bureau, No. 675).

6   ADAMS, FLORENCE DAVENPORT. A home fairy, a play for children.
    Chicago, The dramatic publishing co. [n.d.]. 7p.

7   _____. A king in disguise, a play for children. Chicago,
    The dramatic publishing co. [n.d.]. 7p.

8   _____. The sleepers awakened, a play for children. Chicago,
    The dramatic publishing co. [n.d.]. 8p.

9   ADAMS, JUSTIN. At the picket line, a military drama of the
    civil war, in five acts. Boston, Walter H. Baker and co.,
    1893. 39p.

10 _____. Down East; a comedy in four acts, by Justin Adams...
    Boston, W. H. Baker and co., 1900. 41p. On cover:
    Baker's edition of plays.

1

ADAMS, JUSTIN

11 ADAMS, JUSTIN. T'riss; or, Beyond the Rockies; a drama of western life in four acts, by Justin Adams... Boston, W. H. Baker and co., 1893. 34p. On cover: Baker's edition of plays.

12 ADDISON, H. R. Locked in with a lady. A sketch from life, in one act... New York, Robert M. De Witt [n.d.]. 11p.

13 _____. Lo Zingaro; a melo-dramatic opera, in two acts... London, Thomas Hailes Lacy [n.d.]. 26p. front.

14 ADDISON, JULIA DULANY. Four short playlets in English dealing with the legends of early Rome. [n.p., n.d.]. 4p. (American Classical League Service Bureau, No. 460).

15 AESCHYLUS, 525/4-456 B.C. The Eumenides (The Furies) of Aeschylus. Trans. into rhyming verse by Gilbert Murray. London, George Allen and Unwin, ltd. [n.d.]. 62p.

16 _____. The tragedies of Aeschylus: literally translated. With critical and illustrative notes, and an introduction, by Theodore Alois Buckley... London and New York, Henry G. Bohn, 1849. xx, 234p. front. (port.).

17 AKERMAN, WILLIAM. The cross of sorrow. A tragedy in five acts. By William Akerman. London and New York, G. Bell and sons, 1894. viii p., 1ℓ., 102p.

18 ALBERRY, JAMES. Two roses. An original comedy, in three acts... New York, Samuel French and son [n.d.]. 66p.

19 _____. The two thorns. A comedy in four acts. New York, The De Witt publishing house [n.d.]. 36p.

20 _____. ... Oriana. A romantic legend in three acts. By James Alberry. Produced at the Globe theatre, under the management of H. J. Montague... 15th February, 1873. London, Printed by Judd and co. [1873?]. 38p.

21 ALDRICH, THOMAS BAILEY, 1836-1907. ... Mercedes, and later lyrics. Boston, New York, Houghton, Mifflin and co., 1884. vi p., 2ℓ., [11]-111p.

22 ALFRED, WILLIAM, 1923- . Agamemnon. [1st American ed.] New York, Knopf, 1954. 88p.

23   ALLAN, MARK. The mystery of Ardennes, Le mystère d'Ardennes. A drama in five acts, by Mark Allen... Woburn, Mass., Printed at the Advertiser office, 1888. 62p.

24   ALLEN, ALICE E. The night before Christmas, a Christmas drama. Lebanon, Ohio, March bros., 1906. 16p.

25   ALLEN, ETHAN, 1832-1911. Washington; or, The revolution. A drama. (In blank verse). Founded upon the historic events of the war for American independence. By Ethan Allen. Illustrated by Henry Kratzner. In two parts... Part first: From the Boston massacre to surrender of Burgoyne. Part second: From Red Bank and Valley Forge to Washington's inauguration as President of the United States... London, Chicago [etc.] F. T. Neely [c1899]. 2v. in 1. fronts. (ports.) plates.

26   ALLEN, JOHN H. The fruits of the wine cup, a drama, in three acts. New York, Dick and Fitzgerald [n.d.]. 28p.

27   All's fair in love and war, a comedietta, in three acts. New York, Harold Roorbach [1877]. 18p.

28   ALMAR, GEORGE. The battle of Sedgemoor; or, The days of Kirk and Monmouth: a historical drama, in three acts... London, John Cumberland [n.d.]. 48p. front.

29   _____. The bull-fighter; or, The bridal ring, a romantic drama, in three acts... London, John Cumberland [n.d.]. 39p. front.

30   _____. The charcoal-burner; or, The dropping well of Knaresborough. A drama, in two acts... New York, Samuel French [n.d.]. 32p.

31   _____. ... Crossing the line; or, Crowded houses. A comic drama, in two acts... New York, Samuel French [n.d.]. 21p. (The minor drama, no. xcv).

32   _____. ... Gaspardo, the gondolier; or, The three banished men of Milan! A drama, in three acts. By George Almar, esq. The only ed. correctly marked, by permission, from the prompter's book. Boston, C. H. Spencer [1872]. 27p. (Spencer's universal stage. no. 42).

33   _____. The knights of St. John; or, The fire banner! A melodrama, in two acts... London, Thomas Hailes Lacy [n.d.]. 36p. front.

ALMAR, GEORGE

34   ALMAR, GEORGE. ... Oliver Twist. A serio-comic burletta, in
      four acts... New York, Samuel French [n.d.]. 44p.
      (French's standard drama, no. ccxxviii).

35   _____. The robber of the Rhine: a drama, in two acts, by
      George Almar... Printed from the acting copy, with re-
      marks, biographical and critical, by D.-G. ... As per-
      formed at the Theatres Royal... London, Davidson [n.d.].
      40p. incl. front. (Cumberland's Minor theatre. London
      [ca. 1830-55] v. 10 [no. 3]).
          Remarks by George Daniel, editor of the series.
          Reissued in Davidson's shilling volume of Cumberland's
      plays. v. 25 [no. 3].

36   _____. The rover's bride, or, The bittern's swamp: a roman-
      tic drama, in two acts, by George Almar... Printed from
      the acting copy, with remarks, biographical and critical,
      by D.-G. ... As performed at the Theatres Royal... Lon-
      don, Davidson [n.d.]. 47p. incl. front. (Cumberland's
      Minor theatre. London [ca. 1830-55) v. 11 [no. 5]).
          Remarks by George Daniel, editor of the series.

37   _____. The shadow! A mother's dream: a romantic drama, in
      three acts... London, John Cumberland [n.d.] 56p. front.

38   AMBLENT, MARK, 1860-   . A snug little kingdom; a comedy of
      Bohemia in three acts, by Mark Amblent... New York, S.
      French; London, S. French, 1906. 71p.

39   AMCOTT, VINCENT. Poisoned, a ludicrous farce in one act, for
      male characters only. New York, Dick and Fitzgerald
      [n.d.]. 13p.

40   Americana; or, A new tale of the genii: being an allegorical
      mask, in five acts. Baltimore, Printed by W. Pechin, in
      Second-street, between Gay and South-streets, 1802. 128p.

41   AMES, A. D. Driven to the wall; or, True to the last, a play
      in four acts. Clyde, Ohio, A. D. Ames [n.d.]. 34p.

42   AMESBURY, HOWARD. The fortune teller of dismal swamp. A
      melodrama in four acts. Clyde, Ohio, Ames' publishing
      house [n.d.]. 27p.

43   AMHERST, J. H., 1776-1851. ... The battle of Waterloo, a
      grand military melodrama, in three acts... London, Dun-
      combe [n.d.]. 36p. (Duncombe's edition).

44   _____. ... Will Watch; or, The black phantom: a melo-drama,
      in two acts, by J. H. Amherst... As now performed at the
      London theatres, Embellished with a fine engraving, by Mr.
      Jones... London, J. Duncombe [18--]. 28p. front. (Dun-
      combe's edition [of the British theatre, v. 18].)

45   ANDERSON, EMILY L. The fairy mirror, children's spectacular
      play in three acts. New York, Edgar S. Werner and co.,
      1904. 20p.

46   ANDERSON, ISABEL WELD PERKINS. Everybody and other plays for
      children, by Isabel Anderson; with illustrations by Junius
      Cravens. New York, The Shakespeare press, 1914. 155p.
      incl. front., illus. Reprinted in part from various
      periodicals. CONTENTS. - Everybody. - King Foxy of Muir
      Glacier. - Little Doubt. - Merry Jerry. - The Gee Whiz. -
      Justice Whisker's trial. - The witch of the woods. - Little
      Madcap's journey.

47   ANDERSON, THOMAS F. The trials of a country editor, an
      original sketch. Clyde, Ohio, Ames' publishing co. [n.d.].
      12p.

48   ANDRE, R. Minette's birthday, a vaudeville in one act. Chi-
      cago, The dramatic publishing co. [1890]. 17p.

49   ANDREEV, LEONID NIKOLAEVICH, 1870-1919. Plays, by Leonid
      Andreyeff: The black maskers, The life of man, The Sabine
      women; tr. from the Russian by Clarence L. Meader and Fred
      Newton Scott; with an introductory essay by V. V. Brusya-
      nin. Authorized ed. New York, C. Scribner's sons, 1915.
      xxvi, 2ℓ., 3-214p. front. (port.).

50   ANDREWS, GEORGE H. The scarlet letter. A drama in three
      acts from N. Hawthorne's celebrated novel. Boston, Walter
      H. Baker co. [1871]. 24p.

51   ANZENGRUBER, LUDWIG. The farmer forsworn. 1914. (In Kuno
      Francke, ed., The German classics of the nineteenth and
      twentieth century [New York, The German publication so-
      ciety, 1914], v. 16, p. 112-188). Translated by Adolf
      Busse.

52   ARCHER, THOMAS. ... Asmodeus; or, The little devil's share.
      A drama, in two acts... New York, Samuel French [n.d.].
      32p. (French's standard drama, no. cciv).

ARCHER, THOMAS

53   ARCHER, THOMAS. ... Monseigneur, and the jeweller's appren-
       tice. A drama, in three acts... Boston, Charles H.
       Spencer [n.d.]. 35p. (Spencer's universal stage, no.
       xxxviii).

54   ARDEN, H. T. The belle of the barley-mow; or, The wooer, the
       waitress and the villain... London, Thomas Hailes Lacy
       [n.d.]. 20p.

55   _____. Princess Charming; or, The bard, the baron, the
       beauty, the buffer and the bogey... London, Thomas Hailes
       Lacy [n.d.]. 24p.

56   ARISTOPHANES, ca. 450-ca. 385 B.C. The birds, translated in-
       to corresponding metres by Benjamin Bickley Rogers, Lon-
       don, G. Bell and sons, ltd., 1920. 137p.

57   _____. The comedies of Aristophanes, a new and literal trans-
       lation, from the second revised text of Dindorf, with
       notes and extracts from the best metrical versions. By
       William James Hickie. London, Bell and Baldy, 1865. 2v.
       front. (port.) (Half-title: Bohn's classical library).
       Paged continuously.

58   _____. The comedies of Aristophanes; a new and literal trans-
       lation, from the revised text of Dindorf. With notes and
       extracts from the best metrical versions. By William
       James Hickie... London, Bell and Daldy, 1865, 1860. 2v.
       front. (port.). CONTENTS: I. The Acharnians, Knights,
       Clouds, Wasps, Peace, and Birds. - II. Lysistrata, The
       Thesmophoriazusae, Frogs, Ecclesiazusae, and Plutus.

59   _____. The frogs, translated into English rhyming verse by
       Gilbert Murray. London, George Allen and Unwin, ltd.
       [n.d.]. 136p.

60   ARMSTRONG, LEROY. An Indiana man, a comedy in four acts.
       Chicago, T. S. Denison [1897]. 48p.

61   ARNOLD, SIR EDWIN, 1832-1904. Adzuma, or the Japanese wife,
       a play in four acts, New York, Charles Scribner's sons,
       1893. 170p.

62   ARNOLD, SAMUEL JAMES, 1774-1852. The devil's bridge. An
       opera, in three acts, by Samuel James Arnold... Printed
       from the acting copy, with remarks, biographical and
       critical, by D.-G. ... As performed at the Theatres
       Royal... London, J. Cumberland [n.d.]. 52p. incl. front.

AUBER, DANIEL FRANÇOIS ESPRIT

(ARNOLD, SAMUEL JAMES)
    (In Cumberland's British theatre. London, ca. 1825-55.
    v. 42 [no. 6]).
       Remarks by George Daniel, editor of the series.
       Without the music (by Horn and Braham).

63   _____. Free and easy. A musical farce, in two acts, by
    Samuel James Arnold... Printed from the acting copy, with
    remarks, biographical and critical, by D.-G. ... As per-
    formed at the Theatres Royal... London, J. Cumberland and
    son [n.d.]. 50p. incl. front. (Cumberland's British
    theatre. London, ca. 1825-55. v. 42 [no.3].
       Remarks by George Daniel, editor of the series.
       Without the music (by J. Addison).

64   _____. My aunt: a petit comedy, in two acts, as performed at
    the Theatres Boston, New-York and London. Corrected from
    the prompt-book, Boston. Boston, Published by C. Callender,
    Shakspeare circulating library, 25 School street, 1820.
    35p.
       Without the music (by John Addison).

65   ASHMEAD, HENRY GRAHAM, 1838-1920. The captain's ward; a
    drama in four acts, by Graham Ashmead. [Chester, Pa., J.
    Spencer, printer, 1902]. 35p.

66   [ASHTON, WINIFRED]. Naboth's vineyard; a stage piece, by
    Clarence Dane [pseud.]. New York, The Macmillan co., 1926.
    4 p.ℓ., 90p.

67   _____. The way things happen; a story in three acts, by
    Clemence Dane [pseud.]. New York, The Macmillan co., 1924.
    3 p.ℓ., 93p.

68   AUBER, DANIEL FRANCOIS ESPRIT, 1782-1871. The favourite
    opera, in three acts, entitled The crown jewels, (Les
    diamans de la couronne.). The music by Auber, adapted to
    the English stage by Mr. Tully, the words by E. Fitz-
    ball... As first performed at the Theatre Royal, Drury
    Lane... London, Chappel [etc., 1846?]. 50p.

69   _____. ... Auber's celebrated opera Les diamans de la
    couronne, (The crown diamonds.). Edited for the piano
    forte, by Rudolf Nordmann. London, Boosey and sons [185-
    ?]. 2 p.ℓ., ii p., 1ℓ., 107p. front.

AUSTIN, ALFRED

71   AUSTIN, ALFRED, 1835-1913. Flodden Field, a tragedy, New
      York and London, Harper and bros., publishers, 1903.
      137p.

72   _____. Fortunatus the pessimist. London, Macmillan and co.,
      1892. 179p.

73   _____. Heralds of the dawn, a play in eight scenes, New York,
      John Lane and co., 1912. 93p.

74   AUSTIN, MARY. The arrow maker, a drama in three acts. New
      York, Duffield and co., 1911. 128p.

75   [AYTOUN, WILLIAM EDMONDSTONE]. Firmilian, "spasmodic"
      tragedy, by T. Percy Jones [pseud.]. New York, 1854.
      165p.

76   B., M.   E.
      Dross; or, The root of evil. A domestic drama in three
      acts. New York, The De Witt publishing house [n.d.].
      62p.

77   BABCOCK, CHARLES W. Adrift. A temperance drama, in three
      acts. Clyde, Ohio, A. D. Ames, 1880. 23p.

78   Back from Californy; or, Old clothes, an original darky
      eccentricity. Chicago, T. S. Denison [n.d.]. 8p.

79   BAHR, HERMAN, 1863-1934. The master; adapted for the Ameri-
      can stage by B. F. Glazier. Philadelphia, N. L. Brown,
      1918. 89p.

80   BAILLIE, JOANNA, 1762-1851. Dramas, by Joanna Baillie...
      London, Longman, Rees, Orme, Brown, Green, and Longman,
      1836. 3 v. CONTENTS. - v. 1. Romiero: a tragedy. The
      alienated manor: a comedy. Henriquez: a tragedy. The
      martyr: a drama. - v. 2. The separation: a tragedy. The
      stripling: a tragedy... written in prose. The phantom: a
      musical drama. Enthusiasm: a comedy. - v. 3. Witchcraft:
      a tragedy in prose. The homicide: a tragedy in prose,
      with occasional passages of verse. The bride: a drama.
      The match: a comedy. Appendix [notes, etc.].

81   BAKER, ELIZABETH. Chains: a play, in four acts. Boston,
      Luce, 1913. 80p.

BAKER, GEORGE MELVILLE

82   _____. Miss Robinson; a play in three acts, by Elizabeth
      Baker... London, Sidgwick and Jackson, ltd., 1920. 114p.

83   BAKER, GEORGE MELVILLE, 1832-1890. Above the clouds. By the
      author of "Sylvia's soldier", "Once on a time"... Boston,
      G. M. Baker and co. [1876]. [4], 99-168p. On cover: The
      amateur drama (no. 16).

84   _____. A baker's dozen. Original humorous dialogues. By
      George M. Baker... Boston, W. H. Baker and co. [1900].
      137p.

85   _____. ed. Ballads of bravery. Ed. by George M. Baker.
      With forty full-page illustrations. Boston, Lee and
      Shepard, 1877. 2 p.ℓ., [ix]-xi, [13]-174p. incl. plates.
      front.

86   _____. Better than gold. A drama in four acts. By George
      M. Baker... Boston, G. M. Baker and co., 1879. 58p.

87   _____. The Boston dip. A comedy, in one act. By the author
      of "Sylvia's soldier", "Once on a time"... Boston, G. M.
      Baker and co. [1873]. [4], 215-240p. On cover: The ama-
      teur drama (no. 9).

88   _____. Comrades. A drama in three acts, by George M. Baker.
      [Boston] Printed, not published, 1877. 52p.

89   _____. The duchess of Dublin, a farce. By the author of
      "Sylvia's soldier", "Once on a time"... Boston, G. M.
      Baker and co. [1873]. [4], 241-274p. On cover: The
      amateur drama.

90   _____. ... The exhibition drama: comprising drama, comedy,
      and farce, together with dramatic and musical entertain-
      ments, for private theatricals, home representations,
      holiday and school exhibitions. By George M. Baker...
      Boston, Lee and Shepard; New York, Lee, Shepard and Dill-
      ingham, 1875. [5], 3-24p. front., illus., plates, diagrs.
      The amateur drama series. CONTENTS. - Enlisted for the
      war; or, The home-guard. - Never say die. - The champion
      of her sex. - The visions of freedom. - The merry Christ-
      mas of the old woman who lived in a shoe. - The tournament
      of Idylcourt. - A thorn among the roses. - A Christmas
      carol.

BAKER, GEORGE MELVILLE

91   BAKER, GEORGE MELVILLE. The flower of the family. A comedy in three acts, by the author of "Sylvia's soldier", "Once on a time"... Boston, G. M. Baker and co. [1876]. 72p. On cover: The amateur drama (no. 12).

92   _____. The flowing bowl, a drama in three acts, by George M. Baker. Boston, G. M. Baker and co., 1885. [4], 5-66p.

93   _____. Gentlemen of the jury. A farce. By the author of "Sylvia's soldier", "Once on a time"... Boston, G. M. Baker and co. [1873]. [4], 171-186p. On cover: The amateur drama (no. 6).

94   _____. Gustave the professor, a comedy in one act, translated from the French of M. M. Gaston Maques and Alfred Bertinot. Boston, Walter H. Baker and co. [1888]. 24p.

95   _____. Handy dramas, for amateur actors. New pieces for home, school, and public entertainment. By George M. Baker... Boston, Lee and Shepard; New York, C. T. Dillingham, 1877. 3 p.ℓ., 5-6, 3-356p. front., illus., plates, diagr. CONTENTS. - The flower of the family. - A mysterious disappearance. - Above the clouds. - Shall our mothers vote? - Paddle your own canoe. - One hundred years ago. - The little brown jug. - Seeing the elephant.

96   _____. Little brown jug. By the author of "Sylvia's soldier", "Once on a time"... Boston, G. M. Baker and co. [1873]. 1 p.ℓ. [5]-68p. On cover: The amateur drama (no. 9).

97   _____. Messmates, a drama in three acts, by George M. Baker. Boston, W. M. Baker and co. [1887]. [2], 53p. On cover: The globe drama.

98   _____. My brother's keeper. A drama, in three acts. By the author of "Sylvia's soldier", "Once on a time"... Boston, G. M. Baker and co. [1873]. 67p. On cover: The amateur drama (no. 3).

99   _____. A mysterious disappearance. A farce. By the author of "Sylvia's soldier", "Once on a time"... Boston, G. M. Baker and co. [1876]. [4], 73-97p. On cover: The amateur drama (no. 13).

100   _____. ed. ... Negro dialect recitations, comprising a series of the most popular selections in prose and verse, edited by George M. Baker... Boston, Lee and Shepard; New York. C. T. Dillingham, 1888. 129p. (Baker's dialect series).

BAKER, GEORGE MELVILLE

101   _____. Nevada; or, The lost mine. A drama in three acts.
By George M. Baker... Boston, G. M. Baker and co., 1882.
55p. On cover: The globe drama.

102   _____. An old man's prayer. By George M. Baker. Illustrated
by Hammatt Billings. Boston, Lee and Shepard, 1858. 57,
[2]p. incl. 1 illus., 7 p.ℓ., front.

103   _____. One hundred years ago; or, Our boys of 1776. A patriotic drama in two acts. By the author of "Sylvia's
soldier", "Once on a time"... Boston, G. M. Baker and co.,
1876. 54p. On cover: The amateur drama (no. 11).

104   _____. Our folks. A play in three acts... dramatized from
Running to waste: the story of a tomboy, by the same
author. Boston, Walter H. Baker and co. [1878]. 78p.

105   _____. Paddle your own canoe. A farce. By the author of
"Sylvia's soldier", "Once on a time"... Boston, G. M.
Baker and co. [1876]. 189-215p. diagr. On cover: The
amateur drama (no. 13).

106   _____. Past redemption. A drama in four acts. By George M.
Baker... Boston, G. M. Baker and co., 1975. 47p.

107   _____. Rebecca's triumph. A drama in three acts. (For
female characters only). Written expressly for the "L. O.
C. cooking club" of Chicago. By George M. Baker. Boston,
G. M. Baker and co., 1879. 55p. On cover: The globe
drama.

108   _____. The revolt of the bees. An allegory. By the author
of "Sylvia's soldier", "Once on a time"... Boston, G. M.
Baker and co. [1878]. 1 p.ℓ., 69-84p. On cover: The
amateur drama (no. 9).

109   _____. Seeing the elephant, by the author of "Sylvia's
soldier", "Once on a time"... Boston, G. M. Baker and
co. [1873]. 1 p.ℓ., 69-92p. 1 illus. On cover: The
amateur drama (no. 10).

110   _____. The Seldarte craze, a farce. Boston, Walter H. Baker
and co. [1887]. 32p. On cover: The globe drama.

111   _____. The seven ages, a tableau entertainment. By the
author of "Sylvia's soldier", "Once on a time"... Boston,
G. M. Baker and co. [1873]. [4], 187-213p. illus. On
cover: The amateur drama (no. 3).

BAKER, GEORGE MELVILLE

112   BAKER, GEORGE MELVILLE. Titania; or, The butterflies' carnival, a fairy extravaganza in two acts, by George M. Baker. Boston, G. M. Baker and co., 1880. 38p. On cover: Plays for little folks. By George M. Baker (no. 2).

113   BALCH, WILLIAM LINCOLN. Alice in blunderland, a farce in one act for four male and two female performers [Chicago]. Will Rossiter, 1903. 26p.

114   _____. A true lover's knot, a comedietta for vaudeville team [Chicago] Will Rossiter, 1903. 22p.

115   BALFE, M. W. The Bohemian girl. Opera in three acts. Boston, J. A. Cummings and co., 1875. 32p.

116   BAMBERGER, MICHAEL. About four o'clock, comedietta. Indianapolis, 1910. 11p.

117   BANGS, JOHN KENDRICK, 1862-1922. The bicyclers and three other farces. New York, Harper and bros., 1896. 176p.

118   _____. The real thing, and three other farces, by John Kendrick Bangs... New York and London, Harper and bros., 1909. 4 p.ℓ., 135p. front., 3 p.ℓ. CONTENTS. - The real thing. - The Barringtons' "at home." - The return of Christmas. - The side show.

119   _____. The worsted man; a musical play for amateurs, by John Kendrick Bangs. New York and London, Harper and bros., 1905. 5 p.ℓ., vii, 85, [1] p. front.

120   BANVARD, JOSEPH, 1810-1887. Priscilla; or, Trials for the truth. A historic tale of the Puritans and the Baptists. By Rev. Joseph Banvard... Boston, Heath and Graves, 1854. 11p., 1ℓ., 13-405p. incl. plates., front.

121   [BARBIER, JULES] 1825-1901. Dinorah: the pilgrimage to Ploermel. A romantic opera in three acts, the music by G. Meyerbeer. The English version paraphrased from the original French by Henry F. Chorley... London [Covent Garden theatre, 18--]. 1 p.ℓ., [v]-vi, [7]-50p.

122   _____. Faust, a lyric drama in five acts; book by J. Barbier and M. Carré, music by Charles Gounod. Boston, O. Ditson co.; New York, C. H. Ditson and co.; [etc., etc.], 1906. 47p.

BARKER, JAMES NELSON

123 _____. Jeanne d'Arc. Historical drama in five acts, in verse. By P. J. Barbier. Translated into English verse by Frederic Lyster... New York, F. Rullman, 1891. 1 p.ℓ., [1], 3-33, 3-33p. French and English texts numbered in duplicate.

124 BARCUS, JAMES S. The boomerang; or, Bryan's speech with the wind knocked out. A dialogue, including the full text of Bryan's famous Madison square garden speech, together with complete answers to each argument by various significant characters. By James S. Barcus... New York, J. S. Barcus and co., 1896. 180p.

125 BARING, MAURICE, 1874-1945. Diminutive dramas, by Maurice Baring. London, M. Secker [1919]. 4 p.ℓ., 200p. Reprinted from the "Morning post." CONTENTS. - Catherine Parr. - The drawback. - Pious Aeneas. - The death of Alexander. - The rehearsal. - The blue harlequin. - The member for literature. - Caligylas' picnic. - The Aulis difficulty. - Don Juan's failure. - Calpurnia's dinner-party. - Lucullus' dinner-party. - The stoic's daughter. - After Euripides' "Electra." - Jason and Medea. - King Alfred and the neat-herd. - Rosamund and Eleanor. - Ariadne in Naxos. - Velasquez and the "Venus." - Xantippe and Socrates.

126 _____. Diminutive dramas. Boston and New York, Houghton Mifflin co., 1911. 224p.

127 _____. His Majesty's embassy, and other plays, by Maurice Baring. Boston, Little, Brown, and co., 1923. 3 p.ℓ., 3-222p., 1 ℓ. CONTENTS. - His Majesty's embassy. - Manfroy, Duke of Athens. - June and after.

128 BARKER, HARLEY GRANVILLE. Three plays... The marrying of Ann Leette. The Voysly inheritance. Waste. New York, Mitchell Kennerley [1909]. 351p.

128A BARKER, JAMES NELSON, 1784-1858. The Indian princess; or, La belle sauvage. An operatic melodrame in three acts. By J. N. Barker. Philadelphia, Printed by T. & G. Palmer, for G. E. Blake, no. 1, South Third Street, 1808. iv, 74p.

129 _____. ... Marmion; or, The battle of Flodden Field. A drama in five acts. By James N. Barker, esq. With a portrait of Mr. Duff in the character of Marmion... Philadelphia, A. R. Poole; New York, E. M. Murden [etc., etc., 1826]. 62p. front. (port.)

BARKER, JAMES NELSON

130   BARKER, JAMES NELSON. ... The tragedy of superstition, by
James N. Barker... carefully corrected from the prompt
books of the Philadelphia theatre. By M. Lopez, prompter.
[Philadelphia] A. R. Poole [1826]. 68p. front. (port.)

131   BARNARD, CHARLES, 1838-1920. Alonzo's letter, a monologue
for a lady, in one scene, by Charles Barnard... New York,
E. S. Werner, 1897. 6p.

132   _____. Joe, a comedy of child life in two acts, by Charles
Barnard... Chicago, The Dramatic publishing co. [1897].
22p.

133   _____. The triple wedding. A drama, in three acts, by
Charles Barnard... New York, H. Roorbach, 1887. 36p.

134   _____. The triple wedding; or, The forging of the ring. A
play, designed for a small company, by Charles Barnard...
Printed for private circulation only. [New York, T. L.
De Vinne and co., 1883]. 32p.

135   BERNARD, WILLIAM BAYLE, 1807-1875. ...His last legs, a farce
in two acts, by William Bayle Bernard; with the stage
business, cast of characters, costumes, relative positions,
etc. New York, S. French [187-]. 41p. (The minor drama.
no. vi).

136   BARNES, CHARLOTTE M. S. Plays, prose, and poetry. Philadelphia, E. H. Butler and co., 1848. 491p.

137   BARNETT, MORRIS, 1800-1856. ...The serious family. A comedy
in three acts. By Morris Barnett; with the stage business,
cast of characters, costumes, relative positions, etc.
New York, S. French, [185-?]. 2 p.ℓ., [7]-48p. (French's
standard drama. No. LXXIX).

138   _____. The yankee peddler; or, Old times in Virginia, a
farce in one act. Clyde, Ohio, A. D. Ames [n.d.]. 16p.

139   BARNEY, Mrs. Alice P. About Thebos, a play. Washington,
1909. [28]p.

140   BARNEY, LAURA CLIFFORD. God's heroes, a drama in five acts.
London, Kegan Paul, Trench, Trübner and co.; Philadelphia,
J. B. Lippincott co. [1910]. 107p.

141   Barney the baron. A farce, in one act... New York, Samuel
French [n.d.]. 16p.

142   BARNUM, MADALENE DEMAREST, 1874-   . School plays for all
      occasions, by Madalene D. Barnum... New York, N. Y.,
      Newark, Barse and Hopkins [1922]. 2 p.ℓ., 7-186p.

143   BARR, E. NELSON. Broken links. A drama in five acts. Clyde,
      Ohio, Ames' publishing co. [n.d.]. 23p.

144   _____. Clearing the mists. A drama in three acts, by E.
      Nelson Barr and J. M. Hogan... Clyde, Ohio, Ames' pub-
      lishing co., 1889. 21p.

145   BARRIE, JAMES MATTHEW, 1860-1937. Half hours. London, Hod-
      der and Stoughton [n.d.]. 207p.

146   _____. Der Tag. New York, Hodder and Stoughton [n.d.].
      40p.

147   BARROWS, ELSIE I. Rome and the modern world; a play in En-
      glish, by Elsie I. Barrows and Helen E. Whipple. [n.p.,
      n.d.]. 8p. (American Classical League Service Bureau,
      No. 430).

148   BARRYMORE, WILLIAM, d. 1845. ... The blood red knight! or,
      The fatal bridge! A melodramatic romance, in two acts...
      London, Duncombe and co. [n.d.]. 20p. front. (Duncombe's
      edition).

149   _____. The fatal snow storm; a romantic drama, in two
      acts... London, G. H. Davidson [n.d.]. 34p.

150   _____. Gilderoy; or, The bonnie boy: a melodrama, in two
      acts, by W. Barrymore... Printed from the acting copy,
      with remarks, biographical and critical... As now per-
      formed at the Royal Coburg Theatre... London, T. Richard-
      son [1829]. 54p. incl. front. (On cover: Richardson's
      new minor drama... no. 12).

151   _____. The snow storm; or, Lowina of Tobolskow. A melo-
      dramatick romance... Baltimore, J. Robinson, 1818. 36p.

152   _____. ...Wallace: the hero of Scotland. An historical
      drama in three acts. By W. Barrymore... Boston, W. V.
      Spencer [1856?]. 30p. front. (Added t.-p.: Spencer's
      Boston theatre. [v. 6] no. 48). (Added t.-p. [series
      title] and "Memoir of Mr. J. B. Howe" [with portrait as
      Wallace]: 4p. prefixed).

BARTLETT, ARCHIE ERNEST

153   BARTLETT, ARCHIE ERNEST, 1866-   . Dramas of camp and
      cloister, by Archie E. Bartlett. Boston, R. G. Badger
      [c1907]. 2 p.ℓ., 252p. CONTENTS. - Rahna's triumph. -
      The last judgement. - Five acts of love. - Love's enchant-
      ment. - Empire of Talinis.

154   BARTON, ANDREW. The first comic opera in America; The dis-
      appointment; or, The force of credulity, a new American
      comic opera of two acts, by Andrew Barton... New York
      Federal theatre project, Play bureau, 1936. 4 p.ℓ., 43,
      2 ℓ.

155   BASCOM, LOUISE RAND. The golden goblet. A farce in three
      acts. By Louise Rand Bascom... Lebanon, O., March bros.
      [1911]. 35p. illus. (diagr.)

156   _____. The masonic ring; or, The adventures of a college
      bride. A farce in three acts, by Louise Rand Bascom.
      Lebanon, O., March bros. [1910]. 46p. illus. (diagr.)

157   BATE, RICHARD ALEXANDER, 1871-   . The romance of George
      Rogers Clark and Thérèse de Leyba, by R. Alexander Bate...
      Louisville, The Standard printing co., incorporated [1929].
      51p.

158   The battle of Brooklyn, a farce of two acts: as it was per-
      formed on Long Island, on Tuesday the 27th day of August,
      1776. By the representatives of the tyrants of America,
      assembled at Philadelphia... New York, Printed for J.
      Rivington, in the Year of the Rebellion, 1776. 27p.

159   BAUMAN, E. HENRI. Run in a post office, a farce in one act.
      Clyde, Ohio, A. D. Ames, 1885. 9p.

160   BAUMAN, WILLIAM. Mayflower '76, a one-act play. Louisville,
      1937. 16p.

161   BAX, CLIFFORD, 1886-   . The rose and the cross (studio
      plays: number two). With designs by Dorothy Mullock.
      London, C. Palmer [1918]. 22p. col. illus.

162   BAYLIE, SIMON, 17th cent. The wizard, a play, by Simon Bay-
      lie, edited for the first time from the Durham and London
      manuscripts, with introduction and notes, by Henry de
      Vocht... Louvain, Librairie universitaire, Uystpruyst,
      1930. cvii, [1], 204p. incl. facsims.

163   BAYLY, THOMAS HAYNES, 1797-1839. The barrack room. A comedi-
      etta. In two acts. - Altered from a musical burletta, by
      Thos. Haynes Bayly. Together with a description of the
      costumes - cast of the characters... New York, De Witt,
      1883. 22p. (On cover: De Witt's acting plays, no. 310).

164   _____. ...The ladder of love: a musical drama... By Thomas
      Haynes Bayly... First performed at Madame Vestris' Royal
      Olympic theatre, London. New York, Elton, 1838. 32p.
      (Elton's edition of farces).
        Airs indicated, but no music.

165   _____. ...One hour: or, The carnival ball: an original bur-
      letta, in one act. By Thomas Haynes Bayly... First per-
      formed at Madame Vestris' Olympic theatre, London: January
      11, 1836. New York, Elton, 1838. 30p. (Elton's edition
      of farces).

166   _____. The Swiss cottage; or, Why don't she marry? A vaude-
      ville, in one act. London, Thomas Hailes Lacy [n.d.].
      22p.

167   _____. ...Tom Noddy's secret, a farce, in one act. By
      Thomas Haynes Bayly... Correctly printed from the most
      approved acting copy: with a description of the costume,
      cast of the characters... Baltimore, J. Robinson [ca.
      1840?]. 27p. At head of title: Robinson's edition.

168   BEAUMONT, FRANCIS, 1584?-1616. The knight of the burning
      pestle, by Francis Beaumont and John Fletcher. Edited by
      C. M. Edmonston. London, Wells Gardner, Darton and Co.,
      ltd. [n.d.]. 78p.

169   BEAZLEY, SAMUEL, 1786-1851. ...Is he jealous? an operetta;
      in one act; by Samuel Beazley, esq. ... faithfully marked
      with the stage business, and stage directions, as it is
      performed at the Theatre Royal. English opera. London,
      Pub. for the proprietors, by W. Simpkin and R. Marshall,
      [etc,] 1818. 1 p.ℓ, ii p., 1 ℓ, [2], 25p. front. (port.)
      diagr. (Oxberry, William. The new English drama. London,
      1818. v. 3, no. 3). At head of title: Oxberry's edition.

170   [_____.] 1786-1851. Ivanhoe; or, The knight templar: adapted
      from the novel of that name. First performed the 2nd of
      March, 1820, at the Theatre Royal, Covent Garden. The
      music selected by Dr. Kitchiner, the stage management and
      the whole piece produced under the direction of Mr. Farley.

BEAZLEY, SAMUEL

    (BEAZLEY, SAMUEL)
    London, Printed by W. Smith, sold by Simpkin and Marshall
    [etc.] 1820. 72p. Attributed to Samuel Beazley; cf.
    Theatrical inquisitor, v. 16, p. 125-127, 136, 225; Eitner,
    v. 5, p. 377.
        Without the music.

171   [_____.] The knights of the cross; or, The hermit's prophecy:
    a romantic drama, in three acts, from Sir Walter Scott...
    Printed from the acting copy, with remarks, biographical
    and critical, by D.-G. ... As performed at the Theatres
    Royal... London, J. Cumberland [n.d.]. 43p. incl. front.
    (Cumberland's British theatre. London, ca. 1825-55, v. 34
    [no. 6]).
        Remarks by George Daniel, editor of the series.
        Founded on Scott's "Talisman."
        Without the music (by Bishop).

172   [_____. The lottery ticket; or, The lawyer's clerk: a farce,
    in one act... Printed from the acting copy, with remarks,
    biographical and critical, by D.-G. ... As performed at
    the Theatres Royal... London, J. Cumberland [n.d.]. 35p.
    incl. front. (Cumberland's British theatre. London, ca.
    1825-55. v. 35 [no. 6]).
        Remarks by George Daniel, editor of the series.
        An adaptation of "La maison en loterie", by Picard and
    Radet.

173   BECHER, MARTIN. Hunting the slippers; or, Painless dentistry,
    a farce, in one scene. New York, The De Witt publishing
    house [n.d.]. 14p.

174   _____. In the wrong house; or, No. six Duke Street. A farce.
    New York, The De Witt publishing house [n.d.]. 12p.

175   _____. My uncle's suit; or, In possession. A farce, in one
    act. New York, Robert M. De Witt [n.d.]. 10p.

176   BECK, WILLIAM L. Captured; or, The old maid's triumph. A
    comedy, in four acts... Clyde, Ohio, Ames' Publishing co.
    [n.d.]. 34p.

177   A BECKETT, GILBERT ABBOTT, 1811-1856. O Gemini! or, The
    brothers of course... A new burlesque on a frightfully
    popular subject by Gilbert Abbott A Beckett and Mark
    Lemon... London, Webster and co. [n.d.]. 22p. front.

178   ____. Pascal Bruno; a burletta, in two acts... London, W. Strange, 1838. 29p. front.

179   ____. The Siamese twins. A farce, in one act... New York, Samuel French [n.d.]. 17p.

180   ____. ... Wanted a brigand: or, A visit from Fra Diavolo. A musical burletta, in one act... London, John Duncombe [n.d.]. 25p. front. (Duncombe's edition).

181   BECQUE, HENRI, 1837-1899. The vultures, The woman of Paris, The merry-go-round, three plays by Henry Becque; translated from the French with an introduction by Freeman-Tilden. New York, M. Kennerley, 1913. xiii, [4], 4-266p.

182   BEERY, ADALINE HOHF, comp. The rostrum: a collection of original recitations, dialogues, motion songs, etc. for day-schools and Christmas entertainments. By Adaline Hohf Beery. Cincinnati, O., New York, Fillmore bros., 1900. 40p.

183   BEETE, MR. ... The man of the times; or, A scarcity of cash; a farce by Mr. Beete... New York City, N.Y., Federal theatre project, Play bureau, 1936. 2 p.ℓ., 24, [1] mimeographed ℓ.

184   BEITH, JOHN HAY, 1876-1952. The crimson cocoanut, and other plays, by Ian Hay Beith... Boston, W. H. Baker and co., 1913. 130p. CONTENTS. - The crimson cocoanut. - A late delivery. - The missing card.

185   BELL, MRS. HUGH ("LADY BELL"). Fairy tale plays and how to act them, by Lady Bell... With numerous illustrations by Lancelot Speed. New impression. London [etc., etc.] Longmans, Green, and co., 1910. iv, 366p. illus.

186   [BELL, JOHN KEBLE] 1875-   . The Smiths; a comedy without a plot, by Keble Howard [pseud.]. New York, McClure, Phillips and co., 1907. 3 p.ℓ., v-viii, 318p.,1ℓ.

187   BELL, ROBERT. ... Temper. A comedy, in five acts... New York, William Taylor and co. [n.d.]. 78p. (Modern Standard drama, no. 1i).

188   BELL, VICARS. That night, a play for the nativity. London, Faber and Faber [1959]. 48p.

BELLINGHAM, HENRY

189 BELLINGHAM, HENRY. Bluebeard re-paired. A worn-out subject
     done-up anew. An operatic extravaganza, in one act...
     the music by J. Offenbach... London, Thomas Hailes Lacy
     [n.d.]. 49p.

190 ____. Princess Primrose, and the four pretty princes. A
     burlesque extravaganza, by Primrose and Best. London,
     Thomas Hailes Lacy [n.d.]. 43p.

191 BELOT, ADOLPHE. L'article 47; or, Breaking the ban, a drama,
     in three acts. Chicago, The dramatic publishing co., 1872.
     42p.

192 ____. A life chase. (Le drame de la rue de paix.). A drama,
     in five acts... Translated, with alterations, by John
     Oxenford and Horace Wigan. New York, Robert M. De Witt
     [n.d.]. 34p.

193 BENAVENTE Y MARTÍNEZ, JACINTO, 1866-1954. ... The smile of
     Mona Lisa; a play in one act [by] Jacinto Benavente, tr.
     from the Spanish by John Armstrong Herman. Boston, R. G.
     Badger; [etc., etc., 1915]. 3 p.ℓ., 5-12p. 2 ℓ., 15-34p.
     (Contemporary Dramatists Series).

194 BERNARD, FRANK H. In the shadow of the Rockies. A romance
     of the Golden West, in three acts... New York, Samuel
     French, 1906. 68p.

195 BERNARD, TRISTAN, 1866-1947. I'm going! a comedy in one act,
     by Tristan Bernard, tr. by Barrett H. Clark. New York,
     S. French; [etc., etc., 1915]. 2 p.ℓ., 3-12p. [The
     world's best plays, by celebrated European authors, B. H.
     Clark general ed.].

196 BERNARD, WILLIAM BAYLE, 1807-1875. The farmer's story. A
     domestic drama, in three acts... London, Thomas Hailes
     Lacy [n.d.]. 45p. front.

197 ____. The farmer's story! A dramatic drama, in three acts.
     By Bayle Bernard... London, T. H. Lacy [18--]. 48p incl.
     front. (On cover: The new British theatre (late Duncombe's)
     no. [174]).
     "First produced at the Lyceum, June 13th, 1836."

198 ____. ... The Irish attorney: or, Galway practice in 1770.
     A farce in two acts. By Bayle Bernard... New York, Ber-
     ford and co.; [etc., etc.] 1847. 38p incl. front. (The
     Minor drama. no. 1).

199   _____. ... A maiden's fame! or, A legend of Lisbon! A drama, in two acts... London, J. Duncombe and co. [n.d.]. 40p. front. (Duncombe's edition).

200   _____. The man of two lives! A new romantic play, in three acts and a prologue... London, Thomas Hailes Lacy [n.d.]. 75p.

201   _____. The middy ashore. A farce, in one act. By Bayle Bernard... London, T. H. Lacy [18--]. 24p. front. (On cover: The New British theatre (late Duncombe's no. [177]). "First produced at the English opera house, May 23, 1836."

202   _____. The mummy, a farce, in one act... New York, Samuel French [n.d.]. 24p.

203   _____. ... The nervous man and the man of nerve. A farce, in two acts... New York, William Taylor and co. [n.d.]. 45p. (Modern standard drama, no. xxxvi).

204   _____. The old regimentals: an historical drama, in one act, by William Baile Bernard. Printed from the acting copy, with remarks, biographical and critical, by D.-G. ... As performed at the Theatres Royal... London, J. Cumberland [n.d.]. 34p. incl. front. (Cumberland's British theatre. London, ca. 1825-55. v. 33 [no. 9]).
    Remarks by George Daniel, editor of the series.
    Without the music (by Hawes).

205   _____. ... The passing cloud. A romantic drama, in two acts... New York, Samuel French [n.d.]. 59p. (French's standard drama, no. lxxxv).

206   BERRY, LUCILE BLACKBURN. The melting pot; or, The Americanization of the strangers within our gates. Lebanon, Ohio, March bros. [n.d.]. 16p.

207   _____. Old colony days, by Lucile Blackburn Berry. Lebanon, Ohio, March bros. [1915]. 26p.

208   BESANT, SIR WALTER, 1836-1901. The charm and other drawing-room plays, by Sir Walter Besant and Walter Pollack. New York, Frederick A. Stokes co. [c1897]. 275p. CONTENTS. - The charm. - The voice of love. - Peer and heiress. - Loved I not honour more. - The shrinking shoe. - The glove. - The spy. - The wife's confession.

BESIER, RUDOLF

209   BESIER, RUDOLF, 1878-1942. Don, a comedy in three acts. New
      York, Duffield and co. [1912]. 175p. front. (port.)

210   _____. Lady Patricia, a comedy in three acts, by Rudolf
      Besier... New York, Duffield and co. [1911]. 215, [1]p.
      Half-title: Plays of to-day and to-morrow.

211   BICKERSTAFFE, ISAAC, d. 1812? Love in a village: a comic
      opera, in three acts, by Isaac Bickerstaffe. Printed from
      the acting copy, with remarks, biographical and critical,
      by D.-G. ... As performed at the Theatres Royal... Lon-
      don, G. H. Davidson [n.d.]. 52p. incl. front. (Cumber-
      land's British theatre. London, ca. 1825-55. v. 5 [no.
      4]).

212   _____. The maid of the mill: a comic opera, in three acts...
      London, John Cumberland [n.d.]. 59p. front.

213   BIEN, HERMAN M. The feast of lights; or, Chanukon... Edited
      with an introduction by Paul T. Nolan... Lexington, Ky.,
      1963. x, 45p.

214   BINHAM, FRANK LESTER. Henry Granden; or, The unknown heir,
      a drama, in three acts. Clyde, Ohio, A. D. Ames [n.d.].
      24p.

215   BINYON, LAURENCE, 1869-1943. Attila, a tragedy in four acts.
      London, John Murray, 1907. 134p.

216   BIRCH, SAMUEL, 1757-1841. The adopted child. A musical drama,
      in two acts, by Samuel Birch. Printed from the acting
      copy, with remarks, biographical and critical, by D.-G.
      ... As performed at the Theatres Royal... London, J.
      Cumberland [n.d.]. 34p. incl. front. (Cumberland's
      British theatre. London, ca. 1825-55. v. 29, [no. 11]).

217   BIRCH-PFEIFFER, CHARLOTTE KAROLINA, 1800-1868. 'Twixt axe
      and crown (Elizabeth Prinzessin von England) a historical
      play in five acts... adapted to the English stage by Tom
      Taylor. New York, Robert M. De Witt [n.d.]. 41p.

218   BIRD, CHARLES S. Elmwood folks, a drama in three acts. Bos-
      ton, Walter H. Baker and co., 1910. 49p.

219   BLACHER, SARAH. The conspiracy of Catiline with a western
      setting. [n.p., n.d.]. 4p. (American Classical League
      Service Bureau, No. 683).

220 BLAIR-FISH, WALLACE WILFRID, 1889-   . ... Consarning Sairey
     'Uggins, a one-act farce, by Wilfrid Blair... London, J.
     Williams, ltd.; New York, S. French [1914]. 19p.

221 BLAKE, THOMAS G. Life as it is, or, The convict's child. An
     original domestic drama, in two acts, by T. G. Blake...
     As performed at Sadler's Wells theatre, correctly marked
     from the prompt copy... London, J. Pattie [n.d.]. 40p.
     front. (The Universal stage... London, 1840. v. 1 [no.
     5]).

222 BLAKE, WILLIAM, 1757-1827. Poetical sketches by William Blake,
     now first reprinted from the original edition of 1783, ed.
     and prefaced by Richard Herne Shepherd. London, B. M.
     Pickering, 1868. xiv, 96p. Contains his King Edward the
     Third.

223 BLANCHARD, ARTHUR FRANKLIN. The night after; or, Rameses of
     Mummy Row, a farce in one act. Boston, Walter H. Baker
     and co. [1903]. 21p.

224 BLANCHARD, EDWARD LITT LAMAN, 1820-1889. ... Faith, hope,
     and charity! or, Chance and change! A domestic drama, in
     three acts... London, John Duncombe [n.d.]. 55p.

225 _____. Pork chops; or, A dream at home. A farcical extrava-
     ganza... in one act... London, Thomas Hailes Lacy [n.d.].
     12p.

226 _____. Programme and words of the songs of the seven ages of
     woman; a new lyric entertainment written by E. L. Blan-
     chard, esq., composed expressly for and illustrated by
     Emma Stanley... First produced in America at Niblo's
     Garden, Tuesday, July 8, 1856... [New York, W. Corbyn,
     1856?]. 12p.

227 BLASHFIELD, EVANGELINE WILBOUR, d. 1918. Masques of Cupid,
     by Evangeline Wilbour Blashfield; A surprise party, The
     lesser evil, The honor of the Crequy, In Cleon's garden;
     illustrations by Edwin Howland Blashfield. New York, C.
     Scribner's sons, 1901. viii p., 2 ℓ., 3-264p. front.,
     plates, ports.

228 BLATT, WILLIAM MOSHER, 1876-   . Husbands on approval, a
     comedy in three acts, by W. M. Blatt... Boston, W. H.
     Baker and co., 1914. 197p.

The blockheads

229   The blockheads; or, The affrighted officers. A farce. Boston,
      Printed in Queen-street, M,DCC, LXXVI. 19, [2]p.

229A BLOOR, R. H. U. The enchanted island, an operetta in one act,
      the libretto written by R. H. U. Bloor, the music composed
      by Richard H. Walthew. London, New York, Boosey and co.,
      1900. 1 p.ℓ., 50p.

230   BOCK, ANNIE SARA. The family reunion, a two act comedy, by
      Annie Sara Bock. [Wilkes-Barre, Pa.; Manhattan, Kan.,
      Bock entertainment co., 1909]. cover-title, 1 p.ℓ., 5-25p.

231   BOCK, CAROLYN E. Amor omnia vincit. [n.p., n.d.]. 3p.
      (American Classical League Service Bureau, No. 691).

232   The Bohemians of Paris, a romantic drama, in three acts.
      Adapted from the French. London, Thomas Hailes Lacy
      [n.d.]. 52p. front.

233   BOKER, GEORGE HENRY, 1823-1890. Calaynos: a tragedy, in five
      acts... Printed from the acting copy, with remarks, bio-
      graphical and critical, by D.-G. ... London, G. H. David-
      son [1849?]. 64 (i.e. 68) p. front. (Cumberland's British
      theatre. London, ca. 1825-55. v. 45 [no. 6]).

234   _____. Plays and poems: by George H. Boker... 2d ed. Boston,
      Ticknor and Fields, 1857. 2v. CONTENTS: v.1. Plays:
      Calaynos; Anne Boleyn; Leonor de Guzman; Francesca da
      Rimini. - v.2. Plays: The betrothal; The widow's marriage.
      - Poems.

235   BONDLEY, DORIS. The punishment: a reward to traitors. [n.p.,
      n.d.]. 4p. (American Classical League Service Bureau,
      No. 148).

236   BOOTH, EDWIN, 1833-1893. Edwin Booth's prompt-book of the
      Merchant of Venice. Edited by William Winter. Boston,
      Lee & Shepard; New York, Charles T. Dillingham, 1878.
      86p.

237   BOTTOMLEY, GORDON, 1874-1948. King Lear's wife, The crier by
      night, The riding to Lithend, Midsummer eye. Laodice and
      Danäe, plays, by Gordon Bottomley. Boston, Small, Maynard
      and co. [c1915]. vii, [1], 223, [1]p. illus. (music).

238   _____. Laodice and Danäe; play in one act, by Gordon Bottom-
      ley. Boston, The Four seas co., 1916. 44, [1]p.

239 BOUCICAULT, DION, 1820?-1890. After dark. A drama of London
     life in 1868, in four acts. (Authorized adaptation of
     Messrs. Grangé and Dennery's "Les oiseaux de proie.").
     [New York, The De Witt publishing house, n.d.]. 39p.

240 _____. ... Andy Blake: or, The Irish diamond, a comedy, in
     two acts. By Dion Boucicault... New York [S. French]
     1856. 19p. (Boucicault's dramatic works, forming the
     repertoire of Miss Agnes Robertson. no. II). On cover:
     ... No. 110 of French's edition of the minor drama. Cover
     dated 1857.
          Founded on "Le gamin de Paris, ou L'enfant de Geneviève
     par m^{me} Fanny Richomme... Paris, 1837".
          Produced, London, 1862, as "The Dublin boy."

241 _____. Elfie; or, The Cherrytree inn, a romantic drama, in
     three acts. Chicago, The dramatic publishing co. [n.d.].
     34p.

242 _____. Forbidden fruit; by Dion Boucicault, edited by Allar-
     dyce Nicoll and F. Theodore Cloak. Princeton, N.J.,
     Princeton university press, 1940. viii, 48p.

243 _____. Forbidden fruit, a comedy in three acts, by Dion
     Boucicault, esq. For private use. Not published or sold.
     New York, 1876. 52 numb. 1.

244 _____. Formosa: ("The most beautiful.") or, The railroad to
     ruin, a drama of modern life, in four acts. [n.d.]. 44p.

245 _____. Grimaldi; or, The life of an actress. A drama, in
     five acts, by Dion Boucicault... New York, 1856. 26p.

246 _____. ... How she loves him! A comedy, in five acts...
     New York, Samuel French and son [n.d.]. 48p. (French's
     parlor comedies, no. 2).

247 _____. ... Jean la Poste; drame anglais en cinq actes et dix
     tableaux; traduction d'Arrah na Pogue. Paris, Librairie
     dramatique, 1866. 2 p.l., 104p. Half-title: Bibliothèque
     spéciale de la Société des auteurs et compositeurs drama-
     tiques. At head of title: Dion Boucicault - Eugène Nus.

248 _____. ... Jessie Brown; or, The relief of Lucknow. A drama,
     in three acts. (Founded on an episode in the Indian re-
     bellion.) By Dion Boucicault... .New York, S. French,
     c1858. 32p. (Boucicault's dramatic works. Forming the
     repertoire of Miss Agnes Robertson. no. VI). On cover:
     ... No. 206 of French's edition of the standard drama.

BOUCICAULT, DION

249   BOUCICAULT, DION. The knight of Arva: a comic drama, in two
      acts... New York, Samuel French [n.d.]. 28p.

250   _____. ... Led astray, a comedy in 5 acts. By Dion Bouci-
      cault... New York, S. French and son; [etc., etc.],
      c1873. 57p. (French's standard drama. no. 372. The
      acting edition).
          An adaptation from Feuillet's "La tentation." Cf.
      Stage cyclopedia; Life and reminiscences of E. L. Blanchard,
      1891.

251   _____. London assurance, a comedy in five acts. New York,
      Saumel French [n.d.]. 71p.

252   _____. London assurance, a comedy in five acts, by Dion I.
      Boucicault... Boston, W. H. Baker and co., 1911. 78p.
      On cover: The William Warren ed. of standard plays.

253   _____. London assurance; a comedy in five acts, by Dion I
      Boucicault, acting version of the Yale university dramatic
      association (incorporated) with an introduction by William
      Lyon Phelps... New Haven, Conn., Pub. under the super-
      vision of P. Roberts, 1910. xvii, [3], 87p. front.,
      illus. (facsim) ports.

254   _____. London assurance. A comedy in five acts, by Dion L.
      Boucicault... As produced at Covent Garden theatre, Lon-
      don, in 1841, and at the Park theatre, New York, Oct. 11
      of the same year. An entirely new acting ed. With full-
      stage directions... notes, etc. Ed. by Alfred B. Sedg-
      wick... New York, C. T. De Witt, 1877. 54p. diagrs. On
      cover: De Witt's acting plays (no. 212).

255   _____. ... The long strike, a drama in four acts, by Dion
      Baucicault [!] esq. New York, S. French and son; London,
      S. French [187-?]. 38p. (French's standard drama. No.
      CCCLX).

256   _____. A lover by proxy. A comedietta in one act. By D.
      Boucicault... As performed at the Theatre Royal Haymarket.
      Correctly printed from the prompter's copy... London,
      Webster and co. [etc., 184-]. 28p. (On cover: Webster's
      acting national drama. no. 102).
          "First performed on Thursday, April 21st, 1842."

257   _____. The octoroon; or, Life in Louisiana. A play, in four
      acts... New York, Samuel French and son [n.d.]. 43p.

BOWLAN, MARIAN

258 _____. The O'Dowd, by Dion Boucicault... London, S. French
ltd.; New York, S. French, c1909. 52p.
"Sort of an Irish version of The porter's knot," J.
Oxenford's adaptation of "Les crochets du Père Martin" by
Cormon and Grange, 1858. Published in 1875 as "Daddy
O'Dowd."

259 _____. ... Pauvrette. A drama, in five acts... New York,
Samuel French [n.d.]. 36p.

260 _____. ... The phantom; a drama, in two acts, by Dion Bouci-
cault... New York, [S. French] 1856. 23p.
Boucicault's dramatic works, forming the repertoire of
Miss Agnes Robertson (no. 111).

261 _____. ... The poor of New York, a drama in five acts... New
York, Samuel French [n.d.]. 45p.
At head of title: Boucicault's dramatic works. (no. 5).

262 _____. ... The poor of New York. A drama in five acts. By
the * * * * club. To which are added a description of the
costume - cast of the characters... stage business. As
performed at Wallack's theatre, December, 1857. New York,
S. French [c1857]. 45p. (French's standard drama. The
acting ed. no. CLXXXIX). On cover: Boucicault's dramatic
works, no. 5.
"The original of the play... was 'Les pauvres de Paris'
in seven acts, by E. Brisebarre and Eugène Nus, acted in
1856 at the Paris Ambigu comique." The English adaptation
produced in London by Boucicault has title "Streets of
London." Cf. R. F. Roden, Later Amer. plays, 1900; also
Life of E. L. Blanchard by C. Scott and C. Howard, 1891.

263 _____. The streets of New York, a drama in five acts. Chicago, The dramatic publishing house [n.d.]. 52p.

264 _____. West end; or, The Irish heiress. A comedy - in five
acts. By Dion L. Boucicault... With original casts,
costumes, and all the stage business... New York, S.
French and son; London, S. French [187-?]. 49p. diagr.
(On cover: French's standard drama. The acting ed. No.
CCXXXVI).

265 BOWKER, SUSAN THAYER. His lucky day, a sketch in one act.
Boston, Walter H. Baker and co., 1902. 17p.

266 BOWLAN, MARIAN. Minnie at the movies, a monologue, by Marian
Bowlan... Chicago, T. S. Denison and co., 1913. 8p. On
cover: Denison's monologues.

Box and cox.

267   ... Box and Cox. In one act. Africanized expressly for
       George Christy, by E. Byron Christy... New York, Frederic
       A Brady [n.d.]. 21p. front. (Brady's Ethiopian drama,
       no. ii).

268   BOYD, JACKSON, 1861-1920. The unveiling; a poetic drama in
       five acts, by Jackson Boyd. New York [etc.]. G. P.
       Putnam's sons, 1915. vii, 255p. front. (port.).

269   BRACCO, ROBERTO, 1862-   . The hidden spring, a drama in
       four acts, by Roberto Bracco. Tr. by Dirce St. Cyr. (In
       Poet Lore. Boston, 1907. vol. XVIII, no. II, p. [143]-
       186).

270   [BRACKENRIDGE, HUGH HENRY] 1748-1816. The death of General
       Montgomery, in storming the city of Quebec. A tragedy.
       With an ode, in honour of the Pennsylvania militia, and
       the small band of regular Continental troops, who sus-
       tained the campaign, in the depth of winter, January, 1777,
       and repulsed the British forces from the banks of the
       Delaware. By the author of a dramatic piece, on the Bat-
       tle of Bunker's-hill. To which are added, Elegiac pieces,
       commemorative of distinguished characters. By different
       gentlemen... Philadelphia, Printed and sold by Robert
       Bell, in Third-Street, next door to St. Paul's Church, M,
       DCC,LXXVII. 6 p.ℓ., [9], 79, [2]p. front.

271   [BRAHAM, JOHN] 1774?-1856. The paragraph: a musical enter-
       tainment, in two acts. As it is performed at the Theatre
       Royal, Covent Garden. By Prince Hoare. London, Printed
       for R. Phillips, by C. Mercier and co., 1804. vi, [2],
       52p.

272   BRANEN, JEFF T. The young attorney, a comedy sketch with un-
       expected results. [Chicago] Will Rossiter, 1904. 11p.

273   No Entry.

274   BREAKSPEAR [pseud.]. Melodrame entitled "Treason, strategems,
       and spoils," in five acts, by Breakspear [pseud.], Port-
       land, Ore., Printed by Thos. J. Dryer, "Oregonian" office,
       1852. 32p. illus.

275   BRECK, CHARLES, 1782-1822. The fox chase. A comedy. In
       five acts. As performed at the theatres, Philadelphia and
       Baltimore. By Charles Breck. New York, Published by D.
       Longworth, at the Dramatic repository, Shakespeare Gallery.
       1808. Printed by T. and G. Palmer, Philadelphia. 64p.

BRIDGHAM, GLADYS RUTH

276 _____. The trust. A comedy. In five acts. By Charles
Breck... New York, Published by D. Longworth, at the
Dramatic repository, Shakespeare-gallery, 1808. T. and
G. Palmer, printers, Philadelphia. 82p.

277 BREWER, GEORGE, b. 1766. How to be happy; or, The agreeable
hours of human life; being a series of essays on the in-
fluences which produce happiness, with humorous and satirical characteristics by George Brewer... London, Printed
by W. M. Thiselton, for Sherwood, Neely, and Jones [etc.],
1814. Contains his The dinner party. xxxvi, 351 (i.e.
331)p.

278 [BREWER, STERLING C.]. The dispelling of big Jim [a Negro
farce in one act. Lebanon, Ohio]. March bros., 1905.
8p.

279 ... Brian O'Linn. A farce, in two acts, written for Barney
Williams... New York, Samuel French [n.d.]. 16p. front.
(French's American drama, no. xvi).

280 Bric-a-brac. A comedietta, in one act, translated and adapted
from the French of E. D'Hervilly... New York, Happy Hours
co., 1879. 9p.

281 BRIDGEMAN, J. V. The quicksands of Gotham, a drama in prologue and three acts. Boston, Walter H. Baker and co.,
1899. 43p.

282 _____. The rifle and how to use it: an original farce in one
act. London, Thomas Hailes Lacy [n.d.]. 27p.

283 BRIDGES, ROBERT SEYMOUR, 1844-1930. Achilles in Scyros.
London, Geo. Bell and sons, 1892. 68p.

284 _____. Eight plays. Nero, parts I. and II. Palicio.
Ulysses. Captives. Achilles. Humours. Feast of
Bacchus. 264p.

285 BRIDGHAM, GLADYS RUTH. A case for Sherlock Holmes, a comedy
in two acts for female characters only, by Gladys Ruth
Bridgham... Boston, W. H. Baker and co., 1914. 30p.
On cover: Baker's edition of plays.

286 _____. Cupid's partner, a comedy in three acts, by Gladys
Ruth Bridgham... Boston, W. H. Baker and co., 1914. 47p.
On cover: Baker's edition of plays.

BRIDGHAM, GLADYS RUTH

287   BRIDGHAM, GLADYS RUTH. The girl from upper 7, an original comedy in three acts, by Gladys Ruth Bridgham... Boston, W. H. Baker and co., 1915. 64p. On cover: Baker's edition of plays.

288   _____. Her first assignment, a comedy in one act, by Gladys Ruth Bridgham... Boston, W. H. Baker and co., 1914. 26p. On cover: Baker's edition of plays.

289   _____. Leave it to Polly, a comedy in two acts for female characters only, by Gladys Ruth Bridgham... Boston, W. H. Baker and co., 1914. 35p. On cover: Baker's edition of plays.

290   _____. A modern Cinderella, a comedy in two acts, by Gladys Ruth Bridgham... Boston, W. H. Baker and co., 1915. 30p. On cover: Baker's edition of plays.

291   _____. Mrs. Haywood's help, a comedy in two acts, by Gladys Ruth Bridgham. Philadelphia, The Penn publishing co., 1914. 45p. diagr.

292   _____. On the quiet, a comedy in two acts, by Gladys Ruth Bridgham... Boston, W. H. Baker and co., 1915. 30p. On cover: Baker's edition of plays.

293   _____. A regular rah! rah! boy, a comedy in three acts, by Gladys Ruth Bridgham. Boston, W. H. Baker and co., 1915. 39p. On cover: Baker's edition of plays.

294   _____. A regular scream (royal fetters), a comedy in two acts for male characters only, by Gladys Ruth Bridgham... Boston, W. H. Baker and co., 1913. 41p. On cover: Baker's edition of plays.

295   _____. Ring-around-a-rosie, a comedy in one act, by Gladys Ruth Bridgham... Boston, W. H. Baker and co., 1914. 22p. On cover: Baker's edition of plays.

296   _____. Six times nine, a comedy in two acts for female characters only, by Gladys Ruth Bridgham... Boston, W. H. Baker and co., 1914. 43p. On cover: Baker's edition of plays.

297   _____. The turn in the road, a comedy in two acts, by Gladys Ruth Bridgham... Boston, W. H. Baker and co., 1912. 38p. On cover: Baker's edition of plays.

298 BRIDIE, JAMES. Mr. Bolfry, a play in one act. London, Con-
     stable and co., ltd. [n.d.]. 64p.

299 BRIER, WARREN J. Jedediah Judkins, J. P., a drama in four
     acts. Chicago, T. S. Denison, 1888. 62p.

300 _____. A soldier of fortune, a modern comedy-drama in five
     acts. Chicago, T. S. Denison, 1881. 50p.

301 BRIEUX, EUGÈNE, 1858-1932. Blanchette, and The escape; two
     plays by Brieux; with preface by H. L. Mencken; tr. from
     the French by Frederick Eisemann. Boston, J. W. Luce and
     co., 1913. 2 p.ℓ., xxxvi, [2], 240p.

302 The brigands of Calabria. A romantic drama, in one act.
     London, Thomas Hailes Lacy [n.d.]. 18p.

303 BRIGHT, VIRGINIA. Dido the Tyrian. [n.p., n.d.]. 15p.
     (American Classical League Service Bureau, No. 712).

304 British drama, a collection of the most esteemed dramatic
     productions, with biography of the respective authors; and
     critique on each play by R. Cumberland... London, C.
     Cooke, 1817. 14 v. fronts. (ports.). Added title-pages,
     engraved.

305 BROADHURST, GEORGE H. What happened to Jones; an original
     farce in three acts, by George H. Broadhurst... New York,
     S. French; [etc., etc., 1897?]. 107p. illus. (plan)

306 BROADHURST, THOMAS WILLIAM, 1857-1936. The holy city; a drama,
     by Thomas W. Broadhurst, with an introductory note by
     William Allen Neilson. Philadelphia, G. W. Jacobs and
     co. [1904]. 214p. front., 7 pl. On St. Mary Magdalene.

306A BROOKE, FRANCES MOORE, 1724?-1789. Rosina. A comic opera,
     in two acts, by Mrs. Brooke. Printed from the acting
     copy, with remarks, biographical and critical, by D.-G. ...
     As performed at the Theatres Royal... London, J. Cumber-
     land [n.d.]. 29p. incl. front. (Cumberland's British
     theatre. London, ca. 1825-55. v. 15 [no.7]).
         Remarks by George Daniel, editor of the series.
         Reissued in Davidson's shilling volume of Cumberland's
     plays, v. 12 [no. 3].
         Based on C. S. Favart's Les moissonneurs. Cf. Loewen-
     berg, Annals of opera.

BROOKFIELD, CHARLES H. E.

307   BROOKFIELD, CHARLES H. E. An excellent receipt... New York and London, Samuel French, 1910. 20p.

308   BROOKS, SHIRLEY. Anything for a change. A petite comedy, in one act. Chicago, The dramatic publishing co. [n.d.]. 18p.

309   _____. The Creole; or, Love's letters. An original drama, in three acts... London, Thomas Hailes Lacy [n.d.]. 42p.

310   BROUGH, BROTHERS. The enchanted isle; or, "Raising the wind" on the most approved principles: a drama... London, National Acting Drama Office [n.d.]. 32p. front.

311   _____. The second calendar; and the queen of beauty, who had the fight with the genie. An extravaganza, in two acts... London, National Acting Drama Office [n.d.]. 46p.

312   _____. The Sphinx: a "touch from the ancients," in one act... London, National Acting Drama Office [n.d.]. 33p. front.

313   BROUGH, ROBERT B. ... Crinoline. An original farce, in one act... Boston, William V. Spencer [n.d.]. 21p. (Spencer's Boston theatre, no. xcvi).

314   BROUGH, WILLIAM, 1826-1870. The caliph of Bagdad. An original oriental, operatic extravaganza... London, Thomas Hailes Lacy [n.d.]. 35p.

315   _____. A comical countess. A farce, in one act. By William Brough... London, T. H. Lacy [1866?]. 24p. (On cover: Lacy's acting edition. 769).

316   _____. ... The corsair; or, The little fairy at the bottom of the sea. A new Christmas burlesque and pantomime... New York, Samuel French [n.d.]. 27p. (The minor drama, no. cxxxi).

317   _____. Kind to a fault. An original comedy, in two acts. New York, Robert M. De Witt [n.d.]. 31p.

318   _____. My heart's in the highlands, a farce in one act. By William Brough and Andres Halliday. Clyde, Ohio, A. D. Ames [n.d.]. 11p.

319   _____. ... A phenomenon in a smock frock. A comic drama, in one act... New York, Samuel French [n.d.]. 20p. (The minor drama, no. cxlviii).

BROUGHAM, JOHN

320   _____. Prince Amabel; or, The fairy roses. An original
       fairy extravaganza... London, Thomas Hailes Lacy [n.d.].
       41p.

321   BROUGHAM, JOHN, 1810-1880. ... All's fair in love: an original
       dramatic story, in five acts. By John Brougham, comedian...
       New York, S. French, c1856. 44p. (French's standard drama.
       The acting edition. no. CLXI).
           According to a note in Brougham's diary, altered from
       "The Page." Cf. Life, etc., p. 80.

322   _____. ... Columbus el filibustero!! A new and audaciously
       original historico-plagiaristic, ante-national, pre-patri-
       otic, and omni-local confusion of circumstances, running
       through two acts and four centuries. By John Brougham...
       New York, S. French [185-?]. 24p. (The minor drama. The
       acting ed. No. CXLV).

323   _____. ... A decided case. A darmatic sketch, in one act.
       By John Brougham. New York, S. French [c1857]. 18p.
       (The minor drama. no. 114). On back cover: French's
       minor drama. [v. 15, no. 2].

324   _____. ... Dombey and son. Dramatized from Dickens' novel.
       By John Brougham, esq. In three acts. To which are added,
       a description of the costume - cast of the characters...
       and the whole of the stage business. As performed at the
       New York theatres... New York, S. French [185-]. 31p.
       (French's American drama. The acting edition. no. 126).
       On cover: French's standard drama. no. 126.

325   _____. ... Dred: or The Dismal Swamp. A play in five acts.
       Dramatized (by special permission) from Mrs. Harriet
       Beecher Stowe's novel. By John Brougham... New York,
       S. French, c1856. 43p. (French's American drama. The
       acting ed. no. c).

326   _____. Flies in the web. An original comedy in three acts.
       London, Samuel French, ltd. [n.d.]. 50p.

327   _____. ... Franklin: a new and original historical drama, in
       five acts. By John Brougham, comedian... New York, S.
       French, c1856. 27p. (French's standard drama. no. CLXVI).

328   _____. ... The game of life. An original comedy, in five
       acts. By John Brougham... New York, S. French, c1856.
       44p. (French's American drama. The acting edition, no.
       25).

BROUGHAM, JOHN

329 BROUGHAM, JOHN. ... The game of love. An original comedy, in
     five acts. By John Brougham... As performed at Wallack's
     theatre, N.Y. ... New York, S. French, c1855. 54p.
     (French's American drama. The acting edition, no. 10).

330 _____. ... The great tragic revival. A new and undoubtedly
     original contemporaneous dramatic absurdity, in one act
     and several tableaux. By John Brougham, comedian... As
     performed at Burton's theatre... New York, S. French,
     c1858. 10p. (The minor drama. The acting edition, no.
     154).

331 _____. ... The gun-maker of Moscow: melodrama, in three acts.
     By John Brougham, comedian. To which are added, a descrip-
     tion of the costume - cast of the characters... and the
     whole of the stage business... New York, S. French,
     c1856. 28p. (French's standard drama. no. 164).
         Dramatized from Sylvanus Cobb's novel, The gunmaker of
     Moscow.

332 _____. ... Jane Eyre. A drama, in five acts... New York,
     Samuel French [n.d.]. 32p. (French's American drama, no.
     cxxxvi).

333 _____. ... Life in New York: or, Tom and Jerry on a visit.
     A comic drama, in two acts. By John Brougham... As per-
     formed at the Bowery theatre, N.Y. ... New York, S.
     French, c1856. 26p. (French's American drama. The acting
     edition. no. XCIV).

334 _____. Life in the clouds, or, Olympus in an uproar; a bur-
     lesque burletta, by J. Brougham, as performing at the
     English Opera House. Correctly printed from the prompt
     copy... London, J. Pattie [1840]. vi, [7]-26p. (The
     Universal stage... London, 1840. v. 2 [no. 7]).

335 _____. The lottery of life. A story of New York. An origi-
     nal local drama, in five acts... New York, Samuel French
     and son, 1867. 41p.

336 _____. ... Love and murder: a farce, in one act. By John
     Brougham. To which are added, a description of the cos-
     tume - cast of the characters... and the whole of the
     stage business. As performed at the New York theatres...
     New York, S. French, c1856. 14p. (French's American
     drama. The acting edition. no. 34).

337   ____. Metamora; or, The last of the Pollywogs. A burlesque, in two acts. By John Brougham... Boston, H. W. Swett [1859?]. 18p.

338   ____. ... The miller of New Jersey; or, The prison-hulk. An historic drama-spectacle, in three acts. By John Brougham... New York, S. French, c1858. 28p. (French's standard drama. The acting edition, no. 221).

339   ____. ... The Musard ball; or, Love at the academy. A contemporaneous extrabaganza [!], in one act. By John Brougham... As performed at Burton's theatre... New York, S. French, c1858. 12p. (The minor drama... no. 153).

340   ____. ... Neptune's defeat; or, The seizure of the seas. A new and curiously original allegoric, mythologic, metaphoric filtration of sur-passing events, by John Brougham ... As performed at Wallack's theatre. New York, S. French, c1858. 24p. (The minor drama, no. 165).

341   ____. ... Night and morning: a play, in five acts. Adapted from Bulwer's novel. By John Brougham. As performed at Wallack's theatre... New York, S. French, c1856. 40p. (French's American drama. The acting ed., no. 48).

342   ____. Playing with fire; an original comedy, in five acts, by John Brougham... New York, S. French, c1860. 50p. (On cover: Lacy's acting edition. no. 976). Being v. 66, no. 1 of the series.

343   ____. ...Po-ca-hon-tas: or, The gentle savage. In two acts. By John Brougham... New York, S. French [n.d.]. 32p. (French's American drama. The acting edition. no. 69). On cover: The minor drama, LXIX.

344   ____. ... An original aboriginal erratic operatic semi-civilized and demi-savage extravaganza, being a per-version of ye trewe and wonderrefulle hystorie of ye rennowned princesse, Po-ca-hon-tas: or, The gentle savage. In two acts. By John Brougham, esq. The music dislocated and re-set, by James G. Maeder, M. D.: and presented to public notice through the instrumentality of Signor La Manna... New York, S. French [1856]. 32p. (French's American drama. The acting edition. no. 28).
    Without the music.

BROUGHAM, JOHN

345　BROUGHAM, JOHN.　... The red mask: or, The wolf of Lithuania.
　　　A melodrama, in three acts.　By John Brougham, comedian...
　　　New York, S. French, c1856.　26p.　(French's standard drama.
　　　The acting edition, no. 158).　Cover-title: The red mask;
　　　or, The wolf of Bohemia [etc.].

346　_____.　... Romance and reality, or The young Virginian.　An
　　　original comedy, in five acts...　New York, Samuel French
　　　[n.d.].　54p.　(French's standard drama, no. cix).

347　_____.　... Take care of little Charley.　A farce, in one act.
　　　By John Brougham.　To which are added a description of the
　　　costume - cast of the characters... and the whole of the
　　　stage business as performed at Wallack's theater...　New
　　　York, S. French, c1858.　14p.　(The Minor drama.　The
　　　acting edition. no. 167).

348　_____.　... Temptation: or, The Irish emigrant.　A comic
　　　drama, in two acts.　By John Brougham...　New York, S.
　　　French [185-?].　22p.　(French's American drama.　The
　　　acting edition. no. 65).　On cover: The minor drama. no.
　　　65.

349　BROWN, ALICE, 1857-1948.　Children of earth; a play of New
　　　England, by Alice Brown.　New York, The Macmillan co.,
　　　1915.　7 p.ℓ., 212p. front. (port.).

350　_____.　One act plays, by Alice Brown.　New York, The Mac-
　　　millan co., 1928.　5 p.ℓ., 3-23p.　CONTENTS. - The hero. -
　　　Doctor Auntie. - The Crimson Lake. - Milly dear. - The
　　　web. - The loving cup. - Joint owners in Spain. - The
　　　sugar house. - A March wind.

351　BROWN, ERASTUS.　The trial of Cain, the first murderer, in
　　　poetry, by rule of court; in which a predestinarian, a
　　　Universalian, and an Arminian, argue as attornies at the
　　　bar; the two former as the prisoner's counsel, the latter
　　　as attorney general.　By Erastus Brown...　Boston, Printed
　　　for the purchaser, 1827.　36p.

352　BROWN, J. H.　Katrina's little game.　A Dutch act, with songs
　　　and a dance.　Chicago, The dramatic publishing co., 1876.
　　　8p.

353　BROWN, J. S.　A southern rose.　A military drama, in five
　　　acts.　Clyde, Ohio, Ames' publishing co., 1899.　25p.

354　BROWN, JOHN.　Barbarossa: a tragedy, in five acts...　London,
　　　John Cumberland [n.d.].　46p.

355   BROWN, LEANDO. Mrs. Raford, humanist, a suffrage drama. New
       York and London, L. E. Landone, Inc. [1912]. 137p.

356   BROWN, MARSDEN. ... A bold stratagem. A comedy, in three
       acts... Chicago, Dramatic publishing co. [n.d.]. 26p.
       (American amateur drama).

357   _____. A modern proposal, duologue in one act. Chicago, The
       dramatic publishing co. [1897]. 11p.

358   _____. A passing cloud, a monologue. Chicago, The dramatic
       publishing co. [1897]. 9p.

359   BROWNE, WALTER, 1856-1911. Everywoman, her pilgrimage in
       quest of love, a modern morality play. New York, The
       H. K. Fly company [1908]. 121p. front., illus.

360   BROWNE, WILLIAM MAYNADIER. The trustee, a play in four acts.
       Boston, Walter H. Baker and co. [1891]. 38p.

361   BROWNELL, ATHERTON. The unseen empire; a piece play in four
       acts, by Atherton Brownell... New York and London, Harper
       and bros., 1914. 2 p.ℓ., iii-iv, [6], 176, [1]p.

362   BROWNING, ROBERT, 1812-1889. The poetical works of Robert
       Browning with portraits. In two volumes. Volume I. New
       York, The Macmillan co., 1902. xvi, 748p. front. (port.).
       Includes the following dramas: Strafford, Pippa passes, King
       Victor and King Charles.

363   _____. Browning's Strafford, ed. by Hereford B. George.
       Oxford, At the Clarendon Press, 1908. 90p.

364   BROWNSON, O. A., JR. Annie: a tragic dramina, in four acts...
       Dubuque, Iowa, Palmer and bros., 1869. 23p.

365   BRUEL, EDUARD N. Abishag the Shulamite, drama in three acts
       and four scenes. New Rochelle, N. Y., 1912. 19p.

366   [BUCHANAN, ROBERT] 1785-1873. Tragic dramas from Scottish
       history. Heselrig. Wallace. (2d ed.) James the First of
       Scotland. Edinburgh, T. Constable and co.; [etc., etc.]
       1859. vi p., 1ℓ., 233p.
          "Heselrig" constituted originally the first act of "Wal-
       lace," but was detached on account of the length of the
       play and is here presented as a separate drama of two
       acts; cf. advertisement.

37

BUCHANAN, ROBERT WILLIAMS

367   BUCHANAN, ROBERT WILLIAMS, 1841-1901. Corinne. A romantic
      play, by Robert Buchanan, in four acts. Entirely original.
      Privately printed, not for publication. London, 1876.
      78p.

368   BUCKSTONE, JOHN BALDWIN, 1802-1879. ... Agnes de Vere, or,
      The wife's revenge, a drama, in three acts... Boston,
      William V. Spencer, 1855. 44p. (Spencer's Boston theatre,
      no. xxiii).

369   _____. ... The dead shot. A farce in one act... New York,
      Wm. Taylor and co. [n.d.]. 27p. front. (The minor drama,
      no. v).

370   _____. The flowers of the forest: a gypsy story. An original
      drama, in three acts... New York, Samuel French [n.d.].
      53p.

371   _____. Good for nothing. A comic drama, in one act... New
      York, Samuel French [n.d.]. 17p.

372   _____. The green bushes; or, A hundred years ago. An origi-
      nal drama, in three acts... New York, Samuel French
      [n.d.]. 50p.

373   _____. The happiest day of my life: a farce, in two acts, by
      John Baldwin Buckstone... Printed from the acting copy,
      with remarks, biographical and critical, D.-G. ... As per-
      formed at the Theatres Royal... London, J. Cumberland
      [n.d.]. 35p. incl. front. (Cumberland's British theatre.
      London, ca. 1825-55. v. 23 [no. 2]).
          Remarks by George Daniel, editor of the series.
          Adapted from "Le plus beau jour de la vie," by Scribe
      and Varner.

374   _____. A husband at sight: a farce, in two acts. By J. B.
      Buckstone... Printed from the acting copy, with remarks,
      biographical and critical, by D.-G. ... As performed at
      the Theatres Royal... London, G. H. Davidson [n.d.]. 35p.
      incl. front. (Cumberland's British theatre. London, ca.
      1825-55. v. 26 [no. 3].
          Adapted from "Le mariage impossible" by MM. Mélesville
      [i.e., Duveyrier and Carmouche?].
          Remarks by George Daniel, editor of the series.
          Reissue of Cumberland's earlier edition.

375 _____. The ice witch; or, The frozen hand: a tale of enchant-
ment, in two acts, by J. B. Buckstone... Printed from the
acting copy, with remarks, biographical and critical, by
D.-G. ... As performed at the Theatres Royal... London,
Davidson [n.d.]. 36p. incl. front. (Cumberland's British
theatre. London, ca. 1825-55. v. 28 [no. 6]).
   Remarks by George Daniel, editor of the series.
   Reissue of Cumberland's earlier edition.
   Without the music (by Cooke).

376 _____. The Irish lion. A farce in one act. New York, The
De Witt publishing house [n.d.]. 18p.

377 _____. ... Jack Sheppard. A drama, in four acts... edited
by F. C. Wemyss. New York, Samuel French [n.d.]. 92p.

378 _____. John Jones; or, I'm haunted by a fiend! a farce, in
one act... Philadelphia, Frederick Turner [n.d.]. 26p.

379 _____. Josephine, the child of the regiment; or, The fortune
of war, a musical comedy, in two acts... New York, Samuel
French and son [n.d.]. 45p.

380 _____. ... The lottery ticket; or, The lawyer's clerk. A
farce, in one act... New York, Samuel French [n.d.]. 35p.
(The minor drama, the acting edition, no. cxxxvii).

381 _____. The maid with the milking pail. A comic drama, in
one act. London, Thomas Hailes Lacy [n.d.]. 24p.

382 _____. ... Married life: a comedy in three acts... New York,
Samuel French [n.d.]. 41p. (French's American drama,
no. cxxx).

383 _____. Open house; or, The twin sisters: a farce, in two
acts, by John Baldwin Buckstone... Printed from the
acting copy, with remarks, biographical and critical, by
D.-G. ... As now performed at the Theatres Royal... London, J. Cumberland [n.d.]. 44p. incl. front. (Cumberland's British theatre. London, ca. 1825-55. v. 31 [no.
6]).
   Remarks by George Daniel, editor of the series.

384 _____. The pet of the petticoats; an opera, in three acts...
the music by John Barnett. London, William Strange, 1834.
59p. front.

BUCKSTONE, JOHN BALDWIN

385   BUCKSTONE, JOHN BALDWIN. Popping the question, a farce in
one act. Boston, Walter H. Baker and co., 1890. 19p.

386   _____. ... The rough diamond. A farce, in one act... New
York, Samuel French and son [n.d.]. 26p. (The minor
drama, no. xli).

387   _____. Second thoughts. A comedy, in two acts... London,
William Strange, 1835. 53p. front.

388   _____. Single life: a comedy, in three acts... London and
New York, Samuel French [n.d.]. 56p.

389   _____. Snakes in the grass: a farce, in two acts, by John
Baldwin Buckstone... Printed from the acting copy, with
remarks, biographical and critical, by D.-G. ... As performed at the Theatres Royal... London, J. Cumberland
[n.d.]. 48p. incl. front. (Cumberland's British theatre.
London, ca. 1825-55. v. 24 [no.3]).
    Remarks by George Daniel, editor of the series.

390   _____. The snapping turtles; or, Matrimonial masquerading.
A duologue, in one act... as performed at the Theatre
Royal, Haymarket, Oct. 14, 1845... New York, Robert M.
De Witt [n.d.]. 20p.

391   _____. Uncle John. A petite comedy, in two acts. Philadelphia, Frederick Turner [n.d.]. 36p.

392   _____. ... The wreck ashore. A drama, in two acts... Boston, William V. Spencer, 1856. 39p. (Spencer's Boston
theatre, no. xlv).

393   BUCKSTONE, JOHN COPELAND, 1860-   . Scrooge; adapted from
Charles Dickens' "A Christmas carol," by J. C. Buckstone...
London, S. French, ltd.: New York, S. French, c1927. 48p.
front. diagr. (On cover: French's acting edition, no.
850).

394   BUGBEE, WILLIS NEWTON, 1870-   . Dan Wetherby's prize, a
rural comedy entertainment in 3 acts, by Willis N. Bugbee...
Franklin, O., Eldridge entertainment house, 1914. 48p.
diagrs.

395   _____. The jolly bachelors, a motion song or recitation.
New York, Dick and Fitzgerald, 1908. 6p.

BURNAND, SIR FRANCIS COWLEY

396   _____. The Pikeville centennial, a novelty entertainment in
two acts, by Willis N. Bugbee... Chicago, T. S. Denison
and co. [1914]. 29p. diagr. On cover: Denison's specialties.

397   _____. The Rocky Ridge vaudeville show, a novelty entertainment, by Willis N. Bugbee... Chicago, T. S. Denison and
co. [1913]. 38p. 1 illus., diagrs. On cover: Denison's
specialties.

398   _____. The young patriots' league. A Washington's birthday
play for intermediate grades. By Willis N. Bugbee...
Franklin, O., Eldridge entertainment house, 1918. 14p.

399 BUNGE, MARTIN L. D. Abraham Lincoln, historical drama in
four acts. Milwaukee, Co-operative printery, 1911. 38p.

400 BUNN, ALFRED. My neighbor's wife. A farce, in one act,
adapted from the French... New York, Clinton T. De Witt
[c1877]. 19p.

401 BURGESS, GELETT, 1866-1951. The picaroons, a San Francisco
night's entertainment, by Gelett Burgess and Will Irwin...
London, Chatto and Windus, 1904. 4 p.ℓ., 272p.

402 BURGESS, NEIL, 1851- . Neil Burgess' new play, entitled
Vim; or, A visit to Puffy farm. In three acts (and a
nightmare). By the author of "Widow Bedott." [New York,
1883]. 52p.

403 BURK, JOHN DALY, ca. 1775-1808. Bethlem Gabor, lord of
Transylvania, or, The man hating Palatine; an historical
drama, in three acts. By John Burk. Petersburg [Va.],
Printed by J. Dickson, for Somervell and Conrad, 1807.
49p.

404 BURKE, JAMES, JR. Shannon boys. A romantic Irish drama, in
three acts. Chicago, The dramatic publishing co., 1895.
27p.

405 BURKLEY, ELIZABETH JEAN (ROOT) 1921- . The farce of
Master Pathelin: preface, translation, and director's
book. [Atlanta, Ga.], 1962. vi, 97p. illus.

406 BURNAND, SIR FRANCIS COWLEY, 1836-1917. Black-eyed Susan; or,
The little bill that was taken up, an original burlesque.
London, Thomas Hailes Lacy [n.d.]. 44p.

BURNAND, SIR FRANCIS COWLEY

407   BURNAND, SIR FRANCIS COWLEY. Easy shaving. A farce, in one
       act. By F. C. Burnand and Montagu Williams. New York,
       Robert M. De Witt [n.d.]. 18p.

408   _____. A new and original nautical burlesque, entitled Poll
       and partner Joe; or, The pride of Putney, and the pressing
       pirate. Written by F. C. Burnand... London, Tinsley bros.,
       1871. 40p. No. 4 in a volume of 8 pieces lettered: The
       drama. vol. XIII. H. L. Mencken.

409   BURR, AMELIA JOSEPHINE, 1878-   . Plays in the market-place,
       by Amelia J. Burr. Englewood, N. J., The Hillside press,
       1910. 4 p.ℓ., 7-74, [2]p.

410   BURTON, LENA DALKEITH. Everychild; morality play, by Lena
       Dalkeith Burton, in cooperation with Marian Katherine
       Brown... Boston, C. W. Thompson and co., 1911. [14]p.
       front.

411   BURTON, RICHARD. Rahab, a drama in three acts. New York,
       Henry Holt and co., 1906. 119p.

412   BUSCH, WILLIAM, 1836-   . Brother Jonathan, an acting drama
       in II.acts... by William Busch... [St. Louis, 1877].
       2 p.ℓ., 28p. Title vignette (portrait).

413   _____. Claudius the fickle; or, Fickleness, thy name is man--
       not woman. A comedy, in five acts, by the author of
       "Life's uses and abuses"... Chicago, G. S. Utter and co.,
       printers, 1869. 53p.

414   [_____.] The dawn of liberty; or, Cadunt regum coronae;
       vicit libertas. An original drama, serio-comical, in
       three acts, by Prometheus [pseud.]... Chicago, Co-opera-
       tive print, 1869. 55p. "Addenda and errata" (3 leaves).

415   _____. ... D'ye want a shave! or, Yankee shavings, or, A new
       way to get a wife. A III act comedy. Rev. ed. by William
       Busch... St. Louis, Mo., 1878. 1 p.ℓ., 25 numb. 1. pl.

416   _____. The maid of the lighthouse, a drama in three acts.
       Rev. ed. [St. Louis, 1879]. 36p.

417   _____. Sorosis! or, The onward march to freedom, a dama [!]
       in four acts. Also a poem entitled Reminiscence of the
       immortal Webster. By Wm. Busch... Chicago, S. S. Jones,
       1868. 47p.

418   BUTLER, ELLIS PARKER. The revolt, a play in one act... New York, Samuel French; London, Samuel French, ltd., c1912. 25p.

419   BUTTLE, MYRA. Toynbee in Elysium, a fantasy in one act. London, Thomas Yoseloff, ltd. [n.d.]. 96p.

420   BUXTON, IDA M. Cousin John's album. A pantomime. Clyde, Ohio, Ames' publishing co., 1888. 7p.

421   BYRON, GEORGE GORDON, 6th Baron, 1788-1824. The poetical works of Lord Byron. London, Henry Frowde, Oxford University press [etc., etc.], 1912. x, 924p. front. (port.). Includes the following dramas: Manfred, Marino Faliero, Sardanapalus, The two Foscari, Cain, Heaven and earth, Werner, The deformed transformed.

422   BYRON, HENRY JAMES, 1835-1884. Blow for blow. A drama, in a prologue and three acts. By Henry J. Byron... To which is added a description of the costumes - cast of the characters... and the whole of the stage business. New York, R. M. De Witt [187-]. 41p. diagrs. (On cover: De Witt's acting plays. [No. 160.]).

423   _____. Cyril's success. A comedy, in five acts. Chicago, The dramatic publishing co. [n.d.]. 46p.

424   _____. Daisy farm; an original drama in four acts, by Henry J. Byron. New American ed., correctly reprinted from the original authorized acting ed. ... New York, H. Roorbach, c1889. 53p. diagrs. (On cover: Roorbach's American edition of acting plays, no. 13).

425   _____. Dearer than life. A serio-comic drama, in three acts. By Henry J. Byron... To which is added a description of the costume - cast of the characters... and the whole of the stage business. New York, R. M. De Witt [187-]. 34p. diagrs. (On cover: De Witt's acting plays [No. 16.]). Includes music ("The honest man": p.18-20).

426   _____. How to tame your mother-in-law; a farce in one act, by Henry J. Byron; new American ed., correctly reprinted from the original authorized acting ed. ... New York, H. Roorbach, 1889. 22p. (On cover: Roorbach's American edition of acting plays. no. 8).

BYRON, HENRY JAMES

427   BYRON, HENRY JAMES. A hundred thousand pounds. An original
      comedy in three acts. By Henry J. Byron... To which are
      added a description of the costume-cast of the characters
      ... and the whole of the stage business. New York, R. M.
      De Witt [186-?]. 1 p.ℓ., [5]-38p. diagr. (On cover: De
      Witt's acting plays. [No. 3.]).

428   _____. The Lancashire lass; or, Tempted, tried and true, a
      domestic melodrama, in four acts and a prologue. Chicago,
      The dramatic publishing co. [n.d.]. 44p.

429   _____. Not such a fool as he looks; a comedy in three acts,
      by Henry J. Byron; new American ed., correctly reprinted
      from the original authorized acting ed. ... New York,
      H. Roorbach, c1890. 52p. (On cover: Roorbach's American
      edition of acting plays, no. 35).

430   _____. "Our boys"; a comedy in three acts, by Henry J. Byron;
      new American ed., correctly reprinted from the original
      authorized acting ed. ... New York, H. Roorbach, c1890.
      51p. diagrs. (On cover: Roorbach's American edition of
      acting plays, no. 36).

431   _____. ... Partners for life, an original comedy in three
      acts, by Henry J. Byron... London, S. French; New York,
      S. French and son [188-?]. 48p. (On cover: French's
      acting edition. 1620).

432   _____. Timothy to the rescue. An original farce, in one act.
      New York, The De Witt publishing house [n.d.]. 16p.

433   _____. Uncle, a comedy in three acts, by Henry J. Byron...
      Philadelphia, The Penn publishing co., 1902. 1 p.ℓ., 5-
      47p.

434   Caesar crosses the Rubicon; a burlesque. Written by members
      of the graduating class of Hunter College High School,
      with the help of the faculty advisor, Lillian Corrigan.
      [n.p., n.d.]. 4p. (American Classical League Service
      Bureau, No. 641).

435   CALCRAFT, JOHN WILLIAM. ... The bride of Lammermoor. A
      drama, in five acts... New York, Samuel French [n.d.].
      44p.

436   CALDERÓN DE LA BARCA, PEDRO, 1600–1681.   ... La española de
       Florencia [o Burlas veras, y Amor invencionero] comedia
       Famosa de Don Pedro Calderón de la Barca, edited, with an
       introduction and notes by S. L. Millard Rosenberg. Phila-
       delphia, Pa., 1911. xlii, 132p. Publications of the Uni-
       versity of Pennsylvania, Series on Romantic languages and
       literatures, no. 5.

437   _____. La vida es sueño; comedia famosa de D. Pedro Calderón
       de la Barca. 1636. Ed. by Milton A. Buchanan... [Toronto]
       University of Toronto library, 1909. 2 p.ℓ., 135p. Let-
       tred on cover: University of Toronto studies.

438   _____. Nobility; or, The alcalde of Zalamea. A drama in
       three acts. Adapted from the Spanish of Calderón de la
       Barca. By Adolfo Pierra. Philadelphia, Pa., 1885. vi,
       7–48p.

439   CALLAHAN, CHARLES E. Lambh Darragh; a story of '98. Drama,
       in three acts... Cincinnati, Printed for the author, but
       not published, 1878. 43p.

440   CALMOUR, ALFRED CECIL, 1857?–1912. The amber heart, a poeti-
       cal fancy in three acts, by Alfred C. Calmour... [London,
       Printed by Veale, Chifferiel and co.]. For private circu-
       lation, 1886. 69, [1]p.

441   CALVERT, GEORGE H. Arnold and André, an historical drama.
       Boston, Lee and Shepard, 1876. 95p.

442   CAMERON, MARGARET, i.e. Mrs. Margaret Cameron Smith, 1867–1947.
       A Christmas chime, a play in one act. New York, Samuel
       French, 1910. 22p.

443   _____. Comedies in miniature, by Margaret Cameron; frontis-
       piece by Harrison Fisher. New York, McClure, Phillips and
       co., 1903. ix, 376p. front. CONTENTS. - Miss Doulton's
       orchids. - The burglar. - The kleptomaniac. - A pipe of
       peace. - A Christmas crime. - The committee on matrimony.
       - Her neighbor's creed. - Unexpected guests. - The P. A. I.
       L. W. R. - In a street car. - A patron of art.

444   _____. A loyal renegade, a comedy in one act, by Margaret
       Cameron Smith. Oakland, Calif., Enquirer publishing co.,
       1900. 1 p.ℓ., 7p. illus. (diagr.)

CAMERON, MARGARET

445   CAMERON, MARGARET. A pipe of peace; a comedy in one act, by
          Margaret Cameron Smith. Oakland, Calif., Enquirer pub-
          lishing co., 1900. 1 p.ℓ., 10p. illus. (plan).

446   CAMPBELL, A. L. ... Lyieushee Lovel; or, The gipsey of Ash-
          burnham Dell! a domestic drama, in three acts... London,
          J. Duncombe and co. [n.d.]. 48p. (Duncombe's edition).

447   CAMPBELL, ANDREW LEONARD VOULLAIRE, 1789-1870. The forest
          oracle; or, The bridge of Tresino: an operatic drama, in
          three acts... the music by Mr. Nicholson. London, John
          Cumberland [n.d.]. 48p.

448   CAMPBELL, MARIAN D. An open secret, a farce in two acts. Bos-
          ton, Walter H. Baker and co. [1898]. 16p.

449   CAMPBELL, WILLIAM WILFRED, 1858?-1918. Poetical tragedies.
          Toronto, W. Briggs, 1908. 319p. CONTENTS. - Mordred. -
          Daulac. - Morning. - Hildebrand.

450   CANNAN, GILBERT, 1884-   . Four plays by Gilbert Cannan:
          James and John - Miles Dison - Mary's wedding - A short
          way with authors. London, Sedgwick and Jackson, ltd.,
          1913. 5 p.ℓ., 3-84p.

451   Capuletta. A burlesque... Boston, George M. Baker [n.d.].
          26p.

452   CARMAN, BLISS, 1861-1929. Earth deities, and other rhythmic
          masques, by Bliss Carman and Mary Perry King. New York,
          M. Kennerley, 1914. 4 p.ℓ., 85p. front.

453   CARR, MARK V. Sinatra takes a bow; the fifteenth Idyll of
          Theocritus in an American setting. [n.p., n.d.]. 4p.
          (American Classical League Service Bureau, No. 608).

454   CARTER, WILLIAM. Port wine vs. jealousy. A highly amusing
          sketch... arranged by Charles White... New York, Robert
          M. De Witt, 1875. 8p.

455   CASSILIS, INA LEON. Those landladies, boarding-house comedy
          for two females. New York, Edgar S. Werner and co., 1906.
          7p.

456   CATTELL, WILLIAM F. A valuable fish. A comedy-drama in four
          acts. Clyde, Ohio, Ames' publishing co., 1905. 40p.

BRITISH AND AMERICAN DRAMA

CHAMBERS, CHARLES HADDON

457 CAVERLY, ROBERT BOODEY, 1806-1887. Battle of the Bush.
Dramas and historic legends... Elaborated from the star-
tling events of the New England wars of a hundred years...
By Robert Boodey Caverly. Boston, B. B. Russell, 1886.
5 p.ℓ., 3-346p. front., plates. CONTENTS. - no. 1. The
last night of a nation. - no. 2. Miantonimo. - no. 3.
King Philip. - no. 4. The regicides. - no. 5. Chocorus
in the mountains.

458 _____. ... Chocorus in the mountains. (N. E.) An historical
drama. [Years 1698-1768]. By Robert B. Caverly... Boston,
The author, 1885. 1 p.ℓ., p.251-341. front., plates.

459 _____. ... King Philip. (N. E.) An historical drama, years
1648 to 1698. By Robert B. Caverly... Boston, The author,
1884. 1 p.ℓ., 127-190p. front., pl.

460 _____. ... The last night of a nation. (N. E.) An historical drama, years 1585 to 1637. By Robert B. Caverly...
Boston. The author, 1884. 1 p.ℓ., 57p. front. (port.)
pl.

461 _____. ... Miantonimo. (N. E.) An historical drama, years
1637 to 1649. By Robert B. Caverly... Boston, The author,
1884. 1 p.ℓ., p.61-124. front., pl.

462 _____. ... The regicides. (N. E.) An historical drama.
(Years 1640-1676.) By Robert B. Caverly... Boston, The
author, 1884. 1 p.ℓ., p.193-247. front., 4 pl.

463 CAZAURAN, AUGUSTUS R. French flats. A farcical comedy, in
four acts. Adapted from the French of Henry Chivot by
A. R. Cazauran. [New York, 1879]. 2 p.ℓ., 202 numb. 1.

464 CENTLIVRE, SUSANNAH, 1667-1723. The wonder, a woman keeps a
secret, a comedy, in three acts. London, Thomas Hailes
Lacy [n.d.]. 57p.

465 CHALONER, JOHN ARMSTRONG. "Saul," a tragedy in three acts.
Roanoke Rapids, N. C., Palmetto press, 1915. 69p.

466 CHAMBERS, CHARLES HADDON. The awakening, a play in four acts,
Boston, Walter H. Baker and co., 1903. 160p.

467 _____. Tyranny of tears; a comedy in four acts. Boston,
Baker, 1902. 152p.

CHAMBERS, T. BELL

468   CHAMBERS, T. BELL. A Kentucky belle, a comedy in three acts.
       Philadelphia, The Penn publishing co. [1909]. 35p.

469   CHAMISSO, ADALBERT VON, 1781-1838. Faust; a dramatic sketch,
       by Adalbert von Chamisso (1830) tr. from the German by
       Henry Phillips, Jr., Philadelphia, 1881. v, 23p.

470   CHANDLER, OLIVE. A program for a school assembly: a Roman
       style show and a pageant on Latin derivatives. [n.p.,
       n.d.]. 6p. (American Classical League Service Bureau,
       No. 327).

471   _____. What's the use of Latin? [n.p., n.d.]. 3p. (Ameri-
       can Classical League Service Bureau, No. 699).

472   CHAPIN, BENJAMIN CHESTER. Abraham Lincoln, a drama. New
       York, 1905. Various pagings.

473   CHAPMAN, JOHN JAY, 1862-1933. Cupid and Psyche. New York,
       Laurence J. Gomme, 1916. 92p. CONTENTS. Cupid and Psyche.
       Lafayette, Romulus and Remus.

474   _____. A sausage from Bologna, a comedy in four acts. New
       York, Moffat, Yard and co., 1909. 114p.

475   _____. The treason and death of Benedict Arnold, a play for
       a Greek theatre. [n.p.], Moffat Yard and co., 1910. 76p.

476   CHASE, F. E. A personal matter, a comedy in one act. Boston,
       George M. Baker and co., 1880. 22p.

477   _____. A ready-made suit, a mock trial. Boston, Walter H.
       Baker and co., 1885. 41p.

478   CHASE, GEORGE B. Haunted by a shadow; or, Hunted down, a
       drama in four acts. Clyde, Ohio, Ames' publishing co.,
       1890. 23p.

479   _____. Penn Hapgood; or, The yankee schoolmaster, a drama in
       three acts. Clyde, Ohio, Ames' publishing co., 1890. 34p.

480   _____. Simple Silas: or, The detective from Plunketsville,
       a drama in three acts. Clyde, Ohio, Ames' publishing co.,
       1890. 24p.

481   CHATTERTON, THOMAS, 1752-1770. The works of Thomas Chatter-
       ton... London, T. N. Longman and O. Rees, 1803. 3v.
       fronts., plates (1 fold.) facsim. Contains his Woman of
       spirit. CONTENTS. v.1. Life of Chatterton by G. Gregory.
       Miscellaneous poems. - v.2. Poems attributed to Rowley.
       - v.3. Miscellaneous pieces in prose.

482   CHEKHOV, ANTON PAVLOVICH, 1860-1904. The jubilee, a farce in
       one act, by Anton Chekhov. Tr. from the Russian by Olive
       Frances Murphy. (In Poet lore. Boston, 1920. [vol. XXXI,
       no. 4], p.616-628).

483   _____. Plays... second series. On the high road. The pro-
       posal. The wedding. The bear. A tragedian in spite of
       himself. The anniversary. The three sisters. The cherry
       orchard. Translated with an introduction by Julian West.
       New York, Charles Scribner's sons [n.d.]. 277p.

484   _____. Plays, by Anton Tchekoff... translated from the
       Russian, with an introduction, by Marian Fell. New York,
       C. Scribner's sons, 1912. 4 p.ℓ., 3-233p. front. (port.).

485   _____. The sea-gull, by Anton Tchekoff. Tr. by Fred Eisemann.
       [Boston, R. G. Badger], 1913. p.1-41. (Poet lore plays).

486   _____. That worthless fellow Platonov... Translated from the
       Russian by John Cournos. New York, Dutton [n.d.]. 279p.

487   _____. The three sisters; a drama in four acts, translated
       from the Russian of Anton Chekhov by Stark Young. New
       York, Los Angeles, S. French; [etc., etc.], 1941. xxii,
       110p. 2 pl. on 1ℓ.

488   CHELTNAM, CHALRES SMITH. Deborah (Leah) or, The Jewish
       maiden's wrong, a drama, in three acts. New York, The
       De Witt publishing house [n.d.]. 32p.

489   _____. Edendale. An original drama, in three acts... Lon-
       don, Thomas Hailes Lacy [n.d.]. 42p.

490   CHERRY, A. ... The soldier's daughter. A comedy, in five
       acts... New York, William Taylor and co. [n.d.]. 75p.
       (Modern standard drama, no. xcvii).

491   ... Cherry and fair star. A grand eastern spectacle, in two
       acts... New York, Samuel French [n.d.]. 27p.

CHEW, J. A.

492   CHEW, J. A. That Greenish family. An American comedy (new
      and original) in three acts... Winslow, Bucks., Printed by
      Edwin J. French [c1903]. 63p.

493   CHÉZY, WILHELMINE CHRISTIANE VON, 1783-1856. Euryanthe; a
      grand romantic opera in three acts (in German and English)...
      Manager's ed. London, A. Schloss [18--]. 51p.

494   CHIPMAN, ADELBERT Z. The little wife. A comedy drama, in
      four acts. Clyde, Ohio, Ames' publishing co., 1900. 39p.

495   _____. Ruben Rube; or, My invalid aunt; farce in one act.
      By A. Z. Chipman... Clyde, O., Ames' publishing co.
      [1900]. 15p. On cover: Ames' series of standard and
      minor drama. no. 416.

496   CHIPMAN, ELIZABETH A. Beverly's triumphs, a play in three
      acts. Brookline, Mass., The Riverdale press, 1910. 29p.

497   The Chuckerbutty faction; or, Calcutta preserved. A farce in
      three acts. Calcutta, 1843. 60p.

498   CHURCHILL, WINSTON, 1871-1947. The title-mart, a comedy in
      three acts. New York and London, The Macmillan co., 1905.
      215p.

499   Cicero walks with Washington and Lincoln at midnight, by stu-
      dents of a Cicero class of Sterling Township High School,
      Sterling, Ill. [n.p., n.d.]. 4p. (American Classical
      League Service Bureau, No. 588).

500   Cinderella, a play in three scenes. Illustrated by Arthur
      Rackham [n.d.]. 48p. illus.

501   CLARK, BARRETT HARPER, 1890-1953. ed. One-act plays, edited
      by Barrett H. Clark and Thomas R. Cook... Boston, New
      York [etc.], D. C. Heath and co. [1929]. xix, 288p.
      front., ports.

502   CLARK, MARGERY S. "A wet blanket." [New York and London,
      1910]. 19p.

503   CLARKE, JOSEPH IGNATIUS CONSTANTINE, 1846-1925. The fighting
      race, and other poems and ballads, by Joseph I. C. Clarke...
      New York, The American news co., 1911. 2 p.ℓ., ix-xii p.,
      2ℓ., 13-207p. col. front.

504 _____. Lady Godiva; a play in four acts, by Joseph I. Clarke...
New York, S. French; London, S. French, ltd., 1903. 76p.
(American dramatists club series, no. 2).

505 _____. Luck. A comedy in three acts. By Joseph I. C. Clarke.
Printed but not published. New York, De Lacy and Willson,
printers, 1877. 46p.

506 _____. Mâlmôrda, a metrical romance, by Joseph I. C. Clarke...
New York [etc.], G. P. Putnam's sons, 1893. 2 p.ℓ., 92p.
illus.

507 _____. Robert Emmet, a tragedy of Irish history, by Joseph
I. C. Clarke. New York and London, G. P. Putnam's sons,
1888. vii, p., 1ℓ., 134p. 2 port. (incl. front.) 2 illus.

508 CLARKE, MARY V. Mettius Curtius. [n.p., n.d.]. 2p. (American Classical League Service Bureau, No. 547).

509 CLARKE, N. H. BELDEN. ... O'Neal, the great; or, Cogger na
caillie; a drama in three acts... New York, Samuel French
[n.d.]. 40p. (French's standard drama, no. cccxxi).

510 CLEAVER, E. M. The universal exchange, an entertainment.
Chicago, The dramatic publishing co. [1910]. 32p.

511 CLEMENS, SAMUEL LANGHORNE, 1835-1910. Colonel Sellers, a
drama in five acts. By Saml. L. Clemens, "Mark Twain"
[pseud.] Elmira, N. Y. [1874]. 104p.

512 COALE, GEORGE B. On his devoted head. A domestic scene...
New York, De Witt, 1885. 8p.

512A COBB, JAMES, 1756-1818. Paul and Virginia; a musical entertainment, in two acts, by James Cobb. (In The London
stage. London [1824-27] v. 4 [no. 36] p. [10]-16. 1 illus.).
Caption title. Music by Reeve and Mazzinghi. Cf. Brit.
Mus. Cat. printed mus.

513 COES, GEORGE H. Mistaken identity, an Ethiopian farce in one
scene. Boston, Walter H. Baker and co., 1893. 8p.

514 _____. Scenes in a sanctum, an Ethiopian farce in one act.
Boston, Walter H. Baker and co., 1895. 9p.

515 COFFMAN, T. C. The Coontown musketeers, a minstrel sketch.
Chicago, The Dramatic publishing co. [1901]. 8p.

COLBURN, OTIS LINCOLN

516   COLBURN, OTIS LINCOLN. The path of thorns; or, Anna Karenina,
       a drama by Otis Lincoln Colburn. [Chicago? 1907]. cover-
       title, various pagings.

517   [COLBY, MRS. F. B.] Le triomphe des fées. A comedy for
       juveniles. In four acts and an interlude. Written for
       and dedicated to Jacob A. Mahler, by F.B.C. Original
       dances and ballets arranged by Prof. Jacob A. Mahler...
       [St. Louis, Mo., 1885]. 16p.

518   COLCOUGH, EMMA SHAW. An object lesson in history. New York,
       E. L. Kellogg and co., 1896. 24p.

519   COLE, FRANCIS R. The marriage question, a monologue. Chica-
       go, The dramatic publishing co., 1910. 9p.

520   [COLE, JOHN WILLIAM] d. 1870. The bride of Lammermoor: a
       drama, in three acts, (from Sir Walter Scott) by John
       William Calcraft [pseud.]. Printed from the acting copy,
       with remarks, biographical and critical, by D.-G. ... As
       performed at the Theatres Royal... London, G. H. Davidson
       [n.d.]. 44p. incl. front. (Cumberland's British theatre.
       London, ca. 1825-55. v.45 [no.4]).
           Remarks by George Daniel, editor of the series.
           Reissue of Cumberland's earlier edition.

521   COLERIDGE, SAMUEL TAYLOR, 1772-1834. The dramatic works of
       Samuel Taylor Coleridge. Ed. by Derwent Coleridge. A
       new ed. London, E. Moxon, 1852. 1 p.ℓ., [v]-xivp., 1ℓ.,
       427p. CONTENTS. Remorse. - Zapolya. - The Piccolomini;
       or, The first part of Wallenstein. Tr. from Schiller. -
       The death of Wallenstein.

522   _____. Osorio; a tragedy, as originally written in 1797 by
       Samuel Taylor Coleridge; now first printed from a copy
       recently discovered by the publisher, with the variorum
       readings of "Remorse" and a monograph on the history of
       the play in its earlier and later form, by the author of
       "Tennysonia." London, J. Pearson, 1873. 3 p.ℓ., [v]-
       xxii p., 1 ℓ., 204p.

523   _____. Remorse. A tragedy, in five acts. By S. T. Cole-
       ridge... 2d ed. London, Printed for W. Pople, 1813. vi,
       [2]p., 1ℓ., 73p.

524   COLLIER, WILLIAM. ... The rival sergeants; or, Love and lot-
       tery! A musical burletta, in one act... London, Duncombe
       and Moon [n.d.]. 21p. front.

525   COLLIS, MAURICE. The motherly and auspicious, being the life of the Empress Dowager Tzu Hsi in the form of a drama with an introduction and notes. London, Faber and Faber, 1943. 179p. illus.

526   [COLMAN, GEORGE] 1762-1836. The actor of all work; or, The first and second floor. A farce. In one act. With the comic song of The picture of a London play-house, as introduced by Mr. Mathews, at the New York theatre. New York, E. M. Murden, 1822. 24p.
      Written by George Colman, the younger, "to display the wonderful imitative powers of Mathews" in the character of Multiple. Cf. Memoirs of Charles Mathews, by Mrs. Mathews. 1838, v. 2, p. 414.

527   _____. The Africans; or, War, love, and duty. A play, in three acts, by George Colman, the younger... Printed from the acting copy, with remarks biographical and critical, by D.-G. ... As performed at the Theatres Royal... London, J. Cumberland [n.d.]. 62p. incl. front. (Cumberland's British theatre. London, ca. 1825-55. v. 43 [no. 2]).
      The plot is from Florian's "Selico," one of his "Nouvelles nouvelles." Cf. Baker, Biog. dram.; W. D. Adams, Dict. of the drama; Stage cyclo.
      Remarks by George Daniel, editor of the series.
      Without the music (by Kelly).

527A _____. Blue Beard; a grand dramatic romance, in three acts, by George Colman, the younger... Printed from the acting copy, with remarks, biographical and critical, by D.-G. ... As performed at the Theatres Royal... London, Davidson [n.d.]. 39p. incl. front. (Cumberland's British theatre. London, ca. 1825-55. v.36 [no.5]).
      "Partly founded on a French piece, the Barbebleu, played at Paris, 1746." Cf. Remarks; Baker, Biog. dram.
      In two acts. Produced under title: Blue Beard; or, Female curiosity.
      Remarks by George Daniel, editor of the series.
      Music by Kelly. Cf. Grove, 5th ed.
      Reissue of Cumberland's earlier edition.

528   _____. ... Blue devils. A comedietta, in one act... New York, M. Douglas, 1848. 25p. (Modern standard drama, no. lxxii).

COLMAN, GEORGE

529   COLMAN, GEORGE. The gay deceivers; or, More laugh than love:
      a farce, in two acts. By George Colman, the younger.
      First acted at the Theatre Royal, Haymarket, on the 22d of
      August, 1804. London, J. Cawthorn [etc.] 1808. 46p.
      [Broadhurst, J. Plays. v.2, no. 4].
           Based on "Les événemens imprévus" of d'Hele, or Hales.
      First produced under author's pseud., Arthur Griffin-
      hoof.

530   _____. ... The mountaineers. A play, in three acts... New
      York, Wm. Taylor and co. [n.d.]. 57p. (Modern standard
      drama, no. lxiii).

531   _____. The review; or, The wags of Windsor: a musical farce,
      by George Colman, the younger... Printed from the acting
      copy, with remarks, biographical and critical, by D.-G.
      ... As performed at the Theatres Royal... London, G. H.
      Davidson [n.d.]. 38p. incl front. (Cumberland's British
      theatre. London, ca. 1825-55. v. 36 [n. 9]).
           Based on "Caleb Quotem and his wife," by Henry Lee.
      Cf. Remarks; Genest, Account of the English stage, v. 7,
      p. 490.
           Remarks by George Daniel, editor of the series.
           Originally published under author's pseudonym, Arthur
      Griffinhoof.
           Without the music (by Arnold).
           Reissue of Cumberland's earlier edition.

532   _____. ... Sylvester Daggerwood, an interlude; by G. Colman,
      esq. With prefatory remarks... Faithfully marked with
      the stage business and stage directions, as it is per-
      formed at the Theatres Royal. By W. Oxberry, comedian.
      London, Pub. for the Proprietors, by W. Simpkin, and R.
      Marshall, [etc.] 1823. iv, [5]-12p. front. (port.).
      (Oxberry, William. The new English drama. London, 1818-
      25. v. 21 [no.5]). At head of title: Oxberry's edition.
           "Remarks" signed: P. P.
           From the one act play originally produced under the
      title "New hay at the old market."

533   Columbus, the great discoverer of America. A drama in five
      acts. By an Ursuline... New York, Chicago [etc.], Ben-
      ziger bros., 1892. vii, [3]-55p. front. (port.).

534   CONGREVE, WILLIAM, 1670-1729. The way of the world, a comedy
      as it is acted at the theatre in Lincoln's-Inn-Fields by
      His Majesty's servants. London, W. and G. Foyle, ltd.,
      1924. 95p.

COOLIDGE, HENRY DINGLEY

535   The Connecticut emigrant. A dialogue, between Henry - an in-
        tended emigrant. Mary - his wife. Hezekiah - his father.
        Hepzibah - his mother. George - his son. Also, a song, for
        the anniversary of the Connecticut agricultural societies,
        cattle shows, fairs, and exhibitions of domestic manufac-
        tures, for 1822... By a descendant of the Connecticut pil-
        grims. Hartford, Printed for the purchasers, 1822. 12p.

536   CONRAD, ROBERT TAYLOR, 1810-1858. Aylmere; or, The bondman of
        Kent; and other poems. By Robert T. Conrad. Philadelphia,
        E. H. Butler and co., 1852. x, [11]-329p.

537   The conspiracy of Catiline: a play in English, by the Cicero
        class of Grandview Heights High School, Columbus, Ohio.
        [n.p., n.d.]. 8p. (American Classical League Service
        Bureau, No. 431).

538   CONWAY, H. J. ... Our Jeminy; or, Connecticut courtship. A
        farce, in one act... New York, Samuel French [n.d.]. 25p.
        front. (French's American drama, no. lxxviii).

539   CONWAY, JOHN WILLIAM, 1851-   . Abbe Lawrence, a drama in
        five acts. Norton, Kansas, 1903. 64p.

540   COOK, ESTELLE. The hero of the gridiron, a college comedy in
        five acts. Boston, Walter H. Baker and co., 1908. 34p.

541   COOK, SHERWIN LAWRENCE. A valet's mistake. A comedy, in two
        acts. Clyde, Ohio, Ames' publishing co., 1894. 15p.

542   COOKE, MARJORIE BENTON. Dramatic episodes, by Marjorie Ben-
        ton Cooke... Chicago, Sergel [1919]. 2d.ed. 181p. CON-
        TENTS. - A court comedy. - Manners and modes. - The con-
        fessional. - The child in the house. - The lion and the
        lady. - Success. - Lady Betty's burglar. - A dinner-with
        complications. - Reform. - When love is young.

543   _____. Tit for tat, a play for little folks. Chicago, The
        dramatic publishing co., 1906. 9p.

544   COOLIDGE, CASSIUS MARCELLUS. Guess not, an art pantomine and
        play. In three acts... [Rochester, N. Y., 1875]. 1 p.ℓ.,
        6 numb. ℓ.

545   COOLIDGE, HENRY DINGLEY. Dead reckoning, a farce. Boston,
        Walter H. Baker and co., 1895. 17p.

COOPER, FREDERICK FOX

546 COOPER, FREDERICK FOX. ... The deserted village. A drama, in
    three acts... London, J. Duncombe and co. [n.d.]. 49p.
    front. (Duncombe's edition).

547 COOPER, LANE, ed. Fifteen Greek plays, translated into Eng-
    lish by Gilbert Murray, Benjamin Bickley Rogers, and others.
    With an introduction, and a supplement from the "Poetics"
    of Aristotle by Lane Cooper. New York, Oxford University
    Press, 1943. xxii, 794p. illus. CONTENTS. Aeschylus.
    Prometheus bound. Agamemnon. Choëphore. The Eumenides.
    - Sophocles. Oedipus. Antigone. Oedipus at Colonos.
    Electra. - Euripides. Electra. Iphigenia in Tauris.
    Medea. Hippolytus. - Aristophanes. The Clouds. The Birds.
    The Frogs. - Supplement from the "Poetics" of Aristotle
    [Lane Cooper]. - Aristotle on comedy [Lane Cooper]. - A list
    of useful books [Lane Cooper].

548 CORBIN, JOHN, 1870-   . Husband, and The forbidden guests;
    two plays, by John Corbin... Boston and New York, Houghton
    Mifflin co., 1910. xxxiii p., 5 ℓ., [9]-271, [1]p.

549 CORCORAN, (MRS.) MAY. Persephone; a puppet play in two scenes
    [n.p., n.d.]. 8p. (American Classical League Service
    Bureau, No. 654).

550 _____. Pomona; a puppet play [n.p., n.d.]. 5p. (American
    Classical League Service Bureau, No. 653).

551 CORNEILLE, PIERRE, 1606-1684. Le Cid; a tragedy by P. Corneille;
    ed. with a complete commentary for the use of students by
    Edward S. Joynes... New York, Leypoldt and Holt; [etc.,
    etc.], 1870. 110p. (Student's series of classic French
    plays. v. 1).

552 _____. Horace; tragédie en cinq actes, par P. Corneille. With
    grammatical and explanatory notes by Frederick C. Sumichrast
    ... New York, W. B. Jenkins; [etc., etc.] 1890. viii,
    [2], 102p. Classiques français. no. 5.

553 _____. Horace. Horatius, a tragedy in four acts, (the fifth
    being omitted in representation). By Corneille. The
    original French copy with an English translation, prepared
    expressly for M. Raphael Felix... New York, Darcie and
    Corbyn, 1855. 28p.

554 COUCY, LOUIS DE. The abbot's map, a playlet. New York,
    Frohman, 1907. 18p.

COYNE, JOSEPH STIRLING

555   The courier of Lyons; or, The attack upon the mail. A drama, in three acts. Trans. from the French of ... Moreau, Siraudin, Delacour... New York, Samuel French and son [n.d.]. 44p.

556   COURTNEY, JOHN, 1804-1865. ... Eustache Baudin; an original drama, in three acts. By John Courtney... To which are added a description of the costume - cast of the characters ... and the whole of the stage business... New York, S. French, [185-?]. 45p. (French's standard drama. The acting edition. No. CXLII).

557   _____. Time tries all. An original drama, in two acts. New York, Samuel French [n.d.]. 26p.

558   COURTRIGHT, WILLIAM. The motor bellows. A comedy, in one act and one scene. New York, The De Witt publishing house, 1877. 6p.

559   COWLEY, E. J. The Bohemians, a comedy in three acts. Boston, Walter H. Baker and co., 1896. 43p.

560   COYNE, JOSEPH STIRLING, 1803-1868. ... Box and Cox. Married and settled. An original farce, in one act... New York, Samuel French [n.d.]. 20p.

561   _____. ... Cockneys in California. "A piece of golden opportunity." In one act... New York, M. Douglas [n.d.]. 19p. front. (The minor drama, no. xxxiii).

562   _____. ... Did you ever send your wife to Brooklyn? An original farce, in one act. By J. Stirling Coyne, esq. Correctly printed from the most approved acting copy... To which are added, properties and directions, as performed in the principal theatres. New York and Philadelphia, Turner and Fisher [n.d.]. 18p. (Turner's dramatic library. no. [73]).
      Published in London under title: Did you ever send your wife to Camberwell?

563   _____. Everybody's friend. An original comedy, in three acts. By J. Stirling Coyne... To which is added a description of the costumes, cast of characters... and the whole of the stage business. New York, R. M. De Witt [187-?]. 46p. (On cover: De Witt's acting plays. [No. 135]).

COYNE, JOSEPH STIRLING

564   COYNE, JOSEPH STIRLING. The home wreck. A drama, in three
acts... Suggested by Tennyson's poem of "Enoch Arden."
Partly written by the late J. Stirling Coyne... and com-
pleted by his son, J. Denis Coyne. London, Thomas Hailes
Lacy [n.d.]. 45p.

565   _____. The little rebel. A farce, in one act... New York,
Robert M. De Witt [n.d.]. 19p.

566   _____. ... The love knot. A comedy in three acts... Boston,
William V. Spencer [n.d.]. 39p. (Spencer's Boston theatre,
no. clxiii).

567   _____. The old chateau; or, A night of peril, a drama, in
three acts. London, Thomas Hailes Lacy [n.d.]. 40p.

568   _____. ... Pas de fascination; or, Catching a governor; a
farce, in one act... Originally performed at the Theatre
Royal, Haymarket, under the title of Lola Montes; or, A
countess for an hour... Boston, Wm. V. Spencer [n.d.].
19p. (Spencer's Boston theatre, no. cxcii).

569   _____. ... Separate maintenance. A farce, in one act...
London, Duncombe and Moon [n.d.]. 23p. front. (Duncombe's
eidition).

570   _____. Wanted, 1000 spirited young milliners, for the gold
diggings! A farce, in one act... New York, O. A. Roorbach,
Jr. [n.d.]. 22p.

571   _____. A widow hunt. An original comedy in three acts,
(altered from his own comedy of "Everybody's friend").
Chicago, The dramatic publishing co. [n.d.]. 38p.

572   [CRAIGIE, PEARL MARY-TERESA]. The ambassador, a comedy in
four acts, by John Oliver Hobbes, pseud. Second ed. New
York, Frederick A. Stokes co. [1898]. 173p.

573   _____. The wisdom of the wise, a comedy in three acts. London, T. Fishar Unwin, 1901 151p.

574   CRANE, ELEANOR MAUD. The lost New Year, a play in two scenes
for children. New York, Harold Roorbach, 1897. 23p.

575   CRAVEN, ARTHUR SCOTT. The fool's tragedy, by Arthur Scott
Craven. London, M. Secker [1913]. 275p.

CRAWFORD, JACK RANDALL

576 _____. The last of the English; a play in four acts, by
Arthur Scott Craven. London, E. Mathews, 1910. 159p.

577 CRAVEN, HENRY THORNTON, 1818-1905. The chimney corner. An
original domestic drama, in two acts. By H. T. Craven...
To which are added a description of the costume - cast of
the characters... and the whole of the stage business.
New York, C. T. De Witt [187-?]. 26p diagr. (On cover:
De Witt's acting plays. [No. 219.]).

578 _____. Meg's diversion, a drama in two acts; by H. T. Craven.
New American ed., correctly reprinted from the original
authorized acting ed. ... New York, H. Roorbach [c1890].
46p. diagr. (On cover: Roorbach's American edition of
acting plays, no. 39).

579 _____. Milky white. An original domestic drama. In two acts
... as first performed... September 28, 1864... New York,
Robert M. De Witt [n.d.]. 27p.

580 _____. Milky White; a domestic drama in two acts, by H. T.
Craven. New American ed., correctly reprinted from the
original authorized acting ed. ... New York, H. Roorbach,
c1889. 42p. diagrs. (On cover: Roorbach's American edition of acting plays, no. 5). Song, "Early love": p. 40-42.

581 _____. Miriam's crime. A drama, in three acts. By H. T.
Craven... London, T. H. Lacy [186-]. 39p. (On back
cover: Lacy's acting edition of plays).
   "First performed... October 9th, 1863."

582 _____. Miserrimus; or, The broken heart. A drama, in five
acts, by H. T. Craven... London [etc.] J. Templeman, 1843.
2 p.ℓ., 75p.
   Adapted from "Miserrimus" by F. M. Reynolds.

583 _____. The poet-boy. An original drama, in two acts...
London, Thomas Hailes Lacy [n.d.]. 32p.

584 CRAWFORD, JACK RANDALL, 1878-   . Lovely Peggy; a play in
three acts based on the love romance of Margaret Woffington
and David Garrick, by J. R. Crawford. New Haven, Yale
university press, 1911. 4 p.ℓ., [3]-173p.

585 _____. Robin of Sherwood; a comedy in three acts and four
scenes, by J. R. Crawford. New Haven, Yale university
press, 1912. 5 p.ℓ., 7-150p.

CRESSY, WILL MARTIN

586   CRESSY, WILL MARTIN, 1863-   . Continuous vaudeville, by
           Will M. Cressy; with illustrations by Hal Merritt. Boston,
           R. G. Badger; [etc., etc., 1914]. 181p. front., illus.

587   Crockery's misfortunes; or, Transmogrifications, a burletta
           in one act... New York, E. M. Murden, 1822. 18p.

588   CROFT-COOKE, RUPERT. Tap three times, a comedy thriller in
           one act for seven women. London, Samuel French, ltd. [n.d.].
           16p.

589   CROKER, MRS. BITHIA MARY (SHEPPARD) d. 1920. The real Lady
           Hilda; a sketch, by B. M. Croker... New York, F. M.
           Buckles and co. [etc., etc.] 1899. 266p.

590   CROSWELL, JOSEPH. A new world planted; or, The adventures of
           the forefathers of New England; who landed in Plymouth,
           December 22, 1620. An historical drama--in five acts. By
           Joseph Croswell. Boston, Printed for the author; sold by
           E. Larkin, no. 47, Cornhill, 1802. vi, [7]-45p.

591   CROTHERS, RACHEL, 1878-1958. ... He and she, a play in three
           acts, by Rachel Crothers... Boston, Walter H. Baker and
           co. [c1933]. 126p. illus. (plans). (Baker's professional
           plays).

592   _____. The rector, a play in one act, by Rachel Crothers...
           New York, S. French; London, S. French, ltd., 1905. 2 p.ℓ.,
           3-19p. (On cover: French's international copyrighted...
           edition of the works of the best authors, no. 85).

593   CROZIER, CHALRES. While life shall last. A play by Charles
           Crozier and John Burton. [London, n.d.]. 14p.

594   CRUMPTON, M. NATALINE, 1857-1911. Ceres; a mythological play
           for parlor and school, in three acts; two males and twelve
           females, by M. Nataline Crumpton... New York, E. S. Werner,
           1890. 17p.

595   _____. Pandora, a classical play for parlor and school in
           three acts, four males and three females, by M. Nataline
           Crumpton. New York, E. S. Werner, 1890. 1 p.ℓ., 11p.

596   _____. Theseus, a mythological play for parlor and school in
           five acts... New York, Edgar S. Werner, 1892. 29p.

598   CUMBERLAND, RICHARD, 1732-1811. The Jew of Mogador, a comic
       opera, in three acts. By Richard Cumberland, esq. ...
       New York, Published by David Longworth, at the Dramatic
       repository, Shakspeare-gallery, 1808. 56p. [Dramatic
       pamphlets. v. 24, no. 8].
          Without the music (by Kelly).

599   _____. The posthumous dramatick works of the late Richard
       Cumberland, esq. ... London, G. and W. Nicol, 1813. 2 v.
          "Advertisement to the reader" signed by the author's
       daughter, Frances Marianne Jansen.
          CONTENTS. - v. 1. The sybil, or, The elder Brutus. The
       Walloons. The confession. The passive husband. Torrendal.
       Lover's resolution. - v. 2. Alcanor. The eccentric lover.
       Tiberious in Capreae. The last of the family. Don Pedro.
       The false Demetrius.

600   CUREL, FRANÇOIS, VICOMTE DE, 1854-1928. The beat of the wing
       (Le coup d'aile) (a play in three acts) by François de
       Curel. Tr. from the French by Alice Van Kaathoven. In
       Poet lore. Boston, 1909. vol. XX, no. 5, p. 321-375.

601   [CURT, MRS. ARIANA (RANDOLPH WORMELEY)]. The spirit of
       seventy six; or The coming woman, a prophetic drama, fol-
       lowed by A change of base, and Doctor Mondschein. Seven-
       teenth edition. Boston, Little, Brown and co., 1875.
       141p.

602   CURTIN, H. PELHAM. None so deaf as those who won't hear. A
       comedietta in one act. Boston, Walter H. Baker and co.,
       1880. 22p.

603   CURTIS, H. PELHAM. Uncle Robert; or, Love's labor saved, a
       comedy, in three acts. Boston, Walter H. Baker and co.
       [1861]. 34p.

604   CUSHING, CHARLES CYPRIAN STRONG, 1879-1941. Nathan Hale of
       '73; a drama in four acts, by C. C. S. Cushing... New
       Haven, Conn., Yale publishing association, 1908. x, [2],
       88p., 1ℓ., incl. front., illus. plates.

605   _____. Prehistoric Mable; an hysterical, evolutionary play in
       five ages, by C. C. S. Cushing. Being all about Ding,
       Dong, Bell. [Hartford, Conn., Press of Meyer and Noll,
       c1909]. 6 p.ℓ., 96p. 1ℓ. front., plates.

CUTLER, F. L.

606   CUTLER, F. L.   Hans, the Dutch J. P., a Dutch farce, in one
       act. Clyde, Ohio, A. D. Ames, 1878. 7p.

607   _____. Happy Frank's book of songs, farces, stump speeches,
       gags, lectures, sketches, &c., &c., as produced by the
       inimitable F. L. Cutler, in his entertainments... Clyde,
       O., A. D. Ames [1883]. 35p.

608   _____. The mashers mashed. A farce in two acts. Clyde,
       Ohio, Ames' publishing co., 1891. 10p.

609   _____. Peleg and Peter; or, Around the Horn, a farce-comedy
       in four acts. Clyde, Ohio, Ames' publishing co., 1892.
       23p.

610   _____. A scale with sharps and flats, an operatic and musical
       comedy, in one act. Clyde, Ohio, Ames' publishing co.,
       1888. 15p.

611   DAINGERFIELD, FOXHALL, 1887-1933. Bryan Station, a play in
       four acts, by Foxhall Daingerfield... Lexington, Ky.,
       J. L. Richardson and co., c1908. 2 p.ℓ., 28p.

612   _____. The Southern cross; a play in four acts, by Foxhall
       Daingerfield... Lexington, Ky., J. L. Richardson and co.,
       c1909. 2 p.ℓ., 61, [1] p.

613   DALE, FELIX. He's a lunatic. A farce, in one act... as first
       performed... Oct. 24, 1867... New York, Robert M. De Witt
       [n.d.]. 14p.

614   _____. Six months ago. A comedietta in one act. Chicago,
       The dramatic publishing co. [n.d.]. 15p.

615   DALE, HORACE C. The deacon, an original comedy in five acts.
       New York, Harold Roorbach, 1892. 50p.

616   DALLAS, MRS. MARY KYLE. Aroused at last, a comedy in one act.
       Chicago, The dramatic publishing co. [1892]. 22p.

617   DALRYMPLE, C. LEONA. Mrs. Forrester's crusade, a farce in
       one act. New York, Dick and Fitzgerald, 1908. 8p.

618   DALY, AUGUSTIN, 1838-1899. Divorce. A play of the period in
       five acts. By Augustin Daly. As acted at the Fifth Avenue
       theatre for the first time, September 5th, 1871. New York,
       Printed as manuscript only, for the author, 1884. 93p.

DALY, AUGUSTIN

619 _____. Dollars and sense; or, The heedless ones. A comedy
in three acts. By Augustin Daly. As produced at Daly's
theatre, New York, for the first time, October 2d, 1883.
New York, Printed, as manuscript only, for the author,
1885. 71p.

620 _____. A flash of lightning; a drama of lie in our day, in
five acts. By Augustin Daly. First produced at the Broad-
way theatre (late Wallack's) under the management of Mr.
Barney Williams, June 1868. New York, Printed as manuscript only, for the author, 1885. 72p.

621 _____. ... "Frou frou"; a play of powerful human interest, in
five acts, by Augustin Daly... New York [etc.] S. French,
1897. 59p. (French's standard drama, no. 359).

622 _____. ... Hazardous ground. An original adaptation in four
acts, from Victoria [!] Sardon's [!] "Nos bono [!] ville-
geios [!]" by Augustin Daly... Author's ed. New York, S.
French and son; London, S. French [1868]. 46p. (Wemyss'
acting drama [no. IV]).

623 _____. Horizon; an original drama of contemporaneous society
and of American frontier perils. In five acts and seven
tableaux. By Augustin Daly. As acted at the Olympic
theatre, New York City, for the first time, March 21st,
1871. New York, Printed, as manuscript only, for the
author, 1885. 67p.

624 _____. A legend of "Norwood"; or, Village life in New England.
An original dramatic comedy of American life, in four acts.
Founded on a novel by Rev. Henry Ward Beecher. By Augustin
Daly... New York, Printed for the author, 1867. 79 (i.e.
41)p.

625 _____. Love in tandem, a comedy in three acts, from the
French of Bocage and de Courcy, by Augustin Daly... New
York, Printed as manuscript only, for the author, 1892.
84p.

626 _____. Man and wife, and other plays, by Augustin Daly,
edited with introductory notes and play list by Catherine
Sturtevant. Princeton, N. J., Princeton university press,
1942. xxi, 407p. CONTENTS. List of Daly's plays (p.
[xi]-xxi). - Man and wife. - Divorce. - The big bonanza. -
Pique. - Needles and pins.

DALY, AUGUSTIN

627   DALY, AUGUSTIN. Nancy and company, an eccentric piece in four acts. (From the German of Rosen). By Augustin Daly. As first acted at Faly's theater... February 24, 1886. New York, Printed as manuscript for the author, 1886. 63p.

628   _____. Our English friend. A comedy in 4 acts. By Augustin Daly. As acted at Daly's theatre, for the first time, November 25th, 1882. New York, Printed, as manuscript only, for the author, 1884. 78p.

629   _____. ... Under the gaslight; a totally original and picturesque drama of life and love in these times, in five acts. By Augustin Daly... As originally played at the New York theater in the months of August, Sept., and Oct., 1867. Author's ed. New York, W. C. Wemyss', 1867. 47p. (Wemyss' acting drama).

630   _____. Woffington; a tribute to the actress and the woman, by Augustin Daly... (2d ed.) Troy, N. Y., Nims and Knight [1891]. 4 p.ℓ., 182p. front, illus., plates, ports., facsims.

631   _____. Woffington. A tribute to the actress and the woman... By Augustin Daly. Printed for the author. [Philadelphia, Press of Globe printing house], 1888. 3 p.ℓ., 182p. front., plates, ports., facsims.

632   DALY, JOHN. Married daughters and young husbands. An original comic drama, in two acts... London, S. G. Fairbrother, 1852. 32p.

633   DANCE, CHARLES, 1794-1863. ... Delicate ground; or, Paris in 1793. A comic drama, in one act... New York, Samuel French [n.d.]. 38p. (The minor drama, no. xxxviii).

634   _____. "The dustman's belle": an original comic drama, in two acts, by Charles Dance... First performed at the Theatre Royal, Lyceum, on Monday, June 1st, 1846. London, S. G. Fairbrother; [etc., etc., 1846]. 44p.

635   _____. ... Kill or cure. A farce, in one act... New York, W. Taylor and co. [n.d.]. 29p. (The minor drama, no. xlviii).

636   _____. Marriage a lottery. A comedy, in two acts. Chicago, The dramatic publishing co. [n.d.]. 27p.

DARNLEY, JAMES H.

637   ____. A morning call. An original comedietta, in one act... first performed... March 17, 1851... London, S. G. Fairchild [n.d.]. 18p.

638   ____. ... A morning call. An original comedietta, in one act. By Charles Dance... First performed at the Theatre Royal, Drury Lane, by Her Majesty's servants, on Monday, March 17th, 1851. New York, S. French [186-]. 1 p.ℓ., [5]-24p. (The minor drama. no. 57).

639   ____. Naval engagements. A comedy in two acts. New York, Samuel French [n.d.]. 48p.

640   DANIEL, GEORGE, 1789-1864. Doctor Bolus: a serio-comic-bombastic-operatic interlude: in one act. By George Daniel... Printed from the acting copy, with remarks, biographical and critical, by D.-G. ... As performed at the Theatres Royal... London, Davidson [n.d.]. 30p. incl. front. (Cumberland's British theatre. London, ca. 1825-55. v. 13 [no.6]).
    "The present edition is carefully printed from the author's ms."
    Remarks by the author, editor of the series.
    Airs indicated, but no music.

641   DARGAN, OLIVE TILFORD, 1869-1968. The flutter of the goldleaf, and other plays, by Olive Tilford Dargan and Frederick Peterson. New York, C. Scribner's sons, 1922. 4 p.ℓ., 3-114p.

642   ____. The mortal gods, and other plays, by Olive Tilford Dargan. New York, C. Scribner's sons, 1912. 4 p.ℓ., 3-303p., 1ℓ. CONTENTS. - The mortal gods. - A son of Hermes. - Kidmir.

643   ____. Semiramis, and other plays, by Olive Tilford Dargan. New York, Charles Scribner's sons, 1909. 5 p.ℓ., [9]-255p. CONTENTS. - Semiramis. - Carlotta. - The poet.

644   The darkey tragedian. An Ethiopian sketch, in one scene. New York, Dick and Fitzgerald [n.d.]. 7p.

645   DARLINGTON, ANNE CHARLOTTE. Yelenka the Wise and other folk tales in dramatic form, by Anne Charlotte Darlington. New York, The Womans Press [1926]. 224p. illus. (music).

646   DARNLEY, JAMES H. The balloon, by James H. Darnley and G. M. Fenn. London, Samuel French, 1898. 56p.

DARNLEY, JAMES H.

647   DARNLEY, JAMES H. Facing the music... New York and London,
          Samuel French, 1905. 71p.

648   DARROW, JAMES WALLACE, 1855-   . Patriotic plays, tableaux
          and recitations for use of granges, schools, clubs, or
          other organizations, comp. by J. W. Darrow... Chatham,
          N. Y. [Republican art printery], 1915. 48p.

649   DAVIDSON, JOHN, 1857-1909. Godfrida, a play in four acts, by
          John Davidson. New York and London, J. Lane, 1898. 2 p.ℓ.,
          123p.

650   _____. Mammon and his message, God and Mammon, a trilogy.
          London, Grant Richards, 1908. 173p.

651   _____. Plays by John Davidson, being: An unhistorical pas-
          toral, a romantic farce: Bruce, a chronicle play: Smith,
          a tragic farce: and Scaramouch in Naxos, a pantomine.
          London, E. Mathews and J. Lane; Chicago, Stone and Kimball,
          1894. 4 p.ℓ., 294p. front.

652   _____. The Triumph of Mammon, God and Mammon, a trilogy,
          London, E. Grant Richards, 1907. 170p.

653   DAVIES, HUBERT HENRY. The mollusc, a new and original comedy
          in three acts. Boston, Walter H. Baker and co.; London,
          William Heineman, 1914. 157p.

654   _____. Mrs. Gorringe's necklace, a play in four acts. Bos-
          ton, Walter H. Baker and co.; London, William Heinemann,
          1910. 176p.

655   DAVIS, E. CHRISTINE. How Latin helps in other subjects; a
          playlet in one act. [n.p., n.d.]. 4p. (American Classi-
          cal League Service Bureau, No. 511).

656   DAVIS, MARY EVELYN MOORE, 1852-1909. A bunch of roses, and
          other parlor plays, by M. E. M. Davis. Boston, Small,
          Maynard and co., 1903. 4 p.ℓ., 257p. CONTENTS. - A bunch
          of roses. - Queen Anne cottages. - His Lordship. - Christ-
          mas boxes. - A dress rehearsal. - The new system.

657   _____. A dress rehearsal, comedy for 4 males and 4 females.
          New York, Edgar S. Werner and co., 1899. 68p.

DE MILLE, WILLIAM CHURCHILL

658　DAVIS, OWEN, 1874-1956. Lola, by Owen Davis... illustrated
　　　with scenes from the photo-play produced and copyrighted
　　　by the World film corporation. New York, Grosset and
　　　Dunlap [1915]. 4 p.ℓ., 304p. front., plates, ports.

659　DAVIS, RICHARD HARDING, 1864-1916. "Miss Civilization," a
　　　comedy in one act, by Richard Harding Davis. New York,
　　　C. Scribner's sons, 1905. 3 p.ℓ., 47p.
　　　　"Founded on a story by... James Harvey Smith" entitled
　　　Burglars three.

660　Day in a Roman court, by the students of Mrs. Elizabeth Love.
　　　[n.p., n.d.]. 4p. (American Classical League Service
　　　Bureau, No. 720).

661　DAZEY, CHARLES T. ... In old Kentucky. Foreword by Barrett
　　　H. Clark. Introduction by the author. A historical note
　　　and an all-star cast of players depicted in the leading
　　　roles by Paul McPharlin. Detroit, Fine book circle, 1937.
　　　149p. illus.

662　DEAN, FRANK J. Joe Ruggles; or, The girl miner, a comedy-
　　　drama, in four acts. Chicago, The dramatic publishing co.,
　　　1895. 29p.

663　DELANO, ALONZO, 1806-1874. ... A live woman in the mines; or,
　　　Pike county ahead! A local play in two acts. By "Old
　　　Block." To which are added a description of the costume
　　　... and the whole of the stage business. New York, S.
　　　French [1857]. 36p. The minor drama. The acting edition.
　　　(no. 130).

664　D'ELVILLE, RINALDO. The rescue; or, The villain unmasked.
　　　A farce, in three acts. By Rinaldo D'Elville... New York,
　　　Printed for the author, by C. S. Van Winkle, 1813. 44p.

665　DE MILLE, HENRY CHURCHILL, 1850-1893. John Delmer's daughters.
　　　A comedy in three acts. By Henry C. De Mille. [New York,
　　　1883]. 66p.

666　No Entry.

667　DE MILLE, WILLIAM CHURCHILL, 1878-　　　"Deceivers"; a play
　　　in one act, by William C. de Mille. New York, S. French;
　　　[etc., etc.] c1914. 16p.

DE MILLE, WILLIAM CHURCHILL

668   DE MILLE, WILLIAM CHURCHILL. The genius; a comedy in three
       acts, by William C. and Cecil B. De Mille... New York, S.
       French; [etc., etc.] c1904. 99p. (On cover: French's
       standard library edition).

669   DE NAJAC, EMILE. Babie; a comedy in three acts. Translated
       from the French of Emile de Najac and Alfred Hennquin...
       Boston, Walter H. Baker and co. [1880]. 61p.

670   DENISON, THOMAS STEWART, 1848-1911. Borrowing trouble; a
       farce. By T. S. Denison... Chicago, T. S. Denison, 1878.
       [4], 173-182p. On cover: School and social drama.

671   _____. The danger signal; a drama, by T. S. Denison... Chi-
       cago, T. S. Denison [1883]. 42p. On cover: The Star drama.

672   _____. Exhibition and parlor dramas, containing the following
       plays: Odds with the enemy; Initiating a granger; Seth Green-
       back; Wanted, a correspondent; A family strike; The spark-
       ling cup; The assessor; Two ghosts in white; Country justice;
       Borrowing trouble. By T. S. Denison. Chicago, T. S. Deni-
       son, 1879. 2 p.ℓ., 3-182p.

673   _____. A family strike. A farce. By T. S. Denison... Chi-
       cago, Steam press of Cushing, Thomas and co., 1877. [4],
       [97]-106p. On cover: School and social drama.

674   _____. The great doughnut corporation, a farce. Chicago,
       T. S. Denison and co. [1903]. 19p.

675   _____. Hans von Smash. A farce. By T. S. Denison... Chica-
       go, T. S. Denison, 1878. 1 p.ℓ., [49]-59p.

676   _____. Hard cider; a temperance sketch, by T. S. Denison...
       Chicago, T. S. Denison [1880]. 8p.

677   _____. How not to write a play. By T. S. Denison... Chica-
       go, T. S. Denison, 1904. 8p.

678   _____. Initiating a granger; a farce. By T. S. Denison...
       Chicago, Steam press of Cushing, Thomas and co., 1877.
       [4], 43-51p.

679   _____. The Irish linen peddler. A farce in two acts. By
       T. S. Denison... Chicago, T. S. Denison [1879]. 17p. On
       cover: School and social drama.

DENISON, THOMAS STEWART

680   ____. Is the editor in? A lively one-act farce, by T. S.
       Denison... Chicago, T. S. Denison and co. [1923]. 17p.
       On cover: Amateur series.

681   ____. Is the editor in? A farce. By T. S. Denison... Chi-
       cago, T. S. Denison [1879]. 11p. On cover: School and
       social drama.

682   ____. The Kansas immigrants; or, The great exodus, a farce.
       By T. S. Denison... Chicago, T. S. Denison [1879]. 12p.
       On cover: School and social drama.

683   ____. Lively plays for live people, by Thomas Stewart Deni-
       son... Chicago, T. S. Denison [1895]. 268p. CONTENTS.
       - Topp's twins. - Patsy O'Wang. - Rejected. - The new
       woman. - Only cold tea. - A first-class hotel. - Madame
       Princeton's temple of beauty. - A dude in a cyclone. - It's
       all in the pay streak. - The cobbler.

684   ____. Louva, the pauper. A drama in five acts. By T. S.
       Denison, 1878. 36p. On cover: School and social drama.

685   ____. Odds with the enemy; a drama in four acts. A new
       rev. ed. By T. S. Denison... Chicago, T. S. Denison
       [1898]. 34p. On cover: Amateur series XII.

686   ____. Odds with the enemy; an amateur drama. In five acts.
       By T. S. Denison. Published by the author, De Kalb, Illi-
       nois. Chicago, Press of Cushing, Thomas and co., 1876.
       40p.

687   ____. An only daughter. A drama, in three acts. By T. S.
       Denison... Chicago, T. S. Denison [1879]. 24p. On cover:
       The Star drama.

688   ____. Pets of society; a farce, by T. S. Denison... Chicago,
       T. S. Denison [1880]. 15p.

689   ____. Seth Greenback. An amateur drama in four acts, by T.
       S. Denison... Published by the author De Kalb, Ill. Chi-
       cago, press of Cushing, Thomas and co., 1877. [6], 55-76p.
       On cover: School and social drama.

690   ____. The sparkling cup. A temperance drama, in five acts.
       By T. S. Denison... Chicago, Steam press of Cushing,
       Thomas and co., 1877. [4], [109]-141p. On cover: School
       and social drama.

DENISON, THOMAS STEWART

691 DENISON, THOMAS STEWART. Two ghosts in white. A farce, by
    T. S. Denison... Chicago, T. S. Denison, 1878. [4], 153-
    162p. On cover: School and social drama.

692 _____. Under the laurels; a drama in five acts, by T. S.
    Denison... Chicago, T. S. Denison, 1881. 40p. On cover:
    The star drama.

693 _____. Wanted: a correspondent, a farce, in two acts. By
    T. S. Denison... Chicago, T. S. Denison, 1877. [4], p.
    79-95. On cover: Amateur series.

694 _____. Wide enough for two; a farce, by T. S. Denison [1883].
    On cover: School and social drama.

695 DENNERY, ADOLPHE PHILIPPE, 1811-1899. Belphegor, the mounte-
    bank; or, Woman's constancy: a drama in three acts, (tr.
    and adapted from the French of M. M. Dennery and Marc
    Fournier) by Charles Webb... Printed from the acting copy,
    with remarks, biographical and critical, by D.-G. ... Lon-
    don, The Music publishing co., ltd. [1856]. 6, [4], [5]-
    54p.

696 _____. ... A martyr romance. Rio [de Janeiro] Editora
    Guanabara, Waissman, Reis e cia. ltda. [1932]. 336p.

697 _____. The two orphans; romantic play in four acts, by
    Adolphe d'Ennery and Eugene Cormon, adapted from the
    French by N. Hart Jackson for presentation at the Union
    Square Theatre, New York City, 1874. Now revised and
    edited with an introduction by Glenn Hughes, and illustrated
    from photographs of the 1939 production at the Showboat
    theatre, University of Washington, Seattle. New York,
    Dramatists play service, inc., 1939. 105p. front., plates.

698 DENTON, CLARA JANETTA FORT, comp. All sorts of dialogues; a
    collection of dialogues for young people; with additional
    stage directions by compiler. Comp. from well-known
    authors by Clara J. Denton... Chicago, T. S. Denison
    [1898]. 150p. On cover: Denison's series. vol. VIII,
    no. 52.

699 _____. All the holidays; a collection of recitations, dia-
    logues and exercises for all school holidays, with much
    original matter. Arranged by Clara J. Denton... Chicago,
    A. Flanagan co. [1905]. 201p.

Descart, the buccaneer

700   _____. "Dot pooty gompliment." Franklin, Ohio, Eldridge entertainment house [n.d.]. [3]p.

701   _____. Entertainments for all the year, by Clara J. Denton... Philadelphia, The Penn publishing co., 1910. 220p.

702   _____. The "left-handed" sleeve. Franklin, Ohio, Eldridge entertainment house [n.d.]. [2]p.

703   _____. Little lines for little speakers, containing entirely original short and effective pieces for children between the ages of four and seven and seven and ten, including appropriate pieces for opening and closing school, Christmas, Easter, Thanksgiving, birthday and other special and patriotic occasions; by Clara J. Denton. New York, Dick and Fitzgerald [1891]. 90p.

704   _____. Little people's dialogues. For children of ten years. Everything original and specially written for this book, by Clara J. Denton. Philadelphia, The National school of elocution and oratory, 1888. vi, 7-122p. On cover: National series of juvenile speakers.

705   _____. ... Mademoiselle's mistake. A farce in one act for two girls. By Clara J. Denton... Franklin, O., Eldridge entertainment house [19-]. [8]p.

706   _____. One little chicken. Franklin, Ohio, Eldridge entertainment house [n.d.]. [4]p.

707   _____. comp. "Seeing Uncle Jack"; a two-act comedy for seven girls. [New York, J. Fischer and bro., 1910]. 5-23p. Fischer's edition (no. 3373).

708   _____. Sorry for Billy. Franklin, Ohio, Eldridge entertainment house [n.d.]. [3]p.

709   _____. Waiting for Oscar. Franklin, Ohio, Eldridge entertainment house [n.d.]. [8]p.

710   DERRICK, JOSEPH. Confusion; an entirely new and original farcical comedy in three acts, by Joseph Derrick... New York, London, S. French, 1900. 51p.

711   Descart, the buccaneer, a melo-drama, in two acts, by the author of The smoked miser; The statue lover; Wives by advertisement; Ambrose Gwinet, and co. London, Thomas Hailes Lacy [n.d.]. 22p. front.

DEUTSCH, GOTTHARD

712   DEUTSCH, GOTTHARD. Israel Bruna, an historical tragedy in
        five acts. Boston, Richard G. Badger, The Gorham press,
        1908. 95p.

713   The devil to pay! a ballet pantomime, in two acts. As first
        performed... March 2, 1846. The music by Adolphe Adama...
        Manchester, Lowes and Hill, 1856. 14p.

714   DEY, F. MARMADUKE. H. M. S. Plum (His mollified sugar plum).
        A musical sketch in one act. Clyde, Ohio, A. D. Ames,
        1883. 8p.

715   _____. Passions, an original comedy in four acts. Clyde,
        Ohio, A. D. Ames, 1881. 24p.

715A DIBDIN, CHARLES, 1763-1833. My spouse and I. An operatic
        farce, in two acts, by Charles Dibdin... Printed from the
        acting copy, with remarks, biographical and critical, by
        D.-G. ... As performed at the Theatres Royal... London,
        J. Cumberland and son [n.d.]. 36p. incl. front. (Cumber-
        land's British theatre. London, ca. 1825-55. v. 41 [no.
        9]).
          Remarks by George Daniel, editor of the series.

715B DIBDIN, THOMAS FROGNALL, 1776-1847. The lady of the lake,
        In two acts (from Sir Walter Scott)... London, John Cum-
        berland [n.d.]. 31p.

716   DIBDIN, THOMAS JOHN, 1771-1841. The banks of the Hudson; or,
        The Congress trooper; a transatlantic romance, in three
        acts, by Thomas Dibdin... Printed from the acting copy,
        with remarks, biographical and critical, by D.-G. ... As
        performed at the metropolitan minor theatres... London,
        J. Cumberland [n.d.]. 44p. incl. front. (Cumberland's
        Minor theatre. London [ca. 1830-55] v.4 [no.8]).
          "At the period of General Burgoyne's commanding in Ameri-
        ca, prior to the surrender of Saratoga." Apparently sug-
        gested by Cooper's Spy, but the heroes are British officers,
        not Americans. According to the Dramatic magazine, where
        it is cited as "The banks of the Hudson; or, Jonathan Dob-
        son, the Congress trooper," adapted from a work called the
        "Chelsea pensioner" (by Gleig?) cf. v. 2, p. 26.
          Remarks by George Daniel, editor of the series.
          Reissued in Davidson's shilling volume of Cumberland's
        plays, v. 10 [no.5].

DIBDIN, THOMAS JOHN

717 _____. Don Giovanni; or, A spectre on horseback: a comic,
heroic, oparatic [!] tragic, pantomimic, burletta-spec-
tacular extravaganza, in two acts, by Thomas Dibdin...
Printed from the acting copy, with remarks, biographical
and critical, by D.-G. ... As now performed at the metropolitan minor theatres... London, J. Cumberland [n.d.].
28p. front. (Cumberland's Minor theatre. London [ca.
1830-55] v.2 [no.1]).
"A burlesque on the Italian opera of Don Giovanni."
Remarks by George Daniel, editor of the series.
Without the music.

718 _____. The English fleet, in 1342. An historical comic
opera, in three acts, by Thomas Dibdin... Printed from the
acting copy, with remarks, biographical and critical, by
D.-G. ... As performed at the Theatres Royal... London,
J. Cumberland and son [n.d.]. 49p. incl. front. (Cumberland's British theatre. London, ca. 1825-55. v. 32 [no.
6]).
Remarks by George Daniel, editor of the series.
Without the music (in part by Braham).

719 _____. Five miles off; or, The finger post. A comedy, in
three acts, by Thomas Dibdin... Printed from the acting
copy, with remarks, biographical and critical, by D.-G.
... As performed at the Theatres Royal... London, J.
Cumberland and son [n.d.]. 45p. incl. front. (Cumberland's British theatre. London, ca. 1825-55. v. 42 [no.
5]).
Remarks by George Daniel, editor of the series.

720 _____. Five thousand a year, a comedy, in three acts. As
performed at the Theatre-Royal, Covent-Garden. By Thomas
Dibdin... London, Printed by T. Woodfall for G. G. and J.
Robinson [1799]. 4 p.ℓ., 84p. [Broadhurst, J. Plays.
v. 3, no. 7].

721 _____. Guilty or not guilty: a comedy, in five acts. First
acted at the Theatre-Royal, Haymarket; May 26th 1804.
Written by Thomas Dibdin... 4th ed. London, Printed by
L. Hansard, for Lackington, Allen, and co., 1804. 3 p.ℓ.,
108p.

722 _____. Ivanhoe; or, The Jew's daughter: a romantic melo-drama,
in three acts, by Thomas Dibdin... Printed from the acting
copy, with remarks, biographical and critical, by D.-G. ...
As performed at the Theatres Royal... London, Davidson
[n.d.]. 64p. incl. front. (Cumberland's Minor theatre.

DIBDIN, THOMAS JOHN

(DIBDIN, THOMAS JOHN)
London [ca. 1830-55] v. 2 [no. 8]).
Remarks by George Daniel, editor of the series.

723 _____. The Jew and the doctor: a farce, in two acts, by
Thomas Dibdin... Printed from the acting copy, with re-
marks, biographical and critical, by D.-G. ... London,
Davidson [n.d.]. 31p. incl. front. (Cumberland's British
theatre. London, ca 1825-55. v. 34 [no. 5]).
Remarks by George Daniel, editor of the series.
Reissue of Cumberland's earlier edition.

724 _____. The Lady of the Lake; a melo-dramatic romance, in two
acts (from Sir Walter Scott), by Thomas Dibdin. Printed
from the acting copy, with remarks, biographical and critical, by D.-G. London, G. H. Davidson [n.d.]. 31p. front.
(Cumberland's minor theatre. London [ca. 1830-55] v. 8
[no. 4]).
Libretto by Dibdin; music by Sanderson.
Remarks by George Daniel, editor of the series.

725 _____. Morning, noon, & night; or, The romance of a day.
A comic opera, by Thomas Dibdin. Produced at the Theatre
Royal, Haymarket, on Monday, Sept. 9, 1822. The overture,
and music, with three exceptions, composed by Mr. Perry.
London, W. Simpkin and R. Marshall, 1822. 2 p.ℓ., 61,
[1]p. [Broadhurst, J. Plays. v. 4, no. 1].
Without the music.

726 _____. St. David's day; or, The honest Welshman: a musical
farce, in two acts, by Thomas Dibdin... The music composed
and comp. by T. Attwood. Printed from the acting copy,
with remarks, biographical and critical, by D.-G. ... As
performed at the Theatres Royal... London, J. Cumberland
[n.d.]. 28p. incl. front. (Cumberland's British theatre.
London, ca. 1825-55. v. 37 [no. 9]).
Remarks by George Daniel, editor of the series.
Without the music.

727 _____. Suil Dhuv, the coiner: a melodramatic romance, in
three acts, by Thomas Dibdin... Printed from the acting
copy, with remarks, biographical and critical, by D.-G.
... As performed at the Theatres Royal... London, G. H.
Davidson [n.d.]. 47p. incl. front. (Davidson's shilling
volume of Cumberland's plays. London, ca. 1849-55. v. 9
[no. 4]).
Reissue of Cumberland's minor theatre. no. 6 (v. 1
[no. 6]).
Remarks by George Daniel, editor of the series.

DICKENS, CHARLES

728 _____. Twenty per cent.; or, My father. A farce, in two acts.
As performed at the Theatre Royal, Drury Lane. By Thomas
Dibdin... Correctly given from the author's copy. London,
Printed at the Chiswick press for Whitingham and Ariss,
1816. 32p. illus. (Dibdin, T. J. London theatre. London,
1815 [1814-25] v. 11 [no.6]).
    Title vignette.
    Translated and adapted from the French. Cf. Prelim. note.

729 _____. Two faces under a hood: a comic opera. In three acts.
As performed at the Theatre-Royal, Covent-Garden. Written
by T. Dibdin... London, Printed by Brettell and co. for
Appleyards [1807?]. 2 p.ℓ., 80, [1]p. [Broadhurst. J.
Plays. v. 2, no. 7].
    Without the music (by Shield).

730 _____. The two Gregories; or, Where did the money come from?
A farce, in two acts, by Thomas Dibdin... Printed from the
acting copy, with remarks, biographical and critical, by
D.-G. ... As performed at the Theatres Royal... London,
G. H. Davidson [n.d.]. 28p. incl. front. (Cumberland's
Minor theatre. London [ca. 1830-55] v. 3 [no. 6]).
    Remarks by George Daniel, editor of the series.

731 _____. What next? A farce, in two acts. As performed at the
Theatre Royal, Drury Lane. By Thomas Dibdin... London,
Printed at the Chiswick press for Whittingham and Ariss,
1816. 35p. illus. (Dibdin, T. J. London theatre. London,
1815 [1814-25] v. 12 [no. 1]).
    Title vignette.

732 _____. The will for the deed, a comedy, in three acts: as
performed at the Theatre-Royal, Covent-Garden. Written by
Thomas Dibdin... London, Longman, Hurst, Rees, and Orme,
1805. 64, [2]p. [Broadhurst, J. Plays, v. 10, no. 3].

733 DICKENS, CHARLES, 1812-1870. Is she his wife? or, Something
singular. A comic burletta in one act. By Charles
Dickens. Boston, J. R. Osgood and co., 1877. 80p. illus.

734 _____. Mrs. Camp's tea, a sketch (From Martin Chuzzlewit).
Chicago, T. S. Denison [n.d.]. 5p.

735 _____. ... No thoroughfare: a drama, in five acts and a prologue. By Charles Dickens and Wilkie Collins. (In The
New York drama. New York, 1899. no. 56, p. [1]-17).

DICKINSON, THOMAS H.

736   DICKINSON, THOMAS H., ed. Chief contemporary dramatists.
       Twenty plays from the recent drama of England, Ireland,
       America, Germany, France, Belgium, Norway, Sweden, and
       Russia. Boston [etc.] Houghton, Mifflin [1916]. ix,
       676p. CONTENTS: Wilde, Lady Windemere's fan. Pinero,
       The second Mrs. Tanqueray. Henry Arthur Jones, Michael
       and his lost angel. Galsworthy, Strife. Barker, The
       Madras house. Yeats, The hourglass. Synge, Riders to the
       sea. Lady Gregory, The rising of the moon. Fitch, The
       truth. Moody, The great divide. Thomas, The witching
       hour. MacKaye, The scarecrow. Hauptmann, The weavers, tr.
       by Mary Morison. Sudermann, The vale of content, tr. by
       William Ellery Leonard. Brieux, The red robe, tr. by O.
       Reed. Hervieu, Know thyself, tr. by Barry Cerf. Maeter-
       linck, Pelléas and Mélisande, tr. by Richard Hovey. Bjørn-
       son, Beyond human power, tr. by Lee M. Hollander. Strind-
       berg, The father, tr. by N. Ericksen. Chekov, The cherry
       orchard, tr. by George Calderon.

737   DIETRICHSTEIN, LEO, 1865-1928. Are you a mason? A farcical
       comedy in three acts, by Leo Dietrichstein... New York,
       S. French;[etc., etc., c1901]. 114, [1]p. illus. (plan)
       plates. (On cover: French's standard library edition).

738   _____. Are you a mason? (Die Logenbrüder) farce comedy in
       three acts. Adapted from the German of Carl Laufs and
       Curt Kraatz by Leo Dietrichstein... New York, E. Lederer
       and C. Herrmann, 1901. 83p. incl. plan.

739   DILLON, CHARLES. ... The mysteries of Paris! A drama, in
       two acts... London, John Duncombe [n.d.]. 37p. (Dun-
       combe's edition).

740   DIMOND, WILLIAM, fl. 1800-1830. The broken sword: a grand
       melodrama, in two acts, by William Dimond... Printed from
       the acting copy, with remarks, biographical and critical,
       by D.-G. ... As performed at the Theatres Royal... Lon-
       don, G. H. Davidson [n.d.]. 36p. incl. front. (Cumber-
       land's British theatre. London, ca. 1825-55, v. 41 [no.
       5]).
            An adaptation of "La vallé du torrent ou, L'orphelin
       et le meurtrier," by Frédéric, i.e. Dupetit-Méré.
            Remarks by George Daniel, editor of the series.
            Reissue of Cumberland's earlier edition.

DOIG, AGNES M.

741   [_____.] The carnival at Naples, a play in five acts: as performed at the Theatre Royal, Covent-Garden... By the author of "Adrian and Orrila," "Doubtful son," "Foundling of the forest" &c. &c. &c. London, R. S. Kirby, 1831. 2 p.ℓ., 67p.
      Author's name given in advertisement on verse of last page.
      Without the music (by Barnett).

742   _____. The hunter of the Alps. A drama, in one act... Clyde, Ohio, A. D. Ames [n.d.]. 4p.

743   _____. The peasant boy; an opera, in three acts. New York, The Longworths, 1811. 56p.

744   _____. Stage struck; or, The loves of Augustus Portarlington and Celestina Beverley, a farce in one act. London and New York, Samuel French [n.d.]. 22p.

744A   _____. The young hussar. An operatic drama, in two acts, by William Dimond ... Printed from the acting copy, with remarks, biographical and critical, by D.-G. ... As performed at the Theatres Royal ... London, J. Cumberland [n.d.]. 34p. incl. front. (Cumberland's British theatre. London, ca. 1825-55, v. 41 [no.2]).
      Remarks by George Daniel, editor of the series.
      Music by Kelly. Cf. Grove, 5th ed.

745   DIX, BEULAH MARIE, 1876-   . A Rose o' Plymouth-town: a romantic comedy in four acts by Beulah Marie Dix and Evelyn Greenleaf Sutherland. Boston, The Fortune press, 1903. 4 p.ℓ., 111p. 1ℓ. 4 pl.

746   DODDRIDGE, JOSEPH, 1769-1826. Logan, the last of the race of Shikellemus, chief of the Cayuga nation. A dramatic piece. To which is added, the Dialogue of the backwoodsman and the dandy, first recited at the Buffaloe seminary, July the 1st, 1821. By Dr. Joseph Doddridge... Reprinted from the Virginia ed. of 1823, with an appendix relating to the murder of Logan's family, for William Dodge. Cincinnati, R. Clarke and co., 1868. 1 p.ℓ., 76p.

747   DODSLEY, ROBERT, 1703-1764. The toy-shop. London [1777]. 6p.

748   DOIG, AGNES M. Doig's excellent dialogues for young folks. Lebanon, Ohio, March bros., 1901. 10p.

DONIZETTI, GAETANO

749   DONIZETTI, GAETANO, 1797-1848. La figlia del reggimento, the
       daughter of the regiment; composed by Donizetti: with an
       English version, and the music of the principal airs. Lon-
       don, G. H. Davidson [n.d.]. 23p.

750   _____. Lucia di Lammermoor, Lucy of Lammermoor, a romantic
       opera in three acts. New York, Sheridan Corbyn [n.d.].
       24p.

751   DOREMUS, C. A. ... Mock trial for breach of promise, by C. A.
       Doremus and H. F. Manchester. New York, Samuel French and
       son [n.d.]. 22p. (French's minor drama, no. cccxxxiii).

752   DOWLING, MAURICE G. ... Othello travestie: an operatic bur-
       lesque burletta, in two acts... London, J. Duncombe and
       co. [n.d.]. 33p. front. (Duncombe's edition).

753   DREEBEN, MRS. OCTAVINE LOPEZ, 1886-   . The choice; a play in
       three acts, by Octavine Lopez Dreeben. [Dallas, Oak Cliff
       printing co.] 1914. 2 p.ℓ., 2-27p.

754   DREISER, THEODORE, 1871-1945. Plays of the natural and the
       supernatural. New York and London, John Lane co., 1916.
       228p. CONTENTS: The girl in the coffin. - The blue
       sphere. - Laughing gas. - In the dark. - The spring re-
       cital. - The light in the window. - "Old ragpicker."

755   DRIDEN, PAUL K. The price; a play in three acts. Philadel-
       phia, Printed by G. W. Jacobs and co. [1911]. 129p.

756   DRINKWATER, JOHN, 1882-1937. Abraham Lincoln. London, Sidg-
       wick and Jackson, ltd. [n.d.]. 72p.

757   _____. Oliver Cromwell. London, Sidgwick and Jackson, ltd.
       [n.d.]. 80p.

758   _____. Pawns: three poetic plays by John Drinkwater. London,
       Sidgwick and Jackson, ltd. [n.d.]. 54p.

759   _____. Robert Burns. London, Sidgewick and Jackson, ltd.,
       1925. 93p.

760   _____. Robert E. Lee. London, Sidgwick and Jackson ltd.,
       1923. 95p.

761   _____. The storm, a play in one act. Birmingham, The author,
       1916. 18p.

762 DUBOIS, ALFRED. ... Wilful murder; or, Deeds of dreadful
      note. A romantic tale of terror, in one act. Philadelphia,
      Turner and Fisher [n.d.]. 22p.

763 DUBOURG, A. W. Twenty minutes under an umbrella, comic in-
      terlude. Chicago, T. S. Denison [n.d.]. 11p.

764 [DUCANGE, VICTOR HENRI JOSEPH BRAHAIN] 1783-1833. Thérèse;
      or, The orphan of Geneva: an interesting romance: tr. from
      the French of... M. Victor. By Sarah S. Wilkinson... Lon-
      don, Deam and Munday [1821?]. 1 p.ℓ., [5]-34p. col. front.

764A [_____.] ... Therese, the orphan of Geneva. A drama, in
      three acts... New York, Samuel French [n.d.]. 33p.
      (French's American drama, no. cxi).

765 [_____.] Therese, the orphan of Geneva. A drama in three
      acts: freely tr. from the French, altered and adapted to
      the English stage. By John Howard Payne... London,
      Pinted by J. Tabby, 1821. 1 p.ℓ., [9]-57p.

765A DUDLEY, SIR HENRY BATE, bart., 1745-1824. The woodman; a
      comic opera, in three acts. By Bate Dudley. (In The Lon-
      don state. London [1824-27] v. 4 [no. 6], 16p. 1 illus.).
      Caption title.
         The music is chiefly by Shield.

766 DUGANNE, A. J. H. Woman's vows and mason's oaths. A play, in
      four acts. New York, Robert M. De Witt, 1874. 76p.

767 DUHAMEL, GEORGES, 1884-1966. In the shadow of statues, drama
      in three acts, by Georges Duhamel. Authorized translation
      from the French by Sasha Best. (In Poet lore. Boston,
      1914. vol. XXV, no. V, p. 371-438).

768 _____. The light, a drama in four acts, by Georges Duhamel.
      Tr. from the French by Sasha Best. (In Poet lore. Boston,
      1914. vol. XXV, no. III, p. 161).

769 DUMARS, HORACE. The fire fiend. A pyrotechnic and fire
      drama, in two acts. By Horace Dumars... [n.p., 1891].
      12p.

770 DU MAURIER, GUY. An Englishman's home, a play in three acts.
      New York and London, Harper and bros., 1909. 131p.

771 Dummling, a short play for children [n.d.]. 48p. illus.

DUMONT, FRANK

772   DUMONT, FRANK. The girl from Klondike; or, Wide awake Nell,
       a comedy-drama, in three acts. Chicago, The dramatic pub-
       lishing co., 1898. 26p.

773   _____. The half-breed, a western drama in three acts. Phila-
       delphia, The Penn publishing co., 1909. 32p.

774   _____. Happy Uncle Rufus. A musical sketch, in one scene.
       By Frank Dumont... To which is added, a description of the
       costumes, cast of the characters... and the whole of the
       stage business. Chicago and New York, The dramatic pub-
       lishing co., 1881. 7p. On cover: The Comic drama (no.
       142).

775   _____. Helen's funny babies. An Ethiopian burlesque, in one
       scene. New York, The De Witt publishing house, 1878. 6p.

776   _____. How to get a divorce, a farce in one act. Chicago,
       The Dramatic publishing co. [1897]. 9p.

777   _____. Jack Sheppard and Joe Blueskin; or, Amateur road
       agents, melo-dramatic burlesque in one act. Chicago, The
       Dramatic publishing co. [1897]. 10p.

778   _____. Love in all corners. A farce in one act. Chicago,
       The Dramatic publishing co., 1898. 8p.

779   _____. The midnight intruder. An Ethiopian farce. Chicago,
       The Dramatic publishing co., 1876. 8p.

780   _____. My wife's visitors. A comic drama, in one scene.
       New York, Clinton T. De Witt, 1878. 8p.

781   _____. The serenade party; or, The miser's troubles, a black
       sketch in one act. Chicago, The Dramatic publishing co.
       [1897]. 9p.

782   _____. What shall I take? An Ethiopian farce in one act.
       New York, Robert M. De Witt, 1876. 9p.

783   _____. The wonderful telephone. A black sketch, in one
       scene. New York, The De Witt publishing house [n.d.]. 6p.

784   _____. The yellow kid who lives in Hogan's alley, a burlesque.
       New York, The De Witt publishing house, 1897. 9p.

785 DUNCAN, RONALD. This way to the tomb, a masque and anti-
     masque. London, Faber and Faber [n.d.]. 99p.

786 [DUNLAP, WILLIAM], 1766-1839. André; a tragedy, in five acts:
     as performed by the old American company, New York, March
     30, 1798. To which are added authentic documents respect-
     ing Major André; consisting of letters to Miss Seward, The
     cow chase, Proceedings of the court martial, &c. ... New
     York, Printed by T. and J. Swords, no. 99 Pearl-street,
     1798. viii, [9]-109p.

787 [_____]. The father; or, American Shandyism. A comedy, as
     performed at the New York theatre, by the old American
     company. Written in the year 1788... New York, Printed
     by Hodge, Allen and Campbell, 1789. 56, [2]p.

788 [_____]. The glory of Columbia; her yeomanry. A play in
     five acts. The songs, duets, and choruses, intended for
     the celebration of the fourth of July, at the New York
     theatre. New York, Printed and published by D. Longworth
     at the Shakespeare-gallery, 1803. 56, [3]-12p.

789 _____. The good neighbor; an interlude, in one act. Altered
     from a scene of Iffland's by William Dunlap. As performed
     at the New York theatre. New York, Published by David
     Longworth, at the Dramatic repository, Shakespeare-gallery,
     March, 1814. 12p.

790 _____. A trip to Niagara; or, Travellers in America. A
     farce, in three acts. Written for the Bowery theatre,
     New York. By William Dunlap... New York, E. B. Clayton,
     1830. 54p.

791 _____. Yankee chronology; or, Huzza for the Constitution!
     A musical interlude, in one act. To which are added, the
     patriotic songs of The freedom of the seas, and Yankee
     tsars. By W. Dunlap, esq. New York, Published by D.
     Longworth, at the Dramatic repository, Shakespeare-gallery.
     Dec.--1812. 16p.

792 DUNSANY, EDWARD JOHN MORETON DRAX PLUNKETT, 18th BARON, 1878-
     1957. Plays of gods and men, by Lord Dunsany. Boston,
     J. W. Luce and co. [c1917]. 1 p.ℓ., 7-207p. CONTENTS. -
     The tents of the Arabs. - The laughter of the gods. - The
     queen's enemies. - A night at an inn.

DUPREE, FRANK

793   DUPREE, FRANK. Abyssinia; or, The Negus, a comic opera in
       three acts. Denver, 1902. [58]

794   DURAN, LÉO, 1883-   . Plays of old Japan, tr. by Leo Duran.
       New York, T. Seltzer, 1921. xii, 127p. col. front.

795   DU SOUCHET, HENRY A., 1852-   . My friend from India; a
       farcical comedy in three acts, by H. A. Du Souchet...
       New York, S. French; [etc., etc., 1912?]. 95p.

796   DYRENFORTH, DOUGLAS. The absconder, dramatic composition.
       Chicago, 1910. 64p.

797   E. A. Matchmakers, a comedy in one act. Boston, George M.
       Baker and co., 1884. 30p.

798   Each for himself. A farce, in two acts. As performed at the
       Theatre-Royal, Drury-Lane. New York, Published by David
       Longworth, at the Dramatic-repository, Shakespeare-gallery.
       1817. 41p.

799   EATON, MABEL L. That boy George. An exercise for Washington's
       birthday. Lebanon, Ohio, March bros. [n.d.]. 4p.

800   EBERHART, B. F. Ames' series of medleys, tableaux, panto-
       mimes, recitations, dialogues, etc. suitable for schools,
       church and Christmas entertainments. Clyde, Ohio, Ames'
       publishing co., 1895. 28p.

801   EBIN, ALEXANDER B. ... "Fedia," a comedy in three acts, four
       scenes, from modern life in New York, by Alex. B. Ebin...
       Based in part on Tolstoy's tragedy "The living corpse"...
       [New York], 1912. 59p.

802   _____. ... "Marriageables," a farcical comedy from modern
       life in New York--in three acts, by Alex. B. Ebin...
       [New York], 1912. 64p.

803   _____. ... "Portia in politics," a play in three acts, by
       A. B. Ebin... [New York], 1912. 64p.

804   ECHEGARAY Y EIZAGUIRRE, JOSÉ, 1832 or 3-1916. The great
       Galeoto; Folly or saintliness; two plays done from the
       verse of José Echegaray into English prose by Hannah
       Lynch. London, J. Lane; Boston, L. Wolffe and co., 1895.
       xxxci, 195, [1]p.

ELDRIDGE, HARRY C.

805 _____. Madman or saint, a drama in three acts, by José Echegaray. Translated from the Spanish by Ruth Lansing. (In
Poet lore. Boston, 1912. vol. xxiv (i.e. xxiii), no. iii,
p. 161-220).

806 _____. Mariana; an original drama in three acts and an epilogue, by José Echegaray. Translated by James Graham.
Boston, Roberts bros., 1895. 126p.

807 _____. The son of Don Juan; an original drama in three acts
inspired by the reading of Ibsen's work entitled "Gengangere," by José Echegaray; translated by James Graham.
Boston, Roberts bros., 1895. 131p. front. (port.).

808 ECKERSLEY, ARTHUR. A boy's proposal; a little comedy... New
York and London, Samuel French, 1909. 28p.

809 EDDY, MARION. The outcast's daughter. A drama in four acts.
Chicago, The Dramatic publishing co. [1899]. 32p.

810 EDGCOME, JOHN. A web of lies, a comedy in one act. Chicago
and New York, The Dramatic publishing co., 1899. 18p.

811 EDMONDS, RANDOLPH. Shades and shadows, by Randolph Edmonds.
Boston, Meador publishing co., 1930. 171p.

812 EDWARDS, HENRY SUTHERLAND. ... Noureddin, and the fair
Persian... in two acts... St. Martin's Lane, W. S. Johnson, 1849. 24p.

813 No Entry.

814 No Entry.

815 No Entry.

816 EHRMANN, MAX, 1872-1945. Jesus; a passion play, by Max
Ehrmann... New York, London, The Baker and Taylor co.
[1915]. 282p.

817 _____. The wife of Marobius, a play. New York, Mitchell
Kennerley, 1911. 73p.

818 ELDRIDGE, HARRY C. The wonderful Christmas telescope. A
Christmas dialog and tableaux. Franklin, Ohio, Eldridge
entertainment house, 1909. [8]p.

ELIOT, ANNIE

819   ELIOT, ANNIE. Green-room rivals, one-act comedy. New York,
       Edgar S. Werner and co. [1894]. 16p.

820   ELLIS, EDITH MARY OLDHAM (LEES) "Mrs. Havelock Ellis," 1861-
       1916. Love in danger; three plays by Mrs. Havelock Ellis.
       Boston and New York, Houghton Mifflin co., 1915. 5 p.ℓ.,
       [3]-88p., 1ℓ.

821   ELLIS, KATE F. Fit and Suitemall: fashions, a fantastic enter-
       tainment in two scenes and a tableau. Boston, Walter H.
       Baker and co., 1904. 19p.

822   ELTON, E. W. Paul the poacher: a domestic drama, in two acts.
       London, Thomas Hailes Lacy [n.d.]. 35p.

823   ELWYN, LIZZIE MAY. Rachel, the fire waif. A drama, in four
       acts. Clyde, Ohio, Ames' publishing co., 1900. 29p.

824   ELYOCK, P. ANDREW. Crowned before dawn, a drama in three
       acts for female characters. New York, A. S. Barnes and
       co. [1906]. 20p.

825   EMERSON, W. BURT. The musical captain; or, The fall of Vicks-
       burg, a drama of the late rebellion, in four acts. Clyde,
       Ohio, Ames' publishing co., 1890. 14p.

826   EMERSON, W. D. Humble pie, a comedy in one act. Chicago,
       The Dramatic publishing co. [1910]. 18p.

827   EMMETT, DANIEL D. Hard times, a negro extravaganze--scene.
       Chicago and New York, The Dramatic publishing co., 1874.
       9p.

828   ENELEH, H. B. Tempest tossed. An original drama, in four
       acts. Chicago, The Dramatic publishing co., 1885. 26p.

829   ENGLISH, THOMAS DUNN. The Mormons; or, Life at Salt Lake
       City. A drama in three acts... as performed at Burton's
       Theatre, March, 1858. New York, Samuel French [n.d.].
       43p. (French's standard drama, no. ccv).

830   Enlisted for the war; or, The home-guard, a drama in three
       acts. Boston, Walter H. Baker and co. [n.d.]. 81p.

831   ENSOR, AUBREY. The perfect plot, five variations on an un-
       original theme. London, H. F. W. Deane and sons [n.d.].
       28p.

832 ERLE, TWYNIHOE W., 1828-1908. Don't be too sure, he's a beef-
eater. London, 1861. 42p.

833 ESMOND, HENRY V., 1869-1922. Billy's little love affair; a
comedy in three acts, by H. V. Esmond. ... New York,
[etc.] S. French, 1904. 82p. French's standard library
edition of plays (no. 8).

834 _____. Her vote, a comedy in one act, by H. V. Esmond...
New York, S. French, ltd., 1910. 8p. On cover: French's
international copyrighted... edition of the works of the
best authors (no. 197).

835 _____. One summer's day, by H. V. Esmond... New York [etc.]
S. French, 1900. 63p. On cover: French's international
copyrighted... edition of the works of the best authors
(no. 37).

836 _____. When we were twenty-one; a comedy in four acts, by
H. V. Esmond... New York [etc.] S. French, 1903. 80p.

837 _____. The Wilderness, a comedy in three acts, by H. V.
Esmond... New York, S. French; London, S. French, ltd.,
1901. 65p. On cover: French's international copyrighted
... edition of the works of the best authors (no. 48).

838 ESTEP, E. C. De daughter of de regiment, an Ethiopian burlesque. Chicago, T. S. Denison [1903]. 8p.

839 EURIPIDES, 485?-406? B.C. Euripides translated into English
rhyming verse by George Gilbert Aimé Murray... Fifth
edition. New York, Longmans, Green and co. London,
George Allen and Unwin, 1915. lxviii, 355p. illus.

840 _____. Medea (translated from the Greek of Euripides by
Melba I. MacLeod). Adapted by Lolo Robinson and O. G.
Brockett. [Lexington, Ky., 1949]. 42p.

841 _____. The tragedies of Euripides in English verse, by
Arthur S. Way... London, Macmillan and co., 1894-1898.
3v.

842 EVANS, FLORENCE WILKINSON. Two plays of Israel, David of
Bethlehem. Mary Magdalen. New York, McClure, Phillips
and co., 1904. 333p.

Everyman.

843   Everyman. Jedermann. Englisch und Deutsch. Übersetzt und
mit einem Nachwort von Helmut Wiemken. Stuttgart, Philipp
Reclam Jun. [1970]. [96]p. illus.

844   The exile; or, The coronation of Elizabeth. A drama, in
three acts... London, Hodgson and co. [n.d.]. 24p.
(Hodgson's juvenile drama).

845   FAGAN, JAMES BERNARD. The earth, a modern play in four acts.
London, T. Fisher Unwin [n.d.]. 154p.

846   FALCONER, EDMUND, 1814-1879. Eileen Oge; or, Dark's the hour
before the dawn. An Irish drama, in four acts. By Edmund
Falconer... As performed at the Princess's theatre, London... June 29, 1871... New York, R. M. De Witt, 1876.
44p. diagrs. On cover: De Witt's acting plays (no. 202).

847   _____. Extremes; or, Men of the day. A comedy in three
acts. By Edmund Falconer. London, S. French; New York,
S. French and son [187-]. 72p. (On cover: Lacy's acting
edition [no.] 616).
First performed August 1850.

848   _____. ... Peep o'day; or, Savourneen dheelish. An Irish
romantic drama, in four acts. (Derived from "The tales
of the O'Hara family.") By Edmund Falconer... To which
is added a description of the costumes - cast of the
characters... and the whole of the stage business. New
York, R. M. De Witt [187-?]. 40p. diagr. (On cover:
De Witt's acting plays [no. 82]).
At head of title: New "Drury lane" version.

849   The fall of Algiers. A comic opera, in three acts... London,
John Cumberland [n.d.]. 46p. front.

850   The fall of Troy, by the students of Sister Charles Marie.
[n.p., n.d.]. 5p. (American Classical League Service
Bureau, No. 722).

851   ... Family jars. A musical farce, in two acts... New York,
Samuel French [n.d.]. 21p. (The minor drama, no. cxix).

852   FARLEY, CHARLES, 1771-1859. The Battle of Bothwell Brigg, a
Scottish romance, in two acts, founded on the story of Old
Mortality, in the popular "Tales of my landlord," by Charles
Farley, as performed at the Theatre Royal Covent Garden.
London, Printed by G. Auld, for J. Lowndes, 1820. 2 p.ℓ.,
35p.

(FARLEY, CHARLES)
Playbill of Covent-Garden for May 22, 1820, announcing this and other plays, inserted.
Without the music (by Bishop).

853 FELCH, W. FARRAND. The pet of Parson's ranch. A comedy-drama in five acts... Chicago, T. S. Denison, 1886. 33p.

854 FELTS, WILLIAM B. Elblanke, a tragedy. By Wm. B. Felts. [Russell Springs, Kan.] The author, 1890. 246p.

855 ____. Hernarne, a comedy. By Wm. B. Felts. [Russell Springs, Kans.] The author, 1891. 288p.

856 ____. Romancie, a romance. By Wm. B. Felts. [Russell Springs, Kan.] The author, 1890. 237p. 1ℓ.

857 FENN, GEORGE MANVILLE, 1831-1909. "Land ahead!" or, The Irish emigrant, by G. Manville Fenn. London, 1877. 66p.

858 FENNELL, JAMES, 1766-1816. The hero of the lake; or, The victory of Commodore Perry. By James Fennell. Philadelphia: Published by Moses Thomas, no. 52, Chestnut street. J. Maxwell, printer, 1813. cover-title, 7p.

859 FESSENDEN, THOMAS GREEN, 1771-1837. Original poems. By Thomas Green Fessenden... Philadelphia, Printed at the Lorenzo press of E. Bronson, 1806. xii, 203p.
Contains his A pastoral dialogue; Poetical dialogue.

860 FETTE, W. ELIOT. Dialogues from Dickens, Second series. Boston, Lee and Shepard; New York, Lee, Shepard and Dillingham, 1871. 335p. front.

861 FEUILLET, OCTAVE, 1821-1890. The romance of a poor young man. A drama, adapted from the French of Octave Feuillet, by Messrs. Pierrepont Edwards and Lester Wallack. New York, Samuel French, 1859. 53p.

862 FICKE, ARTHUR DAVISON, 1883-1945. Mr. Faust. New York, Mitchell Kennerley, 1915. 115p.

863 FIELD, A. NEWTON. Reverses, a domestic drama, in five acts. Clyde, Ohio, A. D. Ames, 1882. 26p.

864 ____. School, an Ethiopian farce in one act. Clyde, Ohio, A. D. Ames, 1880. 7p.

FIELD, CHARLES KELLOGG

865   FIELD, CHARLES KELLOGG, 1873-1948. ... The cave man, a play
of the redwoods. Text by Charles K. Field, music by W. J.
McCoy. Introduction and synopses. [San Francisco, 1910].
22p., 1ℓ.

866   FIELD, MICHAEL [pseud.]. The tragic Mary. London, G. Bell
and sons, 1890. viii, 261p.

867   FINCK, EDWARD BERTRAND, 1870-   . Plays. Louisville, John
P. Morton and co., 1902. 40p.

868   _____. Shadows on the wall. Louisville, Kentucky, John P.
Morton and co., inc., 1922. 110p. CONTENTS. - Shadows
on the wall. - The poet. - The house of tragedy. - The unwelcome visitor. - Remorse. - Adversity.

869   ... The first night; or, A peep behind the scenes. A comic
drama, in one act... New York, Samuel French [n.d.].
24p.

870   FITCH, WILLIAM CLYDE, 1865-1909. Captain Jinks of the Horse
marines; a fantastic comedy in three acts by Clyde Fitch.
New York, Doubleday, Page and co., 1902. 7 p.ℓ., 3-166,
[1]p. front., plates.

871   _____. Nathan Hale; a play, in four acts. By Clyde Fitch.
New York, R. H. Russell, 1899. 6 p.ℓ., 100p. front.,
plates, port.

872   _____. The smart set; correspondence and conversations, by
Clyde Fitch, 1897. Chicago and New York, H. S. Stone and
co. [c1897]. 5 p.ℓ., 3-201p., 1ℓ. CONTENTS. - The plaintiff. - The summer. - The children. - Maternity. - A
letter of introduction. - Wagner, 1897. - Sorrow. - The
theatre. - The opera. - A perfect day. - The Westington's
Bohemian dinner. - The gamblers.

873   _____. The woman in the case; a play in four acts, by Clyde
Fitch. Boston, Little, Brown and co., 1915. 195p.
Pub. also, with same pagination, in v. 4 of the
author's Plays... Memorial ed. Boston, 1915.

874   FITZBALL, EDWARD, 1792-1873. Bertha, a tragedy. By Edward
Ball. As performed... at the Theatre-Royal, Norwich.
London, R. Edwards, 1819. 4 p.ℓ., 59 [1]p.

FITZBALL, EDWARD

875 _____. ... Carlmihan; or, The drowned crew! A romantic melo-
drama, in two acts. By Edward Fitzball... As performed
at the Theatre Royal, Covent-Garden. Embellished with a
fine engraving, by Mr. Findlay... London, J. Duncombe and
co. [1835?]. 30p. incl. front. (On cover: Duncombe's
acting edition of the British theatre. no. 131).
At head of title: Duncombe's edition.
"Produced at the Theatre-Royal, Covent-Garden, April 21,
1835."

876 _____. Christmas Eve; or, The duel in the snow. An original
domestic drama in three acts... London, Thomas Hailes
Lacy [n.d.]. 28p.

877 _____. The earthquake; or, The spectre of the Nile: a burletta operatic spectacle, in three acts, by Edward Fitz-
Ball... The music by G. H. Rodwell, esq. Printed from
the acting copy, with remarks, biographical and critical,
by D.-G. ... As now performed at the Theatre Royal,
Adelphi... London, J. Cumberland [n.d.]. 40p. incl.
front. (Cumberland's minor theatre. London [1828-44]
v. 1 [no.7]).
Partly founded on Moore's story of the Epicurean.
Remarks by George Daniel, editor of the series.
First performed at the Adelphi theatre, December 8,
1828. Cf. The Stage; or, Theatrical inquisitor, Dec.
1828, p. 195.
Without the music (by Rodwell).

878 _____. Father and son; or, The rock of Charbonniere. A
drama, in two acts, by Edward Fitzball... Printed from
the acting copy, with remarks, biographical and critical,
by D.-G. ... As performed at the Theatres Royal...
London, G. H. Davidson [n.d.]. 6, [2], [5]-35p. incl.
front. (Cumberland's British theatre. London, ca. 1825-
55. v. 10 [no.3]).
Remarks by George Daniel, editor of the series.

879 _____. The floating beacon; a nautical drama, in two acts,
by Edward Fitzball... Printed from the acting copy, with
remarks, biographical and critical, by D.-G. ... As performed at the Theatres Royal... London, Davidson [n.d.].
32p. incl. front. (Cumberland's minor theatre. London
[1828-44] v. 2 [no. 9].
Remarks by George Daniel, editor of the series.

FITZBALL, EDWARD

880   FITZBALL, EDWARD. Hofer, the Tell of the Tyrol: an historical
drama, in three acts... London, John Cumberland [n.d.].
48p.

881   _____. The Inchcape bell: a nautical burletta, in two acts,
by Edward Fitzball... Printed from the acting copy, with
remarks, biographical and critical, by D.-G. ... As performed at the Theatres Royal... London, G. H. Davidson
[n.d.]. 38p incl. front. (Cumberland's minor theatre.
London [1828-44] v. 1 [no.3]).
    Remarks by George Daniel, editor of the series.
    Without the music (by G. H. Rodwell).

882   _____. The innkeeper of Abbeville; or, The ostler and the
robber: a drama, in two acts, by Edward Fitz-Ball...
Printed from the acting copy, with remarks, biographical
and critical, by D.-G. ... As performed at the Theatres
Royal... London, Davidson [n.d.]. 32p. incl. front.
(Cumberland's minor theatre. London [1828-44] v. 3 [no.
3]).
    Remarks by George Daniel, editor of the series.

883   _____. ... Joan of Arc; or, The maid of Orleans: a melo-drama
in three acts... London, G. H. Davidson [n.d.]. 39p.

884   _____. ... Jonathan Bradford; or, The murder at the road-side
inn. A drama in two acts... New York, Samuel French
[n.d.]. 30p. (French's standard drama, no. cl).

885   _____. The miller of Derwent water. A drama, in three acts.
London and New York, Samuel French [n.d.]. 30p.

886   _____. The momentous question; an original domestic drama,
in two acts... New York, Samuel French [n.d.]. 22p.

887   _____. Pierrette; or, The village rival. A comic operetta
in one act... The music by W. H. Montgomery. London,
Thomas Hailes Lacy [n.d.]. 13p.

888   _____. The pilot: a nautical burletta, in three acts, by
Edward Fitzball... Printed from the acting copy, with remarks, biographical and critical, by D.-G. ... As performed
at the Theatres Royal... London, G. H. Davidson [n.d.].
51p. front. (Cumberland's minor theatre. London [1828-
44] v. 1 [no.1]).
    "Taken from the well-known tale of the Pilot, written
by Mr. Cooper."--Remarks.
    Remarks by George Daniel, editor of the series.
    Portrait and memoir of T. P. Cooke (p. [7]-9).

FITZMAURICE, GEORGE

889   _____. The red rover; or, The mutiny of the dolphin: a nautical drama, in two acts... London, Davidson [n.d.]. 46p.

890   _____. Robin Hood; or, The merry outlaws of Sherwood. A dramatic equestrian spectacle in three acts... London, Thomas Hailes Lacy [n.d.]. 32p.

891   _____. ... The siege of Rochelle: an original opera, in two acts... London, John Duncombe [n.d.]. 38p. front.

892   _____. [...Tom Cringle]; or, Mat of the iron hand. A drama, in two acts. By Edward Fitzball... Printed from the best acting copy, with remarks, biographical and critical... as now performed in the London and American theatres... Philadelphia, F. Turner; New York, Turner and Fisher [1836?]. 38p. front. [Turner's dramatic library. New series. no. 11].
     Imperfect: torn, mutilated, upper part mounted on cover.

893   _____. Waverley; or, Sixty years since: a Scottish drama, in three acts (from Sir Walter Scott), by Edward Fitz-ball... Printed from the acting copy, with remarks, biographical and critical, by D.-G. ... As performed at the metropolitan minor theatres... London, J. Cumberland [n.d.]. 48p. incl. front. (Cumberland's minor theatre. London [1828-44] v. 5 [no. 8]).
     Remarks by George Daniel, editor of the original series. Reissued in Davidson's shilling volume of Cumberland's plays, v. 16 [no.5].

894 FITZGERALD, GERALDINE. Cousin Charlotte's visit; a play in three acts. For girls' schools, by Geraldine Fitzgerald. Halifax, N. S., Halifax printing co., 1900. 19p.

895 FITZMAURICE, GEORGE. The country dressmaker; a play in three acts, by George Fitzmaurice. Dublin and London, Maunsel and co., ltd., 1914. 57p. (Lettered on cover: The Abbey theatre series).

896   _____. Five plays, by George Fitzmaurice: The country dressmaker, The moonlighter, The pie-dish, The magic glasses, The dandy dolls. London and Dublin, Maunsel and co., ltd., 1914. 4 p.ℓ, 3-203p.

FLECKER, JAMES ELROY

897   FLECKER, JAMES ELROY, 1884-1915. Don Juan, a play in three acts, by James Elroy Flecker, with a preface by Helle Flecker. London, W. Heinemann ltd., 1925. xiv, 159, [1]p.

898   The flower of the family. A comedy in three acts. Boston, George M. Baker and co., 1876. 72p.

899   FLOYD, W. R. Handy Andy: a drama, in two acts... New York, Samuel French [n.d.]. 29p. (French's standard drama, the acting edition, no. cccxxxii).

900   FOOTE, SAMUEL, 1720-1777. The liar. A comedy, in two acts, adapted from the French of "Le Menteur" by Corneille by Samuel Foote... as altered and adapted by Charles Mathews. Chicago, The Dramatic publishing co. [n.d.]. 34p.

901   FORTNER, BERTHA C. The spirit of ancient Rome: a pageant-play in English. [n.p., n.d.]. 5p. (American Classical League Service Bureau, No. 400).

902   The fortune hunters; or, Lost and found, comedy in two acts. New York, The Roxbury publishing company, 1899. 21p.

903   FOSTER, CAREY. The moon menagerie. Lebanon, Ohio, March bros. [n.d.]. 5p.

904   FOUCHER, LAURE CLAIRE. Effie's Christmas dream; a play for children; adapted by Laure Clair Foucher from "A Christmas dream and how it came true," by Louisa M. Alcott... Boston, Little, Brown and co., 1912. 53p. front.

905   FOWLE, WILLIAM BENTLEY, 1795-1865. The new speaker; or, Exercises in rhetoric; being a selection of speeches, dialogues, and poetry, from the most approved American and British authors, suitable for declamation: by William B. Fowle... Boston, Hilliard, Gray, Little, and Wilkins, 1829. viii, 376p. CONTENTS. - The American antiquary. - The English traveller. - The fortune teller. - The haunch of mutton. - Pedigree. - Physiognomy. - The revolutionary pensioner. - The sick in his own despite. - The thing that's right. - The will.

906   _____. Parlor dramas; or, Dramatic scenes for home amusement ... Boston, Morris Cotton; New York, J. M. Fairchild and co., 1857. iv, 312p.

FREEMAN, MARY ELEANOR WILKINS

907   FRANK, J. C.   Homeopathy; or, The family cure, a farce in one
        act.   Chicago, T. S. Denison, 1884.   15p.

908   FRANK, LEONHARD, 1882-   .   ... Karl and Anna, a drama in
        three acts by Leonard Frank; translated by Ruth Langner.
        New York, Brentano's, 1929.   5 p.l., 3-108p.

909   FRANK, MAUDE MORRISON, 1870-   .   Short plays about famous
        authors, by Maude Morrison Frank.   New York, H. Holt and
        co., 1915.   vii, 144p.

910   FRASER, JOHN ARTHUR.   Bloomer girls; or, Courtship in the
        twentieth century, a satirical comedy in one act.   Chicago,
        The Dramatic publishing co. [1896].   23p.

911   _____.   A delicate question, an original comedy drama in four
        acts.   Chicago, The Dramatic publishing co. [1896].   64p.

912   _____.   ... The merry cobbler; an original comedy drama in
        four acts, by J. A. Fraser, Jr. ...   Chicago, The Dramatic
        publishing co. [1893].   48p. illus. (plans.).   (On cover:
        American amateur drama).

913   _____.   ... A modern Ananias; a comedy in three acts, by J. A.
        Fraser, Jr. ...   Chicago, The Dramatic publishing co.
        [1895].   66p. illus. (plans).   On cover: American amateur
        drama.

914   _____.   Santiago; or, For the red, white and blue; a war
        drama in four acts, by John A. Fraser...   Chicago, The
        Dramatic publishing co. [1898].   58p. illus. (plans).
        On cover: American acting drama.

915   _____.   The showman's ward, a comedy in three acts.   Chicago,
        The Dramatic publishing co. [1896].   49p.

916   _____.   Wah-na-ton; or, 'Way out West.   Frontier drama, in
        four acts...   Chicago and New York, The Dramatic publishing
        co. [n.d.].   58p.

917   The freedom of the press.   A farce...   Boston, George M.
        Baker and co., 1866.   21p.

918   FREEMAN, MARY ELEANOR WILKINS, 1852-1903.   Giles Corey,
        yeoman; a play by Mary E. Wilkins...   New York, Harper and
        bros., 1893.   3 p.l., [3]-108p. front. 3 pl.

FREUND, E. J.

919   FREUND, E. J.   ... The chiropractor, a serio-comic play for
       nine male and five female actors. By E. J. Freund...
       Antigo, Wis., Antigo publishing co., 1914. 1 p.ℓ., 37p.
       (Dramatic plays for young people's societies.)

920   _____. ... Grapejuice, by E. J. Freund; an international
       farce for seven males... Antigo, Wis., Antigo publishing
       co., c1914. 1 p.ℓ., 23p. (Dramatic plays for young
       people's societies).

921   _____. ... Honesty is the best policy, by E. J. Freund. A
       play for some 20 males, in 4 scenes... Antigo, Wis.,
       Antigo publishing co., 1914. 1 p.ℓ., 40p. (Dramatic plays
       for young people's societies).

922   _____. ... Ruled by suffragettes. A play for 15 female
       characters, in two scenes. By E. J. Freund... Antigo,
       Wis., Antigo publishing co. [1914]. 1 p.ℓ., 29p.
       (Dramatic plays for young people's societies).

923   _____. ... Wanted--a wife. A humorous play for two male and
       two female characters. By E. J. Freund... Antigo, Wis.,
       Antigo publishing co. [1914]. 1 p.ℓ., 20p. (Dramatic
       plays for young people's societies).

924   FREUNDLICH, CHARLES I. The magic toga: a play on derivation.
       [n.p., n.d.]. 5p. (American Classical League Service
       Bureau, No. 563).

925   FREY, MRS. R. E. Eileen; a play in four acts, by Mrs. R. E.
       Frey. [St. Louis, 1898]. 52p.

926   FREYTAG, GUSTAV, 1816-1895. The Journalists. 1914. (In
       Kuno Francke, ed., The German classics of the nineteenth
       and twentieth century [New York, The German publication
       society, 1914], v. 12, p. 11-109).
          Translated by Ernest F. Henderson.

927   FRIARS, AUSTIN. Loved and lost. A drama, in one act.
       Chicago, The Dramatic publishing co., 1884. 8p.

928   FROST, S. A. Aladdin; or, The wonderful lamp, a fairy tale
       drama for the little folks. New York, Dick and Fitzgerald
       [n.d.]. 16p.

929 FROTHINGHAM, MEREDITH S. The princess Tai; or, A China tea
set. A decoction, drawn in two acts, by M. S. Frothingham
... With original dances, ballet and marches, arranged by
Jacob Mahler... Saratoga Springs [N. Y.], The Saratogian
book and job print, 1887. Cover-title, 14p.

930 FROUGHTON, ADOLPHUS CHARLES. Vandyke Brown. A farce in one
act. New York, Robert M. De Witt [n.d.]. 20p.

931 FULLER, ALICE COOK. The gifted givers, a Christmas play, by
Alice Cook Fuller. Lebanon, O., March bros. [1914]. 34p.

932 FULLER, HORACE W. False pretensions. A comedy, in two acts,
adapted from the French "La poudre aux yeux." Chicago and
New York, The Dramatic publishing co., 1887. 35p.

933 FULTON, HARRY CLIFFORD. Jean Valjean; or, The shadow of the
law. A dramatization of Victor Hugo's "Les miserables."
By H. C. Fulton. Davenport, Ia., Glass and Axtman,
printers, 1886. 65p.

934 Furianus gets a father, a two-act play written by students of
Roosevelt High School, Honolulu, under the direction of
Alice Carlson. [n.p., n.d.]. 14p. (American Classical
League Service Bureau, No. 671).

935 FURMAN, ALFRED ANTOINE, 1856-   . Philip of Pokanoket, an
Indian drama, by Alfred Antoine Furman. New York,
Stettiner, Lambert and co., 1894. 136p.

936 FURNISS, GRACE LIVINGSTON. A box of monkeys, and other farce-
comedies, by Grace Livingston Furniss. New York, Harper
and bros., 1891. 3 p.ℓ., 3-257p. CONTENTS. - A box of
monkeys. - The Jack Trust. - The veneered savage. - Tulu.

937 _____. A box of monkeys, a parlor farce in two acts, by
Grace L. Furniss... Boston, W. H. Baker and co., 1889.
31p. On cover: Baker's edition of plays.

938 _____. The corner lot chorus, a farce in one act for female
characters only, by Grace Livingston Furniss... Boston,
W. H. Baker and co., 1891. 19p. On cover: Baker's
edition of plays.

939 _____. Second floor, Spoopendyke, a farce in two acts, by
Grace Livingston Furniss... Boston, W. H. Baker and co.,
1892. 27p. (On cover: Baker's edition of plays).

GABBERT, AUGUST PAUL

940   GABBERT, AUGUST PAUL, 1857-   . The drama of destiny--Karl
       Hanno. 3d rev. ed. A play in IV acts. Written by A. Paul
       Gabbert... Quincy, Ill., The author, 1904. 84p.

941   _____. The drama of destiny--Karl Hanno, revised edition. A
       play of IV acts, written by A. Paul Gabbert... Quincy,
       Ill., The author, 1903. 87p.

942   GADDESS, MARY L. Crowning of Christmas, musical play for 26
       girls, 3 boys, quartet, or for all girls. By Mary L.
       Gaddess and Stanley Schell. New York, Edgar S. Werner,
       1911. 14p.

943   GAFFNEY, MICHAEL HENRY, 1895-   . The stories of Padriac
       Pearse, dramatized by M. H. Gaffney, O. P.; With an intro-
       duction by Miss M. M. Pearse, T. D. Dublin [etc.] The
       Talbot press ltd. [n.d.]. 228p. illus.

944   GAFFNEY, THOMAS J. ... Birds of a feather; a play in four
       acts [by] Thomas J. Gaffney. Boston, The Gorham press;
       [etc., etc., 1915]. 110p. (American dramatists series).

945   GALE, RACHEL E. BAKER. After taps, a drama in three acts,
       completed by Rachel E. Baker from notes and unfinished
       manuscript of the late George M. Baker. Boston, W. H.
       Baker and co., 1891. 45p. On cover: The globe drama.

946   GALLON, TOM. The man who stole the castle, a play in one act,
       by Tom Gallon and L. M. Lion. London, Samuel French, ltd.
       [n.d.]. 40p.

947   GALSWORTHY, JOHN, 1867-1933. Justice; a tragedy in four acts,
       by John Galsworthy. London, Duckworth and co., 1910.
       3 p.ℓ., 111p.

948   _____. Plays. Third series: The fugitive, The pigeon, The
       mob, by John Galsworthy. New York, C. Scribner's sons,
       1914. 6 p.ℓ., 93p., 3ℓ., 30p., 3ℓ., 77p.

949   _____. Plays. Second series: The eldest son, The little
       dream, Justice, by John Galsworthy. New York, C.
       Scribner's sons, 1913. 6 p.ℓ., 3-74p., 2ℓ., 3-34p., 3ℓ.,
       100p.

950   GANTER, FRANZ S. Ravenswood. A romantic tragedy, in five
       acts. Founded on Scott's novel of the Bride of Lammermoor,
       and respectfully dedicated to the Shakespeare club, by the
       authors, F. S. Ganter and George H. Braughn. New Orleans,
       J. W. Madden, print, 1873. 56p.

951   GARNETT, RICHARD, 1835-1906. William Shakespeare, pedagogue
       and poacher. London and New York, John Lane, The Bodley
       Head, 1905. 111p.

952   [GARRAHAN, THOMAS C.]. The catechism, a kindly light, by a
       member of our parish; a playlet for St. Patrick's day
       entertainment. [n.p.] 1915. Cover title, [3]-14p.

953   GARRICK, DAVID, 1717-1779. The guardian. A comedy, in two
       acts. New York, De Witt [n.d.]. 16p.

954   GARTON, J. A. The bowman. Eton, Spottiswoode, Ballantyne and
       co., 1931. 54p.

955   GAY, MAUDE CULBERTSON. The haunted house; an adaptation of
       one of Pliny's letters (VII, 27) [n.p., n.d.]. 5p.
       (American Classical League Service Bureau, No. 555).

956   GAYLER, CHARLES, 1820-1892. ... The love of a prince; or, The
       court of Prussia. A drama, in three acts. Altered and
       adapted from the French. By Charles Gayler... New York,
       S. French [1857]. 45p. (French's standard drama [no.
       168]).

957   _____. ... The son of the night: a drama, in three days; and
       a prologue... New York, Samuel French [n.d.]. 42p.
       (French's standard drama, no. clxix).

958   A gentleman from Idaho, a drama in prologue and three acts.
       Boston, Walter H. Baker and co. [1889]. [50]p.

959   GERSTENBERG, ALICE. A little world; a series of college plays
       for girls, by Alice Gerstenberg. Chicago, The Dramatic
       publishing co. [1908]. 228p.

960   _____. Where are those men! A sketch for girls, by Alice
       Gerstenberg. Chicago, The Dramatic publishing co. [1912].
       14p. (On cover: Segal's acting drama. no. 612).

GHISLANZONI, ANTONIO

961   GHISLANZONI, ANTONIO, 1824-1893. ... Aida, by Antonio
      Ghislanzoni; music by Giuseppe Verdi; edited and with an
      introduction by W. J. Henderson. New York, Dodd, Mead and
      co., 1911. xxiv, 135p.

962   GIACOMETTI, PAOLO, 1816-1882. Elizabeth, queen of England,
      an historical play in five acts, written expressly by
      Paolo Giacometti for Madame Ristori, and her dramatic
      company. Under the management of J. Grau. Translated
      from the Italian by Thomas Williams. New York, J. A. Gray
      and Green, printers, 1867. 40p.

963   _____. Marie Antoinette. A drama in a prologue, five acts,
      and epilogue. Written expressly for Madame Adelaide
      Ristori... The English translation by Isaac C. Pray. New
      York, Théâtre français, 1867. 79p. front.

964   GIACOSA, GIUSEPPE, 1847-1906. "As the leaves" [a drama in
      four acts] by Giacosa. [Chicago?] 1908. 72p.

965   _____. The stronger: Like falling leaves: Sacred ground;
      three plays by Giuseppe Giacosa; tr. from the Italian
      with an introduction by Edith and Allan Updegraff. New
      York, M. Kennerley, 1913. xiv p., 2ℓ., [3], 6-326p. illus.
      (plan). (Half-title: The modern drama series, ed. by E.
      Björkman).

966   No Entry.

967   GIBSON, AD H. Slick and Skinner; or, The barber pards, an
      original sketch in one act. Clyde, Ohio, Ames' publishing
      co., 1889. 9p.

968   GIBSON, WILFRID WILSON, 1878-1962. Daily bread, in three
      books, by Wilfrid Wilson Gibson. New York, The Macmillan
      co., 1922. 2 p.ℓ., 13-62p., 1ℓ. CONTENTS. - The house of
      candles. - On the road. - The betrothal. - The first born.
      - "The family's pride."

969   _____. Daily bread, in three books, by Wilfrid Wilson Gibson.
      New York, The Macmillan co., 1912. 62, [1]p.

970   GIELOW, MRS. MARTHA (SAWYER), 1854-1933. Old Andy, the moon-
      shiner, by Martha S. Gielow... [Washington, D. C., W. F.
      Roberts co., 1910]. 46p., 1ℓ., front. (port.), pl.

GILLETTE, WILLIAM HOOKER

971 _____. Old plantation days, by Martha S. Gielow... New York,
R. H. Russell, 1902. xii p., 1ℓ., 15–183p. front. plates.
ports.

972 GIFFORD, J. WEAR. Supper for two; or, The wolf and the lamb.
A farce... New York, Samuel French and son [n.d.]. 18p.

973 GILBERT, WILLIAM SCHWENCK, 1836–1911. Her Majesty's Ship
"Pinafore"; or, The lass that loved a sailor. An entirely
original comic opera, in two acts... composed by Arthur
Sullivan. Philadelphia, Ledger job print [n.d.]. 31p.

974 _____. The mikado. An entirely new and original Japanese
opera, in two acts... composed by Arthur Sullivan...
Sydney Rosenfeld, 1885. 48p.

975 _____. Original plays... First series containing The wicked
world, Pygmalion and Galatea, Charity, The palace of truth,
The princess, Trial by jury, Iolanthe. London, Chatto and
Windus, 1905. 287p.

976 _____. Original plays. Second series containing Broken hearts,
Engaged, Sweethearts, Dan'l Druce, Gretchen, Tom Cobb, The
Sorcerer, H.M.S. Pinafore, The pirates of Penzance. Lon-
don, Chatto and Windus, 1907. 338p.

977 _____. Princess Ida; or, Castle adamant... music by Arthur
Sullivan... London, J. M. Stoddart, 1884. 49p.

978 _____. Randall's thumb. An original comedy, in three acts.
London and New York, Samuel French [n.d.]. 64p.

979 _____. Sweethearts. An original dramatic contrast, in two
acts... New York, Samuel French and son [n.d.]. 20p.

980 GILL, WILLIAM S. An American hustler, a comedy drama in four
acts. Chicago, T. S. Denison [1906]. 70p.

981 GILLESPIE. Humanity, by Gillespie and Reilly, a clever skit
for two. Chicago and New York, Will Rossiter [n.d.].
10p.

982 GILLETTE, WILLIAM HOOKER, 1855–1937. An American drama
arranged in four acts and entitled Secret service; a
romance of the Southern Confederacy, written by William
Gillette... New York, S. French; [etc., etc., 1898].
183p.

GINGOLD, HELENE

983   GINGOLD, HELENE. Abelard and Heloise. Buffalo, Gingold, 1906. [79]p.

984   GODDARD, CHARLES W. The misleading lady, by Charles W. Goddard and Paul Dickey... New York, Hearst's international library co., 1915. iv p., 2ℓ., 286p. front., plates.

985   GODDARD, MRS. EDWARD. By force of love; or, Wedded and parted, a domestic drama, in five acts. Clyde, Ohio, Ames' publishing co., 1895. 25p.

986   GODFREY, THOMAS, 1736-1763. Juvenile poems on various subjects. With the prince of Parthia, a tragedy. By the late Mr. Thomas Godfrey, jun:... To which is prefixed, Some account of the author and his writings... Philadelphia, Printed by Henry Miller, in Second-street, M DCC LXV. xxvi p., 1ℓ., 223p.

987   GODOY, ARMAND. ... The drama of the passion; English metrical version by Malcolm McLaren. [London and Oxford, Printed by A. R. Mowbray and co., limited, 1935?]. 5 p.ℓ., 126p., 2ℓ. front.

988   GODSEY, EDITH R. The judgment of Paris: a very short play in English. [n.p., n.d.]. 2p. (American Classical League Service Bureau, No. 193).

989   GOETHE, JOHANN WOLFGANG VON, 1749-1832. The Tragedy of Faust, with an introduction; The Faust Legend from Marlowe to Goethe. (In Kuno Francke, ed., The German classics of the nineteenth and twentieth century [New York, The German publication society, 1913] v. 1, pp. 230-497). Translated by Anna Swanwick. Only selected portions of Part II are included.

990   _____. Iphigenia in Tauris. 1787. (In Kuno Francke, ed., The German classics of the nineteenth and twentieth century [New York, The German publication society, 1913], v. 1, pp. 157-229). Translated by Anna Swanwick.

991   GOFF, HENRY. The two drovers. A domestic legendary drama, in two acts... London, Thomas Hailes Lacy [n.d.]. 24p. front.

992   GOLDSMITH, OLIVER, 1730-1774. She stoops to conquer. London and Glasgow, Blackie and son, ltd. [n.d.]. 80p.

993   GONDINET, E. A pleasure trip. A comedy, in three acts, by E.
      Gondinet and A. Bisson, translated from the French by New-
      ton Chisnell... Clyde, Ohio, A. D. Ames, 1885. 45p.

994   GOODLOE, ABBIE CARTER. Antinoüs, a tragedy. Philadelphia,
      Printed by J. B. Lippincott co., 1891. 139p.

995   GORDON, WALTER. A fireside story. A Christmas comedietta,
      in one act. Chicago, The Dramatic publishing co., 1884.
      10p.

996   [GORE, CATHERINE GRACE FRANCES MOODY], 1799-1861. Quid pro
      quo; or, The day of dupes. The prize comedy, in five acts.
      As first performed at the Theatre Royal, Hay-Market. On
      Tuesday, June 18, 1844... London, Pub. at the National
      acting drama office [1844]. v p., 2ℓ., [11]-82p.
      Preface signed: C. F. G.

997   GORE, MRS. CHARLES. ... The maid of Croissey; or, Theresa's
      vow. A drama, in two acts... New York, Samuel French
      [n.d.]. 34p. (The minor drama, no. xxviii).

998   GORKII, MAKSIM, 1868-1936. The lower depths; a play in four
      acts, by Maxim Gorkii, translated from the original Russian
      by Lawrence Irving. New York, Duffield and co. [1912].
      191, [1]p. front. (port.). Half-title: Plays of to-day
      and tomorrow.

999   GOTT, CHARLES. His word of honor, a comedy in three acts.
      Boston, Walter H. Baker and co., 1911. 45p.

1000 GRAHAM, MANTA S. Light weights. Boston, Cornhill publishing
      co., 1921. 102p. CONTENTS. - The goose. - The trend. -
      Two's company. - A by-product. - Allied occupations.

1001 GRANVILLE, EDWARD. 'Enery Brown. London and New York,
      Samuel French, ltd., 1904. 12p.

1002 _____. The three graces, a comedy in one act. Boston,
      Walter H. Baker and co., 1904. 24p.

1003 GRAVES, BELDEN OERTEL TAYLOR. Lydia; a poetical drama in one
      act, by Belden Oertel Taylor Graves. New York, Broadway
      publishing co. [1907]. 5 p.ℓ., 3-43p.

1004 GRAVES, JOSEPH. Cupid. London, Turner and Fisher, 1837.
      22p.

GRAVES, JOSEPH

1005   GRAVES, JOSEPH.   ... The wife; A tale of a Mantua maker!   A
        burlesque burletta, in one act... London, J. Duncombe
        [n.d.]. 24p. front. (Duncombe's edition).

1006   GRAY, NICHOLAS STUART. The imperial nightingale, adapted from
        the story by Hans Christian Andersen. London, Oxford Uni-
        versity Press, 1957. 116p. illus.

1007   GREENE, CLAY MEREDITH, 1850-1933. · The dispensation, and other
        plays, by Clay M. Greene. New York, George H. Doran co.
        [1914]. 4 p.ℓ., 5-96p. CONTENTS. - The dispensation. -
        The star of Bethlehem. - "Through Christmas bells." - The
        awakening of Barbison.

1008   GREENE, HENRY COPLEY, 1871-   . Pontius Pilate, Saint Ronan
        of Brittany, Théophile - three plays in verse by Henry
        Copley Greene. New York, Scott-Thaw co., 1903. 3 p.ℓ.,
        90p. front.

1009   GREENWOOD, FRED L. Our daughters, a society comedy, in four
        acts... from the German... Clyde, Ohio, A. D. Ames, 1883.
        44p.

1010   GREENWOOD, THOMAS. The death of Life in London; or, Tom and
        Jerry's funeral. An entirely new satirical, burlesque,
        operatic parody, in one act, not taken from any thing...
        Performed, for the first time, at the Royal Coburg theatre,
        on Monday, June 2, 1823. Written by T. Greenwood, esq. ...
        Baltimore, J. Robinson, 1823. 24p.
            Founded on Pierce Egan's "Life in London."

1011   GREGORY, ISABELLA AUGUSTA (PERSSE) LADY, 1859-1932. The
        image; a play in three acts, by Lady Gregory. Dublin,
        Maunsel and co., ltd., 1910. 2 p.ℓ., 102p.

1012   _____. Irish folk-history plays, by Lady Gregory... New
        York and London, G. P. Putnam's sons, 1912. 2 v.

1013   _____. Seven short plays, by Lady Gregory. New York and
        London, G. P. Putnam's sons [c1909]. 204p. music.

1014   _____. The travelling man, a miracle play. Dublin, Maunsel
        and co., ltd. [1905]. 19p.

1015   GRIFFIN, G. W. H. Camille, an Ethiopian interlude... New
        York, Samuel French [n.d.]. 8p.

GRIFFITH, HELEN SHERMAN

1016   ____. Feast, an Ethiopian burlesque opera... New York, Samuel French [n.d.]. 8p.

1017   ____. Hamlet the dainty, an Ethiopian burlesque on Shakespeare's Hamlet... New York, Happy hours co. [n.d.]. 8p.

1018   ____. Jack's the Lad; an Ethiopian drama... New York, Samuel French [n.d.]. 8p.

1019   ____. Nobody's son; an Ethiopian act... New York, Samuel French [n.d.]. 8p.

1020   ____. Sports on a lark, an Ethiopian farce. Chicago, T. S. Denison [n.d.]. 7p.

1021   ____. An unhappy pair, an Ethiopian farce, in one act. Chicago, T. S. Denison [n.d.]. 7p.

1022   ____. William Tell; an Ethiopian interlude... New York, Happy hours co. [n.d.]. 8p.

1023   GRIFFITH, BENJAMIN LEASE CROZER. School and parlor comedies ... By B. L. C. Griffith... Philadelphia, The Penn publishing co., 1894. [154]p. various pagings.

1024   GRIFFITH, HELEN SHERMAN, 1873- . An alarm of fire; a comedy in one act, by Helen Sherman Griffith... Boston, W. H. Baker and co., 1911. 17p. (On cover: Baker's edition of plays).

1025   ____. A fallen idol; a farce in one act, by Helen Sherman Griffith... Philadelphia, The Penn publishing co., 1900. 16p.

1026   ____. For love or money; a comedy in three acts, by Helen Sherman Griffith... Philadelphia, The Penn publishing co., 1903. 36p.

1027   ____. A large order, a sketch in one act. Boston, Walter H. Baker and co. [1903]. 16p.

1028   ____. A merry widow hat; a farce in one act for female characters, by Helen Sherman Griffith... Boston, W. H. Baker, 1910. 17p. (On cover: Baker's edition of plays).

1029   ____. Reflected glory; a farce in one act (for female characters), by Helen Sherman Griffith... Philadelphia, The Penn publishing co., 1909. 17p.

GRILLPARZER, FRANZ

1030   GRILLPARZER, FRANZ, 1791-1872. The ancestress, tragedy in
        five acts, by Franz Grillparzer, translated by Herman I.
        Spahr... [Hapeville, Ga., Tyler and co., 1938]. 93p.

1031   _____. A faithful servant of his master, tragedy in five
        acts, by Franz Grillparzer, translated by Arthur Burkhard.
        Yarmouth Port, Mass., The Register press, 1941. 123p.

1032   _____. Family strife in Hapsburg; tragedy in five acts, by
        Franz Grillparzer; translated by Arthur Burkhard. Yarmouth
        Port, Mass., The Register press, 1940. 149p.

1033   _____. Hero and Leander, tragedy in five acts by Franz Grill-
        parzer, translated by Henry H. Stevens. Yarmouth Port,
        Mass., The Register press [1938]. 111p.

1034   _____. The Jewess of Toledo. 1914. (In Kuno Francke, ed.,
        The German classics of the nineteenth and twentieth
        century [New York, The German publication society, 1941],
        v. 6, p. 337-408). Translated by George Henry Danton and
        Annina Periam Danton.

1035   _____. King Ottocar, his rise and fall; tragedy five acts,
        by Franz Grillparzer; translated by Henry H. Stevens.
        Yarmouth Port, Mass., The Register press, 1938. 160p.

1036   _____. Medea. 1914. (In Kuno Francke, ed., The German
        classics of the nineteenth and twentieth century, [New
        York, The German publication society, 1914], p. 235-336).
        Translated by Theodore A. Miller.

1037   _____. Sappho; a tragedy in five acts. After the German of
        Franz Grillparzer, by Edda Middleton. New York, D. Apple-
        ton and co., 1858. 2 p.ℓ., 160p. front.

1038   _____. Sword and queue. 1914. (In Kuno Francke, ed., The
        German classics in the nineteenth and twentieth century
        [New York, The German publication society, 1914], v. 7,
        p. 256-350). Translated by Grace Isabel Colbron.

1039   _____. Thou shalt not lie; comedy in five acts, by Franz
        Grillparzer, translated by Henry H. Stevens. Yarmouth
        Port, Mass., The Register press, 1939. 115p.

1040   GROSKEN, NORMA. "All Gaul---"; a play in two acts, or radio
        script, by Norma Grosken and Rochelle Sussman. [n.p.,
        n.d.]. 18p. (American Classical League Service Bureau,
        No. 639).

1041   GROW, MARGUERITE. The childhood of the Gods. [n.p., n.d.].
       7p. (American Classical League Service Bureau, No. 681).

1042   GRUNDY, SYDNEY, 1848-1914. A fool's paradise; an original
       play in three acts, by Sydney Grundy... London, New York,
       S. French, c1898. 64p. (On cover: French's international
       copyrighted... edition of the works of the best authors.
       no. 1).

1043   _____. The glass of fashion; an original comedy in four acts,
       by Sydney Grundy... London, New York, S. French, 1898.
       60p. On cover: French's international copyrighted...
       edition of the works of the best authors. (no. 3).

1044   _____. The head of Romulus; a comedietta, in one act, founded
       on the French of Eugène Scribe, by Sydney Grundy, 1900.
       24p. On cover: French's international copyrighted...
       edition of the works of the best authors. (no. 3).

1045   _____. A pair of spectacles, a comedy in three acts adapted
       from the French... New York and London, Samuel French,
       1898. 66p.

1046   _____. The silver shield; an original comedy in three acts,
       by Sydney Grundy... London, New York, S. French, 1898.
       62p. On cover: French's international copyrighted...
       edition of the works of the best authors. (no. 2).

1047   _____. Sowing the wind, an original play in four acts, by
       Sydney Grundy... New York, S. French; [etc., etc.] 1901.
       56p. illus. (plans). On cover: French's international
       copyrighted... edition of the works of the best authors.
       (no. 45).

1048   _____. Sympathetic souls; a comedietta in one act, founded
       on the French of Eugène Scribe by Sydney Grundy. New York
       and London, S. French, 1900. 19p. (On cover: French's
       international copyrighted... edition of the works of the
       best authors. no. 33).

1049   GUILD, THATCHER HOWLAND, 1879-1914. Carroty Nell, a farce in
       two acts. Boston, Walter H. Baker and co. [1905]. 25p.

1050   _____. The Clancey kids, a comedy in two acts. Boston,
       Walter H. Baker and co. [1904]. 35p.

GUILD, THATCHER HOWLAND

1051   GUILD, THATCHER HOWLAND. The power of a god, and other one-
       act plays, by Thatcher Howland Guild, with sketches of his
       life and work. Urbana, Ill., University of Illinois press,
       1919. 151p. front. (port.) plates.

1052   _____. Two strikes, a baseball comedy in two acts; by
       Thatcher Howland Guild... Boston, W. H. Baker and co.,
       1910. 27p. (On cover: Baker's edition of plays).

1053   GUIMERÁ, ANGEL, 1847-1924. La pecadora (Daniela); a play in
       three acts, by Angel Guimerá; tr. by Wallace Gillpatrick...
       New York and London, G. P. Putnam's sons, 1916. 162p.

1054   GUION, RIDIE J. Frater bestiarum, or Viae ad sapientiam; a
       Christmas play, by Ridie J. Guion and Ilse M. Zechner.
       [n.p., n.d.]. 9, 2p. (American Classical League Service
       Bureau, No. 618).

1055   GUPTILL, ELIZABETH FRANCES EPHRAIM, 1870-   . Bo Peep's
       Christmas party. A Mother Goose play. By Elizabeth F.
       Guptill... Franklin, O., Eldridge entertainment house,
       1914. 13p.

1056   _____. A brave little tomboy. A play of the revolution. By
       Elizabeth F. Guptill... Franklin, O., Eldridge entertain-
       ment house, 1912. 27p.

1057   _____. ... Christmas at the cross roads. A humorous Christ-
       mas play for high school pupils or adults, by Elizabeth F.
       Guptill... Lebanon, O., March bros., 1909. Cover-title,
       23p.

1058   _____. The dolls' symposium, a captivating play for children,
       by Elizabeth F. Guptill. Lebanon, O., March bros. [1911].
       18p.

1059   _____. Fun at Five Point school, a burlesque, by Elizabeth F.
       Guptill... Franklin, O., Eldridge entertainment house,
       1912. 23p.

1060   _____. Santa's rescue, a Christmas play, by Elizabeth F.
       Guptill... New York, Tullar-Meredith co., 1914. 16p.
       diagr.

1061   _____. The waif's Thanksgiving. Lebanon, Ohio, March bros.
       [1911]. 20p.

1062 HAGEMAN, MAURICE. By telephone, sketch, by Maurice Hageman...
      Chicago, The Dramatic publishing co. [1897]. 1 p.ℓ., 5-
      13p. (On cover: American acting drama).

1063 _____. Hector, a farce in one act, by Maurice Hageman...
      Chicago, The Dramatic publishing co. [1897]. [4], 5-23p.
      On cover: American acting drama.

1064 _____. Oh, that property man! A monologue. Chicago, The
      Dramatic publishing co., 1898. 7p.

1065 _____. Professor Robinson, comedy in one act. Chicago, The
      Dramatic publishing co. [1899]. 18p.

1066 _____. To rent, comedietta in one act. Chicago, The
      Dramatic publishing co. [1898]. 10p.

1067 _____. Two veterans, farce in one act. Chicago, The Dramatic
      publishing co. [1899]. 12p.

1068 HAHN, E. ADELAIDE. "Very tragical mirth": the story of Aeneas
      and Dido. [n.p., n.d.]. 6p. (American Classical League
      Service Bureau, No. 91).

1069 HAINES, JOHN THOMAS, 1799?-1843. Alice Grey, the suspected
      one; or, The moral brand. A domestic drama, in three acts,
      by I. T. Haines, esq. As performed at the Royal Surrey
      theatre... [London] J. Pattie [1839?]. 4 p.ℓ., [7]-59p.
      front. (On cover: Pattie's universal stage, no. 1).
      First performed April 1, 1839.

1070 _____. The factory boy: a drama, in three acts, by I. T.
      Haines... As performing at the Royal Surrey theatre,
      correctly printed from the prompt copy... London, J.
      Pattie [1840]. 50p. front. (The Universal stage... Lon-
      don, 1840. v. 2 [no. 6]).

1071 _____. ... The French spy; or, The siege of Constantina. A
      military drama, in three acts... New York, Samuel French
      [n.d.]. 24p. (French's standard drama, no. cliii).

1072 _____. ... The idiot witness; or, A tale of blood. A melo-
      drama. In three acts. By J. T. Haines, esq. Correctly
      printed from the most approved acting copy... Philadelphia,
      New York, Turner and Fisher [ca. 1844]. 28p. (Turner's
      dramatic library. [New ser., no. 84]).

HAINES, JOHN THOMAS

1073   HAINES, JOHN THOMAS. Jack Sheppard, a domestic drama, in three acts, by J. T. Haines, esq. As performed at the London theatres, correctly printed from the prompt book... [London] J. Pattie, 1839. xx, 70p. front. (The Universal stage... London, 1840. v. 1 [no. 3].
Founded upon Ainsworth's novel "Jack Sheppard."

1074   _____. The life of woman; or, The curate's daughter: a pictorial drama of interest, founded on Hogarth's "Harlot's progress." By J. T. Haines... As performing at the Royal Surrey theatre, correctly printed from the prompt copy... London, J. Pattie [1840]. xi, [12]-56p. (The Universal stage... London, 1840. v.2 [no. 3].

1075   _____. My Poll and my partner Joe. A nautical drama, in three acts. By John Thomas Haines... The music selected and arranged by Mr. Jolly. London, S. French; New York, S. French and son [188-?]. 1 p.ℓ., 5-51p. (On cover: French's acting edition, no. 1058).
Without the music.

1076   _____. The ocean of life; or, "Every inch a sailor!" A nautical drama, in three acts, by John Thomas Haines... The music by Mr. Jolly. Printed from the acting copy, with remarks, biographical and critical, by D.-G. ... As performed at the Royal Surrey theatre... London, J. Cumberland [n.d.]. 57p. incl. front. (Cumberland's minor theatre. London [ca. 1830-55] v. 11 [no. 2]).
Remarks by George Daniel, editor of the series.
Without the music.
Reissued in Davidson's shilling volume of Cumberland's plays, v. 34 [no. 4].

1077   _____. Ruth; or, The lass that loves a soldier. A nautical and domestic drama, in three acts... London, Thomas Hailes Lacy [n.d.]. 49p.

1078   _____. Uncle Oliver; or, A house divided. A farce, in two acts, by J. T. Haines... As performing at the Royal Victoria theatre, correctly printed from the prompt book... [London, J. Pattie, 1839?]. 30p. front. (The Universal stage... London, 1840. v. 1 [no. 2]).
Author's letter to the publisher dated October 9, 1839.

1079   _____. The wizard of the wave; or, The ship of the avenger; a legendary nautical drama, in three acts, by J. T. Haines... As performed at the Victoria theatre, correctly printed from the prompt copy... London, J. Pattie [1840]. vi [7]-54p. (The Universal stage... London, 1840. v. 2 [no. 11]).

1080   _____. The wraith of the lake; a domestic drama, in three acts... London, Thomas Hailes Lacy [n.d.]. 34p. front.

1081   HALBE, MAX. Mother Earth. 1914. (In Kuno Francke, ed., The German classics of the nineteenth and twentieth century [New York, The German publication society, 1914], v. 20, p. 111-233). Translated by Paul H. Grummann.

1082   HALE, RUTH. Stars in their eyes, also published as There'll come a day, a comedy in three acts, by Ruth and Nathan Hale. Cedar Rapids, Iowa, Heuer publishing co., c1953. 88p.

1083   HALEY, E. LUCILLE. The adventures of Ulysses; a play in English in humorous vein. [n.p., n.d.]. 17p. (American Classical League Service Bureau, No. 421).

1084   HALL, WILLIS. The long and the short and the tall; a play in two acts. London, Heinemann [1959]. 104p. illus.

1085   HALLIDAY, ANDREW, 1830-1877. Checkmate. A farcical comedy. In two acts. By Andrew Halliday... London, T. H. Lacy [1872?]. 42p. (On cover: Lacy's acting edition. 1265).

1086   _____. Daddy Gray. A serio-comic drama, in three acts. By Andrew Halliday... To which is added a description of the costume - cast of the characters... and the whole of the stage business. New York, R. M. De Witt [187-?]. 30p. diagrs. (On cover: De Witt's acting plays. (No. 20)).

1087   _____. Notre Dame; or, The gipsy girl of Paris, a grand romantic and spectacular drama (founded on Victor Hugo's celebrated romance) in three acts. Chicago and New York, The Dramatic publishing co. [n.d.]. 33p.

1088   HAMILTON, CICELY. How the vote was won, a play in one act. By Cicely Hamilton and Christopher St. John. Chicago, The Dramatic publishing co. [1910]. 31p.

HAMILTON, COSMO

1089   HAMILTON, COSMO. "Pickwick"; a play in three acts, by Cosmo
       Hamilton and Frank C. Reilly, freely based upon the Pick-
       wick papers, by Charles Dickens. Time - 1827-28. Place -
       England. New York and London, G. P. Putnam's sons, 1927.
       ix, 246p. front., plates.

1090   HAMILTON, GEORGE H. Hotel healthy. Farce in one act. Clyde,
       Ohio, Ames' publishing co., 1896. 13p.

1091   _____. Sunlight; or, The diamond king, a western drama, in
       four acts. Clyde, Ohio, Ames' publishing co., 1896. 29p.

1092   HANDWRIGHT, FLORENCE B. The trial of Latin Language: a
       dramatization. [n.p., n.d.]. 3p. (American Classical
       League Service Bureau, No. 458).

1093   HANKIN, ST. JOHN EMILE CLAVERING, 1869-1909. The plays of St.
       John Hankin, with an introduction by John Drinkwater...
       London, M. Secker [1923]. 2 v.

1094   HANLEY, JOHN. Shann's trust. London and New York, Samuel
       French, 1875. 40p.

1095   HANSEN, ESTHER V. An interview with the poet Horace; a "news-
       paper reporter" of ancient Rome questions the poet laureate.
       [n.p., n.d.]. 4p. (American Classical League Service
       Bureau, No. 535).

1096   HANSHEW, T. W. The forty-niners; or, The pioneer's daughter,
       a picturesque American drama, in five acts, dramatized
       from his own popular story of the same title. Clyde, Ohio,
       A. D. Ames, 1879. 29p.

1097   _____. Oath bound; or, Faithful unto death, a domestic drama,
       in three acts. Clyde, Ohio, A. D. Ames [n.d.]. 20p.

1098   HARDING, C. R. The absinthe fiend, comedy-drama in four acts.
       Atchison, Kansas, 1912. 34p.

1099   HARDT, ERNST. Tristram the Jester. 1914. (In Kuno Francke,
       ed., The German classics of the nineteenth and twentieth
       century [New York, The German publication society, 1914],
       v. 20, p. 398-498). Translated by John Heard, Jr.

1100   HARDY, EDWARD TRUEBLOOD. ... Crowding the season: a comedy in
       three acts, by E. Trueblood Hardy... New York, S. French
       [1870]. 2 p.ℓ., [3]-32p. (French's Minor drama. no. 217).

1101   HARDY, THOMAS, 1840-1928. The dynasts, a drama of the Napole-
        onic wars in three parts, nineteen acts, and one hundred
        and thirty scenes. New York and London, The Macmillan co.,
        1904-1905. 2 v.

1102   HARE, WALTER BEN, 1880-   . Aaron Boggs, freshman, a college
        comedy in three acts, by Walter Ben Hare... Chicago, T. S.
        Denison and co. [1913]. 87p. illus. (diagrs.). (On cover:
        Alta series).

1103   _____. Civil service, an American drama in three acts; a play
        with punch, by Walter Ben Hare... Chicago, T. S. Denison
        and co. [1915]. 68p. illus. (diagr.). (On cover: Alta
        series).

1104   _____. A college town; a college farce comedy in three acts
        by Walter Ben Hare. Chicago, T. S. Denison and co. [1910].
        64p. illus. (diagrs.). (On cover: Alta series).

1105   _____. The fascinators, a musical burlesque entertainment in
        one act; by Walter Ben Hare... Chicago, T. S. Denison and
        co. [1913]. 19p. (On cover: Denison's specialties).

1106   _____. The heiress hunters, a comedy in three acts; by Walter
        Ben Hare... Boston, W. H. Baker and co., 1915. 60p.
        (On cover: Baker's edition of plays).

1107   _____. Mrs. Tubbs of Shantytown, a comedy-drama in three
        acts; by Walter Ben Hare... Chicago, T. S. Denison and
        co [1914]. 70p. illus. (diagr.). (On cover: Alta series).

1108   _____. A poor married man; a farce comedy in three acts, by
        Walter Ben Hare... Chicago, T. S. Denison and co [1915].
        55p. incl. front. (port.) illus. (diagr.). (On cover:
        Alta series).

1109   _____. A rustic Romeo, a musical comedy in two acts, by
        Walter Ben Hare... Chicago, T. S. Denison and co. [1912].
        87p. illus. (diagrs.). (On cover: Denison's specialties).

1110   _____. A southern Cinderella, a comedy-drama in three acts;
        by Walter Ben Hare... Chicago, T. S. Denison and co.
        [1913]. 51p. illus. (diagr.). (On cover: Alta series).

1111   _____. Teddy; or, The runaways, a comedy in three acts; by
        Walter Ben Hare... Boston, W. H. Baker and co., 1913.
        64p. On cover: Baker's edition of plays.

HARKINS, JAMES W.

1112   HARKINS, JAMES W. d. 1910. ... Sydney Carton; a tale of two
        cities... Dramatized by James W. Harkins, Jr. [Holyoke,
        Mass., M. J. Doyle printing co., 1900]. Cover-title, 86,
        [7]p. diagrs. (Shea dramatic series).

1113   ... Harlequin Blue Beard, the Great Pashaw; or, The good fairy
        triumphant over the demon of discord! A grand comic Christ-
        mas pantomine. As performed at Laura Keen's Theatre,
        Thursday, December 24, 1857. New York, Samuel French
        [n.d.]. 16p.

1114   HARRADEN, BEATRICE. Lady Geraldine's speech, a comedietta.
        London, The Women writers' suffrage league, 1911. 31p.
        front.

1115   HARRINGTON, RICHARD. The pedlar boy; or, The old mill ruin.
        A drama, in one act... London, Thomas Hailes Lacy [n.d.].
        20p.

1116   HARRIS, AUGUSTUS GLOSSIP, 1825-1873. ... The little treasure.
        A comedy, in two acts... New York, Samuel French [n.d.].
        29p. (French's American drama, no. cxxv).

1117   _____. ... My son Diana. A farce in one act... Written by
        A. Harris... Boston, W. V. Spencer [1857?]. 17p.
        (Spencer's Boston theatre. [v. 17], no. 133).

1118   HARRIS, EDWARD M. The fatal blow, a melodrama in four acts.
        Philadelphia, The Penn publishing co., 1910. 41p.

1119   HARRIS, FRANK, 1856-1931. Shakespeare and his love, a play
        in four acts and an epilogue. London, Frank Palmer [1910].
        177p.

1120   HARRIS, KATHRYN R. Lovers of all ages. A drama... Lebanon,
        Ohio, March bros., 1906. 12p.

1121   HARRISON, GABRIEL, 1818-1902. A centennial dramatic offering.
        A romantic drama, in four acts, entitled, The scarlet
        letter, dramatized from Nathaniel Hawthorne's masterly
        romance. By Gabriel Harrison... Brooklyn, N. Y., Printed
        by H. M. Gardner, Jr., 1876. 2 p.l., 3-50p. front. (port.)
        pl.

1122   HARRISON, WILMOT. Special performances. A farce, in one act.
        Chicago and New York, The Dramatic publishing co. [n.d.].
        16p.

1123   HARTE, BRET, 1839-1902. Two men of Sandy Bar. American
        comedy drama in three acts, by Bret Harte. Written for
        Stuart Robson... New York, 1876. 1 p.ℓ., 55, 79-107
        numb. l.

1124   HARTNEDY, M. M. A. The World's fair drama. Christopher
        Columbus. A drama in three acts, with tableau, directions
        to amateurs on points of experience, scenery, costumes,
        etc. Written for the quadri-centennial celebration of the
        discovery of America. By V. Rev. M. M. A. Hartnedy, dean.
        Pub. and sold by the Columbus club... Steubenville,
        Ohio... New York, P. J. Kenedy; Chicago, W. H. Sadleir
        [1892]. 3 p.ℓ., [5]-51 (i.e. 49)p. illus.

1125   HARVEY, FRANK. Bought. An original play, in three acts...
        New York, Samuel French and son [n.d.]. 48p.

1126   HASTINGS, BASIL MACDONALD. The new sin: a play in three
        acts. London, Sidgwick, 1916. 86p.

1127   HAUPTMANN, GERHART JOHANN ROBERT, 1862-1946. Before dawn
        (Vor Sonnenaufgang), a social drama, by Gerhart Hauptmann.
        Tr. by Leonard Bloomfield. (In Poet lore. Boston, 1909.
        vol. XX, no. 4, p. 241-315).

1128   _____. Elga, by Gerhart Hauptmann, tr. from the German by
        Mary Harned. (In Poet lore. Boston, 1906. vol. XVII,
        no. X, p. 1-35).

1129   _____. Michael Kramer. 1914. (In Kuno Francke, ed., The
        German classics of the nineteenth and twentieth century
        [New York, The German publication society, v. 18, 1914],
        p. 211-280). Translated by Ludwig Lewisohn.

1130   _____. The reconciliation (a play in three acts) by Gerhart
        Hauptmann. Tr. from the German by Roy Temple House.
        (In Poet lore. Boston, 1910. vol. XXI, no. v. p. 337-
        390).

1131   _____. The sunken bell. 1914. (In Kuno Francke, ed., The
        German classics of the nineteenth and twentieth century
        [New York, The German publication society, 1914], v. 18,
        p. 105-210). Translated by Charles Henry Meltzer.

HAUPTMANN, GERHART JOHANN ROBERT

1132   HAUPTMANN, GERHART JOHANN ROBERT. The sunken bell; a fairy
        play in five acts, by Gerhart Hauptmann, freely rendered
        into English verse by Charles Henry Meltzer. New York,
        Doubleday and McClure co., 1899. 12 p.ℓ., 125p. incl.
        facsim., front (port.).

1133   _____. The weavers. 1914. (In Kuno Francke, ed., The
        German classics of the nineteenth and twentieth century
        [New York, The German publication society, 1914], v. 18,
        p. 16-104). Translated by Mary Morrison.

1134   HAWKINS, ANTHONY HOPE, 1863-1933. Pilkerton's Peerage, a
        comedy in four acts. New York, Samuel French; London,
        Samuel French, ltd., 1908. 112p.

1135   HAWKINS, MICAH, 1777-1825. The saw-mill; or, A Yankee trick.
        A comic opera, in two acts. As performed at the theatre,
        Chatham Garden, with distinguished success. Written and
        composed by Micah Hawkins. New York, Printed by J. and J.
        Harper, 1824. 53p.

1136   HAY, FREDERICK. Caught by the cuff. A farce, in one act...
        as first performed at the Victoria Theatre, London...
        September 30, 1865... New York, Robert De Witt [n.d.].
        14p.

1137   _____. Cupboard love. A farce, in one act... as first per-
        formed at the Vaudeville Theatre, London... April 18,
        1870... New York, Robert M. De Witt [n.d.]. 9p.

1138   _____. A lame excuse. A farce, in one act... as first per-
        formed at the Prince of Wales' Theatre... April 19, 1869
        ... New York, Robert M. De Witt [n.d.]. 14p.

1139   _____. Lodgers and dodgers. A farce, in one act. Chicago,
        The Dramatic publishing co. [n.d.]. 12p.

1140   _____. Our domestics. A comedy-farce, in two acts... as
        first performed at the Royal Standard Theatre, London...
        June 15, 1867... New York, Robert M. De Witt [n.d.].
        26p.

1141   _____. A photographic fix. An original farce, in one act...
        New York, Robert M. De Witt [n.d.]. 14p.

1142   HAZELTON, GEORGE COCHRANE, 1868-1921. Mistress Nell. A
        merry play in four acts. By George C. Hazelton... Phila-
        delphia, 1900. Cover-title, 76p.

1143   _____. The raven; a play in four acts and a tableau, by George C. Hazelton, Jr. ... New York, 1903. 1 p.ℓ., 77p.

1144   _____. The yellow jacket; a Chinese play done in a Chinese manner, in three acts, by George C. Hazelton and Benrimo; illustrated with photographs by Arnold Genthe... Indianapolis, The Bobbs-Merrill co. [1913]. 8 p.ℓ., 190p. col. front., plates.

1145   HAZLEWOOD, COLIN H. Jessy Vere; or, The return of the wanderer. An original domestic drama, in two acts... New York, Samuel French [n.d.]. 34p.

1146   _____. Lady Audley's secret; a drama in two acts, from Miss Braddon's popular novel, by C. H. Hazlewood. New American ed., correctly reprinted from the original authorized acting ed. ... New York, H. Roorbach, c1889. 33p. diagrs. (On cover: Roorbach's American edition of acting plays, no. 9).

1147   _____. Leave it to me. A farce in one act, by Colin H. Hazlewood and Arthur Williams. New York, Samuel French [n.d.]. 20p.

1148   _____. Poul a dhoil; or, The fairy man. An original Hibernian drama, in three acts... London, Thomas Hailes Lacy [n.d.]. 46p.

1149   _____. The staff of diamonds; a nautical drama, in two acts ... New York, Samuel French and son [n.d.]. 37p.

1150   HEATH, GEORGE W. The drummer boy of Shenandoah. A military drama in six acts, by George W. Heath. Dover, N. H., H. H. Goodwin, printer, 1871. 37p.

1151   HEATH, JAMES EWELL. Whigs and democrats; or, Love of no politics. A comedy in three acts... Richmond, T. W. White, 1889. vi, 7-80p.

1152   HEBBEL, FRIEDRICH. Maria Magdalena. 1914. (In Kuno Francke, ed., The German classics of the nineteenth and twentieth century [New York, The German publishing society, 1914], v. 9, p. 22-80). Translated by Paul Bernard Thomas.

1153   _____. Siegfried's death. 1914. (In Kuno Francke, ed., The German classics of the nineteenth and twentieth century [New York, The German publication society, 1914], v. 9, p. 81-165). Translated by Katharine Royce.

HEERMANS, FORBES

1154   HEERMANS, FORBES, 1856-1928. Between two thorns. An original
        scene on a stair-case. By Forbes Heermans... New York,
        The De Witt publishing house [1892]. 15p. illus. On
        cover: De Witt's acting plays. (no. 378).

1155   _____. Love by induction. An original comedy, in one act.
        By Forbes Heermans... New York, The De Witt publishing
        house [1892]. 31p. illus. On cover: De Witt's acting
        plays. (no. 377).

1156   _____. Love by induction, and other plays for private acting.
        By Forbes Heermans... New York, The De Witt publishing
        house [1889]. 4 p.ℓ., [3]-122p. illus. CONTENTS. - Love
        by induction. - Between two thorns. - Two negatives make
        an affirmative. - In the fire-light. - Love's warrant.

1157   _____. Love's warrant. A farce, in one act. By Forbes
        Heermans... New York, The De Witt publishing house [1892].
        32p. illus. On cover: De Witt's acting plays. (no. 361).

1158   _____. Two negatives make an affirmative. A photographic
        comedy, in one act. By Forbes Heermans... New York, The
        De Witt publishing house [1892]. 28p. illus. On cover:
        De Witt's acting plays. No. 379.

1159   HEFFERNAN, FRANK S. When Buckingham met the queen. A play
        in 6 acts and 8 scenes. By F. S. Heffernan. [Springfield?
        Mo., 1901]. Cover-title, 88p.

1160   HEMPSTEAD, JUNIUS LACKLAND, 1842-   . The conspirator. A
        tragedy, in five acts. By Junius L. Hempstead. Memphis,
        Tenn. [1880]. 68p.

1161   _____. The mill of the gods; a tragedy in four acts... By
        J. L. Hempstead... Memphis, Rogers and co., printers,
        1882. Cover-title, 58p.

1162   HENDRICK, WELLAND. Pocahontas, a burlesque operetta in two
        acts... Chicago, T. S. Denison, 1886. 19p.

1163   HENLEY, ANNE. Cinderella; illustrated play in four scenes
        for children, 3 m, 6 f, and supes, by Anne Henley and
        Stanley Scheil. Enl. ed. New York, E. S. Werner and co.,
        1913. 21p. illus.

1164   HENRY, R. A narrow escape, comedietta in one act. Chicago,
        T. S. Denison [n.d.]. 10p.

1165 HERFORD, BEATRICE. Monologues... with pictures by Oliver
      Herford. New York, Charles Scribner and sons, 1908.
      139p. illus.

1166 HERFORD, OLIVER, 1863-1935. McAdam and Eve; or, Two in a gar-
      den; a musical fantasy in three acts, by Oliver Herford.
      New York, C. Scribner's sons, 1900. 109p.

1167 HERVIEU, PAUL ERNEST, 1857-1915. In chains (Les tenailles)
      (a play in three acts) by Paul Hervieu... Translated by
      Ysidor Asckenasy... (In Poet lore. Boston, 1909. vol.
      xx, no. 11, p. 81-112).

1168 _____. Trail of the torch; a play in four acts; tr. by John
      A. Haughton; with an introduction by Brander Matthews.
      Garden City, Doubleday, 1917. 128p.

1169 HEWLETT, MAURICE HENRY, 1861-1923. The birth of Roland, by
      Maurice Hewlett. Chicago, Ralph Fletcher Seymour co.
      [1911]. 3 p.ℓ., [9]-54p.

1170 _____. New Canterbury tales, by Maurice Hewlett... New
      York, The Macmillan co.; London, Macmillan and co., ltd.,
      1901. 6 p.ℓ., 3-262p.

1171 _____. The queen's quair; or, The six years' tragedy, by
      Maurice Hewlett... New York, The Macmillan co.; London,
      Macmillan and co., ltd., 1904. 2 p.ℓ., vii-viii, 509p.

1172 _____. The stooping lady, by Maurice Hewlett... New York,
      Dodd, Mead and co., 1907. viii, 366p. col. front.

1173 HEYSE, PAUL JOHANN LUDWIG VON, 1830-1914. Mary of Magdala;
      an historical and romantic drama in five acts, the original
      in German prose by Paul Heyse, the translation freely
      adapted and written in English verse by William Winter...
      New York, The Macmillan co.; London, Macmillan and co.,
      ltd., 1903. 135p.

1174 HIGGIE, THOMAS. ... A devilish good joke! or, A night's
      frolic! An interlude in one act... London, Duncombe and
      Noon [n.d.]. 19p. (Duncombe's edition).

1175 _____. Laid up in port! or, Sharks along shore! A nautical
      drama, in three acts... London, Thomas Hailes Lacy [n.d.].
      54p.

HIGGIE, THOMAS

1176   HIGGIE, THOMAS. The Tower of London; or, The death omen and
        the fate of Lady Jane Grey. A drama in three acts. By
        T. H. Higgie and T. H. Lacy. London, T. H. Lacy [1850].
        48p. Lacy's acting edition.
            "Founded on the popular work of the same name... by
        W. Harrison Ainsworth." - p. 2.

1177   HIGGINS, DAVID KNOWLES, 1858-   . At Piney Ridge; a play of
        Tennessee life, in four acts, by David K. Higgins...
        [Chicago] 1906. 3 p.ℓ., 4-71 numb. 1.

1178   _____. Darius Green an' his flyin' machine; a comedy-drama,
        in four acts, written by David K. Higgins and Mrs. David
        K. Higgins. [Chicago, 1899]. Cover-title, 61p.

1179   HILAND, F. E. Broken bonds, a drama in four acts. Boston,
        Walter H. Baker and co., 1897. 37p.

1180   _____. Captain Swell, a negro farce in two scenes. Boston,
        Walter H. Baker and co., 1896. 8p.

1181   HILL, DAVID. The granger; or, Caught in his own trap, a
        comedy in three acts. Boston, Walter H. Baker and co.
        [1890]. 63p.

1182   _____. Joining the timpanites; or, Paddy Mcflings' experience,
        a mock initiation for the amusement and instruction of
        secret societies... (in three parts)... part II. Boston,
        Walter H. Baker and co. [1892]. 20p.

1183   HILL, F. S. ... Shoemaker of Toulouse; or, The avenger of
        humble life. A drama, in four acts... Boston, William V.
        Spencer [n.d.]. 48p. (Spencer's Boston theatre, no. xxxix).

1184   _____. The six degrees of crime; or, Wine, women, gambling,
        theft, murder and the scaffold. A melo-drama, in six parts
        ... New York, Samuel French [n.d.]. 50p.

1185   HILL, FREDERICK TREVOR, 1866-1930. High school farces: three
        one act playlets for junior amateurs, by Frederick Trevor
        Hill. New York, Frederick A. Stokes co. [1920]. vi,
        106p.

1186   HILL, ROLAND. Christopher Columbus; an historic drama in four
        acts, by Roland Hill... London, S. Low, Marston and co.,
        ltd., 1913. 2 p.ℓ., [3]-55p. 2 pl. (incl. front.).

HOFMANNSTHAL, HUGO HOFMANN, EDLER VON

1187   ____. In Andalusia long ago; a poetic drama in four acts, by Roland Hill... London, S. Low, Marston and co., ltd. 1914. 47, [1]p. front., plates.

1188   HILLHOUSE, JAMES ABRAHAM, 1789-1841. Scena quarta del quinto atto di Adad, poema drammatico, del signor Giacomo A. Hillhouse. Tradotta in verso italiano da L. Da Ponte... New York, Stampatori Gray e Bunce, 1825. 17p.

1188A HOARE, PRINCE, 1755-1834. Lock and key; a musical farce, in two acts, by Prince Hoare, esq. Printed from the acting copy, with remarks, biographical and critical, by D.-G. ... As now performed at the Theatres Royal... London, J. Cumberland [n.d.]. 38p. incl. front. (Cumberland's British theatre. London, ca. 1825-55. v. 24 [no. 2]). Remarks by George Daniel, editor of the series.

1189   ____. The spoil'd child; a farce, in two acts... Baltimore, J. Robinson, 1828. 27p.

1190   HOBART, GEORGE VERE, 1867-1926. Experience; a morality play of today, by George V. Hobart. Acting version. New York, The H. K. Fly co. [c1915]. 128p. front. (15 port.) plates.

1191   HOBART, MARIE ELIZABETH JEFFERYS. The little pilgrims and the book beloved, a mystery play... New York, Longmans, Green and co., 1906. 53p. illus.

1192   HODGKINSON, JOHN, 1766-1805. The man of fortitude; or, The knight's adventure. A drama. In three acts. Written by the late John Hodgkinson. From the prompt-book. New York, Published by David Longworth, at the Dramatic Repository, Shakespeare-Gallery, 1807. 68p.
    With this is bound: Robin Hood; or, Sherwood forest: a comic opera, in two acts, by Leonard MacNally, New York, 1808. 32p.

1193   HOFMANNSTHAL, HUGO HOFMANN, EDLER VON, 1874-1929. Cristina's journey home, a comedy in three acts, by Hugo von Hofmannsthal. Tr. from the German by Roy Temple House. (In Poet lore. Boston, 1917. vol. xxviii, no. 2, p. 129-186).

1194   ____. Electra, a tragedy in one act, by Hugo von Hofmannsthal; tr. by Arthur Symons. New York, Brentano's, 1908. 83 [1]p.

HOFMANNSTHAL, HUGO HOFMANN, EDLER VON

1195   HOFMANNSTHAL, HUGO HOFMANN, EDLER VON. The Marriage of
        Sobeide. 1914. (In Kuno Francke, ed., The German classics
        of the nineteenth and twentieth century [New York, The
        German publication society, 1914], v. 20, p. 234-288).
        Translated by Bayard Quincy Morgan.

1196   HOGE, PEYTON HARRISON. The divine tragedy, a drama of the
        Christ. New York [etc., etc.], Fleming H. Revel co., 1905.
        146p.

1197   HOLCOMB, WILLARD. A one act play called Her last rehearsal;
        or, Disenchanting an amateur, as written by Willard Hol-
        comb... Washington, D. C., W. A. Page [1897]. 27,[2]p.

1198   HOLCROFT, THOMAS, 1745-1809. Deaf and dumb; or, The orphan
        protected: an historical drama, in five acts, by Thomas
        Holcroft. Printed from the acting copy, with remarks,
        biographical and critical, by D.-G. ... As now performed
        at the Theatres Royal... London, J. Cumberland [n.d.].
        60p. incl. front. (Cumberland's British theatre. London,
        ca. 1825-55. v. 15 [no. 2].
            An adaptation of "L'abbé de l'épée", by Bouilly.
            Remarks by George Daniel, editor of the series.

1199   _____. Hear both sides: a comedy, in five acts. As it is
        performed at the Theatre-Royal, Drury-Lane. By Thomas
        Holcroft. London, R. Phillips, 1803. 4 p.ℓ., [5]-90,
        [2]p. [Broadhurst, J. Plays. v. 4, no. 7].

1200   _____. A tale of mystery, a melo-drama; as performed at the
        Theatre-Royal Covent Garden. By Thomas Holcroft. 2d ed.,
        with etchings after designs by Tresham. London, R.
        Phillips, 1802. 4 p.ℓ., 51p. 3pl.
            Professedly borrowed from the French. Cf. Advertise-
        ment.
            First edition, London, 1802.
            Without the music (by Thomas Busby).

1201   HOLL, HENRY. Grace Huntley: a domestic drama, in three acts...
        London, The Music-Publishing co., ltd. [n.d.]. 44p. front.

1202   HOLLENBECK, B. W. Zion, a drama, in a prologue and four acts.
        Clyde, Ohio, A. D. Ames, 1886. 38p.

1203   HOLLENIUS, L. J. Dollars and cents, an original American
        comedy, in three acts... New York, Nelson Row, 1869. 47p.

HOOGESTEGER, MARIUS D.

1204 _____. ... Maria and Magdalena. A play in four acts.
Adapted for the American stage from the German original
of Paul Lindau... New York, Robert M. De Witt, 1874. 44p.

1205 HOLLEY, HORACE, 1887- . Read-aloud plays, by Horace
Holley. New York, M. Kennerley, 1916. vi, 133p. CONTENTS.
- Her happiness. - A modern prodigal. - The compatibles. -
The genius. - Survival. - The telegram. - Rain. - Pictures.
His luck.

1206 HOLLINGSHEAD, JOHN. The birth place of podgers. A farce, in
one act. New York, Robert M. De Witt [n.d.]. 13p.

1207 HOLMAN, JOSEPH GEORGE, 1764-1817. Abroad and at home; a comic
opera, in three acts. By J. G. Holman. (In The London
stage. London [1824-27]. v. 4 [no. 13], 16p. 1 illus.).
Caption title.
Without the music (by Shield); originally called The
King's bench.

1207A _____. Abroad and at home. A comic opera, in three acts.
Now performing at the Theatre-Royal, Covent-Garden. By
J. G. Holman, 5th ed. London, G. Cawthorn, 1796. 92p.
[Broadhurst, J. Plays. v. 8, no. 2].

1208 _____. The gazette extraordinary: a comedy, in five acts.
By J. G. Holman... (from the first London ed., of 1811).
New York, Published by the Longworths, at the Dramatic
Repository, Shakespeare-Gallery. Nov. - 1811. 76p.

1209 HOLT, FLORENCE TABER. They the crucified and Comrades; two
war plays. Boston and New York, Houghton Mifflin co.,
1918. 84p.

1210 HOLT, HARRISON JEWELL. Absent treatment, a comedy in three
acts. Portland, Maine, 1912. Various pagings.

1211 HONAN, M. B. "The queen's horse," a burletta, in one act, by
M. B. Honan and J. R. Planché... London, Chapman and
Hall [n.d.]. 22p.

1212 HOOGESTEGER, MARIUS D. The convict's daughter. A drama in
three acts, by Marius D. Hoogesteger... [Grand Rapids?
Mich.], 1900. 36p.

HOOK, THEODORE EDWARD

1213   HOOK, THEODORE EDWARD, 1788-1841. Cousin William; or, The
        fatal attachment. By Theodore Hook. London, New York,
        G. Routledge and sons [187-]. 294p. On cover: Hook's
        Sayings and doings.

1214   _____. The fortress; a melo-drama, in three acts, from the
        French... Written by Theodore Edward Hook... The music
        by Mr. Hook, sen. ... London, S. Tipper, 1807. v, [1],
        [7]-68p.
            Without music.

1215   _____. Music mad; a dramatic sketch. By Theodore Edward
        Hook, esq. (From the 1st London ed., of 1808). New York,
        Published by the Longworths, at the Dramatic repository,
        Shakespeare-gallery. May - 1812. 23, [1]p. [Dramatic
        pamphlets. v. 37, no. 3].
            Without the music (by J. Hook).

1216   _____. Safe and sound: an opera, in three acts. By
        Theodore Edward Hook, esq. ... As performed at the
        Lyceum theatre, London. (From the 1st London ed. of 1809).
        New York, Published by D. Longworth, at the Dramatic re-
        pository, Shakespeare-gallery. March - 1810. 44p.
        [Dramatic pamphlets. v. 37, no. 7].
            Without the music (by James Hook).

1217   HOPE, ANTHONY, 1863-1933. The adventure of Lady Ursula, a
        comedy in four acts. London, Samuel French, ltd. [n.d.]
        137p.
            Full name: Anthony Hope Hawkins.

1218   HOUGHTON, STANLEY, 1881-1913. Five one act plays, by Stanley
        Houghton. London, Sidgwick and Jackson, ltd. [etc.].
        New York, S. French, c1913. 111p. CONTENTS. - The dear
        departed. - Fancy free. - The master of the house. -
        Phipps. - The fifth commandment.

1219   _____. Hindle wakes; a play in three acts, by Stanley
        Houghton. Boston, John W. Luce and co.; London, Sidgwick
        and Jackson, ltd., 1913. 109, [1]p.

1220   HOUSMAN, LAURENCE, 1865-1959. Angels and ministers and other
        Victorian plays. London, Jonathan Cape [n.d.]. 95p.

1221   _____. Bethlehem; a nativity play by Laurence Housman, performed with music by Joseph Moorat under the stage-direction of Edward Gordon Craig, December, MCMII. New York, The Macmillan co.; London, Macmillan and co., ltd., 1902. 2 p.ℓ., 76p.

1222   _____. Pains and penalties; an historical tragedy, in four acts by Laurence Housman. London, Sidgwick and Jackson, ltd. [1911]. 3 p.ℓ., 5-89.

1223   [_____]. Prunella; a dramatic composition. New York, Brentano's, 1906. 1 p.ℓ., 89p.

1224   HOVEY, RICHARD, 1864-1900. The birth of Galahad. New York, Duffield and co., 1907. 124p.

1225   [_____]. Launcelot and Guenevere; a poem in dramas. [Boston, Small, Maynard and co., 1898-1907]. 5 v. (Library has only: v. 1-2, 5.). Half-title. Vol. 5 has imprint: New York, Duffield and co. CONTENTS. - The quest of Merlin. - II. The marriage of Guenevere. - III. The birth of Galahad. - IV. Taliesin, a masque. - V. The Holy Graal and other fragments... being the uncompleted parts of the Arthurian dramas; ed. with introduction and notes by Mrs. Richard Hovey and a preface by Bliss Carman.

1226   _____. Taliesin, a masque. New York, Duffield and co., 1907. 58p.

1227   HOWARD, BRONSON, 1842-1908. The amateur benefit. An entertainment in three acts, by Bronson Howard. [New York, 1881]. 3 pt.

1228   _____. ... The autobiography of a play, by Bronson Howard, with an introduction by Augustus Thomas. New York, Printed for the Dramatic museum of Columbia university, 1914. 3 p.ℓ., 53 [1]p. On verson of half-title: Publications of the Dramatic museum of Columbia university in the city of New York. 1st series. Papers on playmaking. II.

1229   _____. The banker's daughter; or, Lilian's last love. A drama in five acts and six tableaux. [New York], 1878. 2 p.ℓ., 24 (i.e. 25), 20, 15, 20, 15, 20, 24 numb. l.

1230   _____. The Henrietta; a comedy in four acts. By Bronson Howard... New York, S. French; [etc., etc.] 1901. 82p.

HOWARD, BRONSON

1231   HOWARD, BRONSON. Kate; a comedy in four acts, by Bronson
        Howard... New York and London, Harper and bros., 1906.
        x, 210 [1]p.

1232   _____. Old love letters, a comedy in one act, by Bronson
        Howard. [New York], 1897. 22p.

1233   _____. One of our girls, a comedy in four acts, by Bronson
        Howard. [New York], 1897. 56p.

1234   _____. Saratoga; or, "Pistols for seven". A comic drama in
        five acts. By Bronson Howard... New York, London, S.
        French, 1898. 68p. On cover: French's standard drama.
        The acting edition. no. CCCLXIX.

1235   _____. Saratoga; or, "Pistols for seven". A comic drama in
        five acts. By Bronson Howard... London, S. French; New
        York, S. French and son [1871?]. 68p. On cover: French's
        acting edition.

1236   _____. Shenandoah, a military comedy in four acts, by Bronson
        Howard. [New York, 1897]. 59p.

1237   _____. Young Mrs. Winthrop; a play in four acts, by Bronson
        Howard... New York, S. French; [etc., etc.], 1899. 56p.
        On cover: French's international copyrighted... edition
        of the works of the best authors. (no. 23).

1238   _____. Young Mrs. Winthrop. A play in four acts. By
        Bronson Howard... New York, Madison Square theatre, 1882.
        47p. 1 illus. (music).

1239   HOWARD, JOSEPH E., 1880-   . His Highness the Bey. A
        musical satire in two acts. Book and lyrics by Will M.
        Hough and Frank R. Adams, music by Joseph E. Howard...
        [Chicago, 1905]. 1 p.ℓ., 55 (i.e. 56) numb. l.

1240   _____. The isle of Bong-Bong. A musical comedy in two acts.
        Book and lyrics by Will M. Hough and Frank R. Adams, music
        by Joseph E. Howard. [Chicago?] 1905. 79ℓ.

1241   _____. The land of Nod. A musical extravaganze in a pro-
        logue and two acts. Book and lyrics by Will M. Hough and
        Frank R. Adams. Music by Joseph E. Howard. Chicago,
        1905. 45ℓ.

HOWELLS, WILLIAM DEAN

1242   _____. The time, the place and the girl, a three act comedy with music, by Will M. Hough and Frank R. Adams, music by Joseph E. Howard. [Chicago?] 1906. 87ℓ.

1243   HOWE, J. B. ... The golden eagle; or, The privateer of '76. A national drama, in three acts, and a prologue... New York, Samuel French [n.d.]. 37p. (French's standard drama, no. clxxi).

1244   HOWE, JULIA WARD, 1819-1910. The world's own. Boston, Ticknor and Fields, 1857. 141p.

1245   HOWELLS, WILLIAM DEAN, 1837-1920. The Albany depot, by W. D. Howells. New York, Harper and bros., 1892 (i.e. 1891). 68p. incl. 7 pl. (On cover: Harper's black and white series).

1246   _____. Bride roses, a scene. Boston and New York, Houghton, Mifflin and co., 1900. 48p.

1247   _____. A counterfeit presentment. Comedy, by W. D. Howells, Boston, J. R. Osgood and co., 1877. 155p.

1248   _____. Different girls... ed. by William Dean Howells and Henry Mills Alden. New York and London, Harper and bros., 1906. vii, 271p. (Harper's novelettes).

1249   _____. The elevator; farce by W. D. Howells. Boston, J. R. Osgood and co., 1885. 84p.

1250   _____. Evening dress; farce by W. D. Howells... New York, Harper and bros., 1893. 2 p.ℓ., 59p. front., pl.

1251   _____. Five o'clock tea; farce by W. D. Howells... New York, Harper and bros., 1894. 46p. front., pl. On cover: Harper's black and white series.

1252   _____. Five o'clock tea, farce. New York and London, Harper and bros. [1885]. 46p. illus.

1253   _____. An Indian giver; a comedy by W. D. Howells. Boston and New York, Houghton, Mifflin and co., 1900. 99p.

1254   _____. Indian summer, by William D. Howells... Boston, Ticknor and co., 1886. 1 p.ℓ., 395p.

HOWELLS, WILLIAM DEAN

1255   HOWELLS, WILLIAM DEAN. A letter of introduction; farce by
       W. D. Howells... New York and London, Harper and bros.,
       1899. 61p. incl. front., 3 pl.

1256   _____. A letter of introduction; farce by W. D. Howells...
       New York, Harper and bros., 1892. 61p. incl. front.,
       3 pl. On cover: Harper's black and white series.

1257   _____. A likely story; farce by W. D. Howells... New York,
       Harper and bros., 1894. 54p. front., pl. On cover:
       Harper's black and white series.

1258   _____. A likely story, farce. New York and London, Harper
       and bros. [1885]. 54p. illus.

1259   _____. The mother and the father, dramatic passages. New
       York and London, Harper and bros., 1909. 55p.

1260   _____. The mouse-trap, and other farces... New York,
       Harper and bros., 1889. 3 p.ℓ., 184p. incl. plates.
       front. CONTENTS. - The garroters. - Five o'clock tea. -
       The mouse-trap. - A likely story.

1261   _____. Out of the question. A comedy... Boston, J. R.
       Osgood and co., 1877. 3 p.ℓ., 5-183p.
          Title in red and black within red line border.
          Appeared originally in Atlantic monthly, Feb.-Apr. 1877.

1262   _____. A pair of patient lovers, by W. D. Howells... New
       York and London, Harper and bros., 1901. 2 p.ℓ., 368p.
       front., (port.).

1263   _____. The parlor car, farce. Boston, James R. Osgood and
       co., 1876. 74p.

1264   _____. A previous engagement; comedy, by W. D. Howells...
       New York, Harper and bros., 1897. 3 p.ℓ., 65, [3]p.
       front., illus., plates.

1265   _____. Room forty-five; a farce, by W. D. Howells. Boston
       and New York, Houghton, Mifflin and co., 1900. 61, [1]p.

1266   _____. A sea-change; or, Love's stowaway, a lyricated farce
       in two acts and an epilogue, by W. D. Howells... Boston,
       Tickner and co., 1888. 151p.

1267 _____. The sleeping-car, and other farces by William D. Howells. Boston and New York, Houghton, Mifflin and co., 1895. 4 p.ℓ., 11-212p. CONTENTS. - The parlor-car. - The sleeping car. - The register. - The elevator.

1268 _____. The smoking car; a farce, by W. D. Howells. Boston, and New York, Houghton, Mifflin and co., 1900. 70p.

1269 _____. The unexpected guest; a farce by W. D. Howells... New York, Harper and bros., 1893. 2 p.ℓ., 54p. front., 5pl.

1270 HOWIE, HELEN MORRISON. His father's son, a farce comedy in one act. Philadelphia, The Penn publishing co., 1900. 20p.

1271 HUFF, L. KEMPER. My ward. Comedy in five acts... Waynesboro, Va., "Semi-weekly Messenger" Print, 1884. 52p.

1272 HUGHES, RUPERT, 1872-1956. Gyges' ring; a dramatic monologue. New York, R. H. Russell, 1901. 4 p.ℓ., 47, [1]p. col. front.

1273 _____. On the road to Yorktown, a dramatic sketch, by Rupert Hughes; written for the National conference of Jews and Christians... New York city, The National conference [193-?]. 11p.

1274 HUGO, VICTOR-MARIE, COMTE, 1802-1885. ... Dramas... by Victor Hugo. Boston, D. Estes and co. [1902?]. 4 v. fronts., plates. CONTENTS. - I. Hernani. The twin brothers. Angelo. Amy Robsart. - II. Mary Tudor. Ruy Blas. Torquemada. Esmeralda. - III. Cromwell. The Burgraves - IV. The fool's revenge (Le Roi s'amuse) as adapted by Tom Taylor. Marion de Lorme. Lucretia Borgia.

1275 _____. Ruy Blas. A romantic drama, in four acts. From the French of Victor Hugo. As first performed... Oct. 27, 1860... New York, Robert M. De Witt [n.d.]. 38p.

1276 HUMBOLDT, ARCHIBALD. A feast in the wilderness. A Christmas dialogue, adapted from a story in the Pacific ensign. Lebanon, Ohio, March bros. [n.d.]. 5p.

1277 _____. The saloon must go. Lebanon, Ohio, March bros., 1909. 16p.

HURD, ST. CLAIR

1278   HURD, ST. CLAIR. Counsel for the plaintiff, a comedy in two
        acts. Boston, Walter H. Baker and co. [1891]. 27p.

1279   HUTCHINSON, M. F. Princess Kiku, a Japanese romance. A play
        for girls, by M. F. Hutchinson... New York, Dick and
        Fitzgerald, 1903. 39p.

1280   _____. ... The terror of a day... London, Joseph Williams,
        ltd.; New York, Edward Schuberth, 1909. 16p.

1281   HUTTON, JOSEPH, 1787-1828. The school for prodigals: a
        comedy. In five acts, as performed at the New theatre,
        Philadelphia. By Joseph Hutton. Philadelphia, Printed
        by Thomas T. Stiles, no. 12 Walnut-street, 1809. 62p.

1282   _____. The wounded hussar; or, Rightful heir: a musical
        afterpiece. In two acts, as performed at the New theatre,
        Philadelphia. By Joseph Hutton... Philadelphia, Printed
        by Thomas T. Stiles, no. 12, Walnut-street, 1809. 24p.

1283   HYDE, ELIZABETH A. An engaged girl, a comedy. Chicago, T.
        S. Denison [1899]. 18p.

1284   [HYER, WILLIAM G.]. Rosa, a melo-drama, in three acts. New
        York, E. Murden, 1822. 2 p.ℓ., [9]-44p.

1285   IBSEN, HENRIK, 1828-1906. Brand: a dramatic poem in five
        acts, by Henrik Ibsen. Translated in the original metres,
        with an introduction and notes, by C. H. Herford...
        London, W. Heinemann, 1901. xcix, [1], 288p.

1286   _____. A doll's house, by Henrik Ibsen. New York and
        London, G. P. Putnam's sons [1911]. 3 p.ℓ., 3-193p.
        front. (port.). The Ariel booklets.

1287   _____. A doll's house; and two other plays... London and
        Toronto, J. M. Dent and sons; New York, E. P. Dutton
        [1910]. xv, 255p.
            "The translation of The Lady from the Sea is that of
        Mrs. Marx-Aveling; for those of A Doll's House and The
        Wild Duck I am responsible. R. Farquharson Sharp."
        p. xiii.

1288   _____. The doll's house (La maison de poupée), a drama in
        three acts, by Henrik Ibsen. English argument by Eliza-
        beth Beall Ginty... New York, F. Rullman [1895]. 21p.

BRITISH AND AMERICAN DRAMA

IBSEN, HENRIK

1289 _____. Early plays: Catiline, The warrior's barrow, Olaf Liljekrans, by Henrik Ibsen, tr. from the Norwegian by Anders Orbeck... New York, The American-Scandinavian foundation; [etc., etc.] 1921. 5 p.ℓ., [vii]-xiv, 238p. Half-title: Scandinavian classics, vol. XVII.

1290 _____. ... Four plays by Ibsen: An enemy of the people, A doll's house, The master builder, Peer Gynt, edited by Clarence Stratton... [Boston, New York, etc.] Ginn and co. [1931]. xxv, 566p. (Modern literature series).

1291 _____. Ghosts. A drama of family life in three acts, by Henrik Ibsen. Tr. from the Norwegian by Henrietta Frances Lord. New ed., rev.... Chicago, Ill., Lily publishing house; London, Griffith, Farran, Okeden and Welsh, 1890. xii, 108p.

1292 _____. Ibsen's prose dramas. [Authorized English ed. Edited by William Archer. New York, Scribner and Welford, 1890]. 5 v. front. (port.). CONTENTS. - [v. 1] Biographical introduction. The league of youth. Tr. by William Archer. The pillars of society. Tr. by William Archer. A doll's house. Tr. by William Archer. - [v. 2] Ghosts. Tr. by William Archer. An enemy of the people. Tr. by Mrs. F. Marx-Aveling. The wild duck. Tr. by Mrs. F. E. Archer - [v. 3] Lady Inger of Østråt. Tr. by Charles Archer. The vikings at Helgeland. Tr. by William Archer. The pretenders. Tr. by William Archer. - [v. 4] Emperor and Galilean... [tr. by William Archer] - [v. 5] Rosmersholm. Tr. by Charles Archer. The lady from the sea. Tr. by Mrs. F. E. Archer. Hedda Gabler. Tr. by William Archer.

1293 _____. The master builder; a play in three acts, by Henrik Ibsen... translated from the Norwegian by Edmund Gosse and William Archer. New York, Tait, sons and co. [1893]. 203p.

1294 _____. Nora. A play. By Henrik Ibsen. Tr. from the Norwegian by Henrietta Frances Lord. London, Griffith and Farran; New York, E. P. Dutton and co., 1882. xxiv, 120p.

1295 _____. Nordische Heerfahrt. Trauerspiel in vier Akten. Unter Mitwirkung von Emma Klingenfeld veranstaltete deutsche Originalausgabe der Haermaendene paa Helgeland... München, Theodor Ackermann, 1876. 128p.

IBSEN, HENRIK

1296   IBSEN, HENRIK. On the heights (Paa vidderne), a tragedy in
lyrical ballads by Henrik Ibsen; English version in the form
of the original by William Norman Guthrie. Sewanee, Tenn.,
Printed for the University of the South [1910]. 7 p.ℓ.,
8-27 numb. l.

1297   _____. The pretenders, by Henrik Ibsen; acting version of the
Yale university dramatic association, with an introduction
by William Lyon Phelps... New Haven [The Tuttle, Morehouse
and Taylor co.] 1907. xx, 8, 103p. front., ports.

1298   _____. When we dead awaken; a dramatic epilogue in three
acts, by Henrik Ibsen. Translated by William Archer.
Chicago and New York, H. S. Stone and co., 1900. 3 p.ℓ.,
157p., 1ℓ. On cover: The green tree library.

1299   [_____]. [The wild duck, The league of youth, Rosmersholm]
[n.p., n.d.]. 342p.

1300   ILLICA, LUIGI, 1857-1919. Iris, an opera in three acts;
Italian libretto by Luigi Illica; English version by W. G.
Day; music by P. Mascagni... New York, Boosey and co.
[1907?]. 39, [2]p.

1301   INCHBALD, ELIZABETH SIMPSON, 1753-1821. Such things are:
a play, in five acts; by Mrs. Inchbald. As performed at
the Theatre Royal, Covent-Garden... With remarks by the
author. London, Longman, Hurst, Rees, Orme, and Brown
[n.d.]. 77p. front. (Inchbald, Mrs. Elizabeth. The
British theatre... London, 1808. v. 23 [no.1]).

1302   _____. To marry, or not to marry; a comedy, in five acts; by
Mrs. Inchbald. As performed at the Theatre Royal, Covent
Garden... with remarks by the author. London, Longman,
Hurst, Rees, Orme, and Brown [n.d.]. 66p. front. (Inch-
bald, Mrs. Elizabeth. The British theatre... London,
1808. v. 23 [no. 5]).

1303   _____. Wives as they were, and maids as they are. A comedy,
in five acts; by Mrs. Inchbald. As performed at the
Theatre Royal, Covent Garden... With remarks by the
author. London, Longman, Hurst, Rees, Orme, and Brown
[n.d.]. 78p. front. (Inchbald, Mrs. Elizabeth. The
British theatre... London, 1808. v. 23 [no. 3]).

1304   INGERSOLL, CHARLES JARED, 1782-1862. Edwy and Elgiva; a
        tragedy, in five acts. Performed at the new theatre.
        Written by Charles Jared Ingersoll... Philadelphia,
        Published by Asbury Dickens, opposite Christ-church.
        H. Maxwell printer, 1801. x, [11]-84p.

1305   INGRAHAM, C. F. Jimmie Jones; or, Our hopeful son; a farce
        in one act. Clyde, Ohio, Ames' publishing co., 1892. 7p.

1306   IRISH, MARIE. Plays and comedies for little folks, by Marie
        Irish... Chicago, A. Flanagan co. [1912]. 172p.

1307   IRVING, WASHINGTON, 1783-1859. Abu Hassan, by Washington
        Irving (hitherto unpublished) with an introduction by
        George S. Hellman. Boston, Printed exclusively for members
        of the Bibliophile Society, 1924. 83p. facsims.

1308   _____. The wild huntsman, by Washington Irving (hitherto un-
        published) with an introduction by George S. Hellman.
        Boston, Printed exclusively for members of the Bibliophile
        Society, 1924. 113p. facsims.

1309   IRWIN, GRACE LUCE. A close call, a farce in one act. Boston,
        Walter H. Baker and co. [1901]. 24p.

1310   _____. Drawing room plays, by Grace Luce Irwin. San Fran-
        cisco, P. Eider and co., 1903. 3 p.ℓ., 165p. CONTENTS.
        - An innocent villain. - Art for art's sake. - An intimate
        acquaintance. - The wedding of Mah Foy. - Music hath charms.

1311   IVES, ALICE EMMA. The village postmaster, a domestic drama
        in four acts, by Alice E. Ives and Jerome H. Eddy...
        New York, S. French; London, S. French, ltd., 1894. 93p.

1312   JACKMAN, ISAAC, fl. 1795. Hero and Leander: a comic burletta,
        in two acts; by Isaac Jackman... London, Printed by D. S.
        Maurice [1819?]. v, [1], [7]-21p. front. [Cabinet
        theatre, v. 7, no. 4]. Title vignette.

1313   JAMESON, ROBERT FRANCIS. A touch at the times; a comedy, in
        five acts, as performed at the Theatre Royal, Covent-
        Garden. By Robert Francis Jameson, esq., of the Inner
        Temple... London, C. Chapple, 1812. vi, [2], 79, [1]p.

1314   JAMIESON, GUY A. Prof. James' experience teaching a country
        school, a comedy, in three acts. Clyde, Ohio, Ames' pub-
        lishing co., 1889. 15p.

JAST, LOUIS STANLEY

1315   JAST, LOUIS STANLEY, 1868-1944. The lover and the dead woman
and five other plays in verse, by L. Stanley Jast. London,
G. Routledge and sons, ltd.; New York, E. P. Dutton and
co., 1923. CONTENTS. - The lover and the dead woman. -
The geisha's wedding. - The loves of the elements. - The
call of the ninth wave. - Venus and the shepherdess. -
Harbour.

1316   JEFFERSON, JOSEPH, 1829-1905, illus. Rip Van Winkle, as
played by Joseph Jefferson. Now for the first time published. New York, Dodd, Mead and co., 1895. 199p. front.
illus., plates, ports.

1317   JENKINS, E. LAWRENCE. Blue Beard; or, The bride, the bogie
and the blood, a burlesque opera in two acts. Lebanon,
Ohio, March bros., 1902. 14p.

1318   _____. The new Aladdin and the same old lamp, a burlesque
opera in two acts and several scenes. New York, Hints
publishing co., 1902. 25p.

1319   _____. The sleeping princess; or, The beauty and the bicycle,
a burlesque opera in three acts. New York, Hints publishing co., 1902. 25p.

1320   _____. The wedding chorus, a comic opera. New York, The
Hints publishing and supply co., 1905. 21p.

1321   _____. The witch's mirror, a tableau entertainment. New
York, Hints publishing co., 1903. 4p.

1322   JENNINGS, GERTRUDE. Between the soup and the savoury, by
Gertrude Jennings... New York, French, c1911. 26p.

1323   JEPHSON, ROBERT, 1736-1803. The Count of Narbonne, a tragedy,
in five acts; by Robert Jephson, esq. As performed at the
Theatre Royal, Covent Garden... With remarks by Mrs. Inchbald. London, Longman, Hurst, Rees, Orme, and Brown
[n.d.]. 63p. front. (Inchbald, Mrs. Elizabeth. The
British theatre... London, 1808. v. 20 [no. 2]).
Founded on Walpole's romance "Castle of Otranto".

1324   _____. The hotel; or, The servant with two masters: a farce,
in two acts. By Robert Jephson, esq. As performed at the
New-theatre. [2nd ed.) New York, Published by D. Longworth, At the Dramatic Repository Shakespeare-Gallery.
April--1810. 36p.

JERROLD, DOUGLAS WILLIAM

1325   _____. Two strings to your bow: a farce, in one act, by
        Robert Jephson... Printed from the acting copy, with re-
        marks, biographical and critical, by D.-G. ... As per-
        formed at the Theatres Royal... London, J. Cumberland
        [n.d.]. 34p. incl. front. (Cumberland's British theatre.
        London, ca 1825-55. v. 30 [no. 6]).
            Remarks by George Daniel, editor of the series.
            An alteration of the author's "The hotel; or, Servant
        with two masters," which may be borrowed from Vaughan's
        "Hotel, or Double valet."

1326   JEROME, JEROME KLAPKA, 1861-1927. Barbara. Play in one act.
        London and New York, Samuel French [n.d.]. 24p.

1327   _____. Fanny and the servant problem, a quite possible play
        in four acts [by] Jerome K. Jerome... New York, S. French;
        London, S. French, ltd., c1909. 2 p.ℓ., [7]-89p. (On
        cover: French's standard library edition).

1328   _____. Woodbarrow farm; play in three acts, by Jerome K.
        Jerome... New York, London, S. French, 1904. 2 p.ℓ.,
        [7]-69. [French's library edition of plays, no. 7].

1329   JERROLD, DOUGLAS WILLIAM, 1803-1857. Ambrose Gwinett; or,
        A sea-side story: a melo-drama, in three acts... London,
        G. H. Davidson [n.d.]. 54p. front.

1330   _____. ... Black-eyed Susan; or, "All in the downs." A
        nautical and domestic drama, in two acts. By Douglas
        Jerrold... With editorial remarks, original casts, cos-
        tumes, scene and property plots, and all the stage
        business. Boston, W. V. Spencer, 1856. iv, [2], 7-36p.
        diagrs. (Spencer's Boston theatre... New series...
        no. vii).

1331   _____. The bride of Ludgate: a comic drama, in two acts, by
        Douglas Jerrold... Printed from the acting copy, with
        remarks, biographical and critical, by D.-G. ... As now
        performed at the Theatres Royal... London, J. Cumberland
        [n.d.]. 47p. front. (Cumberland's British theatre. Lon-
        don, ca. 1825-55. v. 30[no. 1]).
            Remarks by George Daniel, editor of the series.

1332   _____. Bubbles of the day. A comedy, in five acts. By
        Douglas Jerrold... London, How and Parsons, 1842.
        3 p.ℓ., 126p.

JERROLD, DOUGLAS WILLIAM

1333   JERROLD, DOUGLAS WILLIAM. Comedies. By Douglas Jerrold.
        London, Bradbury and Evans, 1853. 3 p.ℓ., 347 p. (Half-
        title: The writings of Douglas Jerrold. Collected edition.
        v. 7). CONTENTS. – Bubbles of the day. – Time works
        wonders. – The catspaw. – The prisoner of war. – Retired
        from business. – St. Cupid; or, Dorothy's fortune.

1334   _____. Comedies and dramas. By Douglas Jerrold. London,
        Bradbury and Evans, 1854. 4 p.ℓ., [3]–287, [1]p. (Half-
        title: The writings of Douglas Jerrold. Collected edition.
        v. 8). CONTENTS. – The rent day. – Nell Gwynne; or, The
        prologue. – The housekeeper. – The wedding gown. – The
        schoolfellows. – Doves in a cage. – The painter of Ghent.
        – Black-ey'd Susan; or, "All in the Downs."

1335   _____. Fifteen years of a drunkard's life, a melo-drama, in
        three acts. Chicago, The Dramatic publishing co. [n.d.].
        32p.

1336   _____. ... The tower of Lochlain; or, The idiot son! A melo-
        drama, in three acts... London, J. Duncombe and co. [n.d.].
        36p. front.

1337   _____. ... Wives by advertisement; or, Courting in the news-
        papers; a dramatic satire, in one act. The only edition
        correctly marked from the prompter's book; with the stage
        business, situations, and directions. As performed at the
        Royal Coburg theatre. London, J. Duncombe [18--]. 22p.
        front. (Duncombe's edition [of the British theatre. no.
        2]).

1338   JERROLD, W. BLANCHARD. ... Cool as a cucumber. A farce, in
        one act... Boston, William V. Spencer [n.d.]. 18p.
        (Spencer's theatre, no. cxlii).

1339   [JEWELL, JAMES WILLIAM]. Pastors versus poets (a reading for
        three) [Frankfort, Ky., n.d.]. 15p.

1340   John Bull; or, The comedy of 1854... London, T. H. Lacy
        [1854]. 49p.

1341   JOHNSON, CHARLES, 1679-1748. The cobbler of Preston. A
        musical farce, in two acts, by Charles Johnson. Printed
        from the acting copy, with remarks, biographical and
        critical, by D.-G. ... As performed at the Theatres
        Royal... London, J. Cumberland and son [n.d.]. 33p.
        incl. front. (Cumberland's British theatre. London,
        ca. 1825-55. v. 42 [no. 4]).

(JOHNSON, CHARLES)
Founded on the Induction to Shakespeare's Taming of the shrew.
Remarks by George Daniel, editor of the series.
According to the Theatrical inquisitor, v. 11, p. 299, adapted with additions, by George Lamb from Johnson's original farce, produced 1716.
Without the music.

1342 JOHNSON, EDWIN. The mouth of gold, a series of dramatic sketches illustrating the times of Chrysostom. New York and Chicago, A. S. Barnes and co., 1873. 109p.

1343 JOHNSON, SAMUEL D. The fireman. A drama, in three acts... New York, Samuel French [n.d.]. 36p.

1344 _____. ... In and out of place; a burletta, in one act. By S. D. Johnson... New York, S. French, c1856. 13p. front. (port.). (The minor drama. [v. 5; no. cvii).

1345 JOHNSTON, MARY, 1870-1936. The goddess of reason. Boston and New York, Houghton, Mifflin and co., 1907. 234p.

1346 JOHNSTONE, JOHN BEER, 1803-1891. Ben Bolt. An original drama. In two acts. By John B. Johnstone... London, T. H. Lacy [185-?]. 24p. (On cover: Lacy's acting edition [of plays. v. 16, no. 228]).
"First performed at the Royal Surrey theatre... March 28th, 1854."
Without the music.

1347 _____. The drunkard's children. A drama, in two acts... New York, Samuel French and son [n.d.]. 27p.

1348 _____. ... Gale Breezely; or, The tale of a tar. A drama in two acts... New York, Samuel French [n.d.]. 23p. (The minor drama, no. xci).

1349 _____. Jack Long; or, The shot in the eye, a drama, in two acts. Chicago, The Dramatic publishing co. [n.d.]. 28p.

1350 _____. ... The sailor of France; or, The republicans of Brest, an original drama, in two acts... New York, Samuel French [n.d.]. 22p. (French's standard drama, no. clvii).

1351 JONES, HENRY ARTHUR, 1851-1929. Carnac Sahib; an original play in four acts, by Henry Arthur Jones... New York, London, The Macmillan co., 1899. vii, 142p.

JONES, HENRY ARTHUR

1352   JONES, HENRY ARTHUR. The case of rebellious Susan; a comedy
        in three acts, by Henry Arthur Jones... New York, Mac-
        millan and co., 1894. x, 118p.

1353   _____. A clerical error; a comedy in one act, by Henry
        Arthur Jones... London, S. French, ltd.; New York, S.
        French, 1906. 2 p.ℓ., [3]-21p. (On cover: French's inter-
        national copyrighted... edition of the works of the best
        authors, no. 80).

1354   _____. The crusaders: an original comedy of modern London
        life; produced at the Avenue theatre, London, on the 2d
        November, 1891, New York, Macmillan, 1911. 115p.

1355   _____. The dancing girl, a drama in four acts. London,
        Samuel French, ltd. [n.d.]. 119p.

1356   _____. The divine gift; a play in three acts, by Henry
        Arthur Jones. New York, George H. Doran co., 1913. 178p.,
        1ℓ.

1357   _____. ... [Dolly reforming herself] A comedy in four acts,
        by Henry Arthur Jones... London, Printed at the Chiswick
        press, 1908. 4 p.ℓ., 97p.

1358   _____. Elopement; a comedy in two acts. By H. A. Jones...
        Ilfracombe, Printed by J. Tait [1879]. 45p.

1359   _____. Joseph entangled; a comedy in three acts, by Henry
        Arthur Jones... New York, S. French: [etc., etc.] 1906.
        2 p.ℓ., 7-141p. 2 diagr.

1360   _____. Judah; an original play in three acts, by Henry
        Arthur Jones... New York and London, Macmillan and co.,
        1894. xxiii, 104p.

1361   _____. The liars; an original comedy in four acts, by Henry
        Arthur Jones... New York, The Macmillan co.; London,
        Macmillan and co., ltd., 1901. vii, 120p.

1362   _____. The manoeuvres of Jane, an original comedy in four
        acts, by Henry Arthur Jones... New York, The Macmillan
        co.; London, Macmillan and co., ltd., 1905. 4 p.ℓ.,
        124p.

JONES, JOSEPH STEVENS

1363 _____. Michael and his lost angel; a play in five acts, by
        Henry Arthur Jones... New York and London, Macmillan and
        co., 1895. vii, 107p.

1364 _____. Mrs. Dane's defence: a play in four acts. New York,
        French, c1905. 144p.

1365 _____. Mrs. Dane's defence; a play in four acts, by Henry
        Arthur Jones. New York, The Macmillan co.; London, Mac-
        millan and co., ltd., 1905. 4 p.l., 127p.

1366 _____. The physician; an original play in four acts, by
        Henry Arthur Jones... New York, The Macmillan co.; London,
        Macmillan and co., ltd., 1899. ix, 114p. plans.

1367 _____. The rogue's comedy, a play in three acts. New York
        and London, The Macmillan co., 1898. 131p.

1368 _____. Saints and sinners, a new and original drama of
        modern English middle-class life, in five acts, by Henry
        Arthur Jones... London and New York, Macmillan and co.,
        1891. xxvi p., 2l., 142p.

1369 _____. The tempter, a tragedy in four acts. New York and
        London. The Macmillan co., 1905. 108p.

1370 _____. The triumph of the Philistines and how Mr. Jorgan
        preserved the morals of Market Pewbury under very trying
        circumstances; a comedy in three acts by Henry Arthur
        Jones... New York, The Macmillan co.; London, Macmillan
        and co., ltd., 1899. xv, 122p.

1371 JONES, JOSEPH STEVENS, 1809-1877. ... Captain Kyd; or, The
        wizard of the sea; a drama, in four acts... Boston,
        William V. Spencer [n.d.]. 44p. (Spencer's Boston
        theatre, no. lxi).

1372 _____. ... The carpenter of Rouen; or, The massacre of St.
        Bartholomew. A romantic drama in four acts... New York,
        Samuel French [n.d.]. 32p. (French's American drama,
        the acting edition, no. cxxiii).

1373 _____. Solon Shingle; or, The people's lawyer, a comedy in
        two acts. New York, Harold Roorbach, 1890. 32p.

JONES, RICHARD

1374   JONES, RICHARD, 1779-1851. The green man; a comedy, in three
        acts. From the French of M. M. d'Aubigny [pseud.] et Poujol,
        by Richard Jones... As performed at the Haymarket and New
        York theatres. (From the 1st London ed., of 1818). New
        York: Published by David Longworth, at the Dramatic reposi-
        tory, Shakespeare-gallery. Jan.--1819. 68p. [Dramatic
        pamphlets. v. 30, no. 5].
            An adaptation of "L'homme gris."

1375   JONES, WINIFRED. Nine mime plays. London, Methuen and co.,
        ltd. [n.d.]. 84p. illus.

1376   Julius Caesar: a musical comedy, by a group of Belhaven
        College students. [n.p., n.d.]. 4p. (American Classical
        League Service Bureau, No. 567).

1377   Jumbo-jum! An original farce, in one act... New York,
        Samuel French [n.d.]. 16p.

1378   Justitia Omnibus, by the students of Mrs. Margaret Graves.
        [n.p., n.d.]. 4p. (American Classical League Service
        Bureau, No. 716).

1379   KAHN, ARTHUR LEE, 1870-   . The one-act plays of Lee Arthur
        [pseud.] Edited with an introduction by Paul T. Nolan.
        Lexington, Ky., 1962. 96p.

1380   KAINE, HELEN. The best laid plans, a farce in one act.
        Philadelphia, The Penn publishing co., 1908. 18p.

1381   _____. A Russian romance, a drama in three acts. Boston,
        Walter H. Baker and co. [1907]. 46p.

1382   KAISER, GEORG. From morn to midnight, a play in seven scenes
        by Georg Kaiser. Trans. from the German by Ashley Dukes.
        London, Hendersons [n.d.]. 58p.

1383   KALIDASA, fl. 5th century. Shakuntala; or, The recovered
        ring; a Hindoo drama by Kalidasa. Translated from the
        Sanskrit by A. Hjalmar Edgren... New York, H. Holt and
        co., 1894. 2 p.ℓ., [iii]-viii, 198p.

1384   KAPLAN, DE WITTE. The madonna and the scarecrow, a phantasy
        in three acts, by De Witte Kaplan. (In Poet lore. Boston.
        1923. vol. XXXIV, no. 2, p. 254-270).

1385   ... Kathleen Mavourneen; or, St. Patrick's eve. A domestic
        Irish drama, in four acts... New York, Samuel French
        [n.d.]. 32p. (French's standard drama).

1386   KAVANAUGH, KATHARINE, 1875-   . A bachelor's baby, a farce
        in one act, by Katharine Kavanaugh... New York, Dick and
        Fitzgerald, 1911. 12p.

1387   _____. Countess Kate, a playlet, by Katharine Kavanaugh...
        Chicago, T. S. Denison and co. [1912]. 15p. diagr. (On
        cover: Half hour dramas).

1388   _____. The dust of the earth, a drama in four acts, by
        Katharine Kavanaugh. Chicago and New York, The Dramatic
        publishing co [1911]. 55p. On cover: Sergel's acting
        drama (no. 611).

1389   _____. From kitchen-maid to actress, a farce in one act, by
        Katharine Kavanaugh. Chicago, The Dramatic publishing
        co. [1910]. 10p. (On cover: The comic drama. [no.] 216).

1390   _____. A gentle touch; vaudeville sketch in one act, by
        Katharine Kavanaugh... New York, Dick and Fitzgerald,
        1912. 10p.

1391   _____. The girl and the outlaw, a dramatic playlet, by
        Katharine Kavanaugh... Chicago, The Dramatic publishing
        co., 1914. 14p. (On cover: Sergel's acting drama.
        no. 631).

1392   _____. A minister pro tem, a comedietta, by Katharine
        Kavanaugh... Chicago, T. S. Denison and co. [1914].
        12p. (On cover: Amateur series).

1393   _____. The professor of love, a comedy in one act, by
        Katharine Kavanaugh... Chicago, The Dramatic publishing
        co., 1914. 19p. diagr. (On cover: Sergel's acting
        drama. no. 633).

1394   _____. The queen of diamonds, by Katharine Kavanaugh...
        Chicago, T. S. Denison and co. [1915]. 11p. diagr.
        (On cover: Half hour dramas).

1395   _____. A stormy night; a comedy in one act, by Katharine
        Kavanaugh... New York, Dick and Fitzgerald, 1912. 12p.

KAVANAUGH, KATHARINE

1396   KAVANAUGH, KATHARINE. Under blue skies, a comedy drama in
        four acts, by Katharine Kavanaugh... Chicago, T. S.
        Denison and co. [1913]. 49p. diagrs.

1397   _____. The wayfarers; a rural play in four acts, by
        Katharine Kavanaugh... New York, Dick and Fitzgerald,
        1912. 56p.

1398   _____. When the worm turned, a comedy, by Katharine
        Kavanaugh... Chicago, T. S. Denison and co. [1912].
        16p. diagr.

1399   KEATINGE, ELLA. The legend of the Christmas tree, a play for
        children. Chicago and New York, The Dramatic publishing
        co., 1899. 12p.

1400   KEATS, JOHN, 1795-1821. ... The poetical works of John Keats,
        edited with an introduction and textual notes by H.
        Buxton Forman. London [etc.] Oxford University press,
        1920. lxxxii, 491p. illus. Includes the following dramas:
        Otho the Great, King Stephen.

1401   KEFFER, BILLY. A strange book. [n.p., n.d.]. 3p. (American
        Classical League Service Bureau, No. 271).

1402   KEISER, ELIZABETH. Perseus and the Gorgon's head, by Eliza-
        beth Keiser and Alexander Hamilton. [n.p., n.d.]. 14p.
        (American Classical League Service Bureau, No. 630).

1403   KELLEY, HALL JACKSON, 1790-1874. The American instructor,
        second book. Designed for the common schools in America;
        containing the elements of the English language; lessons
        in orthography and reading, and the pronunciation of
        Walker's critical pronouncing dictionary... By Hall J.
        Kelley... 2d ed. ... Boston, Lincoln and Edmands, 1826.
        168p. incl. front., illus. Contains his The colonists.

1404   KELLEY, JESSIE A. Squire Judkins' apple bee, an old-
        fashioned entertainment in one scene. Boston, Walter H.
        Baker and co. [1905]. 18p.

1405   No Entry.

1406   KELLY, MICHAEL, 1764?-1826. Illusion; or, The trances of
        Nourjahad: an oriental romance, in three acts. Founded
        on a Persian tale, written by Mrs. Sheridan. The music
        composed and selected by Mr. Kelly. (From the first
        London edition of 1813.) New York, Published by David

KEMBLE, MARIE THÉRÈSE DE CAMP

(KELLY, MICHAEL)
Longworth, at the Dramatic respository, Shakespeare-gallery,
1815. 36p. [Dramatic pamphlets, v. 32, no. 4]. Librettist
not named.

1407   No Entry.

1408   KEMBLE, CHARLES, 1775–1854. Plot and counterplot; or, The
portrait of Cervantes: a farce, in two acts. By Charles
Kemble. Printed from the acting copy, with remarks,
biographical and critical, by D.-G. ... As performed at
the Theatres Royal... London, Davidson [n.d.]. 39p.
incl. front. (Cumberland's British theatre. London, ca.
1825–55. v. 41 [no. 7]).
An alteration of "Le portrait de Michel Cervantes" by
Dieulafoy.
Remarks by George Daniel, editor of the series.
Reissue of Cumberland's earlier edition.

1409   KEMBLE, MRS. CHARLES. The day after the wedding. A farce,
in one act. Chicago, The Dramatic publishing co. [n.d.].
16p.

1410   KEMBLE, FRANCES ANNE, 1800–1893. Francis the First. A
tragedy in five acts. With other poetical pieces. By
Frances Ann Kemble. 6th American ed. In which is in-
cluded an original memoir and a full length portrait.
New York, Peabody and co., 1833. 1 p.ℓ., 15p., 1l.,
[17]–56, 61–79, [65]–72p.
"Memoir of the dramatic life of Miss Fanny Kemble"
signed: S. D. L.
Text abridged from 1832 London edition.
Imperfect: portrait wanting.

1411   KEMBLE, MARIE THÉRÈSE DE CAMP, 1774–1838. Personation; or,
Fairly taken in a comic interlude, in one act, by Mrs.
Charles Kemble. Printed from the acting copy, with remarks, biographical and critical, by D.-G. ... As performed at the Theatres Royal... London, Davidson [n.d.].
19p. incl. front. (Davidson's shilling volume of Cumberland's plays. London, ca. 1849–55. [v. 19, no. 5]).
"Alteration from a French piece by Dieulafoy, called
Défiance et malice."--Baker's Biog. dram.
Reissue of Cumberland's British theatre, no. 246
(v. 32 [no. 9]).
Remarks by George Daniel, editor of the original
series.

KEMP, HARRY

1412   KEMP, HARRY, 1883-   . Boccaccio's untold tale, and other
       one-act plays, by Harry Kemp. New York, Brentano's [c1924].
       5 p.ℓ., 252p. CONTENTS. - A few words beforehand. - The
       plays themselves. - Boccaccio's untold tale. - The game
       called Kiss. - The white hawk. - Solomon's song. - Judith.
       - Don Juan's Christmas eve. - Don Juan in a garden. -
       Calypso. - Their day. - The period of the moon.

1413   ... Kenilworth. A melo-drama. With prefatory remarks...
       Faithfully marked with the stage business, and stage
       directions, as it is performed at the Theatres Royal. By
       W. Oxberry, comedian. London, Pub. for the Proprietors,
       by W. Simpkin and R. Marshall [etc.] 1824. iv, [2], 61p.
       front. (port.). (Oxberry, William. The new English drama.
       London, 1818-25. v. 19 [no. 5]). At head of title: Ox-
       berry's edition.
          Compiled from Scott's novel and plays founded on it.
       Cf. "Remarks"; Genest, v. 9, p. 171-172.

1414   KENNEDY, CHARLES RANN, 1871-1950. The necessary evil, a one-
       act stage play for four persons: to be played in the light.
       New York and London, Harper and bros., publishers, 1913.
       111p.

1415   _____. Servant in the house; illus. with portraits of the
       characters in the play. New York, Harper, 1908. 151p.

1416   _____. The terrible meek, a one-act play for three voices,
       to be played in darkness. New York and London, Harper
       and bros., 1912. 44p.

1417   _____. The winterfeast. New York and London, Harper and
       bros., publishers, 1908. 159p.

1418   KENNEY, JAMES, 1780-1849. The Alcaid; or, The secrets of
       office, a comic opera, in three acts, by James Kenney...
       Printed from the acting copy, with remarks, biographical
       and critical, by D.-G. ... As performed at the Theatres
       Royal... London, G. H. Davidson [n.d.]. 6, [2], [7]-58p.
       front. (port.) pl. (Cumberland's British theatre. London,
       ca. 1825-55. v. 8 [no. 1]).
          Remarks by George Daniel, editor of the series.
          Reissue of Cumberland's earlier edition.
          Without the music (by Nathan).

1419   [_____]. The blind boy: a melo-drama, in two acts. As per-
       formed at the Theatre Royal, Covent-Garden. London,
       Longman, Hurst, Rees and Orme, 1808. 2 p.ℓ., 36p. [Longe,
       F. Collection of plays. v. 311, no. 11].
            Adapted from Caigniez's "L'illustre aveugle". Ascribed
       also to William B. Hewetson.

1420   _____. ... Ella Rosenberg, a grand melodrama, in two acts.
       Written by Mr. Kenny. As it is performed at the Theatre
       Royal, Drury Lane. London, J. Scales [1807?]. 26p. incl.
       col. front.
            No. 2 in a volume lettered: Tracts and chap-books.
            At head of title: Scales' edition.

1421   _____. False Alarms; or, My cousin, a comic opera, in three
       acts. Performed at the Theatre Royal, Drury-Lane, on
       Monday, Jan. 12, 1807. By James Kenney. London, Printed
       for Longman, Hurst, Rees and Orm[e] by C. Stower, 1807.
       2 p.ℓ., 48 + p. [Broadhurst, J. Plays. v. 9, no. 4].
            Without the music (by Braham and King).

1422   _____. The fortune of war. A comic piece, in two acts; as
       performed at the Theatre Royal, Covent Garden. Tr. from
       the French by James Kenney... New York, D. Longworth,
       1816. 40p.

1423   _____. The illustrious stranger; or, Married and buried: an
       operatic farce, in two acts, by James Kenney... Printed
       from the acting copy, with remarks, biographical and
       critical, by D.-G. ... As performed at the Theatres
       Royal... London, Davidson [n.d.]. 36p. incl. front.
       (Cumberland's British theatre. London, ca. 1825-55.
       v. 23 [no. 6]).
            Remarks by George Daniel, editor of the series, ascribe
       the play to Kenney, but in those prefixed to Millingen's
       Beehive in v. 30, he lists it as a play of Millingen's
       "to which Mr. Kenny's name has been erroneously attached."
            Borrowed in part from "Le naufrage, ou, La pompe
       funèbre de Crispin."
            Without the music (by Nathan).
            Reissue of Cumberland's earlier edition.

1424   _____. John Buzzby; or, A day's pleasure. A comedy in
       three acts. As performed at the Theatre-Royal, Haymarket.
       By James Kenney... New York, E. M. Murden, 1822. 63p.

KENNEY, JAMES

1425   KENNEY, JAMES. Love, law, and physic. A farce, in two acts,
       by James Kenney... Printed from the acting copy, with
       remarks, biographical and critical, by D.-G. ... As per-
       formed at the Theatres Royal... London, J. Cumberland
       [n.d.]. 41p. incl. front. (Cumberland's British theatre.
       London, ca. 1825-55. v. 24 [no. 4]).
          Remarks by George Daniel, editor of the series.

1426   _____. Match-breaking; or, The prince's present. A comedy,
       in three acts; with airs. As first acted at the Theatre
       Royal, Haymarket, on Thursday, September the 20th, 1821.
       By James Kenney... London, W. Simpkin, and R. Marshall
       [etc.] 1821. 2 p.ℓ., 48 + p. [Broadhurst, J. Plays.
       v. 8, no. 1].
          Without the music.
          Imperfect: all after p. 48 wanting.
          Based on "Le présent du prince; ou, L'autre fille
       d'honneur" by Decomberousse and Baudouin.

1427   _____. Matrimony: a petite opera, in two acts, by James
       Kenney... Printed from the acting copy, with remarks,
       biographical and critical, by D.-G. ... As performed at
       the Theatres Royal... London, Davidson [n.d.]. 36p. incl.
       front. (Cumberland's British theatre. London, ca. 1825-55.
       v. 26 [no. 2]).
          From Marsollier des Vivetières' opera, Adolphe et Clara;
       perhaps based on an earlier translation, "by Eleanor
       H____" in the Lady's magazine, Feb.-July, 1804: Adolphus
       and Clara; or, The two prisoners.
          Remarks by George Daniel, editor of the series.
          Without the music (by King).
          Reissue of Cumberland's earlier edition.

1428   _____. Raising the wind: a farce, in two acts, by James
       Kenney ... Printed from the acting copy, with remarks,
       biographical and critical, by D.-G. ... As performed at
       the Theatres Royal... London, G. H. Davidson [n.d.]. 35p.
       incl. front. (Cumberland's British theatre. London, ca.
       1825-55. v. 19 [no. 7]).
          Remarks by George Daniel, editor of the series.
          Reissue of Cumberland's earlier edition.

1429   _____. The Sicilian vespers: an historical tragedy. By
       James Kenney... London, J. Miller, 1840. 66p.

1430   [____]. ... Sweethearts and wives. In three acts. With a
        portrait of Mr. Barnes, in the character of Billy Lackaday
        ... carefully corrected from the prompt books of the Phil-
        adelphia theatre, by M. Lopez, prompter. Philadelphia,
        A. R. Poole [etc.]; Washington, P. Thompson; [etc., etc.,
        1827]. 66p. front (port.). (Added t.-p.: Lopez and
        Wemyss' edition. Acting American theatre. [no. 10]).
            Series title also at head of t.-p.
            Added t.-p., dated 1827.
            Without the music.

1431   KERR, G. H. A. D. 2000; or, The century plants, a comic
        opera in two acts. Music by Bowness Briggs. Wilmington,
        Delaware, 1894. 102p.

1432   [KERR, JOHN]. The wandering boys; or, The castle of Olival.
        A melo-drama. In two acts. Boston, Richardson and Lord,
        1821. 44p.

1433   KIDDER, EDWARD E. A lively legacy; a fantastic farce-comedy
        in three acts and six scenes, written by E. E. Kidder.
        Motive, situations, and scenic effects supplied by Hanlon
        bros. [New York?] 1900. 82p.

1433A   KIND, FRIEDRICH, 1768-1843. Der Freischütz; or, The seventh
        bullet. An opera, in three acts, by Carl Maria von Weber.
        Printed from the acting copy, with remarks, biographical
        and critical, by D.-G. ... Embellished with a fine en-
        graving, by Mr. White, from a drawing taken in the theatre,
        by Mr. R. Cruikshank. London, J. Cumberland [18--]. 7,
        [1], [11]-41p. incl. front.
            Libretto by Friedrich Kind, based on J. A. Apel's story
        of the same name. Translated and adapted by W. McGregor
        Logan. Cf. Loewenberg, Alfred. Annals of opera, 1943.
            Reissued in Davidson's shilling volume of Cumberland's
        plays, v. 10 [no. 8].
            Another issue. [Cumberland's British theatre. London,
        ca. 1825-55. v. 9 [no. 7]].

1434   KIRALFY, IMRE, 1845-1919. Grand historical spectacle America,
        in four acts, and seventeen scenes... Music by Angelo
        Venanzi. [Chicago] Abbey, Schoeffel and Grau, 1893. 36p.
        illustrated.

KIRALFY, IMRE

1435   KIRALFY, IMRE. ... Imre Kiralfy's Columbus and the discovery
        of America... adapted and arranged for production with
        Barnum and Bailey's greatest show on earth... Buffalo,
        N. Y., The Courier co., show printers [1892]. 24p. illus.,
        fold. col. pl.

1436   _____. ... Nero; or, The fall of Rome. A grand dramatic
        historical spectacle, conceived, designed and produced by
        Imre Kiralfy... [New York] 1888. 24p. fold. col. pl.

1437   KIRBY, HARRIET GRISWOLD. Barbesieu; or, The troubadour, a
        libretto. Louisville, John P. Morton and co., 1913. 21p.

1438   KNIGHT, EDWARD, 1774-1826. The veteran; or, The farmer's
        sons: a comic opera, in three acts, as performed at the
        Theatre Royal, Drury Lane, with the most distinguished
        applause. By E. Knight, comedian... London, Printed by
        W. Glindon, 1822. vii, [1], 9-68p. [Broadhurst, J. Plays.
        v. 2, no. 1].
            Without the music (by T. Cooke and others).

1438A   KNIGHT, THOMAS, d. 1820. The turnpike gate: a musical farce,
        in two acts. By T. Knight. Printed from the acting copy,
        with remarks, biographical and critical, by D.-G. ... As
        performed at the Theatres Royal... London, G. H. Davidson
        [n.d.]. 36p. incl. front. (Cumberland's British theatre.
        London, ca. 1825-55, v. 20 [no. 6]).
            Remarks by George Daniel, editor of the series.
            Reissue of Cumberland's earlier edition.
            Music by Mazzinghi and Reeve. Cf. Brit. Mus. Cat.
        print. mus.

1439   KNOWLES, JAMES SHERIDAN, 1784-1862. ... Brian Boroihme; or,
        The maid of Erin. A historical Hibernian melo-drama, in
        three acts. By James Sheridan Knowles... To which are
        added, a description of the costume - cast of the charac-
        ters... and the whole of the stage business. As performed
        at the New York theatres. New York, S. French [1856?].
        27p. (French's American drama. The acting edition.
        no. 23).
            An adaptation of Daniel A. O'Meara's drama of the same
        name.

1440   _____. The dramatic works of James Sheridan Knowles... A
        new ed. in one volume. London, New York, Routledge,
        Warnes, and Routledge, 1859. vi p., 1ℓ., 448, 457p.
        CONTENTS. - Pt. I. Caius Gracchus. Virginius. William
        Tell. Alfred the Great; or, The patriotic king. The

KOOGLE, EFFIE LOUISE

(KNOWLES, JAMES SHERIDAN)
hunchback. The wife: a tale of Mantua. The beggar of
Bethnal green. The daughter. - Pt. II. The love-chase.
Women's wit; or, Love's disguises. The maid of Marien-
dorpt. Love. John of Procida; or, The bridals of Messina.
Old maids. The rose of Aragon. The secretary.

1441 _____. Virginius, a tragedy in five acts. New York, Samuel
French and son; London, Samuel French [n.d.]. 72p.

1442 KOCH, FREDERICK HENRY, 1877-1944. Raleigh, the shepherd of
the ocean; a pageant drama, by Frederick Henry Koch...
designed to commemorate the Tercentenary of the Execution
of Sir Walter Raleigh, with a foreword by Edwin Greenlaw.
Raleigh, N. C., Edwards and Broughton printing co., 1920.
95p. front., plates, ports.

1443 KOCK, CHARLES PAUL DE, 1794-1871. ... The works of Charles
Paul de Kock, with a general introduction by Jules
Claretie... Boston, London [etc.] The F. J. Quinby co.
[1902-   ]. v. fronts., illus., plates (part col.)
ports., facsim. CONTENTS - [v. 1-2] Sister Anne. - [v. 3-
4] Monsieur Dupont. - [v. 5-6] Frère Jacques. [v. 7-8] The
barber of Paris. - [v. 9] The child of my wife. - [v. 10-
11] The Gogo family. - [v. 12] The memoirs of Charles Paul
de Kock. - [v. 13-14] My neighbor Raymond. - [v. 15] The
damsel of three skirts. - [v. 16-17] Jean. - [v. 18]
Friquette. - [v. 19] Scenes of Parisian life. - [v. 20]
Edmond and his cousin, etc. - [v. 21] Madame Pantalon. -
[v. 22] Gustave, v. 1. - [v. 23] Gustave, v. 2. M. Martin's
donkey. - [v. 24] Adhemar. - [v. 25] Little Lise. - [v. 26-
27] André the Savoyard. - [v. 28-29] The flower girl. -
[v. 30-31] Milkmaid of Montfermeil. - [v. 32-33] Monsieur
Cherami. - [v. 34-35] Mustache. - [v. 36] A queer legacy
(L'homme aux trois culottes) - [v. 37-38] Frédérique. -
[v. 39-   ] Sans-cravate. - [v. 41-42] Paul and his dog. -
[v. 43-   ] Cerisette.

1444 KOOGLE, EFFIE LOUISE. Cupid's joke, a play for young folks.
Lebanon, Ohio, March bros., 1906. 20p.

1445 _____. The heir of Mt. Vernon, a colonial play. Lebanon,
Ohio, March bros., 1906. 49p.

1446 _____. The knickerbockers at school, an historical play for
young folks. Lebanon, Ohio, March bros., 1906. 28p.

KOOGLE, EFFIE LOUISE

1447   KOOGLE, EFFIE LOUISE. Master George Washington, his sixth
        birthday party, an historical play for children. Lebanon,
        Ohio, March bros., 1906. 13p.

1448   _____. Up to date America; or, The sweet girl graduate's
        dream, drama-caprice. Lebanon, Ohio, March bros., 1907.
        46p.

1449   KOPSCH, (MRS.) H. E. Why elect Latin? [n.p., n.d.]. 2p.
        (American Classical League Service Bureau, No. 539).

1450   KOSOR, JOSIP, 1879-   . People of the universe; four Serbo-
        Croatian plays, by Josip Kosor. London, Hendersons [1917].
        339p. CONTENTS. - The woman, tr. by P. Selver. - Passion's
        furnace, tr. by F. S. Copeland. - Reconciliation, tr. by
        J. N. Duddington. - The invincible ship, tr. by P. Selver.

1451   KOTZEBUE, AUGUST FRIEDRICH FERDINAND VON, 1761-1819. The
        beautiful unknown, a dramatic history. Translated from
        the German of Augustus von Kotzebue. By Charles Smith.
        New York, Published by Burnton and Darling, 116, Broadway.
        Seare and Andrews, printers.....1808. 50p.

1452   _____. False shame; a comedy, in four acts. Translated from
        the German of Kotzebue. Newark, Printed by John Wallis,
        for Charles Smith, no. 56, Maiden-Lane, New York, 1801.
        63p.

1453   _____. Lovers' vows: a play, in five acts, tr. from the
        German of Kotzebue, by Mrs. Inchbald... Printed from the
        acting copy, with remarks, biographical and critical, by
        D.-G. ... As performed at the Theatres Royal... London,
        J. Cumberland [n.d.]. 58p. incl. front. (Cumberland's
        British theatre. London, ca. 1825-55. v. 17 [no. 7]).
            "A sort of paraphrase on Kotzebue's 'Child of love.'"--
        Remarks by George Daniel, editor of the series.

1454   _____. Lover's vows; or, The child of love, a play in five
        acts... Edinburgh, Oliver and Boyd [n.d.]. 38p. front.

1455   [_____]. Pizarro: a tragic play, in five acts, by Richard
        Brinsley Sheridan... Printed from the acting copy, with
        remarks, biographical and critical, by D.-G. ... As per-
        formed at the Theatres Royal... London, Davidson [n.d.].
        60p. incl. front. (Cumberland's British theatre. London,
        ca. 1825-55. v. 1 [no. 4]).
            Adaptation of Kotzebue's Die Spanier in Peru, oder
        Rolla's tod.
            Remarks by George Daniel, editor of the series.

LACY, ERNEST

1456 _____. The stranger: a drama, in five acts, tr. from the German of Kotzebue, by Benjamin Thompson, esq. Printed from the acting copy, with remarks, biographical and critical, by D.-G. ... As performed at the Theatres Royal... London, Davidson [n.d.]. 60p. incl. front. (Cumberland's British theatre. London, ca. 1825-55. v. 14 [no.2]).
   Remarks by George Daniel, editor of the series.
   Title of original: Menschenhass und Reue.

1457 KRAFT, IRMA. The power of Purim, and other plays; a series of one act plays designed for Jewish religious schools, by Irma Kraft. Philadelphia, The Jewish publication society of America, 1915. 189 [1]p. illus. CONTENTS. - The power Purim (Purim)--A Maccab cure (Ilanukkah)--To save his country (Peaah)--Ambition in Whitechapel (Shahout)--Because he loved David so (closing of school).

1458 KREBS, PAT. The prize apple; or, Apples that glitter like gold may be green. [n.p., n.d.]. 6p. (American Classical League Service Bureau, No. 667).

1459 KVAPIL, JAROSLAV. The clouds (a play in three acts) by Jaroslav Kvapil. Tr. from the Bohemian by Charles Recht. (In Poet lore. Boston, 1910. vol. xxi, no. vi, p. 417-466).

1460 KYNE, ESTELLA. Pyramus and Thisbe à la mode. [n.p., n.d.]. 3p. (American Classical League Service Bureau, No. 600).

1461 LABICHE, EUGÈNE MARIN, 1815-1888. La grammaire and Le baron de Fourchevif, two comedies by Labiche; ed. with intro-duction and notes by Herman S. Piatt... Boston, U.S.A., Ginn and co., 1901. v, 130p. (On cover: International modern language series).

1462 _____. Under a spell; a comedy in one act, tr. from the French of Labiche and Jolly [pseud.] by J. De W. Gibbs. Boston, W. H. Baker and co., 1888. 24p.

1463 LACY, ERNEST, 1863-1916. Plays and sonnets by Ernest Lacy; etchings of Julia Marlowe as Chatterton, and Joseph Haworth as Rinaldo, by Stephan J. Ferris. Philadelphia, Printed by Sherman and co., 1900. 2 p.ℓ., v-vii, 237p. 2 port. (incl. front.).

LACY, THOMAS HAILES

1464   LACY, THOMAS HAILES. A silent woman. A farce, in one act...
        first performed August 17, 1835... New York, Robert M.
        De Witt [n.d.]. 8p.

1465   The ladies' battle. Translated from the celebrated French
        drama, "Un duel en amour," a comedy, in three acts... New
        York, Samuel French [n.d.]. 35p.

1466   LAIDLAW, ALEXANDER HAMILTON, 1869-1908. The charms of music;
        farce in one act and one scene, by Alex. H. Laidlaw, Jr.
        111 New York, T. H. French; London, S. French [1894].
        20p. (On cover: French's minor drama. The acting edition.
        no. 358).

1467   LAIDLAW, F. ALLAN. True! An entirely new and original play.
        In one act. New York, Dewitt, 1884. 12p.

1468   LAMSON, C. A. Grandmother Hildebrand's legacy; or, Mae
        Blossom's reward, a drama in five acts... Clyde, Ohio,
        Ames' publishing co., 1892. 25p.

1469   LANCASTER, CHARLES SEARS. Advice to husbands, an original
        comedietta, in one act. London, John Duncombe [n.d.].
        19p. front.

1470   LANCASTER, EDWARD. ... The manager's daughter. An interlude,
        in one act. By Edward Lancaster, esq. (In The New York
        drama. New York, c1880. no. 53, p. [18]-25). Caption
        title.

1471   LANE, CHRIS. A country visitor, a laughable one-act farce.
        Chicago, Will Rossiter, 1903. 11p.

1472   _____. A lunatic pro tem. An original sketch for male and
        female. Will Rossiter, 1903. 7p.

1473   LANGE, STELLA L. The slave girl. [n.p., n.d.]. 10p.
        (American Classical League Service Bureau, No. 87).

1474   LANGLOIS, FANNIE MYERS. Suite B, sketch in one scene. Chi-
        cago, The Dramatic publishing co. [n.d.]. 14p.

1475   LANGNER, LAWRENCE, 1890-1962. Another way out, a play in one
        act, by Lawrence Langner. New York, F. Shay, The Washing-
        ton Square players, 1916. 36p.

1476 _____. Five one-act comedies, by Lawrence Langner, introduction by St. John Ervine. Cincinnati, Stewart Kidd
company [c1922]. 165p. CONTENTS. - Matinata. - Another
way out. - The family exit. - Pie. - Licensed.

1477 LANIGAN, JOHN ALPHONSUS, 1854-1919. Eithne; or, The siege of
Armagh, a drama, in four acts. By John A. Lanigan... To
which are added a description of costumes, dramatic
personae, and stage business... Buffalo, Express steam
printing house, 1878. 1 p.ℓ., [5]-49p.

1478 The last loaf, a drama... Boston, George M. Baker and co.
[1870]. 56p.

1479 LAW, ARTHUR, 1844-1913. A country mouse, a satirical comedy
in three acts, by Arthur Law... New York, S. French;
London, S. French, ltd. [191-]. 60p. diagrs. On cover:
French's standard library edition.

1480 _____. The new boy; a farcical play in three acts, by Arthur
Law... New York, London, S. French, 1904. 66p.

1481 _____. Three blind mice; or, Marjorie's lovers, a play in
three acts, by Arthur Law... New York, S. French; London,
S. French, ltd., 1910. [4], 5-100p.

1482 LAWLER, LILLIAN B. The gifts of Mother Lingua. [n.p., n.d.].
3p. (American Classical League Service Bureau, No. 184).

1483 _____. In honor of Vergil; a playlet for eleven girls.
[n.p., n.d.]. 12p. (American Classical League Service
Bureau, No. 378).

1484 _____. Sabine moonlight: a pageant-play with Horace and his
poetry. [n.p., n.d.]. 8p. (American Classical League
Service Bureau, No. 503).

1485 LAWRENCE, DAVID HERBERT, 1885-1930. David. London, Martin
Secker, 1930. 127p.

1486 LAWRENCE, SLINGSBY. Sunshine through the clouds. A drama in
one act... London, Thomas Hailes Lacy [n.d.]. 29p.

1487 [LEACOCK, JOHN]. The fall of British tyranny; or, American
triumphant. The first campaign. A tragi-comedy of five-
acts, as lately planned at the Royal theatrum pandemonium,
at St. James's. The principal place of action in America.

[LEACOCK, JOHN]

([LEACOCK, JOHN])
Pub. according to act of Parliament... Philadelphia,
Printed by Styner and Cist, in Second-street, near Arch-
street, 1776. viii, 66p.

1488   LEAVITT, ANDREW J. The academy of stars. An Ethiopian
sketch, by A. J. Leavitt and H. W. Eagan. New York, Samuel
French [n.d.]. 8p.

1489   _____. The black Ole Bull. An Ethiopian sketch, by A. J.
Leavitt and H. W. Eagan. New York, Samuel French [n.d.].
8p.

1490   _____. The blackest tragedy of all; or, A peep behind the
scenes, by A. J. Leavitt and H. W. Eagan. New York, Samuel
French [n.d.]. 8p.

1491   _____. Blinks and Jinks. An Ethiopian sketch, by A. J.
Leavitt and H. W. Eagan. New York, Samuel French [n.d.].
8p.

1492   _____. Boarding school. An Ethiopian sketch, by A. J.
Leavitt and H. W. Eagan. New York, Samuel French [n.d.].
8p.

1493   _____. The coming man. An Ethiopian sketch in two scenes...
arranged by Charles White... Chicago, The Dramatic publishing co., 1877. 6p.

1494   _____. The dead alive. An Ethiopian sketch, by J. A. Leavitt
and H. W. Eagan. New York, Samuel French [n.d.]. 8p.

1495   _____. Deaf as a post. An Ethiopian sketch, by A. J. Leavitt
and H. W. Eagan. New York, Samuel French [n.d.]. 8p.

1496   _____. Echo band. An Ethiopian sketch, by A. J. Leavitt and
H. W. Eagan. New York, Samuel French [n.d.]. 8p.

1497   _____. High Jack, the heeler. An Ethiopian sketch, in one
scene. Arranged by Charles White. New York, The De Witt
publishing house, 1875. 6p.

1498   _____. High Jack, the heeler. An Ethiopian sketch, in one
scene... arranged by Charles White... Chicago and New
York, The Dramatic publishing co., 1875. 6p.

1499   _____. The intelligence office. An Ethiopian sketch, by
A. J. Leavitt and H. W. Eagan. New York, Samuel French
[n.d.]. 8p.

LECOCQ, CHARLES

1500 _____. The lucky number. An Ethiopian sketch, by A. J. Leavitt and H. W. Eagan. New York, Samuel French [n.d.]. 8p.

1501 _____. No tator; or, Man-fish. An Ethiopian sketch, by A. J. Leavitt and H. W. Eagan. New York, Samuel French [n.d.]. 8p.

1502 _____. Running the blockade. An Ethiopian sketch, by A. J. Leavitt and H. W. Eagan. New York, Samuel French [n.d.]. 8p.

1503 _____. Somebody's coat. An Ethiopian sketch, by A. J. Leavitt and H. W. Eagan. New York, Samuel French [n.d.]. 8p.

1504 _____. Squire for a day. A negro sketch. Arranged by Charles White... New York, Robert M. De Witt, 1875. 7p.

1505 _____. Tom and Jerry, and Who's been here since I've been gone, by A. J. Leavitt and H. W. Eagan. New York, Samuel French [n.d.]. 8p.

1506 _____. A trip to Paris. An Ethiopian sketch, by A. J. Leavitt and H. W. Eagan. New York, Samuel French [n.d.]. 8p.

1507 _____. The two Pompeys. An Ethiopian sketch, by A. J. Leavitt and H. W. Eagan. New York, Samuel French [n.d.]. 8p.

1508 _____. The upper ten thousand. An Ethiopian sketch, by A. J. Leavitt and H. W. Eagan. New York, Samuel French [n.d.]. 8p.

1509 _____. Who stole the chickens? An Ethiopian sketch, by A. J. Leavitt and H. W. Eagan. New York, Samuel French [n.d.]. 6p.

1510 LE BRANDT, JOSEPH. My Lady Darrell; or, A strange marriage. A drama in four acts, by Joseph Le Brandt... New York, H. Roorbach, 1898. 62p.

1511 LECOCQ, CHARLES, 1832-1918. Heart and hand. Opéra-comique in three acts... trans. and adapted by Theodore T. Barker. Boston, Oliver Ditson, 1883. 72p.

LEE, SOPHIA

1512   LEE, SOPHIA, 1750-1824. The chapter of accidents. A comedy.
        By Miss Lee. Correctly given, from copies used in the
        theatres, by Thomas Dibdin... London, Printed at the Chis-
        wick press for Whittingham and Arliss, 1816. 75p. illus.
        (Dibdin, T. J. London theatre. London, 1815 [1814-25]
        v. 2 [no. 3]). Title vignette.
            "Built on Diderot's Père de famille."--Prelim. note.

1513   LEFUSE, M. For lack of evidence. A play for ladies, in one
        act... London and New York, 1910. 12p.

1514   _____. Mistress Runaway, a comedy for ladies in one act...
        New York and London, Samuel French, 1910. 18p.

1515   LE GALLIENNE, RICHARD, 1866-1947. Orestes, a tragedy. New
        York, Mitchell Kennerley, 1910. 50p.

1516   LEGGE, ARTHUR E. J. The silver age, a dramatic poem, by
        Arthur E. J. Legge. London, John Lane; New York, John
        Lane co., 1911. 136p.

1517   LEGOUVÉ, ERNEST, 1807-1903. The broken seal. A dramatic
        sketch, in one act, by E. Legouvé. Translated and adapted
        from the French, by André Arnold... New York, Happy hours
        co., 1879. 6p. (On cover: The acting drama. no. 111).

1518   _____. La cigale chez les fourmis; comédie en un acte [par]
        Legouvé et Labiche; edited with notes and vocabulary by
        Thomas J. Farrar... New York, Cincinnati [etc.] American
        book co. [1898]. 56p.

1519   _____. Foresight; or, My daughter's dowry. A comedy, in two
        acts, translated from the French of Ernest Legouvé.
        Adapted for the American stage by John H. Delafield...
        New York, Happy hours co. [1879]. 28p.

1520   _____. Medea; a tragedy in three acts, by Ernest Legouvé,
        translated from the Italian version of Joseph Montanelli,
        by Thomas Williams. Represented by Madame Ristori, and
        her Italian dramatic company under the management of J.
        Grau. New York, John A. Gray and Green, 1867. 35p. front.

1521   LEIGH, WILLIAM ROBINSON, 1866-   . Clipt wings; a drama in
        five acts, being an explanation of the mystery concerning
        the authorship of the works attributed to Shakespeare,
        the parentage of Francis Bacon, and the character of
        Shaxper, by William R. Leigh. New York, Thornton W. Allen
        co., 1930. xi p., 21, 12-159p. front., ports.

1522   LEMON, HARRY. Up for the cattle show. A farce, in one act. Chicago and New York, The Dramatic publishing co. [n.d.]. 12p.

1523   LEMON, MARK, 1809-1870. ... The ancestress! or, The doom of Barostein! A melo-drama, in two acts, by Mark Lemon... London, J. Duncombe and co. [ca. 1840]. 30p. front. (On cover: Duncombe's acting edition of the British theatre. no. 220).
        Imperfect: frontispiece wanting.
        "Produced at the City of London theatre, April 27, 1837."

1524   _____. ... Arnold of Winkelried; or, The fight of Sempach! A drama, in five acts... London, J. Duncombe and co. [n.d.]. 49p. front.

1525   _____. The demon gift; or, Visions of the future; a melo-drama, in two acts, by Mark Lemon... Correctly printed from the prompt copy... London, J. Pattie [n.d.]. iv, [5]-24p. front. (The Universal stage... London, 1840. v. 2 [no. 9]).
        Written in collaboration with John Brougham.

1526   _____. A familiar friend. A farce, in one act, by Mark Lemon... First performed at the Royal Olympic theatre, 8th, of February, 1840. Correctly printed from the prompt copy... [London] J. Pattie [1840]. 23p. front. (The Universal stage... London, 1840. v. 1 [no. 6]).
        Error in paging: p. 13-14 misplaced in binding to follow 22.

1527   _____. The gentleman in black, a burletta in one act, by Mark Lemon... As performing at the Royal Olympic theatre, correctly printed from the prompt copy... London, J. Pattie [1840?]. 20p. front. (The Universal stage... London, 1840. v. 2 [no. 2]).

1528   _____. Gwynneth Vaughan, a drama, in two acts, by Mark Lemon... The overture and incidental music, by W. L. Phillips. As performing at the Royal Olympic theatre, correctly printed from the prompt copy... London, J. Pattie [1840?]. iv, 5-31p. front. (The Universal stage... London, 1840. v. 2 [no. 1]).
        Without the music.

LEMON, MARK

1529   LEMON, MARK. Honesty is the best policy: a drama in two acts, (adapted to the English stage,) by Mark Lemon, esq. Printed from the acting copy, with remarks, biographical and critical, by D.-G. ... As performed at the Theatres Royal... London, G. H. Davidson [n.d.]. 40p. incl. front. (Cumberland's British theatre. London, ca. 1825-55. v. 45 [no. 5]).
        Adapted from the French.
        Remarks by George Daniel, editor of the series.

1530   _____. The house of ladies; a burletta, in one act; by Mark Lemon... As performed at the Royal Olympic theatre. Correctly printed from the prompt book... London, J. Pattie [n.d.]. 22p. front. (The Universal stage... London, 1840. v. 2 [n. 4]).
        Frontispiece dated 1845.

1531   _____. Ins and outs; a burletta, in two acts; by Mark Lemon... As performed nightly at the Royal English Opera House. Correctly printed from the prompt book... London, J. Pattie [n.d.]. 30p. (The Universal stage... London, 1840. v. 2 [no. 10]).

1532   _____. The ladies' club; a burletta, in two acts; by Mark Lemon... As performed at the Royal Olympic theatre. Correctly printed from the prompt book... London, J. Pattie [n.d.]. 32p. front. (The Universal stage... London, 1840. v. 1 [no. 9]).

1533   _____. Mind your own business. An original drama, in three acts, by Mark Lemon... Splendidly illustrated with an engraving, by Mr. J. P. Wall... London, Webster and co.; [etc., etc., 1852?]. 59p. front. [Webster, B. The Acting national drama. no. 185; v. 17, no. 6].
        "First performed... April 24th, 1852."

1534   _____. A moving tale, a farce, in one act. By Mark Lemon... London, T. H. Lacy [185-]. 23p. (On cover: Lacy's acting edition. no. 227).
        "First performed... June 7th, 1854."

1535   _____. The petticoat parliament. An extravaganza, in one act... as first performed... Dec. 26, 1867... New York, Robert M. De Witt [n.d.]. 19p.

LESSING, GOTTHOLD EPHRAIM

1536   _____. The pupil of Da Vinci! An operatic burletta, in one act, by Mark Lemon... As performed at the Theatre Royal, St. James's, correctly printed from the prompt book... [London] J. Pattie [n.d.]. 24p. front. (The Universal stage... London, 1840. v. 1 [no. 1]).

1537   _____. ... Self accusation; or, A brother's love! A melodrama, in two acts... London, J. Duncombe [n.d.]. 26p. front. (Duncombe's edition).

1538   _____. The three secrets, a drama, in two acts, (partly taken from the French,) by Mark Lemon... Correctly printed from the prompt copy... [London] J. Pattie [n.d.]. iv, [5]-24p. (The Universal stage... London, 1840. v. 2 [no. 8]).

1539   LEON, (MRS.) HARRY J. Tivoli mists; a Horatian play. [n.p., n.d.]. 4p. (American Classical League Service Bureau, No. 504).

1540   LEONCAVALLO, RUGGIERO, 1858-1919. ... Pagliacci (Punchinello) drama in two acts; words and music by R. Leoncavallo, English version by Henry Grafton Chapman. New York, G. Schirmer [1907]. 4 p.ℓ., [3]-67p.

1541   LESLIE, HENRY. The orange girl. A drama, in a prologue and three acts... New York, Robert M. De Witt [n.d.]. 42p.

1542   _____. The sin and sorrow. An entirely original drama, in a prologue and three acts... London, Thomas Hailes Lacy [n.d.]. 59p.

1543   _____. Time and tide. A drama, in three acts and a prologue. Chicago, The Dramatic publishing co. [n.d.]. 36p.

1544   LESPERANCE, JOHN. One hundred years ago. An historical drama of the war of independence in four acts and 20 tableaux. Montreal, "La Minerva" steam presses, 1876. 108p.

1545   LESSING, GOTTHOLD EPHRAIM, 1729-1781. Emilia Galotti; a tragedy, in five acts. Translated from the German of G. E. Lessing, by Miss Fanny Holcroft. Published by Bradford and Innskeep, Philadelphia; Inskeep and Bradford, New York; Wm. M'Ilhenny, Boston; Edward J. Coale, Baltimore; and Morford, Willington and co., Charleston, South Carolina. J. Maxwell, printer, 1810. 18p. (The Mirror of taste and dramatic censor. Philadelphia, 1810-11. v. 2 [no. 3]).

LESSING, GOTTHOLD EPHRAIM

1546 LESSING, GOTTHOLD EPHRAIM. Nathan the Wise; a dramatic poem
      in five acts. By Gotthold Ephraim Lessing. Tr. from the
      German, with a biography of Lessing, and a critical survey
      of his position, writings, etc., by Adolphus Reich. London,
      A. W. Bennett, 1860. xxv, [1], 219p.

1547 LESTER, FRANCIS. The new squire, comedy in one act (male
      characters). Chicago, The Dramatic publishing co., 1899.
      31p.

1548 LEWIS, EDWARD. Precious bane, a play in a prologue and three
      acts. Adapted from the novel of Mary Webb. London, New
      York, Samuel French, c1932. 64p.

1549 LEWIS, EDWIN A., d. 1888. Newbern; or, The old flag. A drama
      of the southern rebellion, in prologue and three acts. By
      Edwin A. Lewis. [Clinton, Mass., W. J. Coulter, 1884].
      49p.

1550 LEWIS, LEOPOLD. The bells. A drama, in three acts... New
      York, Samuel French and son [n.d.]. 30p.

1551 _____. The bells, a drama in three acts. London, Samuel
      French, ltd. [n.d.]. 34p.

1552 LEWIS, MATTHEW GREGORY, 1775-1818. Alfonso, king of Castile:
      a tragedy, in five acts. By M. G. Lewis... London, J.
      Bell, 1801. vii, [1] 111, [1]p.

1553 _____. One o'clock; or, The knight and wood demon: a grand
      operatic romance, in three acts, by M. G. Lewis... Printed
      from the acting copy, with remarks, biographical and
      critical, by D.-G. ... As performed at the Theatres Royal
      ... London, G. H. Davidson [n.d.]. 54p. incl. front.
      (Cumberland's British theatre. London, ca. 1825-55.
      v. 32 [no. 2]).
         Appeared also under title: The wood daemon; or, The
      clock has struck.
         Remarks by George Daniel, editor of the series.
         Without the music (by King and Kelly).
         Reissue of Cumberland's earlier edition.

1554 _____. Rugantino; or, The bravo of Venice: a grand romantic
      melo-drama, in two acts, by Matthew Gregory Lewis...
      Printed from the acting copy, with remarks, biographical
      and critical, by D.-G. ... As performed at the Theatres
      Royal... London, J. Cumberland [n.d.]. 38p. incl. front.

(LEWIS, MATTHEW GREGORY)
    (Cumberland's British theatre. London, ca. 1825-55.
    v. 34 [no. 9]).
        Remarks by George Daniel, editor of the series.
        A dramatization of the author's "The bravo of Venice"
    (translated from Zschokke's "Aballino der grosse Bandit").
    Without the music (by Busby).

1555   _____. Timour the Tartar: a grand romantic melo-drama. In
    two acts, by Matthew Gregory Lewis... Printed from the
    acting copy, with remarks biographical and critical, by
    D.-G. ... As performed at the Theatres Royal... London,
    J. Cumberland [n.d.]. 41p. incl. front. (Cumberland's
    British theatre. London, ca. 1825-55. v. 29 [no. 3]).
    Remarks by George Daniel, editor of the series.

1556   LEWIS, PERCY WYNDHAM, 1884-1957. At the sign of the blue
    moon. London, Andrew Melrose, ltd. [n.d.]. 136p.

1557   LILLE, HUBERT. As like as two peas. A farce, in one act...
    London, Thomas Hailes Lacy [n.d.]. 28p.

1558   LILLIBRIDGE, GARDNER R. Tancred; or, The rightful heir to
    Rochdale castle. A drama, in three acts. Altered from a
    tale of ancient times. By Gardner R. Lillibridge. Provi-
    dence [R. I.] 1824. 68p.

1559   LILLO, GEORGE, 1693-1739. ... George Barnwell. A tragedy,
    in five acts... New York, William Taylor and co. [n.d.].
    36p. (Modern standard drama, no. lxxxviii).

1560   LINCOLN, LOUISE. The twilight of the gods; a one act playlet
    in two scenes. [n.p., n.d.]. 6p. (American Classical
    League Service Bureau, No. 660).

1561   LINDSLEY, A. B. Love and friendship; or, Yankee notions: a
    comedy, in three acts. By A. B. Lindsley. New York,
    Published by D. Longworth, at the Dramatic repository,
    Shakespeare-gallery, 1809. 58p.

1562   LINKLATER, ERIC. The cornerstones, a conversation in Elysium.
    London, Macmillan and co., ltd., 1942. 85p.

1563   _____. The raft and Socrates asks why, two conversations.
    London, Macmillan and co., ltd., 1942. 121p.

LION, KATHLEEN CRIGHTON

1564   LION, KATHLEEN CRIGHTON. The wiles of the widow, a Yorkshire
       comedy in one act... New York and London, Samuel French,
       1911. 24p.

1565   Little brown jug. Boston, Walter H. Baker and co. [n.d.].
       267-332p.

1566   LITTLETON, MARY L. Christopher Columbus, an historical
       spectacle, presenting the most magnificent scenes and
       dramatic events in connection with the discovery of
       America, arranged for presentation during the World's fair
       at Chicago. By M. L. Littleton, Nashville, Tenn. [Nash-
       ville] 1891. 10p., 1ℓ.

1567   LIVIUS, CHARLES BARHAM, d. 1865. Maid or wife; or, The
       deceiver deceived: a musical comedy, in two acts, by
       Barham Livius, esq. The music composed by the author.
       Printed from the acting copy, with remarks, biographical
       and critical, by D.-G. ... As now performed at the
       Theatres Royal... London, J. Cumberland [n.d.]. 34p.
       front. (Cumberland's British theatre. London, ca. 1825-
       55. v. 33 [no. 1]).
           Remarks by George Daniel, editor of the series.
           Without music.
           Reissued in Davidson's shilling volume of Cumberland's
       plays, v. 29 [no. 1].

1568   LLOYD, AUGUSTUS PARTLETT. Cranks' retreat. A comedy-drama,
       in four acts. By A. Parlett Lloyd... Baltimore, O. W.
       Clay and co. (ltd.) 1885. 85p.

1569   LLOYD, S. O. For myself alone. A drama, in three acts. By
       "Marius" [pseud.] New York, The De Witt publishing house,
       1884. 20p.

1570   LOCKE, BELLE MARSHALL. Breezy Point, a comedy in three acts
       for female characters only. Boston, Walter H. Baker co.
       [1898]. 50p.

1571   LOCKE, FRED. Goody two shoes, with lyrics and topical
       allusions by Thos. H. Hardman [n.p., n.d.]. 104p.

1572   _____. Robinson Crusoe, with lyrics and allusions by Thos.
       H. Hardman.[n.p., n.d.]. 100p.

1573   LOCKE, HELEN M. All due to the management, monologue for a
       gentleman. Chicago, The Dramatic publishing co., 1897.
       6p.

1574 LOCKE, NELLIE M. A victim of woman's rights. A monologue. Clyde, Ohio, Ames' publishing co., 1896. 4p.

1575 LODGE, GEORGE CABOT, 1873-1909. Cain; a drama, by George Cabot Lodge. Boston and New York, Houghton, Mifflin and co., 1904. 6 p.ℓ., 154, [2]p.

1576 _____. Herakles, by George Cabot Lodge. Boston and New York, Houghton Mifflin co. [1908]. v, [2], 271, [1]p.

1577 LOGAN, ALGERNON SYDNEY. Messalina, a tragedy in five acts. Philadelphia, J. B. Lippincott co., 1890. 147p.

1578 LONGFELLOW, HENRY WADSWORTH, 1809-1882. Christus, a mystery ... in three parts. Boston, James R. Osgood and co., 1873. 159, 215, 186p. CONTENTS: The divine tragedy. - The golden legend. - The New-England tragedies.

1579 _____. Hiawatha, the Indian passion play. Souvenir program. Longfellow's immortal poem dramatized for Indian players by F. E. Moore... [Middletown, Ohio, The Journal press] 1913. Cover-title, [16]p. illus.

1580 _____. The New-England tragedies, by Henry Wadsworth Longfellow. I. John Endicott. II. Giles Corey of the Salem Farms. Ed. by George Cabot Lodge. Boston, Ticknor and fields, 1868. 179p.

1581 LORD, WILLIAM WILBERFORCE. André, a tragedy in five acts. New York, Charles Scribner, 1856. 138p.

1582 ... Lost in London. A drama, in three acts... Boston, Charles H. Spencer [n.d.]. 22p. (Spencer's universal stage, no. i).

1583 LOTHROP, GEORGE EDWIN, 1869- . Historical, dramatic, and romantic ballads, by George E. Lothrop, Jr. Boston, Mass., 1908. 2v.

1584 LOVELL, GEORGE WILLIAM, 1804-1878. ... Look before you leap; or, Wooings and weddings. A comedy in five acts... New York, William Taylor and co. [n.d.]. 79p. (Modern standard drama, no. xxxiv).

1585 _____. ... Love's sacrifice; or, The rival merchants; a play in five acts. By George Lovell... With the stage directions, cast of characters, and costumes, marked and corrected by J. B. Addis, prompter. First American edition.

LOVELL, GEORGE WILLIAM

    (LOVELL, GEORGE WILLIAM)
    New York, W. Taylor; Baltimore, Taylor, Wilde, and co.,
    1846. 1 p.ℓ., [iv]-v p., 1ℓ., [7]-72p. (Modern standard
    drama, edited by Epes Sargent. [vol. II] no. XII).

1586   _____. The wife's secret. An original play, in five acts.
    Boston, Charles H. Spencer, 1871. 48p.

1587   LOVELL, MARIA. ... Ingomar, the barbarian. A play, in five
    acts... New York, William Taylor and co. [n.d.]. 65p.
    (Modern standard drama, no. lxxxix).

1588   LOVER, SAMUEL, 1797-1868. The happy man. An extravaganza, in
    one act... New York, Samuel French [n.d.]. 17p.

1589   _____. ... The happy man. Founded on the popular drama by
    Samuel Lover... New York, G. Munro [1883]. 21p. (Sea-
    side library, v. 81, no. 1637).

1590   _____. ... Rory O'Moore: a drama in three acts... New York,
    Samuel French [n.d.]. 47p. (French's standard drama,
    no. clxx).

1591   A lover's stratagem. A comedy, in three acts... New York,
    The De Witt publishing house, 1884. 15p.

1592   LUDWIG, OTTO. The hereditary forester. 1914. (In Kuno
    Francke, ed., The German classics of the nineteenth and
    twentieth century [New York, The German publication society,
    1914], v. 9, p. 280-376). Translated by Alfred Remy.

1593   LUNN, JOSEPH, 1784-1863. Fish out of water. A farce, in one
    act... London, Thomas Hailes Lacy [n.d.]. 32p.

1594   _____. Hide and seek: a petite opera, in two acts, by Joseph
    Lunn... Printed from the acting copy, with remarks, bio-
    graphical and critical, by D.-G. ... As now performed at
    the Theatres Royal... London, J. Cumberland [n.d.]. 36p.
    incl. front. (Cumberland's British theatre. London, ca.
    1825-55. v. 12 [no. 2]).
      "Almost a literal translation from the French - except
    the songs." -- Remarks.
      Remarks by George Daniel, editor of the series.

1595   _____. Roses and thorns; or, Two houses under one roof: a
    comedy, in three acts, by Joseph Lunn... Printed from the
    acting copy, with remarks, biographical and critical, by
    D.-G. ... As now performed at the Theatres Royal...

LYTTON, EDWARD GEORGE EARLE LYTTON BULWER-LYTTON

(LUNN, JOSEPH)
London, J. Cumberland [n.d.]. 57p. incl. front. (Cumberland's British theatre. London, ca. 1825-55. v. 12 [no. 5]).
Remarks by George Daniel, editor of the series.

1596 LUPTON, THOMAS, d. 1583. ... All for money, by Thomas Lupton, 1578. [London?] Issued for subscribers by the editor of the Tudor facsimile texts, 1910. 3 p.ℓ., facsim. (1 p.ℓ., [36]p.).

1597 LYNCH, THOMAS J. ... The rose of Ettrick Vale; or, The bridal of the borders. A drama, in two acts... New York, Samuel French [n.d.]. 31p.

1598 LYTTELTON, EDITH. Peter's chance; a play in three acts, by Edith Lyttelton. London, Duckworth and co., 1912. 4 p.ℓ., 74p., 1ℓ.

1599 LYTTON, EDWARD GEORGE EARLE LYTTON BULWER-LYTTON, 1st Baron, 1803-1873. The dramatic works of the Right Hon. Lord Lytton... New ed. London, New York, G. Routledge and sons [1873?]. 4 p.ℓ., [3]-496p. front. (port.). Added t. - p., engraved with vignette. CONTENTS. - The Duchess de la Vallière. - The lady of Lyons; or, Love and pride. - Richelieu; or, The conspiracy. - Money. - Not so bad as we seem; or, Many sides to a character.

1600 _____. The lady of Lyons; or, Love and pride. A play in five acts. New York, S. French [186-]. 59p.

1601 _____. Not as bad as we seem; or, Many sides to a character. A comedy in five acts, by Sir Edward Bulwer Lytton, bart. As first performed at Devonshire House... New York, Harper and bros., 1851. vi, 1ℓ., [9]-166p.

1602 _____. ... Bulwer's drama of Richelieu, as presented by Edwin Booth... New York, Printed for W. Winter, by F. Hart and co., 1878. 1 p.ℓ., 5, [3] p., [9]-92 numb. 1., [93]-104p. ([Booth, Edwin] The prompt-book. Ed. by W. Winter. [v. 4]).
Text of play printed on one side of leaf only.

1603 [_____]. The sea-captain; or, The birthright; a drama in five acts. By the author of "The lady of Lyons," "Richelieu" and c. London, Saunders and Otley, 1839. viii, 112p.

LYTTON, EDWARD GEORGE EARLE LYTTON BULWER-LYTTON

1604   LYTTON, EDWARD GEORGE EARLE LYTTON BULWER-LYTTON. Walpole;
       or, Every man has his price. A comedy in rhyme, in three
       acts... New York, Robert M. De Witt [n.d.]. 33p.

1605   MACAULEY, WARD, 1879-1938. Examination day at Wood Hill School,
       a farcical entertainment in one act, by Ward Macauley...
       Philadelphia, The Penn publishing co., 1911. 31p. diagr.

1606   _____. Graduation day at Wood Hill school; a farcical school
       entertainment in two scenes, by Ward Macauley... Phila-
       delphia, The Penn publishing co., 1909. 34p.

1607   _____. The Wheatville candidates, a rural political play in
       four acts. Philadelphia, The Penn publishing co., 1911.
       64p.

1608   MCAVOY, BALLARD BROWNLEE. Prince Richard [a drama] by Ballard
       Brownlee McAvoy. [Trenton? N. J.] 1902. 97p.

1609   _____. Richard Coeur de Lion [a drama] by Ballard Brownlee
       McAvoy... [Trenton? N. J.] 1903. 103p.

1610   MCBRIDE, H. ELLIOTT. A bad job. A farce, in one act. By H.
       Elliott McBride... Chicago, T. S. Denison, 1878. 1 p.ℓ.,
       p. 51-64. (On cover: School and social drama).

1611   _____. The cow that kicked Chicago, a farce, by H. Elliott
       McBride... Chicago, T. S. Denison, 1882. 10p. On cover:
       School and social drama.

1612   _____. Humorous dialogues. Designed for school exhibitions,
       literary entertainment, and amateur theatricals, by H.
       Elliott McBride... New York, Happy hours co. [1879]. vi,
       7-192p.

1613   _____. I'll stay awhile, a farce, by H. Elliott McBride...
       Chicago, T. S. Denison, 1882. 10p. On cover: School and
       social drama.

1614   _____. Lucy's old man, a farce. Chicago, T. S. Denison and
       co., 1882. 9p.

1615   _____. McBride's all kinds of dialogues. A collection of
       original humorous dialogues. Introducing Yankee, French,
       Irish, Dutch and other characters. Designed for amateur
       performance. By H. Elliott McBride... New York, Dick and
       Fitzgerald [1874]. 180p.

MCBRIDE, H. ELLIOTT

1616   _____. McBride's choice dialogues, containing original and characteristic dialogues for school exhibitions and other amateur juvenile entertainments, by H. Elliott McBride... New York, Dick and Fitzgerald [1893]. 180p.

1617   _____. McBride's funny dialogues: a collection of original humorous dialogues, especially designed for amateur juvenile entertainments and school exhibitions, by H. Elliott McBride... New York, Dick and Fitzgerald [1889]. 178p.

1618   _____. McBride's new dialogues, especially designed for school and literary entertainments. Containing entirely new and original dialogues; introducing Irish, Yankee and other eccentric characters. By H. Elliott McBride... New York, Dick and Fitzgerald [1883]. 178p.

1619   _____. My Jeremiah, a farce, by H. Elliott McBride... Chicago, T. S. Denison, 1882. 12p. On cover: School and social drama.

1620   _____. New temperance dialogue. A boy's rehearsal. By H. Elliott McBride. New York, National temperance society and publication house, 1879. 20p.

1621   _____. Old time humorous dialogues for young people and adults, by H. Elliott McBride... Chicago, A. Flanagan co. [1906]. 127p.

1622   _____. On the brink; or, The reclaimed husband. A temperance drama, in two acts. By H. Elliott McBride... Chicago, T. S. Denison, 1878. 34p. On cover: School and social drama.

1623   _____. Out of the depths, a temperance drama in three acts. New York, Dick and Fitzgerald, 1877. 49-61p.

1624   _____. A parlor entertainment. A sketch for boys and girls, by H. Elliott McBride... Chicago, T. S. Denison, 1878. [5], p. 37-48.

1625   _____. Played and lost, a farce. Chicago, T. S. Denison, 1882. 8p.

1626   _____. Temperance dialogues designed for the use of schools, temperance societies, Bands of hope divisions, lodges, and literary circles. By H. Elliott McBride... New York, Happy hours co. [1877]. vi, 7-183p. CONTENTS. - Acting drunk. - Banishing the bitters. - The poisoned darkys. -

MCBRIDE, H. ELLIOTT

(MCBRIDE, H. ELLIOTT)
A meeting of liquor dealers. - Out of the depths. -
Arresting the march of intemperance. - Maud's command; or,
Yielding to temptation. - A beer drinker's courtship. -
Ralph Coleman's reformation . - Barney's resolution. -
Commencing to work. - A temperance meeting. - The closing
of the "Eagle". - Don't marry a drunkard to reform him. -
Obtaining a promise.

1627 _____. Two drams of brandy. A temperance play. In one act.
By H. Elliott McBride... New York, O. A. Roorbach [1881].
12p.

1628 _____. Under the curse. A temperance drama, in one act. By
H. Elliott McBride... New York, O. A. Roorbach [1881].
8p.

1629 MCCABE, JAMES DABNEY, 1842-1883. The guerrillas: an original
domestic drama, in three acts. By James D. McCabe, Jr.
111 Richmond, Va., West and Johnston, 1863. 44p.

1630 MCCARTHY, JUSTIN HUNTLY, 1860-   . If I were king; a
romantic drama in five acts by Justin Huntly McCarthy; E.
H. Sothern as François Villon; published with the authori-
zation of Daniel Frohman. New York, R. H. Russell, 1901.
16p. illus.
Photographs of Sothern and his company, accompanied by
passages taken from McCarthy's dramatization of his novel
"If I were king."

1631 MCCLELLAND, J. L. Santa Claus, a monologue. Boston, Walter
H. Baker and co., 1901. 11p.

1632 [MCCLINTIC, CHARLES]. Reviewing for examination. Lebanon,
Ohio, March bros. [n.d.]. 6p.

1633 MCCRARY, BEN. Aaron and Theodosia; or, The fate of the Burrs,
a drama in five acts. Salt Lake City, 1902. 69p.

1634 MCDONALD, CAMPBELL. The collapse of the Catilinian Conspiracy. 5p. (American Classical League Service Bureau,
No. 736).

1635 MCFADDEN, ELIZABETH APTHORP, 1875-   . A selected list of
plays for amateurs and students of dramatic expression in
schools and colleges, comp. by Elizabeth A. McFadden and
Lilian E. Davis; with an introduction by Ludella L. Peck...
Cincinnati, E. A. McFadden, 1908. 6p., 2ℓ., 9-100p.

1636   MCFALL, B. G.   Among the moonshiners; or, A drunkard's legacy,
        a temperance drama, in three acts...   Clyde, Ohio, Ames'
        publishing co., 1897.   26p.

1637   MACFARREN, GEORGE, 1788-1843.   Gil Blas; or, The boy of San-
        tillane: a romantic drama, in three acts, by George Mac-
        farren...   Printed from the acting copy, with remarks,
        biographical and critical, by D.-G.   ...   As performed at
        the Theatres Royal...   London, J. Cumberland [n.d.].   50p.
        incl. front.   (Cumberland's British theatre.   London, ca.
        1825-55.   v. 36 [no. 3]).
            Based on Le Sage's novel.
            Remarks by George Daniel, editor of the series.
            Also appeared under title: The boy of Santillane; or,
        Gil Blas and the robbers of Asturias.

1638   _____.   Guy Faux; or, The gunpowder treason: an historical
        melo-drama, in three acts...   London, John Cumberland
        [n.d.].   50p. front.

1639   _____.   Lestocq; or, The fete at the Hermitage: an historical
        opera, in three acts, adapted to the stage from the cele-
        brated piece of M. Scribe, by George Macfarren...   The
        music by M. Auber.   Printed from the acting copy, with
        remarks, biographical and critical, by D.-G.   ...   As per-
        formed at the Theatres Royal...   London, J. Cumberland
        [n.d.].   68p. incl. front.   (Cumberland's British theatre.
        London, ca. 1825-55.   v. 33 [no. 7]).
            Remarks by George Daniel, editor of the series.
            Adapted from Scribe's "Lestocq; ou L'intrigue et
        l'amour."
            Without the music.

1640   _____.   Malvina: an opera, in three acts, by George Macfarren
        ...   The music by Mr. T. Cooke.   Printed from the acting
        copy, with remarks, biographical and critical, by D.-G.
        ...   As performed at the Theatres Royal...   London, J.
        Cumberland [n.d.].   52p. incl. front.   (Cumberland's
        British theatre.   London, ca. 1825-55.   v. 36 [no. 8]).
            Remarks by George Daniel, editor of the series.
            Without the music.

1641   _____.   The march of intellect: a mono-dramatic bagatelle, in
        one act, by George Macfarren...   Printed from the acting
        copy, with remarks, biographical and critical, by D.-G.
        ...   As performed at the metropolitan minor theatres...
        London, J. Cumberland [n.d.].   31p. incl. front.   (Cumber-
        land's Minor theatre.   London [ca. 1830-55] v. 12 [no. 3]).
            Remarks by George Daniel, editor of the series.

MACKAY, CONSTANCE D'ARCY

1642   MACKAY, CONSTANCE D'ARCY. Patriotic plays and pageants for
       young people... New York, Henry Holt and co. [c1912].
       223p.

1643   MACKAY, ETHEL. Philemon and Baucis. [n.p., n.d.]. 6p.
       (American Classical League Service Bureau, No. 368).

1644   MACKAYE, MARY KEITH MEDBERY, "MRS. STEELE MACKAYE," 1845-1924.
       Pride and prejudice; a play, founded on Jane Austen's novel
       by Mrs. Steele MacKaye. New York, Duffield and co., 1906.
       vii p., 3ℓ., 168p. col. front.

1645   MACKAYE, PERCY WALLACE, 1875-1956. Anti-matrimony, a satiri-
       cal comedy. New York, Frederick A. Stokes co., 1910.
       160p.

1646   _____. The Canterbury pilgrims, a comedy. New York, The
       Macmillan co., 1903. 210p.

1647   _____. Fenris, the wolf, a tragedy. New York, The Macmillan
       co., 1905. 150p.

1648   _____. A garland to Sylvia, a dramatic reverie with a pro-
       logue. New York, The Macmillan co., 1910. 177p.

1649   _____. Jeanne d'Arc. New York and London. The Macmillan
       co., 1906. 165p. front.

1650   _____. Mater, an American study in comedy. New York, The
       Macmillan co., 1908. 163p.

1651   _____. Sanctuary, a bird masque... Illustrated with photo-
       graphs in color and monotone by Arnold Genthe. New York,
       Frederick A. Stokes co. [1914]. 71p. illus.

1652   _____. Sappho and Phaon, a tragedy. New York and London,
       The Macmillan co., 1907. 225p. front.

1653   _____. This fine-pretty world; a comedy of the Kentucky
       mountains. New York, Macmillan, 1924. 197p.

1654   _____. Tomorrow, a play in three acts. New York, Frederick
       A. Stokes co. [1912]. 176p.

MACNUTT, FRANCIS A.

1655 _____. Wakefield, a folk-masque of America; being a mid-winter night's dream of the birth of Washington, by Percy MacKaye, with illustration designs by Arvia MacKaye; together with three monographs on the masque written by the author, the illustration-designer, and John Tasker Howard, adapter and composer of the music, designed and written for the United States commission for the celebration of the two-hundredth anniversary of the birth of George Washington 1732-1799. [Washington, D. C., George Washington bicentennial commission, c1932]. 173p. plates.

1656 MACKAYE, STEELE, 1844-1894. Hazel Kirke, a domestic comedy drama in four acts, by Steele MacKaye... [New York] 1908. 95p. incl. front. (port.).

1657 MCKIERNAN, WILLIAM J. The wardrobe of the king, a burlesque, by William J. McKiernan... originally produced by the boy scouts of the first city playground, 1911... New York, Dick and Fitzgerald, 1911. 13p.

1658 MCKINNEL, NORMAN. Dick's sister. London, 1911. 11 p.

1659 MACKLIN, CHARLES, 1697?-1797. Love à la mode: an afterpiece, in two acts; by Charles Macklin... London, Printed by D. S. Maurice [1819?]. 42p. front. [Cabinet theatre. v. 7, no. 6]. Title vignette.
    Owes something to "The lover" of Theophilus Cibber.

1660 MCLACHLAN, CHARLES. ... I dine with my mother. A comedietta, in one act, adapted by Charles McLachlan. As performed at Laura Keene's theatre. To which are added, a description of the costume... and the whole of the stage business... New-York, S. French [1857?]. 15p. (The minor drama, no. 108).
    Adapted from Decourcelle's "Je dine chez ma mère."

1661 MACLEAN, EDA W. The absent-minded suffragette. New York, 1908. 5p.

1662 MACMILLAN, MARY LOUISE. Third book of short plays, by Mary MacMillan. Cincinnati, Stewart Kidd co. [c1922]. 265p.

1663 MACNUTT, FRANCIS A. Three plays; Balboa, Xilona, The victorious duchess, by Francis A. MacNutt. New York, L. J. Gomme, 1916. 3 p.l., 425p.

MACRAE, CHARLES

1664   MACRAE, CHARLES. Abduction, an American romance in five acts.
        New York, MacRae, 1874. Various pagings.

1665   MACREADY, WILLIAM, d. 1829. The Irishman in London: a farce,
        in two acts, by William Macready, esq. Printed from the
        acting copy, with remarks, biographical and critical, by
        D.-G. ... As performed at the Theatres Royal... London,
        J. Cumberland [n.d.]. 31p. front. (Cumberland's British
        theatre. London, ca. 1825-55. v. 22 [no. 1]).
            In part "borrowed from 'The intriguing footman, or The
        humours of Harry Humbug', a piece attributed to James
        Whiteley."--Remarks.
            Remarks by George Daniel, editor of the series.

1666   MACVAY, ANNA PEARL. Mnemosyne and the Muses: a drama in verse.
        Oxford, Ohio, American Classical League Service Bureau,
        Miami University, 1941. iii, 16p.

1667   MADDOX, J. M. The king and deserter. A drama, in two acts...
        New York, Samuel French [n.d.]. 22p.

1668   MAETERLINCK, MAURICE, 1862-1949. Aglavaine and Selysette, a
        drama in five acts, by Maurice Maeterlinck, tr. by Alfred
        Suto, with an introduction by J. W. Mackail. London,
        George Allen, 1904. xxv, 2ℓ., 104p.

1669   _____. Blind. The intruder. Tr. from the French of Maurice
        Maeterlinck, by Mary Vielé. Only authorized translation.
        Washington, D. C., W. H. Morrison, 1891. 3 p.ℓ., [9]-145p.

1670   _____. The blue bird; fairy play in six acts, by Maurice
        Maeterlinck, tr. by Alexander Teixera de Mattos. New York,
        Dodd, Mead and co., 1929. 287p.

1671   _____. Joyzelle, tr. by A. Teixera de Mattos; Monna Vanna,
        tr. by Alfred Sutro... New York, Dodd, Mead and co., 1920.
        3 p.ℓ., 277p.

1672   _____. The miracle of Saint Anthony, trans. by Alexander
        Teixeira de Mattos. London, Methuen and co., ltd. [n.d.].
        77p.

1673   _____. Old fashioned flowers, and other out-of-doors studies,
        by Maurice Maeterlinck; with illustrations by Charles B.
        Falls. New York, Dodd, Mead and co., 1905. 5 p.ℓ., 3-105,
        [1]p. col. front., 5 col. pl.

MAKEE, WALTER

1674   _____. Pelléas and Mélisande; lyric drama in five acts, taken
from the play by Maurice Metterlinck [!] and done into
English by Charles Alfred Byrne. Music by Claude Debussy
... New York, C. E. Burden, 1907. 59p.

1675   _____. ... Pigeons and spiders (The water spider) translated
by Bernard Miall. New York, W. W. Norton and co., inc.
[1936]. 128p.

1676   _____. The plays of Maurice Maeterlinck... tr. by Richard
Hovey. Chicago, Stone and Kimball, 1894-96. 2 v.

1677   MAGGIONI, MANFREDO. Masaniello; a lyric drama, in five acts,
the music by Auber. London, J. Miles and co. [n.d.]. 64p.

1677A   _____. Songs, duets, concerted pieces, and choruses, in
Masaniello; or, The dumb girl of Portici; a grand opera,
in three acts... The music by Auber. Boston, Dutton and
Wentworth, printers, 1833. 12p.

1678   The magpie; or, The maid of Palaiseau. A melo-drama. With
prefatory remarks... faithfully marked with the stage
business, and stage directions, as it is performed at the
Theatres royal. By W. Oxberry, comedian. London, Pub.
for the Proprietors, by W. Simpkin, and R. Marshall [etc.]
1820. 1 p.l., ii, [2], 36p. front. (port.). (Oxberry,
William. The new English drama. London, 1821. v. 11
[no. 1]).
    At head of title: Oxberry's edition.
    Translation and adaptation of the "La pie voleuse, ou
La servante de Palaiseau" of L. C. Caigniez and J. M. T.
Baudoin.
    According to Genest, the adaptation has been attributed
to Thomas Dibdin, but he does not claim it. See his
Reminiscences. London, 1827, v. 2, p. 55, 67.
    Two other adaptations ascribed to S. J. Arnold and
Isaac Pocock appeared about the same time.

1679   MAGUIRE, JOHN. Honesty is the best policy; or, True to the
core. A play, in one act and one scene... New York,
Clinton T. De Witt, 1877. 8p.

1680   MAKEE, WALTER. A scratch race, a comedy in one act. Boston,
Walter H. Baker and co., 1900. 13p.

MALLESON, MILES

1681   MALLESON, MILES. 'D' company and Black 'ell, two plays by
Miles Malleson. London, Hendersons [n.d.]. 64p.

1682   MALTBY, ALFRED. Just my luck, an entirely original farce.
Chicago, T. S. Denison [n.d.]. 12p.

1683   MALTBY, C. A. Borrowed plumes, an original farce. London,
Thomas Hailes Lacy [n.d.]. 16p.

1684   _____. For better or worse. A farce in one act... New York,
Samuel French and son [n.d.]. 12p.

1685   MANKOWITZ, WOLF. Five one-act plays. London, Evans bros.,
ltd. [n.d.]. 72p.

1686   MANNING, KATHRYN. Francesco Carrara, a drama in three acts
from the French by Kathryn Manning. Chicago, The Dramatic
publishing co., 1899. 32p.

1687   MARBLE, THOMAS LITTLEFIELD. The Hessian, a revolutionary
drama in three acts. Philadelphia, The Penn publishing
co., 1910. 34p.

1688   MARCH, GEORGE. Who's the heir? An operetta, in one act...
the music composed by Virginia Gabriel. London, Thomas
Hailes Lacy [n.d.]. 20p.

1689   [MARCH, GEORGE OTIS] 1859-   . With trumpet and drum; a
patriotic compendium, arranged by Archibald Humboldt.
Lebanon, Ohio, March bros. [1911]. 146p.

1690   Marion; or, The page. London, C. Mitchell, 1844. 64p.

1691   MARRIOTT, J. W., ed. The best one-act plays of 1932. London,
George G. Harrap and co., ltd. [n.d.].

1692   _____. ed. One-act plays of today. London, George G.
Harrap and co., ltd. [n.d.]. 278p.

1693   _____. ed. One-act plays of to-day, second series. London,
George G. Harrap and co. [1925]. 266p. illus.

1694   _____. ed. One-act plays of to-day, third series. London,
George G. Harrap and co. [1926]. 253p. illus.

1695   MARRIOTT, WILLIAM, ed.   A collection of English miracle-plays
        or mysteries; containing ten dramas from the Chester,
        Coventry, and Towneley series, with two of latter date.
        To which is prefixed, An historical view of this descrip-
        tion of plays. By William Marriott, Ph.Dr. Basel, Schweig-
        hauser and co.; [etc., etc.] 1838. lxiii, 271p. CONTENTS:
        Historical view of English miracle-plays or mysteries. -
        Chester miracle-plays: The deluge. Antichrist. - Coventry
        miracle plays: Joseph's jealousy. The trial of Mary and
        Joseph. The pageant of the company of shearman and
        tailors. - Towneley miracle plays: Pharao. Pastores.
        Crucifixio. Extractio animarum ab inferno. Juditium. -
        Candlemas-day; or, The killing of the children of Israel.
        - God's promises. - Glossary.

1696   MARSHALL, R.   His excellency the governor, a farcical romance
        in three acts. Boston, Walter H. Baker and co. [1901].
        152p.

1697   _____.   Shades of night, a fantasy in one act.   New York and
        London, Samuel French [n.d.]. 20p.

1698   MARSTON, JOHN WESTLAND, 1819-1890.   The dramatic and poetical
        works of Westland Marston... Collective ed. London,
        Chatto and Windus, 1876. 2 v. CONTENTS. - v. 1.
        Strathmore. Marie de Méranie. Life for life. A life's
        ransom. The patrician's daughter. Anne Blake. - v. 2.
        Donna Diana. The favourite of fortune. Pure gold. The
        wife's portrait. A hard struggle. Borough politics.
        Dramatic scenes and fragments. Sonnets. General poems.

1699   MARTIN, W. H.   Servants vs. master; or, A father's will, a
        comedy drama, in three acts. Clyde, Ohio, Ames' publishing
        go., 1898. 23p.

1700   MARTIN, WILLIAM.   Chang-Ching-Fou! Cream of Tartar; or, the
        prince, the princess, and the mandarin. An original
        Chinese burlesque extravaganza... London, Thomas Hailes
        Lacy [n.d.]. 24p.

1701   MARTYN, EDWARD, 1859-1924.   The heather field, a play in three
        acts. London, Duckworth and co.; New York, Brentano's,
        1917. 92p.

1702   MASEFIELD, JOHN, 1878-1967.   Mrs. Gorringe's necklace, a play
        in four acts. Boston, Walter H. Baker and co.; London,
        William Heinemann, 1910. 176p.

MASEFIELD, JOHN

1703   MASEFIELD, JOHN. The tragedy of Nan, and other plays. New
        York, Mitchell Kennerley, 1910. 114p.

1704   _____. The tragedy of Pompey the Great. New York, The Mac-
        millan co., 1914. 138p.

1705   MASSINGER, PHILIP. ... A new way to pay old debts. A comedy
        in five acts... New York, Wm. Taylor and co. [n.d.].
        75p. (Modern standard drama, no. xxxiii).

1706   MASTERS, EDGAR LEE, 1868-1950. The bread of idleness; a play
        in four acts, by Edgar Lee Masters... Chicago, The Rooks
        press, 1911. 173p.

1707   _____. Eileen; a play in three acts, by Edgar Lee Masters...
        Chicago, The Rooks press, 1910. 84p.

1708   _____. The locket; a play in three acts, by Edgar Lee Masters
        ... Chicago, The Rooks press, 1910. 110p.

1709   _____. Maximilian; a play in five acts, by Edgar Lee Masters.
        Boston, R. C. Badger, 1902. 154p.

1710   _____. The trifler, a play, by Edgar Lee Masters... Chicago,
        The Rooks press, 1908. 131p.

1711   MATHER, MABEL J. Latin is practical. [n.p., n.d.]. 4p.
        (American Classical League Service Bureau, No. 579).

1712   MATHEWS, CHARLES. The adventures of a love letter; a comedy,
        in two acts. New York, Samuel French [n.d.]. 48p.

1713   _____. ... The bachelor's bedroom; or, Two in the morning.
        A comic scene. Boston, William V. Spencer, 1855. 21p.
        (The Boston theatre, no. iv).

1714   _____. ... Used up. A petit comedy, in two acts... New York,
        Samuel French [n.d.]. 38p. (The minor drama, no. vi).

1715   _____. ... Who killed Cock Robin? A farce, in two acts...
        New York, Samuel French [n.d.]. 34p. (French's minor
        drama, no. ccxcviii).

1716   _____. Why did you die? A petite comedy, in one act... New
        York, Harold Roorbach [n.d.]. 33p.

1717   MATHEWS, CORNELIUS, 1817-1889. The politicians: a comedy, in
        five acts. By Cornelius Mathews... New York, B. G.
        Trevett [etc.] 1840. 118p.

1718   _____. Witchcraft: a tragedy, in five acts. By Cornelius
        Mathews. New York, S. French, 1852. 3 p.ℓ., [9]-99p.

1719   MATHEWS, FRANCES AYMAR. Teacups, comedy for three males and
        two females. New York, Edgar S. Werner and co., 1889.
        13p.

1720   MATTHEWS, BOB E. Absinthe, dramatic conception. New York,
        1910. [7]p.

1721   MATTHEWS, JAMES BRANDER, 1852-1929, ed. The chief European
        dramatists. Twenty-one plays from the drama of Greece,
        Rome, Spain, France, Italy, Germany, Denmark and Norway
        from 500 B.C. to 1879 A.D. Selected and edited, with notes,
        biographies, and bibliographies... Boston [etc.] Houghton
        Mifflin [1916]. xi, 786p. CONTENTS. Aeschylus, Agamemnon,
        tr. by E. D. A. Morshead. - Sophocles, Oedipus the king,
        tr. By Sir Richard Claverhouse Jebb. - Euripides, Medea,
        tr. by Gilbert Murray. - Aristophanes, The frogs, tr. by
        J. Hookham Frere. - Plautus, The captives, tr. by Edward
        H. Sugden. - Terence, Phormio, tr. by Morris H. Morgan. -
        Lope de Vega, The star of Seville, tr. by Philip M. Hayden.
        - Calderon, Life is a dream, tr. by Denis Florence MacCarthy.
        - Corneille, The Cid, tr. by Florence Kendrick Cooper. -
        Molière, Tartuffe, tr. by Curtis Hidden Page. - Racine,
        Phaedra, tr. by Robert Bruce Boswell. - Beaumarchais, The
        barber of Seville, tr. by Arthur B. Myrick. - Hugo, Hernani,
        tr. by Mrs. Newton Crosland. Augier and Sandeau, the son-in-
        law of M. Poirier, tr. by Barrett H. Clark. - Dumas fils,
        The outer edge of society, tr. by Barrett H. Clark. -
        Goldoni, The mistress of the inn, tr. by Merle Pierson. -
        Lessing, Minna von Barnhelm, tr. by Ernest Bell. - Goethe,
        Goetz von Berlichingen, tr. by Sir Walter Scott. - Schiller,
        William Tell, tr. by Sir Theodore Martin. - Holberg,
        Rasmus Montanus, tr. by Oscar James Campbell and Frederic
        Schenck. - Ibsen, A doll's house, tr. by William Archer.

1722   _____. ed. ... Comedies for amateur acting. Ed., with a
        prefatory note on private theatricals, by J. Brander
        Matthews. New York, D. Appleton and co., 1880. 245p.
        (Appletons' new handy-volume series. [no. 46].).
            Arthur Penn, pseud. of James Brander Matthews.
            CONTENTS. - A trumped suit, by J. Magnus [from Les
        deux timides, by M. E. Labiche. - A bad case, by J. Magnus

MATTHEWS, JAMES BRANDER

(MATTHEWS, JAMES BRANDER)
and H. C. Bunner. - Courtship with variations, by H. C.
Bunner [from Le monde renversé, by M. H. de Bornier] - A
teacher taught, by A. H. Oakes [from Le Roman d'une pupille,
by M. P. Ferrier] - Heredity, by A. Penn [from La postérité
d'un bourgmestre, by M. M. Uchard] - Frank Wylde, by M. B.
Matthews [from Le serment d'Horace, by M. H. Mürger].

1723   _____. The decision of the court; a comedy, by Brander
Matthews... New York, Harper and bros., 1893. 4 p.ℓ.,
[11]-60p. front., 2 pl., port. (On cover: Harper's black
and white series).

1724   _____. This picture and that; a comedy, by Brander Matthews...
New York, Harper and bros., 1899. 4 p.ℓ., [11]-76, [1]p.
front., 2 pl.

1725   MATURIN, CHARLES ROBERT, 1789-1824. Bertram: a tragedy, in
five acts, by The Rev. R. C. Maturin. Printed from the
acting copy, with remarks, biographical and critical, by
D.-G. ... As performed at the Theatres Royal... London,
G. H. Davidson [n.d.]. 51p. incl. front. (Cumberland's
British theatre. London, ca. 1825-55. v. 43 [no. 8].
Remarks by George Daniel, editor of the series.
Reissue of Cumberland's earlier edition.

1726   [_____]. Manuel; a tragedy, in five acts. As performed at
the Theatre Royal, Drury-Lame. By the author of Bertram.
New-York, Published by David Longworth, at the Dramatic
repository, Shakespeare-gallery. May--1817. 64p.

1727   MAY, GORDAN V. Bar Haven, a comedy drama in three acts.
Boston, Walter H. Baker and co. [1906]. 47p.

1728   MAYHEW, AUGUSTUS. The goose with the golden eggs, by August
Mayhew and Sutherland Edwards. A farce, in one act...
as first performed... September 1, 1859... New York,
Robert M. De Witt [n.d.]. 17p.

1729   MAYHEW, EDWARD, 1813-1868. Make your wills. A farce, in one
act, by Edward Mayhew and G. Smith. Printed from the
acting copy, with remarks, biographical and critical, by
D.-G. ... As performed at the Theatres Royal... London,
J. Cumberland [n.d.]. 29p. incl. front. (Cumberland's
British theatre. London, ca. 1825-55. v. 35 [no. 9]).
Remarks by George Daniel, editor of the series.

1730   _____. ... Make your wills! A farce, in one act, by E. Mayhew and G. Smith... New York, Samuel French [n.d.]. 29p. (The minor drama, no. cxxiv).

1731   MAYHEW, HENRY, 1812-1887. "But however--" A farce, in one act, by Henry Mayhew and Henry Baylis. London, Chapman and Hall [n.d.]. 24p. front.

1732   _____. ... The wandering minstrel. A farce, in one act... Boston, William V. Spencer [n.d.]. 19p.

1733   No Entry.

1734   No Entry.

1735   MEDINA, LOUISA. ... Ernest Maltravels. A drama, in three acts... New York, Samuel French [n.d.]. 37p. (French's standard drama, no. cxliii).

1736   MEDWALL, HENRY, fl. 1486. ... Fulgens and Lucres, by Henry Medwall: from the unique copy in the Henry E. Huntington library, with an introductory note by Seymour De Ricci. New York, G. D. Smith, 1920. 15p., facsim. 1ℓ., [76]p.

1737   _____. ... Nature, by Henry Medwall [c. 1486-1500] London, W. C. and Edinburg, Issued for subscribers by T. C. and E. C. Jack, 1908. viii p., facsim: [71]p., 1ℓ., [4]p.

1738   MEILHAC, HENRI, 1831-1897. The bachelor's box. (Le petit hôtel.) A comedietta in one act. Tr. from the French of Messrs. Meilhac and Halévy. By Henry L. Williams... New York, Pub. for the trade, 1880. 18p.

1739   _____. La cigale. A comedy, in three acts, tr. from the French of Henry Meilhac and Ludovic Halévy... Adapted for the American stage by John H. Delafield... New York, Happy hours co. [1879]. viii, [9]-72p.

1740   _____. A cigarette from Java. Comedy in one act. Tr. from the French of Messrs. Meilhac and Narrey, by T. R. Sullivan. Boston, 1879. 21p.

1741   _____. Frou-Frou. A comedy in five acts. By Meilhac and Halévy... New York, F. Rullmann [1880]. 49p. front.

MEILHAC, HENRI

1742   MEILHAC, HENRI. ... The widow. A comedy, in three acts. By
       Henry Meilhac and Ludovic Halévy. Tr. and adapted from the
       original by Harriet Hubbard Ayer... New York, C. T. De Witt
       [1877]. 29p.

1743   MERINGTON, MARGUERITE. Captain Lettarblair; a comedy in three
       acts written for E. H. Sothern, by Marguerite Merington;
       arranged from the prompt-book used in the original Lyceum
       production; illustrated with photographs of the play.
       Indianapolis, The Bobbs-Merrill co. [1906]. 9 p.ℓ., 212p.
       front. 18 pl.

1744   _____. Cranford; a play; a comedy in three acts made from
       Mrs. Gaskell's famous story, by Marguerite Merington...
       New York, Fox, Duffield and co., 1905. [7], 90p. col.
       front.

1745   _____. Daphne; or, The pipes of Arcadia. Three acts of
       singing nonsense, by Marguerite Merington. New York, The
       Century co., 1896. 5 p.ℓ., 166p. 5 pl. (incl. front.).

1746   _____. Festival plays; one-act pieces for New Year's day,
       St. Valentine's day, Easter, All Hallowe'en, Christmas and
       a child's birthday, by Marguerite Merington. New York,
       Duffield and co., 1913. 6 p.ℓ., 9-302p. front. plates.
       CONTENTS. - Father Time and his children (New Year's day).
       - Tertulia's garden; or, The miracle of good St. Valentine
       (Valentine's day). - The seven sleepers of Ephesos (Easter).
       - Princess Moss Rose (for every child's birthday). - The
       testing of Sir Gawayne (Hallowe'en). - A Christmas party
       (Christmas).

1747   MERIVALE, HERMAN CHARLES, 1839-1906. The lord of the manor.
       A drama in three acts. Written by Herman Merivale, and
       founded upon Goethe's Wilhelm Meister. Kingston-on-Thames,
       G. Phillipson, printer, 1879. 54p.

1748   _____. ... The queen's proctor. A comedy, in three acts.
       By Herman Merivale. (Adapted from "Divorçons" by Victorien
       Sardou and E. de Najac.) London, Printed at the Chiswick
       press, 1896. 2 p.ℓ., 89, [1] p.
       "Privately printed and not for circulation."

1749   _____. A son of the soil. A romantic play, in three acts...
       New York, Samuel French and son [n.d.]. 48p.

1750   _____. The white pilgrim. A romantic play, in four acts. Written by Herman Merivale. The story by Gilbert. A. Beckett. London, Nassau steam press, 1874. 48p.

1751   MERRIMAN, EFFIE WOODWARD, 1857-   . Comedies for children, by Effie W. Merriman... A collection of one-act plays written for presentation in the home or school-room, by the children of the family and their friends... Chicago, The Dramatic publishing co., 1898. 100p.

1752   _____. A pair of artists, a comedy in three acts. Chicago, The Dramatic publishing co., 1892. 48p.

1753   _____. Their first meeting, a comedietta in one act. Chicago, The Dramatic publishing co., 1899. 10p.

1754   MEYER, ANNIE NATHAN. The dominant sex, a play in three acts. New York, Brandu's, 1911. 112p.

1755   MEYERS, ROBERT CORNELIUS V., 1858-1917. A forced friendship; a farce in one act, by Robert C. V. Meyers... Philadelphia, The Penn publishing co., 1903. 12p.

1756   _____. A lady's note, a farce in one act. Philadelphia, The Penn publishing co., 1905. 13p.

1757   _____. Monsieur, a farce in two acts. Philadelphia, The Penn publishing co., 1902. 23p.

1758   _____. On account of the lobster; a farce in one act, by Robert C. V. Meyers... Philadelphia, The Penn publishing co., 1903. 15p.

1759   MIDDLETON, EDGAR. Banned by the censor. London, T. Werner Laurie, ltd., 1929. 126p.

1760   MIDDLETON, GEORGE, 1880-   . Masks, with Jim's beast, Tides, Among the lions, The reason, The house; one-act plays of contemporary life, by George Middleton... New York, H. Holt and co., 1920. 227p.

1761   _____. Nowadays; a contemporaneous comedy, by George Middleton... New York, H. Holt and co., 1914. v, 218p.

1762   _____. Possession, with The groove, The unborn, Circles, A good woman, The black tie; one-act plays of contemporary life, by George Middleton... New York, H. Holt and co., 1915. ix, 1ℓ., 217p.

179

MIDDLETON, GEORGE

1763   MIDDLETON, GEORGE. Tradition, with On bail, Their wife,
       Waiting, The cheat of pity, and Mother; one-act plays of
       contemporary life, by George Middleton... New York, H.
       Holt and co., 1913. 5 p.ℓ., 3-173p.

1764   MILES, GEORGE HENRY, 1824-1871. ... Mary's birthday; or, The
       cynic. A play, in three acts... Boston, William V.
       Spencer, 1858. 36p. (Spencer's Boston theatre, no. ccii).

1765   _____. Mohammed, the Arabian prophet. A tragedy, in five
       acts. By George H. Miles. Boston, Phillips, Sampson and
       co., 1850. viii p., 2ℓ., 166p., 1ℓ.

1766   MILLER, CHESTER GORE. Chihuahua, a new and original social
       drama in four acts. Chicago, Kehm, Fietsch and Wilson co.,
       1891. 95p.

1767   _____. Father Junipero Serra, a new and original historical
       drama, in four acts. By Chester Gore Miller... Chicago,
       Press of Skeen, Baker and co., 1894. 160p. 1ℓ., front.
       (port.) illus. (incl. port.).

1768   MILLER, JOAQUIN, 1841-1913. The Danites in the Sierras (in
       four acts) by Joaquin Miller. San Francisco, Whitaker
       and Ray-Wiggin co., 1910. 1 p.ℓ., 62p.

1769   _____. Forty-nine; an idyl drama of the Sierras (in four
       acts) by Joaquin Miller. San Francisco, Whitaker and
       Ray-Wiggin co., 1910. 1 p.ℓ., p. [63]-120.

1770   _____. The silent man; a comedy-drama, in four acts. By
       Joaquin Miller... [New York] 1888. 61p.

1771   _____. The silent man; a comedy-drama, in four acts. By
       Joaquin Miller... [New York] 1883. 61p.

1772   MILLET. All at C; or, The captive, the coffee and the cocoa-
       tina. An original modern musical melodrama, by Major
       Millet and Lieutenant Wilcox. New York, Samuel French and
       son [n.d.]. 18p.

1773   MILMAN, HENRY HART, 1791-1868. Belshazzar: a dramatic poem.
       By the Rev. H. H. Milman... Boston, Wells and Lilly, 1822.
       iv, [5]-125, [1]p.

1774   _____. The fall of Jerusalem, a dramatic poem by the Rev.
       H. H. Milman. New ed. London, J. Murray, 1820. vii, 167,
       [1] p.

MILNER, HENRY M.

1775   _____. Fazio; or, The Italian wife. A tragedy, in five acts.
          By H. H. Milman... Baltimore, J. Robinson, Circulating
          library, 1833. 59p.
             First acted under the title: The Italian wife.

1776   _____. The martyr of Antioch: a dramatic poem. By the Rev.
          H. H. Milman... New York, Printed for the booksellers, W.
          Grattan, printer, 1822. vii, [1]p., 1ℓ., [11]-108p.
          [With his Samor, lord of the bright city... New York,
          1818].

1777   MILNE, ALAN ALEXANDER, 1882-1956. Four plays. Harmondsworth,
          Penguin Books, ltd. [n.d.]. 254p. CONTENTS. To have the
          honour. - Belinda. - The Dover road. - Mr. Pim passes by.

1778   MILNER, HENRY M. ... The gambler's fate; or, Thirty years in
          a gamester's life. A drama, in two acts... New York,
          Samuel French [n.d.]. 37p. (French's standard drama, no.
          cxcii).

1779   _____. Gustavus the Third; or, The masked ball! An historical
          drama, in three acts... Baltimore, Jos. Robinson, 1834.
          36p.

1780   _____. Masaniello; or, The dumb girl of Portici: a musical
          drama, in three acts, by H. M. Milner, esq. Printed from
          the acting copy, with remarks, biographical and critical,
          by D.-G. ... As performed at the metropolitan minor
          theatres... London, Davidson [n.d.]. 40p. incl. front.
          (Cumberland's Minor theatre. London [ca. 1820-55] v. 1
          [no. 9]).
             Founded on M. Auber's opera La muette de Portici. Cf
          Remarks by George Daniel, editor of the series.
             Without the music.

1781   _____. Mazeppa: a romantic drama, in three acts, dramatized
          from Lord Byron's poem, by H. M. Milner, and adapted to
          the stage under the direction of Mr. Ducrow. Printed
          from the acting copy, with remarks, biographical and
          critical, by D.-G. ... As performed at the Royal amphi-
          theatre, Westminster... London, J. Cumberland [n.d.].
          52p. incl. front. (Cumberland's Minor theatre. London
          [ca. 1830-55] v. 5 [no. 2]).
             Remarks by George Daniel, editor of the series.

1782   _____. The temple of death. A melodrama, in three acts...
          London, Thomas Hailes Lacy [n.d.]. 45p.

MINSHULL, JOHN

1783   MINSHULL, JOHN. A comedy, entitled The sprightly widow, with
        the frolics of youth; or a speedy way of uniting the
        sexes, by honorable marriage. By John Minshull... New
        York, The author, 1803. vi, [5], 12-64p.

1784   _____. A comic opera, entitled Rural felicity: with the humour
        of Patrick, and marriage of Shelty. By John Minshull...
        New York, Printed for the author, 1801. viii, [2], [11]-
        68p., 1ℓ., [4]p. front. (port.).

1785   _____. He stoops to conquer; or, The virgin wife triumphant;
        a comedy in three acts. By John Minshull... New York,
        Printed for the author, by G. and R. Waite, no. 64, and
        no. 38, Maiden-Lane, 1804. 33, [1]p.

1786   MITCHELL, EDMUND, 1861-1917. The outlaw of El Tejón, a tale
        of California; film drama in six parts, by Edmund Mitchell
        from a novel by Willis George Emerson... Los Angeles,
        California, Times-Mirror printing and binding house, 1914.
        58p.

1787   _____. The redemption of Bill Gunther; or, Making Bill an
        elk; film drama in four parts, story by Willis George
        Emerson, dramatized by Edmund Mitchell... Los Angeles,
        California, Times-Mirror printing and binding house, 1914.
        28p., 1ℓ.

1788   _____. The treasure of Hidden valley, a tale of Wyoming;
        film drama in five parts, by Edmund Mitchell from a novel
        by Willis George Emerson. Los Angeles, California, Times-
        Mirror printing and binding house, 1914. 56p.

1789   MITCHELL, LANGDON ELWYN. In the season, a one act comedy.
        London and New York, Samuel French [n.d.]. 17p.

1790   MITCHELL, WILLIAM LOUIS. The conscript, a play in six acts.
        by W. L. Mitchell. Chicago [1877]. Cover-title, 1 p.ℓ.,
        27p.

1791   MITFORD, MARY RUSSELL, 1787-1855. The dramatic works of Mary
        Russell Mitford... London, Hurst and Blackett, 1854. 2 v.
        fronts. (v. 1: port.) pl. CONTENTS. - v. 1. Introduction.
        Rienzi Foscari. Julian. Charles I. - v. 2. Sadak and
        Kalasrade. Inez de Castro. Gaston de Blondeville. Otto
        of Wittelsbach. Dramatic scenes: Cunigunda's vow. The
        fawn. The wedding ring. Emily. The painter's daughter.
        Fair Rosamond. Alice Henry Talbot. The siege. The
        captive. The masque of the seasons.

MÖLLER, EBERHARD WOLFGANG

1792   The model house. A comedy, in five acts. Albany, New York,
C. Van Benthuysen and sons, 1868. 110p.

1793   Modern one-act plays. Harmondsworth, Penguin Books, ltd.
[n.d.]. 151p. CONTENTS. J. B. Fagan, Doctor O'Toole. –
Evan John, The king's march. – Arthur Watkyn, "Wanted–Mr.
Stuart". – Mabel Constanduros and Howard Agg, The lady from
abroad. – Alfred Sangster, Boney. – J. A. Ferguson, Such
stuff as dreams. – Michael Redgrave, The seventh man.

1794   [Molière, Jean Baptiste Poquelin] 1622-1673. The cheats of
Scapin; a comedy, in three acts. By Thomas Otway. (In the
London Stage. London [1823-27] v. 4, no. 26, 10p. 1 illus.).

1795   _____. The miser; a comedy in three acts. (For male characters only). Tr. and adapted from the French of Molière.
By Joseph A. Lyons, A.M. Notre Dame, Indiana, 1886. 36p.

1796   _____. The miser; a comedy in three acts. (For male charac-
ters only). Tr. and adapted from the French of Molière.
By Joseph A. Lyons, A.M. Notre Dame, Indiana, 1886. 36p.
Variant.

1797   [_____]. The mock doctor; or, The dumb lady cured. A comedy,
in two acts. As performed at the Theatre-Royal, Drury-
Lane. By Henry Fielding, esq. (In Inchbald, Mrs. Elizabeth. A collection of farces... London, 1815. v. 5, p.
[73]-106).

1798   _____. The mock doctor; or, The dumb lady cur'd. A comedy.
Done from Molière. As it is acted at the Theatre Royal in
Drury-Lane. By His Majesty's servants. With the musick
prefix'd to each song. A new ed. With additional songs
and alterations. London, A. Millar, 1761. 3 p.ℓ., 33,
[1]p.

1799   _____. Tartuffe; or, The imposter. A comedy in five acts.
By Molière... New York, F. Rullman [1888]. 43p.

1800   _____. Tartuffe; or, The French puritan. A comedy, acted at
the Theatre-Royal. Written in French by Molière, and
render'd into English, with much addition and advantage,
by M. Medbourne... London, Printed for R. Wellington,
1707. 3 p.ℓ., 65, [1]p.

1801   MÖLLER, EBERHARD WOLFGANG. Douaumont; or, The return of the
soldier Ulysses, by Eberhard Wolfgang Mueller; English
version by Graham and Tristan Rawson. London, V. Gollancz
ltd., 1930. 96p.

MONCRIEFF, W. J.

1802   MONCRIEFF, W. J. The scamps of London; or, The cross roads of
        life! A drama of the day... London, Thomas Hailes Lacy
        [n.d.]. 45p.

1803   MONCRIEFF, WILLIAM THOMAS, 1794-1857. All at Coventry; or,
        Love and laugh: a musical farce, in two acts, by W. T.
        Moncrieff... Printed from the acting copy, with remarks,
        biographical and critical, by D.-G. ... As performed at
        the Theatres Royal... London, G. H. Davidson [n.d.]. 44p.
        incl. front. (Cumberland's British theatre. London, ca.
        1825-55. v. 33 [no. 4]).
            Remarks by George Daniel, editor of the series.
            Without the music.

1804   _____. The bashful man; a comic drama. By W. T. Moncrieff.
        (In The London stage. London [1824-27] v. 4 [no. 21]. 12p.,
        1 illus.). Caption-title.

1805   _____. The cataract of the Ganges; or, The Rajah's daughter:
        a grand romantic drama, in two acts, by W. T. Moncrieff...
        Printed from the acting copy, with remarks, biographical
        and critical, by D.-G. ... As performed at the Theatres
        Royal... London, J. Cumberland [n.d.]. 41p. incl. front.
        (Cumberland's British theatre. London, ca. 1825-55, v. 33
        [no. 8]).
            Remarks by George Daniel, editor of the series.

1806   _____. Eugene Aram; or, Saint Robert's cave: a drama, in
        three acts, by W. T. Moncrieff... Printed from the
        acting copy, with remarks, biographical and critical, by
        D.-G. ... As performed at the Theatres Royal... London,
        Davidson [n.d.]. 7, [1], [11]-68p. incl. front. (Cumber-
        land's Minor theatre. London [ca. 1830-55] v. 10 [no. 4]).
            Founded on the romance by Edward, Lord Bulwer-Lytton.
            Remarks by George Daniel, editor of the series.

1807   _____. Giovanni, in London; or, The libertine reclaimed. An
        operatic extravaganza, in two acts, by W. T. Moncieff [!]
        ... Printed from the acting copy, with remarks, biographi-
        cal and critical, by D.-G. ... As performed at the Theatres
        Royal... London, J. Cumberland [n.d.]. 47p. incl. front.
        (Cumberland's British theatre. London, ca. 1825-55, v. 17
        [no. 5]).
            Remarks by George Daniel, editor of the series.
            Without the music.

MONCRIEFF, WILLIAM THOMAS

1808 _____. ... The Jewess; or, The council of Constance. An
historical drama, in three acts. By W. T. Moncrieff...
As performed at the London and New-York theatres... New-
York, O. Phelan [ca. 1840]. 62p.
    At head of title: Phelan's edition.
    Based on Scribe's opera, "La juive."

1809 _____. Joconde; or, The festival of the Rosiere: a musical
comedy, in three acts, by W. T. Moncrieff... Printed from
the acting copy, with remarks, biographical and critical,
by D.-G. ... As performed at the metropolitan minor
theatres... London, J. Cumberland [n.d.]. 48p. incl.
front. (Cumberland's minor theatre. London [ca. 1830-55]
v. 12 [no. 4]).
    Borrowed in part from M. Étienne's comic opera "Joconde,
ou Les coureurs d'aventures." Cf. Remarks by George Daniel,
editor of the series.
    Without music.

1810 _____. Monsieur Tonson: a farce, in two acts, by W. T. Moncrieff... Printed from the acting copy, with remarks,
biographical and critical, by D.-G. ... As now performed
at the Theatres Royal... London, J. Cumberland [n.d.].
40p. front. (Cumberland's British theatre. London, ca.
1825-55. v. 16 [no. 1]).
    Remarks by George Daniel, editor of the series.
    "Founded on the well-known poetical tale," by John
Taylor. Cf. Remarks.
    Reissued in Davidson's shilling volume of Cumberland's
plays, v. 20 [no. 1].

1811 _____. Monsieur Tonson. A farce, in two acts. By William
T. Moncrieff... As performed at the Theatre-royal, Drury-
lane. New York, E. M. Murden, 1822. 42p.
    Founded on the poetical tale by John Taylor.

1812 _____. ... The party wall; or, In and out! A comic interlude, in one act; altered from the German of Kotzebue's
"Gefährliche Nachbarshaft." By W. T. Moncrieff... The
only edition correctly marked from the prompter's book...
Printed from Duncombe's London edition. As performed at
the London theatres. New-York, E. B. Clayton; Philadelphia, C. Neal, [ca. 1842] 24p.
    At head of title: Clayton's edition.

MONCRIEFF, WILLIAM THOMAS

1813   MONCRIEFF, WILLIAM THOMAS. Rochester; or, King Charles the
Second's merry days: a burletta, in three acts. As performed at the Olympic new theatre... Written by William
Thomas Moncrieff... London, J. Lowndes, 1819. 2 p.ℓ.,
63p.

1814   _____. Sam Weller; or, The Pickwickians. A drama, in three
acts... By W. T. Moncrieff... London [T. Stagg, printer]
1837. viii, 153, iii p.
    "Founded on the... 'Posthumous papers of the Pickwick
club,' written by Mr. Dickens."--Advertisement.

1815   [_____]. The secret; or, The hole in the wall. A farce in
one act... New York, W. Taylor and co. [1854?]. 3 p.ℓ.,
[5]-22p. (The Minor drama. no. xvii).

1816   _____. The somnambulist; or, The phantom of the village. A
dramatic entertainment, in two acts, by W. T. Moncrieff...
Printed from the acting copy, with remarks, biographical
and critical, by D.-G. ... As performed at the Theatres
Royal... London, J. Cumberland [n.d.]. 40p. incl. front.
(Cumberland's British theatre. London, ca. 1825-55.
v. 18 [no.6]).
    Remarks by George Daniel, editor of the series.
    Founded on the ballet "La somnambule," by Scribe and
Aumer. Cf. Remarks.

1817   _____. The spectre bridegroom; or, A ghost in spite of himself: a farce, in two acts, by W. T. Moncrieff... Printed
from the acting copy, with remarks, biographical and
critical, by D.-G. ... As performed at the Theatres
Royal... London, G. H. Davidson [n.d.]. 32p. incl. front.
(Cumberland's British theatre. London, ca. 1825-55.
v. 16 [no. 3]).
    "Founded on a story in the Sketch book, which Mr. Irving
himself borrowed from the French."--Remarks.
    Remarks by George Daniel, editor of the series.

1818   _____. Tom and Jerry; or, Life in London: an operatic extravaganza, in three acts, by W. T. Moncrieff... Printed from
the acting copy, with remarks, biographical and critical,
by D.-G. ... As performed at the Theatres Royal... London, J. Cumberland [n.d.]. 72p. incl. front. (Cumberland's British theatre. London, ca. 1825-55. v. 33
[no. 5]).
    Remarks by George Daniel, editor of the series.
    Founded on Pierce Egan's "Life in London."
    Without the music.

1819   _____. Wanted a wife; or, A checque on my banker, a comedy,
        in five acts: as performed at the Theatre Royal, Drury
        Lane... By W. T. Moncrieff, esq. London, J. Lowndes,
        1819. vi, [2], 68p.

1820   MONROE, HARRIET, 1860-1938. The passing show; five modern
        plays in verse, by Harriet Monroe. Boston and New York,
        Houghton, Mifflin and co., 1903. 4 p.ℓ., 125 [1]p.
        CONTENTS. - The thunderstorm. - At the goal. - After all.
        A modern minuet. - It passes by.

1821   Monte Cristo. A drama, in five acts. New York, Samuel French
        and son [n.d.]. 79p.

1822   MONTENEGRO, CARLOTA. Alcestis, a drama. Boston, The poet
        lore co., 1909. 110p.

1823   MOODY, WILLIAM VAUGHN, 1869-1910. The faith healer, a play in
        three acts, by William Vaughn Moody... New York, The Mac-
        millan co., 1910. 4 p.ℓ., 3-164p.

1824   _____. The fire-bringer, by William Moody, Boston and New
        York, Houghton, Mifflin and co., 1904. 4 p.ℓ., 107, [1]p.

1825   MOORE, BERNARD FRANCIS. Ferguson, of Troy; a farce comedy in
        three acts, by Bernard Francis Moore... Boston, W. H.
        Baker and co., 1900. 50p. (On cover: Baker's edition of
        plays).

1826   _____. The government detective, a play in four acts. Boston,
        Walter H. Baker and co., 1910. 51p.

1827   _____. The haunted mill; or, Con O'Ragen's secret. An Irish
        drama in three acts. By Bernard F. Moore. To which is
        added a description of the costumes, cast of the charac-
        ters... and the whole of the stage business... Clyde,
        Ohio, Ames publishing co. [1893]. 28p. (On cover: Ames'
        series of standard and minor drama, no. 314).

1828   _____. Winning a wife. Farce in one act... Clyde, Ohio,
        Ames' publishing co., 1898. 13p.

1829   MOORE, EDWARD, 1712-1757. The gamester. A tragedy in five
        acts. New York, Samuel French [n.d.]. 56p.

MOORE, FRANK FRANKFORT

1830   MOORE, FRANK FRANKFORT, 1855-1931. "I forbid the banns!" The
        story of a comedy which was played seriously by Frank
        Frankfort Moore... New York, Cassell publishing co. [1893].
        vi, 404p.

1831   _____. Kitty Clive. Comedy in one act. London and New York,
        Samuel French [n.d.]. 19p.

1832   MOORE, GEORGE, 1852-1933. The bending of the bough; a comedy
        in five acts, by G. Moore. Chicago and New York, H. S.
        Stone and co., 1900. xxvi, 192p. Half-title: The green
        tree library.

1833   _____. Elizabeth Cooper; a comedy in three acts, by George
        Moore. Dublin and London, Maunsel and co., ltd., 1913.
        80p.

1834   MOORE, IRENE CLEMENTINE. Around the calendar plays, by Irene
        Clementine Moore... A collection of plays to be used as a
        dramatic reader, an auditorium text and an assembly guide;
        drawings by Chester Snowden. Dallas, Texas, Manfred, Van
        Nort and co. [c1939]. 2 p.ℓ., xii, 443p. incl. front.
        illus., plates.

1835   MOORE, JOHN. Mad dogs; or, The two Caesars. A farce in one
        act... New York, Samuel French [n.d.]. 15p.

1836   MOORE, LA MONT. Juno tries to change the decrees of fate; a
        one-act playlet based upon an episode from Vergil's
        Aeneid. [n.p., n.d.]. 5p. (American Classical League
        Service Bureau, No. 383).

1837   MOORE, MARION E. A. D. 1912, one-act comedy. Stapleton,
        New York, 1912. 18p.

1838   MORE, HANNAH, 1745-1833. Percy. A tragedy, in five acts. By
        Mrs. Hannah More... London, D. S. Maurice [1819?]. 58p.
        incl. front. [Cabinet theatre. v. 4, no. 5]. Title
        vignette.

1839   MORRIS, EDWIN BATEMAN, 1881-   . The freshman, a college
        comedy in three acts, by Edwin Bateman Morris... Phila-
        delphia, Pennsylvania, 1919. 44p.

1840   _____. The freshman, a college comedy in three acts, by
        Edwin Bateman Morris... Philadelphia, The Penn publishing
        co., 1909. 44p. diagrs.

MORTON, JOHN MADDISON

1841   _____. In the line of duty, a military drama in two acts.
        Philadelphia, The Penn publishing co., 1910. 19p.

1842   _____. The junior; a college comedy in three acts, by Edwin
        Bateman Morris... Philadelphia, The Penn publishing co.,
        1911. 42p.

1843   _____. The senior; a college comedy in three acts, by Edwin
        Bateman Morris... Philadelphia, The Penn publishing co.,
        1911. 44p. diagrs.

1844   _____. The sophomore, a college comedy in three acts, by
        Edwin Bateman Morris... Philadelphia, The Penn publishing
        co., 1910. 43p. diagrs.

1845   MORRIS, FELIX J. Electric love. A farce in one act. From
        the French... New York, De Witt, 1883. 9p.

1846   MORRISON, GEORGE AUSTIN, 1864-1916. "Lafayette," or, "The
        maid and the marquis," an original burlesque in three acts.
        By George Austin Morrison, Jr. ... New York [Press of
        A. E. Chasmar and co.] 1899. 86p.

1847   MORSE, M. A foolish investment. A comedietta, in one act.
        Adapted from the German. New York, De Witt, 1888. 15p.

1848   MORSE, SALMI. The passion: a miracle play in ten acts, by
        Salmi Morse. Revised and approved by the Most Reverend
        Joseph S. Alemany, archbishop of California. San Francisco,
        E. Bosqui and co., printers, 1879. 69p.

1849   MORTIMER, JAMES. ... Sundown to dawn; or, London forty years
        ago. A drama, in six tableaux... London, Published at
        the "Figaro" office, 1875. 54p.

1850   MORTON, EDWARD. The Eton boy. A farce, in one act... New
        York, Samuel French [n.d.]. 16p.

1851   _____. The windmill; a farce, in one act... London, Thomas
        Hailes Lacy [n.d.]. 24p. front.

1852   MORTON, JOHN MADDISON, 1811-1891. After a storm, comes a
        calm. A comedietta, in one act, by John Maddison Morton...
        Together with a description of the costumes... and the
        whole of the stage business. New York, De Witt, 1886.
        14p. On cover: De Witt's acting plays (no. 340).

MORTON, JOHN MADDISON

1853   MORTON, JOHN MADDISON. The "Alabama," ... a transatlantic
        nautical extravaganza... London, Thomas Hailes Lacy [n.d.].
        22p.

1854   _____. Atchi! A comedietta in one act, by John Maddison
        Morton. New American edition correctly reprinted from the
        original authorized acting edition, with the original cast
        of the characters... and all of the stage business... New
        York, H. Roorbach, 1889. 21p. On cover: Roorbach's
        American edition of acting plays (no. 20).

1855   _____. The attic story: a farce, in one act, by John Maddison
        Morton... Printed from the acting copy, with remarks,
        biographical and critical, by D.-G. ... As performed at
        the Theatres Royal... London, Davidson [n.d.]. 28p. incl.
        front. (Cumberland's British theatre. London, ca. 1825-
        55. v. 42 [no. 8]).
            Remarks by George Daniel, editor of the series.
            Reissue of Cumberland's earlier edition.

1856   _____. The attic story: a farce, in one act... London,
        Davidson [n.d.]. 28p. front.

1857   _____. The barbers of Bassora. A comic opera, in two acts...
        the music by John Hullah... London, Chapman and Hall
        [n.d.]. 32p. front.

1858   _____. Brother Ben: a farce, in one act... London, J. Pattie
        [n.d.]. 22p.

1859   _____. A capital match, a farce in one act. Clyde, Ohio,
        Ames' publishing co. [n.d.]. 18p.

1860   _____. ... Comediettas and farces, by John Maddison Morton...
        New York, Harper and bros., 1886. Cover-title, xi, [11]-
        171p. 1 illus. (port.). (Harper's handy series, [no. 95]).
        CONTENTS. - Box and Cox. - First come, first served. -
        Pepperpot's little pets. - After a storm comes a calm. -
        Express! - Taken from the French. - Declined--with thanks.

1861   _____. ... Cousin Lambkin: an original farce, in one act...
        London, J. Duncombe and co. [n.d.]. 20p. front. (Dun-
        combe's edition).

BRITISH AND AMERICAN DRAMA

1862   _____. Declined--with thanks. An original farcical
comedietta, in one act and one scene. By John Maddison
Morton, esq. ... Adapted to the American stage by H. I.
Williams, together with a description of the costumes...
and the whole of the stage business. New York, De Witt,
1886. 17p. On cover: De Witt's acting plays (no. 342).

1863   _____. A desperate game. A comic drama, in one act...
London, Thomas Hailes Lacy [n.d.]. 22p.

1864   _____. Don't judge by appearances. A farce, in one act...
London, Thomas Hailes Lacy [n.d.]. 23p.

1865   _____. ... The double-bedded room. A farce, in one act...
New York, Samuel French [n.d.]. 16p. (The minor drama,
no. clxxi).

1866   _____. First come, first served, a comedietta, in one act,
by John Maddison Morton, esq. ... Together with a description of the costumes... and the whole of the stage business.
New York, De Witt, 1886. 16p. On cover: De Witt's acting
plays.

1867   _____. A husband to order. A serio-comic drama, in two acts.
Boston, Walter H. Baker and co. [n.d.]. 32p.

1868   _____. If I had a thousand a year. A farce, in one act...
as first produced at the Royal Olympic Theatre, London...
October 21, 1867... New York, Robert M. De Witt [n.d.].
25p.

1869   _____. ... The Irish tiger: a farce, in one act. By John
Madison Morton... To which are added, A description of
the costume - cast of the characters... and the whole of
the stage business. As performed at the American
theatres. New-York, S. French [1856?]. 19p. (French's
American drama. The acting edition. no. 84).

1870   _____. John Dobbs. A farce, in one act. By John Maddison
Morton... London, T. H. Lacy [1859?]. 22p. front. On
cover: Lacy's acting edition.

1871   _____. ... Lend me five shillings. A farce in one act...
New York, William Taylor and co. [n.d.]. 31p. (Modern
standard drama, no. xxiv).

MORTON, JOHN MADDISON

1872   MORTON, JOHN MADDISON. ... The midnight watch! An original
       drama, in one act. By John Maddison Morton... The only
       edition correctly marked, by permission, from the prompter's
       book. To which is added, a description of the costume--
       cast of the characters--the whole of the stage business,
       situations--entrances--exits--properties, and directions
       as performed at the London theatres. Embellished with a
       fine engraving by Mr. T. Jones from a drawing, taken ex-
       pressly in the theatre. London, Duncombe and Moon [1848?].
       29p. incl. front. Duncombe's edition of the British
       theatre (no. 62).

1873   _____. ... The mother and child are doing well. A farce, in
       one act. By J. M. Morton, esq. ... Correctly printed from
       the most approved acting copy, with a description of the
       costume... and the whole of the stage business... New
       York and Philadelphia, Turner and Fisher [184-]. 25p.
       (Turner's dramatic library. [no. 75]).

1874   _____. The muleteer of Toledo; or, King, queen, and knave.
       A comic drama, in two acts. By John Maddison Morton...
       London, T. H. Lacy [185-]. 28p. (On cover: Lacy's acting
       edition no. 264).
           Vol. 18, no. 9 of series. cf. back cover.
           "First performed... April 9th, 1855."

1875   _____. My bachelor days. A farce, in one act... New York,
       Samuel French and son [n.d.]. 16p.

1876   _____. My husband's ghost! A comic interlude, in one act,
       by John Maddison Morton, esq. Printed from the acting
       copy, with remarks, biographical and critical, by D.-G. ...
       As performed at the Theatres Royal... London, J. Cumber-
       land [n.d.]. 25p. incl. front. (Cumberland's British
       theatre. London, ca. 1825-55. v. 35 [no. 10]).

1877   _____. My wife's bonnet. A farce in one act. By John
       Maddison Morton... London, T. H. Lacy [1864?]. 27, [1]p.
       diagr. (On cover: Lacy's acting edition, no. 94).
           "First performed... on Wednesday, the 2nd day of
       November, 1864."

1878   _____. My wife's second floor, an original farce in one act,
       by John M. Morton... London, T. H. Lacy [185-]. 24p.
       front. [Lacy's acting edition. no. 659 (v. 44, no. 14)].
           "First produced... June 22, 1853."

MORTON, JOHN MADDISON

1879   _____. ... Old Honesty! a comic drama, in two acts. By John Maddison Morton... The only edition correctly marked, by permission, from the prompter's book. To which is added, a description of the costume, cast of the characters... As performed at the London theatres... London, Duncombe and Moon [1848]. 49p. incl. front. (On cover: Duncombe's acting edition of the British theatre, no. 489).

1880   _____. On the sly! A farce, in one act... London, Thomas Hailes Lacy [n.d.]. 30p.

1881   _____. The pacha of Pimlico, a little eastern farcical extravaganza in one act. By John Maddison Morton, esq. ... London, T. H. Lacy [186-?]. 22p.

1882   _____. Pepperpot's little pets. A comedietta, in one act. By John Maddison Morton... Together with a description of the costumes... and the whole of the stage business. New York, De Witt, 1886. 16p. On cover: De Witt's acting plays (no. 341).

1883   _____. Poor Pillicoddy. A farce, in one act. By John Maddison Morton... To which are added a description of the costume... and the whole of the stage business. New York, C. T. De Witt [c1877]. 22p. (On cover: De Witt's acting plays. no. 217).

1884   _____. ... Sent to the tower. A farce, in one act... Boston, William V. Spencer [n.d.]. 16p. (Spencer's theatre, no. cix).

1885   _____. She would and he wouldn't. A comedy in two acts... London, Thomas Hailes Lacy [n.d.]. 40p.

1886   _____. ... The spitfire. A farce in one act... Philadelphia and New York, Turner and Fisher [n.d.]. 24p. (Turner's dramatic library).

1887   _____. Thirty-three next birthday, a farce in one act. London, Thomas Hailes Lacy [n.d.]. 24p.

1888   _____. ... The two Bonnycastles: a farce, in one act, by John Maddison Morton. New York, S. French [185-?]. 32p. diagr. (The minor drama. Ed. by F. C. Wemyss, No. XLIV).

MORTON, JOHN MADDISON

1889   MORTON, JOHN MADDISON. The two buzzards; or, Whitebait at
        Greenwich. A farce, in one act... New York, Samuel French
        [n.d.]. 24p.

1890   _____. The two puddifoots. A farce, in one act... Boston,
        Charles H. Spencer, 1870. 20p.

1891   _____. Which of the two? A comedietta, in one act... New
        York, Robert M. De Witt [n.d.]. 20p.

1892   _____. Who stole the pocket-book? or, A dinner for six, a
        farce, in one act... London, Thomas Hailes Lacy [n.d.].
        19p.

1893   _____. Woodcock's little game, a comedy-farce in two acts,
        by John Maddison Morton. New American edition correctly
        reprinted from the original authorized acting edition,
        with the original casts of the characters... and all of
        the stage business... New York, H. Roorbach, c1889.
        36p. (On cover: Roorbach's American edition of acting
        plays. no. 7).

1894   MORTON, THOMAS, 1764?-1838. All that glitters is not gold;
        or, The poor girl's diary. A comic drama in two acts, by
        Thomas and J. M. Morton. New American ed. ... reprinted
        from the original authorized acting ed., with the original
        casts of the characters... and all of the stage business...
        New York, H. Roorbach, 1889. 46p. On cover: Roorbach's
        American edition of acting plays (no. 1).

1895   _____. ... All that glitters is not gold. A comic drama, in
        two acts. By Thomas and J. M. Morton... New York, S.
        French [185-]. 52p. The minor drama, ed. by F. O. Wemyss
        (no. 40).

1896   _____. ... The angel of the attic: a serio-comic drama, in
        one act... New York, Samuel French [n.d.]. 16p. (French's
        minor drama, no. ccxciii).

1897   _____. Another glass. A drama, in one act... Boston,
        Charles H. Spencer [n.d.]. 17p.

1898   _____. ... The children in the wood. An opera, in two acts
        ... New York, Samuel French [n.d.]. 28p. (The minor
        drama, no. cxxi).

MORTON, THOMAS

1899 _____. The children in the wood: a musical piece, in two acts.
By Thomas Morton, esq. As performed at the New York
Theatre. From the prompt-book--by permission. 2nd. ed.
New York, Published by D. Longworth, at the Dramatic
repository, Shakespeare-gallery, May--1816. 31p.

1900 _____. Columbus; or, A world discovered. An historical play.
As it is performed at the Theatre-Royal, Covent-Garden.
By Thomas Morton... London, W. Miller, 1792. 2 p.ℓ.,
66, [2]p. [Broadhurst, J. Plays. v. 3, no. 4].
Founded in part upon Marmontel's "Les Incas; ou, La
destruction de l'Empire du Pérou."

1901 _____. A cure for the heartache: a comedy, in five acts, by
Thomas Morton... Printed from the acting copy, with
remarks biographical and critical, by D.-G. ... As performed at the Theatres Royal... London, Davidson [n.d.].
68p. incl. front. (Cumberland's British theatre. London,
ca. 1825-55. v. 16 [n.d.]).
Remarks by George Daniel, editor of the series.
Reissue of Cumberland's earlier edition.

1902 _____. A cure for the heart ache; a comedy in five acts; by
Thomas Morton, esq. As performed at the Theatre Royal,
Covent-Garden... With remarks by Mrs. Inchbald. London,
Longman, Hurst, Rees, Orme, and Brown [n.d.]. 84p. front.
Inchbald, Mrs. Elizabeth, The British theatre...
London, 1808. v. 25 [no. 8].

1903 _____. ... A cure for the heartache. A comedy, in five acts.
By Thomas Morton. With the stage directions, cast of
characters, costumes, & c. New York, W. Taylor and co.
[185-?]. v, [1], 7-66p.
Modern standard drama, ed. by Epes Sargent. (no. XIV).

1904 _____. Education: a comedy, in five acts, by Thomas Morton...
Printed from the acting copy, with remarks, biographical
and critical, by D.-G. ... As performed at the Theatres
Royal... London, J. Cumberland [n.d.]. 65, [1] p. incl.
front. (Cumberland's British theatre. London, ca. 1825-55.
v. 16 [no. 7]).
Remarks by George Daniel, editor of the series.
Borrowed in part from "Conscience," a play by Iffland,
translated by Benjamin Thompson. Title of original: Das
Gewissen.

1905 _____. ... Go to bed Tom. A farce, in one act..; New York,
William Taylor and co. [n.d.]. 26p. (The minor drama,
no. li).

195

MORTON, THOMAS

1906   MORTON, THOMAS. The invincibles: a musical farce, in two
        acts, by Thomas Morton... Printed from the acting copy,
        with remarks, biographical and critical, by D.-G. ... As
        now performed at the Theatres Royal... London, J. Cumber-
        land [n.d.]. 38p. incl. front. (Cumberland's British
        theatre. London, ca. 1825-55. v. 36 [no. 7]).
           Remarks by George Daniel, editor of the series.
           Without the music (by Lee).

1907   _____. 'Methinks I see my father!' or, 'Who's my father?'
        A farce, in two acts, by Thomas Morton... Printed from the
        acting copy, with remarks, biographical and critical, by
        D.-G. ... As performed at the Theatres Royal... London,
        G. H. Davidson [n.d.]. 29p. incl. front. (Cumberland's
        British theatre. London, ca. 1825-55. v. 45 [no. 7]).
           Remarks by George Daniel, editor of the series.
           Reissue of Cumberland's earlier edition.

1908   _____. A pretty piece of business; a comedietta in one act,
        by Thomas Morton. New American ed. ... reprinted from the
        original authorized acting edition, with the original cast
        of the characters... and all of the stage business... New
        York, H. Roorbach, 1889. 26p. On cover: Roorbach's
        American edition of acting plays. [no. 15].

1909   _____. The school of reform; or, How to rule a wife, a comedy,
        in five acts, by Thomas Morton... Printed from the acting
        copy, with remarks, biographical and critical by D.-G. ...
        As performed at the Theatres Royal... London, Davidson
        [n.d.]. 65p. incl. front. Cumberland's British theatre.
        London, ca. 1825-55, v. 17. (no. 6).

1910   _____. ... The school of reform; or, How to rule a husband.
        A comedy, in five acts. By Thomas Morton, esq. With a
        portrait of Mr. Hilson, in the character of Tyke. The
        play carefully corrected from the prompt books of the
        Philadelphia theatre. By M. Lopez, prompter. Philadel-
        phia, A. R. Poole, and Ash and Mason; New York, E. M.
        Murden; [etc., etc., 1826]. 75p. front. (port). (Added
        t.-p.: Lopez and Wemyss' edition. Acting American
        theatre. [no. 8]).

1911   _____. The school of reform; or, How to rule a husband. A
        comedy, in five acts, as performed at the Theatre-Royal,
        Covent-Garden. By Thomas Morton, esq. Philadelphia,
        Printed by Wm. Duane, No. 106, Market Street. For George
        E. Blake, Cook's Buildings. 1805. 86p.

MORTON, THOMAS

1912 _____. Secrets worth knowing: a comedy, in five acts, by
Thomas Morton... Printed from the acting copy, with
remarks, biographical and critical, by D.-G. ... As now
performed at the Theatres Royal... London, J. Cumberland
[n.d.]. 57p. incl. front. (Cumberland's British theatre.
London, ca. 1825-55. v. 18 [no. 4]).
Remarks by George Daniel, editor of the series.

1913 _____. Sink or swim! A comedy. In two acts. By Thomas
Morton... London, T. H. Lacy [1832?]. 26p. On cover:
Lacy's acting edition (no. 96).

1914 _____. The slave: an opera, in three acts, by Thomas Morton
... Printed from the acting copy, with remarks, biographi-
cal and critical, by D.-G. ... As performed at the
Theatres Royal... London, Davidson [n.d.]. 60p. incl.
front. (Cumberland's British theatre. London, ca. 1825-
55. v. 22 [no. 3]).
Remarks by George Daniel, editor of the series.
Without the music (by Bishop).

1915 _____. Speed the plough: a comedy, in five acts, by Thomas
Morton... Printed from the acting copy, with remarks,
biographical and critical, by D.-G. ... As performed at
the Theatres Royal... London, G. H. Davidson [n.d.].
69p. incl. front. (Cumberland's British theatre. London,
ca. 1825-55. v. 15 [no. 6]).
Remarks by George Daniel, editor of the series.
Reissue of Cumberland's earlier edition.

1916 _____. ... Speed the plough. A comedy in five acts. By
Thomas Morton. With the stage business, cast of characters,
costumes, relative positions, etc. New York, S. French
[18--]. v, 7-67p. French's standard drama. (no. XLX).

1917 _____. Speed the plough: a comedy, in five acts. As per-
formed with universal applause, at the Theatre-Royal,
Covent-Garden. By Thomas Morton, esq. ... 4th ed. Dublin,
Printed by W. Porter, for G. Burnet [etc.] 1800. 81p.

1918 _____. Town and country; a comedy, in five acts. By Thomas
Morton... Printed from the acting copy, with remarks,
biographical and critical, by D.-G. ... As performed at
the Theatre Royal... London, G. H. Davidson [n.d.].
67p. incl. front. Cumberland's British theatre. London,
ca. 1825-55. v. 23. (no. 9).

MORTON, THOMAS

1919   MORTON, THOMAS. ... Town and country, a comedy. In five acts.
        By Thomas Morton, esq. With the stage business, cast of
        characters, relative positions, etc. New York, S. French
        [18--]. iv, 7-68p. 1 illus. French's standard drama.

1920   _____. ... Town and country, a comedy in five acts. By
        Thomas Morton, esq. With the stage business, cast of
        characters, costumes, relative positions, etc. New York,
        Douglas, 1848. iv, p. 1ℓ., 7-68p. Modern standard drama...
        [vol. IX] (no. LXX).

1921   _____. Town and country; a comedy, in five acts. By Thomas
        Morton, esq. 2d ed. New York, Published by David Long-
        worth, at the Dramatic repository, Shakespeare-gallery.
        1814. 72p. [Broadhurst, J. Plays. v. 18, no. 4].

1922   _____. Town and country. A comedy, in five acts. As per-
        formed at the Theatre-Royal, Covent-Garden. By Thomas
        Morton, esq. Carlisle [Pa.], Printed by A. Loudon, for
        Conrod and co., and sold at their stores in Philadelphia,
        Baltimore, Petersburg and Norfolk. 1807. 98, [2]p.

1923   _____. The way to get married. A comedy, in five acts, by
        Thomas Morton... Printed from the acting copy, with re-
        marks, biographical and critical, by D.-G. ... As per-
        formed at the Theatres Royal... London, J. Cumberland and
        son [n.d.]. 67p. incl. front. (Cumberland's British
        theatre. London, ca. 1825-55. v. 20 [no. 5]).
            Remarks by George Daniel, editor of the series.
            Reissued in Davidson's shilling volume of Cumberland's
        plays, v. 7 [no. 4].

1924   _____. The way to get married; a comedy, in five acts; by
        Thomas Morton, esq. As performed at the Theatre Royal,
        Covent Garden... With remarks by Mrs. Inchbald. London,
        Longman, Hurst, Rees, Orme, and Brown [n.d.]. 83 (i.e.
        82)p. front.
            Inchbald, Mrs. Elizabeth. The British theatre... Lon-
        don, 1808. v. 25 (no. 1).

1925   _____. The writing on the wall; a melo-drama in three acts,
        by Thomas and J. M. Morton. New York, W. Taylor; S.
        French, general agent [185-?]. 64p. (Modern standard
        drama [v. 12] no. 95).

BRITISH AND AMERICAN DRAMA

1926 [_____]. Zorinski. [London, 1800?]. [3]-72p. [Broadhurst, J. Plays, v. 3, no. 2].
Imperfect: t.-p. and preliminary matter wanting.
First produced in 1795.
Without the music (by Arnold).

1927 MOSER, GUSTAV VON, 1825-1903. An Arabian might in the nineteenth century. A comedy in four acts from the German of von Moser. By Augustin Daly. As acted at Daly's theatre for the first time, November 29th, 1879. New York, printed as manuscript only, for the author, 1884. 84p.

1928 _____. The white horse, a comedy in one act, literally translated from the German of G. von Moser. Cambridge, Mass., W. H. Wheeler, printer, 1887. 18p.

1929 MOWATT, ANNA CORA. ... Fashion; or, Life in New York. A comedy, in five acts... New York, Samuel French [n.d.]. 62p. (French's standard drama, no. ccxv).

1930 MOZART, WOLFGANG AMADEUS, 1756-1791. Don Giovanni. [n.p.] Wm. C. Bryant and co., 1871. 40p.

1931 MUNFORD, ROBERT, 1730?-1784. A collection of plays and poems, by the late Col. Robert Munford, of Mecklenburg county, in the state of Virginia. Now first published together. Petersburg, Printed by William Prentis, 1798. xii, 13-192p. CONTENTS. - The candidates; or, The humors of a Virginia election. - The patriots. - The first book of Ovid's Metamorphoses, translated. - Miscellaneous poems, consisting of: The ram, a cosmic poem; Letters from the Devil to his son; Answer to "The winter piece"; Colin and Celio, a pastoral poem; A dream; and A patriotic song.

1932 MUNSON, A. J. A midnight mistake. A melo-drama, in four acts... Clyde, Ohio, A. D. Ames, 1886. 25p.

1933 [MURDOCK, JOHN] 1790-1800. The politicians; or, A state of things. A dramatic piece. Written by an American and a citizen of Philadelphia. Philadelphia, Printed for the author, 1798.

1934 MURPHY, ARTHUR, 1727-1805. All in the wrong; a comedy, in five acts; by Arthur Murphy, esq. As performed at the Theatre Royal, Drury-Lane... With remarks by Mrs. Inchbald. London, Longman, Hurst, Rees, Orme, and Frown [n.d.]. 97p. front. (Inchbald, Mrs. Elizabeth. The British theatre... London, 1808. v. 15 [no. 8]).
Based on Molière's "Sganarelle, ou, Le cocu imaginaire."

MURPHY, ARTHUR

1935   MURPHY, ARTHUR. The apprentice: a farce, in two acts; by
Arthur Murphy... London, Printed by D. S. Maurice [1819?].
vi, [2], [9]-34p. front. [Cabinet theatre. v. 12, no. 5].
Title vignette.

1936   _____. The citizen; a farce, in two acts, by Arthur Murphy.
Printed from the acting copy, with remarks, biographical
and critical, by D.-G. ... As performed at the Theatres
Royal... London, J. Cumberland [n.d.]. 34p. incl. front.
(Cumberland's British theatre. London, ca. 1825-55. v. 24
[no. 9]).
    Remarks by George Daniel, editor of the series.
    Originally produced as a three act comedy, later
reduced to a farce.

1937   _____. The Grecian daughter; a tragedy, in five acts; by
Arthur Murphy, esq. As performed at the Theatre Royal,
Covent Garden... With remarks by Mrs. Inchbald. London,
Longman, Hurst, Rees, Orme, and Brown [n.d.]. 58p. front.
(Inchbald, Mrs. Elizabeth. The British theatre... London,
1808. v. 15 [no. 4]).

1938   _____. Know your own mind; a comedy, in five acts; by Arthur
Murphy, esq. As performed at the Theatre Royal, Drury
Lane... With remarks by Mrs. Inchbald. London, Longman,
Hurst, Rees, Orme, and Brown [n.d.]. 105p. front.
(Inchbald, Mrs. Elizabeth. The British theatre... London,
1808. v. 15 [no. 5]).
    Founded on the "Irrésolu" of Destouches.

1939   _____. The orphan of China. A tragedy. By Arthur Murphy,
esq. Correctly given, from copies used in the theatres,
by Thomas Dibdin... London, Printed at the Chiswick press
for Whittingham and Arliss, 1816. 63, [1]p. illus.
(Dibdin, T. J. London theatre. London, 1815 [1814-25]
v. 8 [no. 9]). Title vignette.
    Based on the Chinese tragedy in Du Halde's Description
géographique, historique... de l'empire de la Chine. (cf.
the English translation, v. 3: Tchao chi con ell; or, The
little orphan of the family of Tchao). Differs much from
Voltaire's L'orphelin de la Chine, from the same source.
Cf. Murphy's letter to Voltaire usually prefixed to the
play, and Voltaire's dedication to his play.

NEWBOLT, HENRY JOHN

1940 ____. The upholsterer; or, What news? A farce. In two
acts. Written by Mr. Murphy. Taken from the manager's
book at the Theatre Royal, Covent-Garden. London,
Printed for H. D. Symonds [180-?]. 27p.
"Avowedly taken from the 'Tatler' [nos. 155 and 160 by
Addison and Steele] but owing more to Fielding's 'Coffee-
house politician.'"--Dict. nat. biog. Cf. also Genest,
v. 4, p. 516-517.
No. 5 in a volume lettered: Plays.

1941 MURPHY, ETHEL ALLEN. The watcher for the dawn, a masque of
heritage, dedicated to the Pilgrim tercentenary. [Louis-
ville, Mayes printing co., 1920]. 20p.

1942 MURRAY, GILBERT, 1866-1957. Andromache; a play in three acts.
Portland, Maine, T. B. Mosher, 1913. 88p.

1943 MUSKERRY, WILLIAM. London Bridge; or, The mysteries of the
old mint. A sensational drama, in a prologue and three
acts... London, Edward Hastings [n.d.]. 47p.

1944 ____. Three blind mice; a predicament in one scene... London and New York, Samuel French [c1911]. 15p.

1945 MUSSET, ALFRED DE, 1810-1857. Fantasio, a comedy in two acts,
by Alfred de Musset, translated by Maurice Baring. [New
York] The Pleiad, 1929. 57, [1]p. col. front. illus.,
col. pl.

1946 My next door neighbor, a character sketch in one act and one
scene. New York, Dick and Fitzgerald [n.d.]. 14p.

1947 The mystic charm; or, A wonderful cure, a farce in one act.
Clyde, Ohio, Ames' publishing co. [n.d.]. 26p.

1948 Narcissus, a Twelfth Night merriment played by youths of the
parish at the College of S. John the Baptist in Oxford,
A.D. 1602, with appendix; now first ed. from a Bodleian
ms. by Margaret L. Lee... London, D. Nutt, 1893. xxxii,
51p.

1949 Nature and philosophy. Adapted from the French, by a citizen
of Richmond (Va.)... New York, R. Hobbs, 1830. 33p.

1950 NEWBOLT, HENRY JOHN, 1862-1938. Mordred, a tragedy. London,
Unwin, 1895. 125p.

NEWTON, HARRY LEE

1951   NEWTON, HARRY LEE, 1872-   . A bogus detective, a comedy
sketch with awkward situations. Chicago, Will Rossiter,
1904. 13p.

1952   _____. The burglar's welcome, a sketch in one act. Chicago
and New York, The Dramatic publishing co., 1902. 10p.

1953   _____. Chatter, a monologue for males, by Harry L. Newton...
Chicago, San Francisco [etc.] M. Whitmark and sons, 1913.
8p.

1954   _____. A comedy sketch "The jumpkins jumble" two male--two
female. Chicago, Will Rossiter, 1903. 17p.

1955   _____. The corner drug store, a musical comedy prescription
in one dose. Chicago, T. S. Denison and co. [1909]. 29p.

1956   _____. For rent to-morrow, comedy sketch. By Harry L.
Newman and A. S. Hoffman. Chicago and New York, The
Dramatic publishing co. [1903]. 10p.

1957   _____. The goddess of love, a vaudeville sketch. Chicago,
T. S. Denison and co. [1904]. 12p.

1958   _____. His fifty kids, a comedy sketch for male and female.
Chicago, Will Rossiter, 1904. 16p.

1959   _____. Messrs. Grin & Barrett, a sketch for two Irish
comedians. Chicago, Will Rossiter, 1903. 11p.

1960   _____. Mr. Niagara's fall, a comedy sketch for male and
female. Chicago, Will Rossiter, 1903. 15p.

1961   _____. The new cook, an exciting two-character comedy sketch.
Chicago, Will Rossiter, 1904. 18p.

1962   _____. O'Toole's battle of ante-up, a vaudeville sketch.
Chicago, T. S. Denison [1906]. 13p.

1963   _____. An oyster stew, a rapid-fire talking act by Harry L.
Newton and A. S. Hoffman... Chicago, T. S. Denison and
co. [1904]. 6p.

1964   _____. The Pacific slope. Chicago, Will Rossiter, 1903. 11p.

1965   _____. The second-hand man, a two-character sketch for Jew
and rube. Chicago, Will Rossiter, 1903. 11p.

1966   _____. Some vaudeville monologues, by Harry L. Newton... illustrations by Buckton Nendick. Chicago, T. S. Denison and co. [c1917]. 148p. front. (port.) illus.

1967   _____. Twixt midnight and morn. A comedietta in one act. By Newton and Hoffman. Chicago, H. L. Newton pub. co., 1902. 7p.

1968   _____. What every woman thinks she knows, a suffragette monologue, by Harry L. Newton... Chicago, San Francisco [etc.] M. Whitmark and sons, 1913. 10p.

1969   NICHOLS, ADELAIDE. The haunted circle, and other outdoor plays, by Adelaide Nichols. New York, E. P. Dutton and co. [c1924]. xx, 279p.

1970   NIELD, THOMAS, 1834-1913. Master and man: a play in a pro- logue and four acts. By Francis Howard Williams... Philadelphia, D. F. Gillin [1886]. Cover-title, 23p.

1971   No Entry.

1972   _____. Oliver Cromwell, lord protector of England, a drama, by Thomas Nield. New York, The Argyle press [1890]. 168p.

1973   NIEMEIER, MINNIE A. New plays for every day the schools celebrate, by Minnie A. Niemeier... Enl. ed. New York, Noble and Noble [c1936]. viii, 383p. illus.

1974   [NOAH, MORDECAI MANUEL] 1785-1851. The fortress of Sorrento: a petit historical drama, in two acts... New York, Published by D. Longworth, at the Dramatic repository, Shakespeare-gallery. 1803. 28p.

1975   NOBLES, MILTON, 1847-1924. The actor; or, A son of Thespis. An original comedy-drama in four acts. By Milton Nobles... Philadelphia, Ledger job print., 1891. Cover-title, 104p. plan.

1976   _____. From sire to son; or, The hour and the man. An original drama in four acts, by Milton Nobles... Phila- delphia, Ledger job print., 1887. 85p.

1977   _____. Interviews; or, Bright Bohemia. An American comedy in four acts. By Milton Nobles. Philadelphia, Ledger job print., 1881. 77p.

NOBLES, MILTON

1978   NOBLES, MILTON. Love and law. An original comedy-drama in
        four acts. By Milton Nobles... Philadelphia, Ledger job
        print., 1884. 78p.

1979   _____. The phoenix; a drama in four acts, by Milton Nobles...
        Chicago, The Dramatic publishing co., 1900. 3 p.ℓ., 128p.

1980   NOMAD [pseud.]. "Caught at last." A comedietta, in one act,
        by Nomad. The blue stocking. A comedietta, in one act.
        By Delissa Joseph. New York, De Witt, 1884. 11p.

1981   NORCROSS, FREDERIC WALTER. When a woman loves, a romantic
        play in 3 acts, by Frederic Walter Norcross. [Philadel-
        phia, 1909]. 1 p.ℓ., 15-68p.

1982   NORTON, ALLEN. The convolvulus; a comedy in three acts, by
        Allen Norton. New York, Claire Marie, 1914. 72p.

1983   NORTON, FRANKLIN P. Abraham Lincoln; or, The rebellion,
        drama in five acts. New York, 1911. 61p.

1984   NUTTER, CHARLES. A cup of tea. A comedietta, in one act...
        by Charles Nutter and J. Derley. As performed... February
        11, 1869... New York, Robert M. De Witt [n.d.]. 16p.

1985   Oberon; or, The charmed horn. A romantic fairy tale, in two
        acts. Printed from the acting copy, with remarks, bio-
        graphical and critical, by D.-G. ... As performed at the
        Theatres Royal... London, J. Cumberland [n.d.]. 36p.
        front. (port.) (Cumberland's British theatre. London,
        ca. 1825-55. v. 13 [no. 3]).
            Remarks by George Daniel, editor of the series.
            Founded on Wieland's poem. Brought out in opposition
        to Weber's opera of the same name. Cf. J. R. Planché,
        Recollections, v. 1, p. 86.
            Without the music (adapted by Cooke).

1986   O'BRIEN, CONSTANCE. Love in a flue; or, The sweep and the
        magistrate, a comedy, in two acts. New York, De Witt
        [n.d.]. 35p.

1987   _____. A lover and a half. A comedy, in two acts. New York,
        The De Witt publishing house [n.d.]. 30p.

1988   O'BRIEN, SEUMAS. Duty, and other Irish comedies, by Seumas
        O'Brien. Boston, Little, Brown, and co., 1916. 5 p.ℓ.,
        5-134p. front. (port.).

[O'KEEFFE, JOHN]

1989 O'BRIEN, WILLIAM, d. 1815. Cross purposes; a farce, in two
      acts... (In The London stage. London [1824-27]. v. 2
      [no. 38], 9-16p., 1 illus.).

1990 O'BRIEN, WILLIAM L., d. 1908. Aaron Burr, a play in four
      acts. By William L. O'Brien. [Minneapolis, Minnesota,
      Review publishing co., 1908]. 82p.

1991 The obstinate family. A farce, in one act. Translated and
      adapted from the German... New York, Samuel French [n.d.].
      14p.

1992 O'CALLAGHAN, P. P. The married bachelor; or, Master and man:
      a comic piece, in one act, by P. P. O'Callaghan, esq.
      Printed from the acting copy, with remarks, biographical
      and critical, by D.-G. ... London, G. H. Davidson [n.d.].
      28p. incl. front. (Cumberland's Minor theatre. London
      [ca. 1830-55] v. 10 [no. 7]).
          Remarks by George Daniel, editor of the series.

1993 O'CASEY, SEAN, 1884-1964. Within the gates, a play of four
      scenes in a London park. London, MacMillan and co., ltd.,
      1934. 203p.

1994 O'CONNELL, DANIEL, 1844-1899. ... King Hal; a romantic opera
      in three acts for mixed voices. Book and lyrics by Daniel
      O'Connell, rev. by Allan Dunn; music by H. J. Stewart...
      New York, J. Fischer and bro.; [etc., etc.] 1911. 32p.

1995 Of arms and the man, we sing! by the students of Waltham High
      School, Waltham, Massachusetts. [n.p., n.d.]. 5p.
      (American Classical League Service Bureau, No. 724).

1996 O'HARA, KANE. Midas: a burletta, in two acts... London,
      John Cumberland [n.d.]. 32p. front.

1997 _____. Tom Thumb: a burletta, in two acts... altered from
      Henry Fielding... London, John Cumberland [n.d.]. 27p.

1998 [O'KEEFFE, JOHN] 1747-1833. The basket-maker. In two acts.
      Performed at the Theatre-Royal, Hay-market, in 1789. The
      musick by Dr. Arnold.
          (In his Dramatic works... London, 1798. v. 2, p. [335]-
      376).
          Without the music.
          Scene, on the banks of the St. Lawrence River, and in
      the forests of the Iroquois country. Cf, p. [336].

[O'KEEFFE, JOHN]

1999   [O'KEEFFE, JOHN]. The blacksmith of Antwerp. In two acts.
        Performed at the Theatre-Royal, Covent-Garden, in 1788.
            (In his Dramatic works... London, 1798. v. 2, p. [377]-
        423).

2000   _____. The castle of Andalusia; a comic opera, in three acts;
        by John O'Keeffe, esq. As performed at the Theatre Royal,
        Covent-Garden... With remarks by Mrs. Inchbald. London,
        Longman, Hurst, Rees, Orme, and Brown [n.d.]. 70p. front.
        (Inchbald, Mrs. Elizabeth. The British theatre... London,
        1808. v. 22 [no. 1]).
            Appeared first under title: The banditti; or, Love's
        labyrinth. Altered and brought out with new title at
        Covent Garden on November 2, 1782.
            Without the music (by Arnold and others).

2000A   _____. Fontainbleau; a comic opera, in three acts, by John
        O'Keeffe, esq. As performed at the Theatre Royal, Covent
        Garden... With remarks by Mrs. Inchbald. London, Long-
        man, Hurst, Rees, Orme, and Brown [n.d.]. 75p. front.
        (Inchbald, Elizabeth. The British theatre, London, 1808.
        v. 22 [no. 2]).
            The music composed and compiled by Shield.
            Produced under title: Fontainbleau; or, Our way in France.

2000B   _____. The highland reel. A musical farce, in two acts, by
        John O'Keeffe... Printed from the acting copy, with re-
        marks, biographical and critical, by D.-G. ... As per-
        formed at the Theatres Royal... London, J. Cumberland
        [n.d.]. 35p. front. (Cumberland's British theatre. Lon-
        don, ca. 1825-55. Vol. 18 [no. 1]).
            Remarks by George Daniel, editor of the series.
            The music composed and compiled by Shield.
            Reissued in Davidson's shilling volume of Cumberland's
        plays, v. 8 [no. 1].

2001   _____. The highland reel; a comic opera, in three acts...
        New York, D. Longworth, 1813. 64p.

2002   _____. Modern antiques; or, The merry mourners: a farce, in
        two acts, by John O'Keeffe... Printed from the acting
        copy, with remarks, biographical and critical, by D.-G.
        ... As now performed at the Theatres Royal... London,
        J. Cumberland [n.d.]. 43p. incl. front. (Cumberland's
        British theatre. London, ca. 1825-55. v. 29 [no. 4]).

O'KEEFFE, JOHN

2003 _____. Peeping Tom of Coventry: a musical farce, in two acts, by John O'Keeffe... Printed from the acting copy, with remarks, biographical and critical, by D.-G. ... As now performed at the Theatres Royal... London, J. Cumberland [n.d.]. 36p. incl. front. (Cumberland's British theatre. London, ca. 1825-55. v. 31 [no. 9]).
     Remarks by George Daniel, editor of the series.
     Without the music (by S. Arnold).

2004 _____. The poor soldier: a musical farce, in two acts... Baltimore, J. Robinson, 1827. 35p.

2004A _____. The poor soldier. A musical farce, in two acts, by John O'Keeffe... Printed from the acting copy, with re- marks, biographical and critical, by D.-G. ... As per- formed at the Theatres Royal... London, J. Cumberland [n.d.]. 42p. incl. front. (Cumberland's British theatre. London, ca. 1825-55. v. 20 [no. 8]).
     Remarks by George Daniel, editor of the series.

2005 _____. The prisoner at large: a comedy, in two acts, by John O'Keeffe... Printed from the acting copy, with remarks, biographical and critical, by D.-G. ... As performed at the Theatres Royal... London, J. Cumberland [n.d.]. 31p. incl. front. (Cumberland's British theatre. London, ca. 1825-55. v. 26 [no. 7]).
     Remarks by George Daniel, editor of the series.

2005A _____. The Wicklow mountains. In three acts. Performed at the Theatre-Royal, Covent-Garden, in 1795. The music by Mr. Shield.
     (In O'Keefe, John. Dramatic works... London, 1798. v. 2, p. [109]-192).
     Originally produced under title: The lad of the hills; or, The Wicklow gold mine.

2006 _____. The young Quaker: a comedy, in five acts, by John O'Keeffe... Printed from the acting copy, with remarks, biographical and critical, by D.-G. ... As performed at the Theatres Royal... London, J. Cumberland [n.d.]. 59p. incl. front. (Cumberland's British theatre. London, ca. 1825-55. v. 37 [no. 6]).
     Remarks by George Daniel, editor of the series.

Old and young

2007   Old and young: a farce, in one act. Printed from the acting
        copy, with remarks, biographical and critical, by D.-G. ...
        As performed at the Theatres Royal... London, J. Cumber-
        land [n.d.]. 30p. incl. front. (Cumberland's British
        theatre. London, ca. 1825-55. v. 30 [no. 3]).
            Remarks by George Daniel, editor of the series.
            Based on "Le vieux garçon et la petite fille" by Scribe
        and Delavigne.

2008   The (old clothes) merchant of Venice; or, The young judge and
        ole jewry, a burlesque sketch, for the drawing-room. New
        York, De Witt [n.d.]. 15p.

2009   ... The old guard. A drama, in one act... New York, Samuel
        French [n.d.]. 2op. (The minor drama, no. xxix).

2010   One, two, three, four, five; by advertisement. A musical
        entertainment, in one act. Printed from the acting copy,
        with remarks, biographical and critical, by D.-G. ... As
        performed at the Theatres Royal... London, J. Cumberland
        [n.d.]. 23p. incl. front. (Cumberland's British theatre.
        London, ca. 1825-55. v. 31 [no. 8]).
            Remarks by George Daniel, editor of the series.
            Without the music.

2011   O'NEILL, CLEMENT. ... Wanted: a housekeeper, a humorous play
        in one act... London, Joseph Williams, 1911. 11p.

2012   O'NEILL, I. R. Aladdin; or, The wonderful lamp: a piece of
        Oriental extravaganza, in one act... London, G. H.
        Davidson [n.d.]. 19p.

2013   ORANGE, B. Acacia cottage, a comedy in one act. New York,
        French, 1906. 11p.

2014   Order of the fan. [New York] Edgar S. Werner and co., 1905.
        6p.

2015   An original idea. A duologue... Boston, George M. Baker and
        co. [n.d.]. 27p.

2016   ORNE, MARTHA RUSSELL. A black diamond. A comic drama in
        two acts, by M. R. Orne... Boston, W. H. Baker and co.,
        1890. 24p.

2017   _____. The donation party; or, Thanksgiving eve at the
        parsonage, a comedy in three acts. Boston, Walter H.
        Baker and co. [1894]. 43p.

OULTON, WALLEY CHAMBERLAIN

2018 _____. A limb o' the law. A comedy in two acts, by M. R. Orne... Boston, W. H. Baker and co., 1892. 18p.

2019 _____. Timothy Delano's courtship; a comedy in two acts, by Martha Russell Orne... New York, H. Roorbach, 1892. 27p.

2020 OSBALDISTON, D. W. Naomie; or, The peasant girl's dream. A romantic drama, in two acts... London, James Pattie [n.d.]. 24p. front.

2021 OSBORN, LAUGHTON, 1809-1878. The Montanini; The school for critics; comedies, being in continuation and completion of the fourth volume of the dramatic series by Laughton Osborn. New York, J. Miller, 1868. 2 p.ℓ., p. [265]-517.

2022 OSBORNE, HARRY WILDER, 1880- . After the play, a dramatic sketch. Chicago, T. S. Denison and co. [1910]. 13p.

2023 _____. The deacon entangled, a comedy, by Harry Osborne... Chicago, T. S. Denison and co. [1914]. 63p. diagrs. On cover: Alta series.

2024 "Othello," a burlesque, as performed by Griffin & Christy's ministrels, at their opera house. New York, Samuel French [n.d.]. 8p.

2025 OTT, GRACE. In Gallia: a one-act play in Latin, French and English. [n.p., n.d.]. 3p. (American Classical League Service Bureau, No. 88).

2026 OTWAY, THOMAS. ... Venice preserved. A tragedy, in five acts... New York, Samuel French [n.d.]. 58p. (French's standard drama, no. xx).

2027 OULTON, WALLEY CHAMBERLAIN, 1770?-1820? My landlady's gown. A farce, in two acts. As performed at the Theatre-royal, Haymarket, and at the Philadelphia and Baltimore theatres. By W. C. Oulton... Baltimore, Printed and published by J. Robinson, Circulating library and dramatic repository, 94 Market-street. 1817. 47, [1]p.

2028 _____. The sixty-third letter, a musical farce, in two acts, as performed at the Theatre Royal, Hay-Market. By Walley Chamberlain Oulton. The overture and music by Doctor Arnold. London, Baker and son, 1802. 44p.

2029 _____. The sleep-walker; or, Which is the lady? A farce in two acts. As performed at the Theatre Royal, Covent-Garden. By W. C. Oulton... 3rd ed. London, J. Roach [1812?]. 39p.

OULTON, WALLEY CHAMBERLAIN

2030   OULTON, WALLEY CHAMBERLAIN. The sleep-walker; or, Which is
       the lady? A farce. In two acts. As performed at the
       Theatre-Royal, Haymarket. By W. C. Oulton. London, Printed
       by and for J. Roach, 1812. 44p.

2031   Our clerks; or, No. 3 Fig Tree Court, Temple, a farce, in one
       act. New York, Robert M. De Witt [n.d.]. 24p.

2032   Our country aunt; or, Aunt Jerusha's visit, a domestic drama,
       in two acts. Clyde, Ohio, Ames publishing co. [n.d.]. 9p.

2033   [OWEN, ROBERT DALE] 1801-1877. Pocahontas: a historical drama,
       in five acts; with an introductory essay and notes. By a
       citizen of the West. New York, G. Dearborn, 1837. 2 p.ℓ.,
       [7]-240p.

2034   OXBERRY, WILLIAM, 1784-1824, ed. The new English drama...
       being the only edition existing which is faithfully marked
       with the stage business, and stage directions, as per-
       formed at the Theatres Royal. London, Published for the
       proprietors by W. Simkin and R. Marshall, 1818-1828. 22 v.
       fronts.

2035   OXENFORD, JOHN, 1812-1877. A cleft stick. A comedy, in three
       acts... London, Thomas Hailes Lacy [n.d.]. 52p.

2036   _____. A day well spent. A farce, in one act... London,
       Thomas Hailes Lacy [n.d.]. 24p.

2037   _____. Twice killed. A farce. Chicago, The Dramatic
       publishing co. [n.d.]. 16p.

2038   _____. ... The two orphans. A drama, in eight tableaux,
       divided into six acts, by John Oxenford, esq. First pro-
       duced at the Royal Olympic theatre... September 14, 1874.
       New York, S. French and son; London, S. French [187-].
       71p. (French's standard drama. The acting edition. no.
       365).

2039   PAINTON, EDITH F. A. U. PALMER, 1878- . As a woman
       thinketh, a comedy of the period in three acts, by Edith
       F. A. U. Painton... Chicago, T. S. Denison and co. [1914].
       96p. diagrs. (On copy: Alta series).

2040   _____. The class ship; or, "Launched but not anchored," a
       dramatization of Longfellow's "The building of the ship,"
       for the use of graduating classes, embodying the above motto
       by Edith F. A. U. Painton... Chicago, T. S. Denison and co.
       [1914]. 20p. (On cover: Amateur series).

PARKER, LEM B.

2041 _____. Clubbing a husband, a comedy in three acts for women's clubs, by Edith F. A. U. Painton... Chicago, T. S. Denison and co. [1915]. 54p. diagrs. (On cover: Alta series).

2042 _____. The graduate's choice, a commencement playlet in one act, by Edith F. A. U. Painton... Chicago, T. S. Denison and co. [1914]. 20p. (On cover: Amateur series).

2043 _____. Just plain Dot. A commencement playlet for children children, in three scenes, by Edith P. [!] A. U. Painton... Franklin, Ohio, Eldridge entertainment house, 1912. 2 p.ℓ., [3]-51p.

2044 _____. A prairie rose, a comedy-drama of the Kansas prairies, in four acts, by Edith F. A. U. Painton... Chicago, T. S. Denison and co. [1913]. 77p. diagrs. (On cover: Alta series).

2045 _____. Sister Angela, a drama for female characters only, by Edith F. A. U. Painton... San Diego, California, The Paintons, 1912. 4 p.ℓ., 5-37p., 1ℓ.

2046 _____. Star bright, a comedy drama in three acts, by Edith F. A. U. Painton... Chicago, T. S. Denison and co. [1915]. 83p. diagrs. (On cover: Alta series).

2047 PALMER, BELL ELLIOTT. Dodging an heiress; or, His uncle's choice, a two act comedy. Franklin, Ohio, Eldridge entertainment house [n.d.]. 41p.

2048 _____. A social crisis; or, Almost a tragedy of tongues, a comedy in one act. Franklin, Ohio, Eldridge entertainment house [n.d.]. 11p.

2049 PARDEY, HENRY OAKE. ... Nature's nobleman. A comedy, in five acts... first produced in Burton's Theatre, N. Y., October 7, 1851. New York, Samuel French [n.d.]. 79p. (French's standard drama, no. c).

2050 PARKER, HARRY. Gertrude Wheeler, M. D., a comedy in one act (female characters). Chicago, The Dramatic publishing co., 1899. 18p.

2051 PARKER, LEM B. Up Vermont way, a rural comedy-drama, in four acts. Chicago, The Dramatic publishing co. [1903]. 83p.

PARKER, MARY MONCURE

2052   PARKER, MARY MONCURE. Black art, a minstrel sketch in one
        act, a take-off on mind-reading and thought-transference
        exhibitions. Chicago, Frederick J. Drake and co., 1903.
        7p.

2053   _____. "Love behind the scenes," a comedy in one act.
        Chicago, Frederick J. Drake and co., 1903. 8p.

2054   PARKER, MAUD MAY. The missive, a dramatic poem. Boston, The
        poet lore co., 1907. 48p.

2055   PARKER, W. COLEMAN. The bank cashier, a sensational melo-
        drama in four acts. Chicago, T. S. Denison [1903]. 57p.

2056   _____. Breaking the engagement, a farce in one act, by W. C.
        Parker... Boston, W. H. Baker and co., 1910. 10p.

2057   _____. Brother Josiah, a comedy in three acts. Chicago,
        T. S. Denison and co. [1903]. 52p.

2058   _____. The congressman, a comedy in three acts, by W. C.
        Parker... Philadelphia, The Penn publishing co., 1914.
        60p. diagrs.

2059   _____. The face at the window, a drama in three acts, by
        W. C. Parker... Chicago, T. S. Denison and co. [1904].
        39p. diagrs. (On cover: Denison's miscellaneous plays).

2060   _____. Those dreadful twins; a farce comedy, by W. C.
        Parker... Chicago, T. S. Denison [1900]. 46p. illus.
        (plans). (On cover: Denison's series. vol. x, no. 61
        Alta series).

2061   _____. Those red envelopes, a farce in one act. Chicago,
        T. S. Denison [1908]. 14p.

2062   _____. "William," a farce in one act, by W. C. Parker...
        Boston, Walter H. Baker co., 1910. 9p. (On cover:
        Baker's edition of plays).

2063   PARRY, TOM. The lucky horse shoe; or, Woman's trials. A
        domestic drama, in three acts... London, Thomas Hailes
        Lacy [n.d.]. 32p.

2064   PARSONS, LAURA MATILDA STEPHENSON, 1855–   . Colloquy of the
       holidays; a play for children, by Laura M. Parsons repre-
       senting New Year's day, St. Valentine's day, Washington's
       birthday, April fool's day, May day, Decoration day,
       Fourth of July, Thanksgiving day, Christmas day. Dansville,
       N. Y., Bunnell and Oberdorf, printers, 1889. 23p.

2065   _____. The district school at Blueberry Corners. A farce in
       three scenes... By Laura M. Parsons... Danville, N. Y.,
       Bunnell and Oberdorf press, 1889. 31p.

2066   _____. Scenes and songs of ye olden time; an old folks'
       entertainment, by Laura M. Parsons... Boston, W. H.
       Baker and co., 1894. 20p. On cover: Baker's novelties.

2067   _____. A variety contest; a humorous entertainment in one
       scene, by Laura M. Parsons... Boston, W. H. Baker and co.,
       1901. 25p. On cover: Baker's novelties.

2068   PASTON, GEORGE. Feed the brute... New York and London, T. H.
       Lacy, 1909. 21p. George Paston is pseud. of Emily Morse
       Symonds.

2069   PAUL, JOHN HOWARD. ... The mob cap; or, Love's disguises.
       A domestic drama, in two acts... New York, William Taylor
       and co. [n.d.]. 33p. (The minor drama, no. lx).

2070   _____. Opposite neighbors. An original farce, in one act.
       New York, Samuel French [n.d.]. 14p.

2071   _____. Thrice married. A personation piece, in one act...
       as first performed at Drury Lane Theatre, London, Thursday,
       March 12, 1854... New York, Robert M. De Witt [n.d.]. 15p.

2072   ... Pauline; a drama, in five acts and seven tableaux... New
       York, Samuel French [n.d.]. 43p. (French's American drama,
       no. cxxxv).

2073   PAYNE, JOHN HOWARD, 1791-1852. Ali Pacha; or, The signet-
       ring. A melo-drama, in two acts. By John Howard Payne...
       As performed at Covent-Garden Theatre, London. New York,
       E. M. Murden, 1823. 36p.

2074   _____. Brutus; or, The fall of Tarquin. An historical
       tragedy, in five acts. By John Howard Payne. First repre-
       sented at the Theatre Royal, Drury-Lane. On Thursday
       evening, December 3, 1818. London, R. White, 1818. viii,
       56p. 1st edition.
          "In the present play I have had no hesitation in
       adopting the conceptions and language of my predecessors,

PAYNE, JOHN HOWARD

(PAYNE, JOHN HOWARD)
wherever they seemed likely to strengthen the plan which
I had prescribed."--Pref.
Some entire scenes and portions of others are from
Downman's Lucius Junius Brutus, 1779, and from Cumberland's
The Sybil, or The elder Brutus, pub. in 1813 in the
posthumous dramatic works of Cumberland. Cf. Genest,
Account of the English stage.

2075   _____. ... Charles the Second; or, The merry monarch. A
comedy, in two acts, (with some songs) By John Howard
Payne. Printed from the acting copy, with remarks. To
which are added, a description of the costume, cast of the
characters... and the whole of the stage business, as now
performed at the Theatre Royal, Covent-Garden... London,
Printed and pub. by T. Dolby [1824]. 45p. front., diagr.
(Dolby's British theatre). [Broadhurst, J. Plays. v. 11,
no. 6].
Founded on Duval's "La jeunesse de Henri V."
Reissued, with remarks by George Daniel, as no. 59 (v. 9,
no. 3) of Cumberland's British theatre.

2076   _____. Clari; or, The maid of Milan, an opera, in two acts,
by John Howard Payne... Printed from the acting copy,
with remarks, biographical and critical, by D.-G. ... As
performed at the Theatres Royal... London, G. H. Davidson
[n.d.]. 40p. incl. front. (Cumberland's British theatre.
London, ca. 1825-55. v. 24 [no. 6]).
Remarks by George Daniel, editor of the series.
Contains the famous song, Home, sweet home.
Without the music (by Bishop).

2077   _____. The fall of Algiers: a comic opera, in three acts,
by John Howard Payne... Printed from the acting copy with
remarks, biographical and critical, by D.-G. ... As performed at the Theatres Royal... London, J. Cumberland
[n.d.]. 6, [2], [5]-47p. incl. front. (Cumberland's
British theatre. London, ca. 1825-55. v. 9 [no. 6]).
Remarks by George Daniel, editor of the series.
Without the music (by Bishop).

2078   _____. The lancers. An interlude, in one act, by John
Howard Payne... Printed from the acting copy, with remarks, biographical and critical, by D.-G. ... As performed at the Theatres Royal... London, C. Cumberland
[n.d.]. 27p. incl. front. (Cumberland's British theatre.
London, ca. 1825-55. v. 19 [no. 3]).
Remarks by George Daniel, editor of the series.

PEAKE, RICHARD BRINSLEY

2079   _____. Love in humble life: a petite comedy, in one act, by
John Howard Payne... Printed from the acting copy, with
remarks, biographical and critical, by D.-G. ... As performed at the Theatres Royal... London, G. H. Davidson
[n.d.]. 2 p.ℓ., [9]-31p. front. (Cumberland's British
theatre. London, ca. 1825-55. v. 11 [no. 5]).
    Adapted from Scribe and Dupin's "Michel et Christine."
Remarks by George Daniel, editor of the series.
Reissue of Cumberland's earlier edition.

2080   _____. ... Love in humble life. A petite comedy, in one
act... New York, Samuel French [n.d.]. 24p. (The minor
drama, no. cxviii).

2081 No Entry.

2082   _____. The two galley slaves: a melo-drama, in two acts, by
John Howard Payne... Printed from the acting copy, with
remarks, biographical and critical, by D.-G. ... As performed at the Theatres Royal... London, Davidson [n.d.].
33p. incl. front. (Cumberland's British theatre. London,
ca. 1825-55. v. 10 [no. 7]).
    Remarks by George Daniel, editor of the series.

2083 PEABODY, JOSEPHINE PRESTON, 1874-1922. Marlowe, a drama in
five acts. Boston and New York, Houghton Mifflin co.,
1901. 156p.

2084   _____. The piper, a play in four acts. Boston and New York,
Houghton Mifflin co., 1910. 201p.

2085   _____. The piper, a play in four acts. Boston and New York,
Houghton Mifflin co. [1909]. 201p.

2086   _____. The wolf of Gubbio, a comedy in three acts. Boston
and New York, Houghton Mifflin co., 1913. 195p.

2087 PEACOCK, THOMAS LOVE, 1785-1866. Plays, Published for the
first time. Edited by A. B. Young. London, P. Nutt,
1910. xiii, 157p.

2088 PEAKE, RICHARD BRINSLEY, 1792-1847. Amateurs and actors. A
musical farce, in two acts, by Richard Brinsley Peake...
Printed from the acting copy, with remarks, biographical
and critical, by D.-G. ... As performed at the Theatres
Royal... London, J. Cumberland [n.d.]. 36p. incl. front.
(Cumberland's British theatre. London, ca. 1825-55.
v. 16 [no. 5]).

PEAKE, RICHARD BRINSLEY

(PEAKE, RICHARD BRINSLEY)
Remarks by George Daniel, editor of the series.
Without the music (by J. B. Hart).
Reissued in Davidson's shilling volume of Cumberland's
plays. v. 6 [no. 4].

2089 _____. The chancery suit! A comedy in five acts. First performed at the Theatre royal, Covent Garden, Tuesday,
November 30, 1830. By R. B. Peake. Baltimore, J. Robinson,
1831. 76p.

2090 _____. Comfortable lodgings; or, Paris in 1750: a farce, in
two acts, by Richard Brinsley Peake... Printed from the
acting copy, with remarks, biographical and critical, by
D.-G. ... As performed at the Theatres Royal... London,
Davidson [n.d.]. 36p. incl. front. (Cumberland's
British theatre. London, ca. 1825-55. v. 29 [no. 8]).
Remarks by George Daniel, editor of the series.

2091 _____. Court and city. A comedy, in five acts. Adapted
from scenes in Sir Richard Steele's "Tender husband" and
Mrs. Frances Sheridan's "Discovery", by Richard Brinsley
Peake... Printed from the acting copy, with remarks,
biographical and critical, by D.-G. ... As performed at
The Theatre Royal, Covent Garden... London, J. Cumberland
and son [n.d.]. 72p. incl. front. (Cumberland's British
theatre. London, ca. 1825-55. v. 49, no. 2]).
Remarks by George Daniel, editor of the series.

2092 _____. The haunted inn. A farce, in two acts. First performed at the Theatre Royal, London, February 21, 1828...
London, John Dicks [n.d.]. 14p. (Dicks' standard plays,
no. 677).

2093 _____. The haunted man. A farce, in two acts, by Richard
Brinsley Peake... Printed from the acting copy, with re-
marks, biographical and critical, by D.-G. ... As per-
formed at the Theatres Royal... London, G. H. Davidson
[n.d.]. 40p. incl. front. (Cumberland's British theatre.
London, ca. 1825-55. v. 30 [no. 7]).
Remarks by George Daniel, editor of the series.
Reissue of Cumberland's earlier edition.

2094 _____. The hundred pound note: a farce, in two acts, by
Richard Brinsley Peake... Printed from the acting copy,
with remarks, biographical and critical, by D.-G. ... As
now performed at the Theatres Royal... London, J. Cumberland [n.d.]. 43p. incl. front. (Cumberland's British

PELHAM, NETTIE H.

(PEAKE, RICHARD BRINSLEY)
    theatre. London, ca. 1825-55. v. 34 [no. 8]).
        Remarks by George Daniel, editor of the series.

2095   _____. In the wrong box; a farce, in two acts... London,
    John Miller, 1834. 54p.

2096   _____. Uncle Rip. A farce, in two acts, by Richard Brinsley
    Peake... Printed from the acting copy, with remarks, bio-
    graphical and critical, by D.-G. ... As performed at the
    Theatres Royal... London, J. Cumberland and son [n.d.].
    40p. incl. front. (Cumberland's British theatre. London,
    ca. 1825-55. v. 42 [no. 7]).
        Remarks by George Daniel, editor of the series.
        Borrowed from Picard's Les deux Philibert.

2097   _____. Walk for a wager; or, A bailiff's bet. A musical
    farce, in two acts, first performed at the Theatre Royal,
    English Opera House. On Monday, August 2, 1819. By R. B.
    Peake... The overture and new music composed by Mr.
    Pindar. London, W. Fearman, 1819. 72p. [Broadhurst,
    J. Plays, v. 2, no. 2].
        Without the music.

2097A PEARCE, WILLIAM. Hartford bridge; or, The skirts of the camp:
    an operatic farce, in two acts. By William Pearce, printed
    from the acting copy, with remarks, biographical and
    critical, by D.-G. ... As performed at the Theatres Royal
    ... London, G. H. Davidson [n.d.]. 36p. incl. front.
    (Cumberland's British theatre. London, ca. 1825-55. v. 30
    [no. 5]).
        Remarks by George Daniel, editor of the series.
        Reissue of Cumberland's earlier edition.
        The music composed and compiled by Shield.

2098   The peddler of very nice; a burlesque. Boston, Walter H.
    Baker and co. [1866]. 201-214p.

2099   PEGUY, CHARLES, 1873-1914. The mystery of the charity of
    Joan of Arc. Translated by Julian Green. London, Hollis
    and Carter [n.d.]. 216p.

2100   PELHAM, NETTIE H. The Christmas ship, a Christmas entertain-
    ment, by Nettie H. Pelham. Chicago, T. S. Denison [1888].
    10p. On cover: Amateur series.

PELHAM, NETTIE H.

2101   PELHAM, NETTIE H. The old fashioned husking bee; an old
       folks' entertainment in one scene, by Nettie H. Pelham.
       Boston, W. H. Baker and co., 1891. 17p. On cover: Baker's
       edition of plays.

2102   _____. The realm of time, a pageant for young people and
       children. By Nettie H. Pelham... Chicago, T. S. Denison
       [1890]. 20p. On cover: Amateur series.

2103   PEMBERTON, HARRIET L. CHILDE. Nicknames. A comedietta, in
       one act. Chicago, The Dramatic publishing co. [n.d.].
       16p.

2104   PEMBERTON, THOMAS EDGAR, 1849-1905. Don't be too quick to
       cry "wolf." A comedietta, in one act. By T. Edgar Pem-
       berton... New York, De Witt, 1884. 12p. (On cover: De
       Witt's acting plays. no. 330).

2105   PENLEY, SAMSON. The sleeping-draught: a farce, in two acts,
       by S. Penley. Printed from the acting copy, with remarks,
       biographical and critical, by D.-G. ... As performed at
       the Theatres Royal... London, Davidson [n.d.]. 38p.
       incl. front. (Cumberland's British theatre. London, ca.
       1825-55. v. 29 [no. 2]).
           Founded on The Decameron of Boccaccio (Fourth day,
       novel x).
           Remarks by George Daniel, editor of the series.
           Reissue of Cumberland's earlier edition.

2106   PENN, ARTHUR. Too much Smith; or, Heredity, a physiological
       and psychological absurdity in one act. Boston, Walter H.
       Baker and co., 1902. 51p.

2107   PEPLE, EDWARD HENRY, 1869-1924. The prince chap, a comedy in
       three acts, by Edward Peple... [French's standard library
       ed.] New York, S. French; [etc., etc.] 1914. 101p.

2108   _____. The prince chap; a comedy in three acts, by Edward
       Peple... New York, S. French; [etc., etc.] 1904. 101p.

2109   PERCIVAL, JAMES GATES, 1795-1856. Poems by James G. Percival
       III. New Haven, Pub. for the author, A. H. Maltby and co.,
       printers, 1821. xii, [9]-346p., 1ℓ. Contains his Zamor.

2110   Peregrine Pickle: a biographical play, in five acts. Oxford,
       Henry Slatter, 1851. 73p.

2111   PÉREZ GALDOS, BENITO, 1815-1920. ... The grandfather (drama
        in five acts) by Pérez Galdos... tr. from the Spanish by
        Elizabeth Wallace. [Boston, R. G. Badger] 1910. p. 161-
        233. (Poet lore, vol. xxi, no. III).

2112   PERLEY, MAE CLEMENT. The quilt; pageant of Kentucky's Jewry.
        Louisville, Kentucky, Jewish Tercentenary Committee of the
        Conference of Jewish Organizations, 1954. 56p.

2113   No Entry.

2114   PETERSON, HENRY, 1818-1891. Caesar; a dramatic study. In
        five acts. By Henry Peterson... Philadelphia, H. Peter-
        son and co., 1879. 72p.

2115   _____. Columbus. By Henry Peterson... In six acts...
        Cincinnati, W. Peterson, 1893. 65p.

2116   PFEIL, HELENA A. Bill Perkins' proposin' day, a rustic
        comedy in one act. Chicago, The Dramatic publishing co.,
        1910. 12p.

2117   PHELPS, PAULINE. A cyclone for a cent, a farce in one act,
        by Pauline Phelps. Boston, W. H. Baker and co., 1894.
        17p. (On cover: Baker's edition of plays).

2118   _____. Deacon Slocum's presence of mind; monologue for a
        woman, by Pauline Phelps... [New York, E. S. Werner
        publishing and supply co. (incorporated)] 1904. [3]-7p.

2119   _____. Her Cuban tea. Humorous monologue for a woman. By
        Pauline Phelps. [New York, E. S. Werner publishing and
        supply co. (incorporated) 1902]. 6p.

2120   _____. A Shakespearian conference [a drama]. By Pauline
        Phelps. [New York] E. S. Werner publishing and supply
        co. (incorporated), 1901. 15p.

2121   _____. ... Sixteen 2-character plays, also encores. Text
        and stage-business ed. and rev. by Pauline Phelps and
        Marion Short. New York. E. S. Werner and co., 1906.
        192p. (Werner's readings and recitations, no. 36).

2122   _____. The sweet girl-graduate. Humorous monologue for a
        lady. By Pauline Phelps. New York, E. S. Werner pub. and
        supply co., 1900. Cover-title, 7p. 12°.

PHELPS, PAULINE

2123   PHELPS, PAULINE. A telephone romance. Humorous monologue for a lady. New York, Edgar S. Werner and co., 1899. 8p.

2124   PHILLIPS, BERTINE K. Aunt Dinah's quilting party, an original entertainment in one act and one scene. New York, Fitzgerald publishing corp., 1903. 25p.

2125   PHILLIPS, STEPHEN, 1868-1915. Herod; a tragedy, by Stephen Phillips. London and New York, J. Lane, 1901. 3 p.ℓ., [5]-126p.

2126   _____. Nero, by Stephen Phillips. New York, The Macmillan co.; London, Macmillan and co., ltd., 1906. v, 200p.

2127   _____. The new inferno, by Stephen Phillips. New York, John Lane co., 1910. 151p.

2128   _____. Paolo and Francesca; a tragedy in four acts, by Stephen Phillips... [4th ed.] London and New York, John Lane, 1911. 120p.

2129   _____. Paolo and Francesca, a tragedy in four acts. London and New York. John Lane, The Bodley Head, 1900. 120p.

2130   _____. Pietro of Siena, a drama, by Stephen Phillips... New York, The Macmillan co., 1910. 4 p.ℓ., 3-82p.

2131   _____. The sin of David, New York, The Macmillan co., 1904. 141p.

2132   _____. Ulysses; a drama, by Stephen Phillips... in a prologue and three acts. New York, London, The Macmillan co., 1908. vii, 137p.

2133   PHILLIPS, WATTS, 1825-1874. A golden fetter. Fettered. A drama, in three acts. New York, Robert M. De Witt [n.d.]. 40p.

2134   _____. A lion at bay. A drama, in one act... London, Thomas Hailes Lacy [n.d.]. 19p.

2135   _____. Lost in London. A new and original drama. In three acts. By Watts Phillips... London, S. French; New York, S. French and son [1880?]. 58p. (On cover: French's acting edition, 1195).

2136 _____. Maud's peril. A drama in four acts. By Watts
Phillips... To which is added a description of the costume,
cast of the characters... and the whole of the stage business. New York, R. M. De Witt [187-]. 4, 7-28p. (On
cover: De Witt's acting plays. (No. 7.)).

2137 _____. Nobody's child. A romantic drama, in three acts. By
Watts Phillips... [To] which are added a description of the
costume - cast of the characters... and the whole of the
stage business. New York, R. M. De Witt [187-?]. 38p.
diagr. (On cover: De Witt's acting plays. No. 2).

2138 _____. Not guilty. A drama, in four acts. By Watts
Phillips... To which is added a description of the costume - cast of the characters... and the whole of the stage
business. New York, R. M. De Witt [187-?]. 50p. diagrs.
(On cover: De Witt's acting plays. [No. 84.]).

2139 PHILLPOTTS, EDEN, 1862-1960. Curtain raisers, by Eden Phillpotts. London, Duckworth and co., 1912. 4 p.ℓ., 3-53p.,
Il. CONTENTS. - The point of view. - Hiatus. - The carrier-
pigeon.

2140 PICKETT, A. ST. J. The sublime tragedy of the lost cause, by
A. St. J. Pickett. A tragic poem of the war. In four
acts... Columbus [Ohio] The Westbote printing co., 1884.
238, [2]p.

2141 PICTON, THOMAS. A hard case. A farce, in one act... New
York, Robert M. De Witt, 1873. 13p.

2142 _____. 'Tis better to live than to die. A petite comedy, in
one act. New York, Robert M. De Witt, 1874. 12p.

2143 PIDGIN, CHARLES FELTON, 1844-1923. Blennerhassett, a dramatic
romance in a prologue and four acts; founded upon incidents
in the life of Harman Blennerhassett, his wife Margaret,
Aaron Burr, his daughter Theodosia, and Alexander Hamilton.
Boston, C. M. Clark pub. co., 1901. 2 p.ℓ., 69p.

2144 PIERCE, L. FRANCE. Aaron Burr, a romantic drama in four acts.
Chicago, Pierce, 1901. Various pagings.

2145 [PIERRA, ADOLFO]. The Cuban patriots, a drama of the struggle
for independence actually going on in the gem of the
Antilles. In three acts. Written in English by a native
Cuban. Philadelphia, 1873. iv, [5]-45, [1]p., 1ℓ.

PIERRON, EUGÈNE ATHANASE

2146   PIERRON, EUGÈNE ATHANASE, 1819-1865. Book the third, chapter
        the first. A comedy, in one act. Tr. and adapted from the
        French of mm. Eugène Pierron et Adolphe Laferrière. Lon-
        don, T. H. Lacy [1852?]. 21p.

2147   _____. Two can play at that game. A petit comedy, in one act.
        Translated and adapted from the French of Eugène Pierron
        and Adolphe Laferrière... New York, Samuel French [n.d.].
        20p.

2148   PILGRIM, JAMES, d. 1879. Eveleen Wilson, the flower of the
        Erin. An original drama, in three acts... New York,
        Samuel French [n.d.]. 32p.

2149   _____. ... Katty O'Sheal: a farce, in two acts, by James
        Pilgrim, esq. ... As now performed at the principal
        English and American theatres. New York, S. French
        [1870?]. 22p. (French's Minor drama. The acting edition.
        no. 295).

2150   _____. ... Paddy the piper. A comic drama, in one act...
        New York, Samuel French [n.d.]. 16p.

2151   _____. Robert Emmet, the martyr of Irish liberty, an his-
        torical drama, in three acts. New York, Samuel French,
        London, Samuel French [n.d.]. 28p.

2152   _____. Servants by legacy. A farce, in one act... New York,
        Samuel French [n.d.]. 10p.

2153   PILON, FREDERICK, 1750-1788. He would be a soldier. A
        comedy, in five acts; by Frederic Pilon... London,
        Printed by D. S. Maurice [1819?]. 74p. front. [Cabinet
        theatre. v. 1, no. 4]. Title vignette.

2154   PINERO, SIR ARTHUR WING, 1855-1934. The benefit of the
        doubt; a comedy in three acts, by Arthur W. Pinero.
        Rahway, N. J., The Mershon co., 1895. 4 p.ℓ., 229p.

2155   _____. The cabinet minister; a farce in four acts, by Arthur
        W. Pinero. New York, J. W. Lovell co. [c1891]. 3 p.ℓ.,
        188p.

2156   _____. Dandy Dick; a play in three acts, by Arthur Pinero...
        New York, Chicago, United States book co. [c1893]. 1 p.ℓ.,
        5-162p.

PINERO, SIR ARTHUR WING

2157 _____. His house in order, a comedy, in four acts, by Arthur W. Pinero. London, W. Heinemann, 1906. 3 p.ℓ., 224p.

2158 _____. The hobby-horse; a comedy in three acts, by Arthur W. Pinero. New York, United States book co. [c1892]. 3 p.ℓ., 168p.

2159 _____. In chancery; an original fantastic comedy in three acts, by Arthur W. Pinero... New York, London, S. French, c1905. 4 p.ℓ., 5-72p. incl. plans. On cover: French's standard library edition.

2160 _____. Iris; a drama in five acts, by Arthur W. Pinero. New York, R. H. Russell, 1902. 3 p.ℓ., 224p.

2161 _____. Lady Bountiful, a story of years; a play in four acts, by Arthur W. Pinero... New York, Chicago, United States book co. [c1892]. 2 p.ℓ., [7]-203p.

2162 _____. The magistrate; a farce in three acts, by Arthur W. Pinero. New York, Chicago, United States book co. [c1892]. x p., 2ℓ., 164p.

2163 _____. The money spinner; an original comedy in two acts, by Arthur W. Pinero. New York, S. French; London, S. French, ltd., c1900. 43p. (On cover: French's international copyrighted... edition of the works of the best authors, no. 35).

2164 _____. The notorious Mrs. Ebbsmith, a drama in four acts, by Arthur W. Pinero... Boston, W. H. Baker and co., 1895. 200p.

2165 _____. The profligate, a play in four acts, by Arthur W. Pinero... New York, United States book co. [c1891]. 3 p.ℓ., 123p.

2166 _____. The rocket, an original comedy in three acts, by Arthur W. Pinero... London, New York, S. French, ltd., c1905. 3 p.ℓ., 5-80p. incl. plans. (On cover: French's standard library edition).

2167 _____. The schoolmistress; a farce in three acts, by Arthur W. Pinero. Boston, W. H. Baker and co., 1894. 177p.

PINERO, SIR ARTHUR WING

2168   PINERO, SIR ARTHUR WING. The squire; an original comedy in
        three acts, by Arthur W. Pinero. New York, London, S.
        French, c1905. 3 p.ℓ., 5-81p. incl. plans. On cover:
        French's standard library edition.

2169   _____. Sweet Lavender; a comedy in three acts, by Arthur W.
        Pinero... Boston, Mass., W. H. Baker and co. [c1893].
        184p.
        "Printed as manuscript only."

2170   _____. The thunderbolt, an episode in the history of a pro-
        vincial family in four acts. Boston, Walter H. Baker and
        co., London, William Heinemann, 1909. 237p.

2171   _____. The times; a comedy, by A. W. Pinero. New York,
        United States book co. [c1891]. x, 192p.

2172   _____. Trelawny of the "Wells"; a comedietta in four acts,
        by Arthur W. Pinero. New York, The De Witt publishing
        house; [etc., etc.] 1898. 4 p.ℓ., 215p. (On cover:
        Green-room edition of copyrighted plays).

2173   _____. The weaker sex; a comedy in three acts, by Arthur W.
        Pinero... Boston, W. H. Baker and co., 1894. 133p.

2174   _____. A wife without a smile; a comedy in disguise, in
        three acts, by Arthur W. Pinero... Boston, W. H. Baker and
        co.; [etc., etc.] 1905. 166p.

2175   PINKOPKI, PHILLIP. A colonel's mishap. A farce comedy in
        one act. Clyde, Ohio, Ames' publishing co., 1891. 8p.

2176   PITT, GEORGE DIBDIN. The drunkard's doom; or, The last nail,
        a romantic drama, in two acts. Clyde, Ohio, A. D. Ames
        [n.d.]. 23p.

2177   _____. The Eddystone elf: a melodrama, in two acts... Lon-
        don, G. H. Davidson [n.d.]. 36p. front.

2178   _____. ... The whistler! or, The fate of the lily of St.
        Leonard's. A melodrama, in three acts... London, J.
        Duncombe and co. [n.d.]. 35p. front. (Duncombe's edition).

2179   PLANCHE, ELIZA. ... A pleasant neighbor. A farce, in one
        act... New York, Samuel French [n.d.]. 16p. (French's
        American drama, no. lxi).

PLANCHÉ, JAMES ROBINSON

2180 PLANCHÉ, JAMES ROBINSON, 1796-1880. All in the dark; or, The
banks of the Elbe. A musical farce, in two acts, adapted
to the English stage from the French of Victor... London,
Printed for C. Chapple, 1822. 47p.

2181 _____. Amoroso, king of Little Britain. A serio-comic,
bombastic, operatic interlude, in one act, by J. R.
Planché... Printed from the acting copy, with remarks,
biographical and critical, by D.-G. ... As performed at
the Theatres Royal... London, J. Cumberland [n.d.]. 19p.
incl. front. (Cumberland's British theatre. London, ca.
1825-55. v. 43 [no. 7]).
    Remarks by George Daniel, editor of the series.
    Without the music.

2182 _____. The brigand. A romantic drama, in two acts, by J. R.
Planché... Printed from the acting copy, with remarks,
biographical and critical, by D.-G. ... As performed at
the Theatres Royal... London, J. Cumberland [n.d.]. 36p.
incl. front. (Cumberland's British theatre. London, ca.
1825-55. v. 24 [no. 7]).
    Based on a French piece, "Le bandit" [by Théaulon,
Saint-Laurent, and Théodore?]. Cf. Remarks.
    Remarks by George Daniel, editor of the series.

2183 _____. A cabinet question. A comic drama in one act...
London, S. G. Fairbrother, 1845. 28p.

2184 _____. The captain of the watch. A comedietta, in one act.
By J. R. Planché. <Freely rendered from the French piece
entitled, "Le chevalier du guet," by M. Lockroy.> As performed at Covent Garden theatre, London, in 1841. To
which are added, a description of the costumes... and the
whole of the stage business. New York, R. M. De Witt,
c1876. 23p. (On cover: De Witt's acting plays. no.
199).

2185 _____. Cortez; or, The conquest of Mexico. An historical
drama in three acts... The music by Henry R. Bishop.
London, Printed by and for John Lowndes [n.d.]. 50p.

2186 _____. The court beauties: a dramatic sketch, in one act...
London, John Miller, 1835. 30p.

PLANCHÉ, JAMES ROBINSON

2187   PLANCHÉ, JAMES ROBINSON. A day of reckoning. A drama, in
three acts... first performed at the Royal Lyceum Theatre,
Wednesday, December 4, 1851... London, S. G. Fairbrother
[n.d.]. 42p.

2188   _____. ... The extravaganzas of J. R. Planché, esq., (Somerset herald) 1825-1871. Ed. by T. F. Dillon Croker and
Stephen Tucker (Rouge croix)... London, S. French, 1879.
5 v. fronts., ports.
     At head of title: Testimonial edition.
     Imperfect: List of subscribers wanting.
     CONTENTS. - v. 1. Note by the editors. Author's
preface. Success; or, A hit if you like it. Olympic re-
vels; or, Prometheus and Pandora. Olympic devils; or,
Orpheus and Eurydice. The Paphian bower; or, Venus and
Adonis. High, low, jack, and the game; or, The card
party. Deep, deep sea; or, Perseus and Andromeda. Tele-
machus; or, The island of Calypso. Riquet with the tuft.
Puss in boots. Appendix. - v. 2. The drama's levée; or,
A peep at the past. Blue Beard. The sleeping beauty in
the wood. Beauty and the beast. The white cat. Fortunio,
and his seven gifted servants. The fair one with the
golden locks. The drama at home; or, An evening with Puff.
Graciosa and Percinet. - v. 3. The golden fleece; or,
Jason in Colchis and Medea in Corinth. The bee and the
orange tree; or, The four wishes. "The birds" of Aristoph-
anes. The invisible prince; or, The island of Tranquil
Delights. The new planet; or, Harlequin out of place.
The golden branch. Theseus and Ariadne; or, The marriage
of Bacchus. The king of the peacocks. The seven champions
of Christendom. - v. 4. The island of Jewels. Cymon and
Iphigenia. King Charming; or, The blue bird of paradise.
The queen of the frogs. The prince of Happy Land; or, The
fawn in the forest. The good woman in the wood. Mr.
Buckstone's ascent of Mount Parnassus. The camp at the
Olympic. Once upon a time there were two kings. - v. 5.
Mr. Buckstone's voyage round the globe (in Leicester square).
The yellow dwarf and the king of the gold mines. The new
Haymarket spring meeting. The discreet princess; or, The
three glass distaffs. Young and handsome. Love and
fortune. Orpheus in the Haymarket. King Christmas.
Appendix. A complete list of the dramatic productions of
J. R. Planché. List of subscribers to the Testimonial
edition.

2189   _____. ... Faint heart never won fair lady. A comedy in one
act... New York, William and co. [n.d.]. 31p. (Modern
standard drama, no. lxviii).

PLANCHÉ, JAMES ROBINSON

2190   . The fair Gabrielle; an operatic anecdote, in one act...
London, Printed for C. Chapple, 1822. 31p.

2191   . The follies of a night, a vaudeville, comedy, in two
acts... London, S. G. Fairbrother [1842]. 48p.

2192   . The fortunate isles; or, The triumphs of Britannia.
An allegorical national masque... The music composed and
selected by H. R. Bishop. London, Chapman and Hall, 1840.
16p.

2193   . The golden fleece; or, Jason in Colchis and Medea in
Corinth; a classical extravaganza in two parts. London,
Thomas Hailes Lacy [n.d.]. 32p.

2194   . The green-eyed monster; a comedy, in two acts, by
J. R. Planché... Printed from the acting copy, with remarks, biographical and critical, by D.-G. ... As performed at the Theatres Royal... London, J. Cumberland
[n.d.]. 45p. incl. front. (Cumberland's British theatre.
London, ca. 1825-55. v. 21 [no.3]).
    Founded in part on "Les deux jaloux" of Vial.
    Remarks by George Daniel, editor of the series.

2195   . Grist to the mill. A comic drama, in two acts...
London, S. G. Fairbrother [etc., etc.] 1844. 36p.

2196   . ... The invisible prince; or, The island of Tranquil
Delights. A fairy extravaganza in one act. (Founded on
the Countess d'Aulnoy's Fairy tale, "Prince Lutin.") By
J. R. Planché. With the stage business, cast of charac-
ters... New York, W. Taylor and co.; Baltimobe [!] Md.,
W. and H. Taylor [1847?]. 35p. (The Minor drama. no. 7).

2197   . The island of jewels. An original grand comic, fairy
extravaganza... London, Thomas Hailes Lacy [n.d.]. 38p.

2198   . The Jacobite: a comic drama in two acts... London,
S. G. Fairbrother [etc., etc.] [1847]. 32p.

2199   . The Jewess, a grand operatic drama, in three acts,
founded on M. Scribe's opera, "La juive," by J. R. Planché
... First performed at the Theatre royal, Drury-Lane,
Monday, November 16, 1835. London, Porter and Wright,
1835. vii, [1], 48p. [With his Shere Afkun. London,
1823].

PLANCHÉ, JAMES ROBINSON

(PLANCHÉ, JAMES ROBINSON)
"Although I have adhered pretty closely... to the plot
of Mons. Scribe's drama, the language, such as it is, is
my own."--Note at end, signed J. R. P.

2200 _____. King Charming; or, The blue bird of paradise. A new
and original grand comic fairy extravaganza, in two acts...
London, Published by S. G. Fairbrother [n.d.]. 38p.

2201 [_____]. Songs, duets, chorusses, &c. in the new and original
fairy extravaganza, of The king of the peacocks. By the
author of The golden branch... London, Printed by S. G.
Fairbrother [n.d.]. 14p.

2202 _____. The loan of a lover. A vaudeville, in one act.
Boston, Walter H. Baker and co. [n.d.]. 21p.

2203 _____. ... The loan of a lover. A vaudeville in one act.
By J. R. Planché. With the stage business, cast of characters... New York, Baltimore, W. Taylor and co., 1847.
29p. front. (The Minor drama. no. 4).

2204 _____. Songs, duets, etc., in the new dramatic tableau (in
Watteau colors) entitled Love and fortune... London,
Thomas Hailes Lacy [1859]. 11p.

2205 _____. Maid Marian; or, The huntress of Arlingford. A
legendary opera, in three acts... The overture and music
entirely new, composed by Mr. [H. R.] Bishop. London,
Printed for John Lowndes [n.d.]. 52p.

2206 _____. The merchant's wedding; or, London frolics in 1638:
a comedy, in five acts, principally founded on Jasper
Mayne's "City match," and W. Rowley's "Match at midnight,"
by J. R. Planché... London, J. Cumberland, 1828. viii,
[9]-79p.

2207 _____. My daughter, Sir! or, A daughter to marry: a farce,
in one act, by J. R. Planché... Printed from the acting
copy, with remarks, biographical and critical, by D.-G.
... As performed at the Theatres Royal... London, J.
Cumberland [n.d.]. 28p. incl. front. (Cumberland's
British theatre. London, ca. 1825-55. v. 37 [no. 5]).
Remarks by George Daniel, editor of the series.
Produced under title: A daughter to marry.

PLANCHÉ, JAMES ROBINSON

2208   . My great aunt; or, Relations and friends, a comedy in one act... London, S. G. Fairbrother [etc., etc.] 1846. 24p.

2209   . Norma; a grand tragic drama, in two acts, freely rendered from the Italian... The music composed by Bellini... London, Printed by S. G. Fairbrother, 1848. 31p.

2210 [   ]. Oberon, opéra en 3 actes, musique de M. [Carl Maria von Weber] [Paris] Vinchon [n.d.] 14p.

2211   . ... Oberon: a romantic and fairy opera, in three acts... with the music of the Baron Carl Maria von Weber... London, published by Hunt and Clarke, 1826. 53p. front. (port.).

2212   . Orpheus in the Haymarket. An opera buffe, in three tableaux and a last scene... The music by J. Offenbach. London, Thomas Hailes Lacy [1865]. 40p.

2213   . The pirate; a musical drama in three acts... London, Printed for John Lowndes [1822]. 70p.

2214   . ... The pride of the market. A comic drama, in three acts... New York, William Taylor [n.d.]. 47p. (The minor drama, no. ix).

2215   . The printer's devil. A farce, in one act... Illustrated with an engraving, by Pierce Egan the younger... London, Chapman and Hall [1838]. 19p. front.

2216   . Reputation; or, The state secret. A play in five acts... London, published by J. Andrews [1833]. 60p.

2217   . Rodolph the wolf; or, Columbine Red Riding-Hood; a comic melodramatic pantomime... London, Printed for John Lowndes, 1819. 23p.

2218   . ... Secret service. A drama in two acts. From the French of Messrs. Mélesville [pseud.] and Duveyrier. By J. R. Planché. New York, S. French [185-]. 2 p.ℓ., 7-46p. (The Minor drama. no. 25).
    Translated and adapted from "Michel Perrin."
    First acted April, 1834.

PLANCHÉ, JAMES ROBINSON

2219   PLANCHÉ, JAMES ROBINSON. Spring gardens: a farce, in one
        act... London, Published by S. G. Fairbrother [etc., etc.]
        [1846]. 28p.

2220   _____. The two Figaros, a musical comedy, in two acts, by
        J. R. Planché... As performed at the Royal Olympic theatre.
        Correctly printed from the prompter's copy... Prefaced by
        A dedication to Madame Vestris; and an original biographi-
        cal sketch of John Liston, esq. Splendidly illustrated
        with two engravings, by Orrin Smith, and Pierce Egan, the
        younger... London, Chapman and Hall [1837]. iv, [5]-44p.
        front., pl. (Webster, B. The acting national drama...
        London, 1837-52. v. 1, no. 2).
            Biographical sketch of Liston (p. [5]-9) signed: B.-W.
        (i.e., Benjamin Webster.
            Based on Martelly's "Les deux Figaro; ou, Le sujet de
        comédie."
            Without the music (selected from "The barber of Seville"
        and "The marriage of Figaro").

2221   PLAUTUS, TITUS MACCIUS, ca. 251-184 B.C. The comedies of
        Plautus, literally translated into English prose, with
        notes by Henry Thomas Riley... vol. I. Containing the
        Trinummus, Miles Gloriosus, Bacchides, Stichus, Pseudolus,
        Menaechmi, Aulularia, Captivi, Asinaria, and Curculio.
        London, G. Bell and sons, 1912. 564p.

2222   _____. Comedies of T. Maccius Plautus (Amphitruo, Asinaria,
        Aulularia, Bacchides, Captivi) Tr. in the original metres
        by Edward H. Sugden... London, S. Sonnenschein and co.;
        New York, Macmillan and co., 1893. viii p., 2ℓ., 315p.
        illus.

2223   PLEASANT, LILLIAN. Their godfather from Paris, comedy in one
        act. New York, Ernest A. Fink [1905]. 28p.

2224   PLOWMAN, THOMAS FORDER, 1844-1919. ... Isaac of York; or,
        Saxons and Normans at home. A new burlesque extravangnza,
        by Thomas F. Plowman. Produced at the Royal court theatre,
        November 29th, 1871. London, Printed by J. W. Last and
        co. [1871]. 24p.
            Based on Sir Walter Scott's Ivanhoe.

2225   PLUMMER, FRANK EVERETT. Gracia; a social tragedy... illus-
        trations designed by the author; F. W. Webster, artist.
        Chicago, C. H. Kerr and co., 1900 [1899]. 124p. pl.

2226   PLUNKETT, HENRY WILLOUGHBY GRATTAN, 1808-1889. ... The
minerali; or, The dying gift. A romantic drama, in two
acts. By Henry Grattan Plunkett... To which are added,
a description of the costume - cast of the characters...
and the whole of the stage business... New-York, S. French,
[185-]. 27p. (French's standard drama. no. 152).

2226A POCOCK, ISAAC, 1782-1835. Hit or miss: a musical farce, in
two acts, by I. Pocock... Printed from the acting copy,
with remarks, biographical and critical, by D.-G. ... As
performed at the Theatres Royal... London, J. Cumberland
[n.d.]. 34p. incl. front. (Cumberland's British theatre.
London, ca. 1825-55. v. 34 [no. 3]).
     Remarks by George Daniel, editor of the series.

2227   . Hit or miss! A musical farce, in two acts. As performed at the theatres royal, English opera house, &c. By
I. Pocock, esq. ... Correctly given, from copies used in
the theatres, by Thomas Dibdin... London, Printed at the
Chiswick press for Sherwood, Neely, and Jones, 1818. 40p.
illus. (Dibdin, T. J. London theatre. London, 1815
[1814-25] v. 6 [no. 1]). Title vignette.
     Without music.

2228   . John of Paris. A comic opera, in two acts, by I.
Pocock... Printed from the acting copy, with remarks,
biographical and critical, by D.-G. ... As performed at
the Theatres Royal... London, J. Cumberland [n.d.]. 39p.
incl. front. (Cumberland's British theatre. London, ca.
1825-55. v. 26 [no. 5]).
     Remarks by George Daniel, editor of the series.
     Adapted from Saint-Just's "Jean de Paris."
     Without the music (adapted from Boieldieu by Bishop).

2229   . The magpie, or the maid? A melodrama, in three acts.
Translated and altered from the French, by I. Pocock...
First performed at the Theatre-royal, Covent-Garden, on
Friday, September 15, 1815. From the original London copy
by permission of the managers. Baltimore, J. Robinson,
1831. 48p.
     Adapted from the French of L. C. Caigniez and J. M.
Baudouin.

2230   . The miller and his men: a melodrama, in two acts, by
I. Pocock... Printed from the acting copy, with remarks,
biographical and critical, by D.-G. ... As performed at
the Theatres Royal... London, Davidson [n.d.]. 48p. incl.
front. (Cumberland's British theatre. London, ca. 1825-
55. v. 26 [no. 6]).

POCOCK, ISAAC

       (POCOCK, ISAAC)
           Remarks by George Daniel, editor of the series.
           Without the music (by Bishop).
           Reissue of Cumberland's earlier edition.

2231   ____. Montrose; or, The children of the mist. A musical drama, in three acts. Founded on the Legend of Montrose. First performed at the Theatre-Royal, Covent-Garden. Thursday, February 14, 1822. By I. Pocock, esq. ... Baltimore, J. Robinson, 1822. 60p.
           Without the music (by Bishop).

2232   [____]. Nigel; or, The crown jewels, a play, in five acts, as first performed, at the Theatre Royal Covent Garden, January 28, 1823. London [R. Wilks, printer] 1823. v, [1], 97, 1p. [Broadhurst, J. Plays. v. 2, no. 9].
           By Pocock, founded on Scott's "The fortunes of Nigel." cf. E. Fitzball, Thirty-five years of a dramatic author's life, p. 89-90, 108.

2233   [____]. ... The omnibus. A farce in one act... New York, Douglas, 1848. 23p. front. (The Minor drama, no. XXVI).
           By Isaac Pocock. Cf. Brown's Guide to books on Ireland; Dict. nat. biog.
           "The omnibus, or, A convenient distance', is an adaptation from... [R. J. Raymond's] farce called "Cherry bounce', and was produced during the zenith of power and fame, with his alterations."--Editorial introd.

2234   ____. Rob Roy; a national drama, founded on the celebrated novel of the same name, by the author of "Waverley," &c., &c., as performed at the Theatre-Royal, Edinburgh... [n.p., n.d.]. 68p. front. (In The Waverley dramas, from the novels... London, 1845. [no. 2]).
           Published also under title: Rob Roy Macgregor; or, Auld lang syne.
           Without the music (by John Davy).

2235   ____. Rob Roy Macgregor; or, "Auld Lang Syne," an operatic play, in three acts. New York, Wm. Taylor and co. [n.d.]. 60p.

2236   ____. The robber's wife. A romantic drama, in two acts, by I. Pocock... Printed from the acting copy, with remarks, biographical and critical, by D.-G. ... As performed at the Theatres Royal... London, J. Cumberland [n.d.]. 40p. front. (port.). (Cumberland's British theatre. London, ca. 1825-55. v. 28 [no. 1]).

(POCOCK, ISAAC)
Founded on one of the Tales of the Munster festivals,
by Gerald Griffin.

2237   _____. Robinson Crusoe; or, The bold buccaneers: a romantic
drama, in three acts, by I. Pocock... Printed from the
acting copy, with remarks, biographical and critical, by
D.-G. ... As performed at the Theatres Royal... London,
J. Cumberland [n.d.]. 41p. incl. front. (Cumberland's
British theatre. London, ca. 1825-55. v. 28 [no. 9]).
Remarks by George Daniel, editor of the series.

2238   _____. Yes, or no? A musical farce, in two acts. By I.
Pocock, esq. The music composed by Mr. G. [!] Smith. Per-
formed with universal applause at the Theatre Royal, Hay-
market. New-York, Published by D. Longworth, At the
Dramatic Repository, Shakspeare-Gallery, 1809. 32p.
Without the music.

2239 POEL, WILLIAM, 1852-1934, ed. ... Lillies that fester, and
Love's constancy; arranged by William Poel... New York,
Brentano's [c1906]. 2 p.ℓ., [iii]-vii p., 1ℓ., [2], 109p.
(The playhouse series).
Modified versions of the older plays: the first has
been almost entirely reconstructed and the second consists
only of an episode from the chronicle, adapted to the
modern stage. Cf. Introd.
CONTENTS. - Lilies that fester, a tragedy adapted from
the play Arden of Feversham - Love's constancy, an episode
in the play of "Edward the Third."

2240 POGSON, BERTHA. Absorbing passion, a comedy in three acts.
Hamburg, Germany, 1906. Various pagings.

2241 POLLOCK, JOHN. Twelve one-acters. London, The Cayme Press,
1926. 330p.

2242 POLSON, MINNIE. Our Kittie. A comedy drama in three acts.
Clyde, Ohio, Ames' publishing co., 1894. 20p.

2243 POOLE, JOHN, 1786?-1872. ... Deaf as a post, a farce, in one
act. By T. [!] Poole, esq. Printed from the acting copy,
with stage directions. New-York, E. B. Clayton; Philadelphia, C. Neal [1833?]. 31p. At head of title: Clayton's
edition.

POOLE, JOHN

2244   [_____]. Hamlet travestie: in three acts. With annotations
        by Dr. Johnson and Geo. Steevens, esq., and other commen-
        tators... London, J. M. Richardson, 1810. 1 p.ℓ., [v]-
        xiii, [2], 94p.
            With ms. marginal notes and 4 pages of ms. annotations
        at end signed: Editor.
            Burlesque notes.

2245   _____. The hole in the wall: a farce, in two acts. By John
        Poole... <From the first London edition, of 1813.> New-
        York, Published by D. Longworth, at the Dramatic repository,
        Shakspeare-gallery, Dec. 1813. 36p.

2246   _____. Intrigue; or, Married yesterday. A comic interlude,
        in one act. As performed at the Theatre Royal, Drury Lane.
        By John Poole, esq. ... New York, Published by D. Long-
        worth, at the Dramatic repository, Shakspeare-gallery,
        Jan. 1816. 27p.

2247   _____. Married and single. A comedy. In three acts... To
        which is prefixed, an exposure of a recent little proceeding
        of the great director of the Theatre royal at the corner
        of Brydges street. By John Poole... London, J. Miller,
        1824. xv, [1], 67p.
            Adapted from the French drama called "Le célibataire et
        l'homme marié."

2248   _____. Paul Pry, a comedy, in three acts, by John Poole, esq.
        ... As performed at the Hay-market theatre, London, and
        Park and Chatham theatres, New York... New-York, E. M.
        Murden, 1827. 72p.
            Advertising matter, list of plays published by Murden:
        p. [70]-72.

2249   _____. The scape-goat; a farce, in one act. By John Poole.
        (In The London stage. London [1824-27]. v. 4 [no. 49]
        7p. 1 illus.).
            Caption title.
            An adaptation of Duveyrier's "Le précepteur dans l'em-
        barras." Cf. Dict. nat. biog.

2250   _____. The scape-goat; a farce, in one act... By John Poole
        ... London, Sherwood, Gilbert, and Piper, 1826. 31p.
            "A French piece, called 'Le précepteur dans l'embarras,'
        furnished the groundwork of the following farce."

POOLE, JOHN

2251   ____. Simpson and co: a comedy in two acts, by John Poole...
Printed from the acting copy, with remarks, biographical
and critical, by D.-G. ... As performed at the Theatres
Royal... London, Davidson [n.d.]. 39p. incl. front.
(Cumberland's British theatre. London, ca. 1825-   v. 43
[no. 10]).

2252   [____]. Simpson & co.; a comedy, in two acts. As performed
at the New-York, and Drury lane theatres. New York, Circulating library and dramatic repository, 1823. 48p.

2253   ____. Tribulation; or, Unwelcome visitors: a comedy, in two
acts, by John Poole... Printed from the acting copy, with
remarks, biographical and critical, by D.-G. ... As now
performed at the Theatres Royal... London, J. Cumberland
[n.d.]. 2 p.ℓ., [9]-42p. front. (Cumberland's British
theatre. London, ca. 1825-55. v. 12 [no. 3]).

2254   ____. Tribulation; or, Unwelcome visitors. A comedy, in
two acts. By John Poole... Printed from the author's
ms., with the cast of the characters... and the whole of
the stage business, as performed at the Theatre-Royal,
Haymarket... London, T. Dolby, 1825. 42p. incl. front.,
diagr. (On frontispiece: Dolby's British theatre).
[Broadhurst, J. Plays. v. 12, no. 7].
     Based on "Un moment d'imprudence" by Wafflard and Bury.
     Reissued, with different preliminary matter, as no. 80
(v. 12, no. 3) of Cumberland's British theatre.

2255   ____. ... Turning the tables; an original farce, in one act.
By John Poole... The only edition correctly marked, by
permission from the prompter's book. To which is added,
a description of the costume - cast of the characters, the
whole of the stage business, situations - entrances -
exits - properties, and directions, as performed at the
London theatres. Embellished with a fine engraving by Mr.
Findlay, from a drawing, taken expressly in the theatre.
London, J. Duncombe [18--]. 28p. (Duncombe's edition [of
the British theatre]).

2256   ____. ... 'Twould puzzle a conjurer. A comic drama, in two
acts... New York, Wm. Taylor and co. [n.d.]. 36p.
(Modern standard drama, no. xlvii).

POOLE, JOHN

2257   POOLE, JOHN. The wealthy widow; or, They're both to blame.
       A comedy. In three acts. By John Poole... London, J.
       Miller [1827]. 1 p.ℓ., [v]-vi p., 1ℓ., 61p.
          "...Partly derived from a play, called Le jeune mari."--
       Advertisement.

2258   _____. A year in an hour; or, The cock of the walk. A
       farce... By John Poole... London, J. Miller, 1824.
       2 p.ℓ., 28p.

2259   ... The poor of New York. A drama, in five acts. By the
       **** Club... as performed at Wallack's Theatre, December,
       1852. New York, Samuel French [n.d.]. 45p.

2260   POWER, THOMAS F. The Virginia veteran. A military drama, in
       four acts... Boston, Lee and Shepard, 1874. 57p.

2261   POWER, TYRONE, i.e. WILLIAM GRATTON TYRONE, 1797-1841.
       ... Born to good luck; the Irishman's fortune. A farce in
       two acts... New York, Samuel French [n.d.]. 39p. (The
       minor drama, no. xlv).

2262   _____. Married lovers: a petite comedy, in two acts; as per-
       formed at the Theatres Royal, Covent Garden, on February 2,
       1831. By T. Power... Baltimore, J. Robinson, 1831. 42p.

2263   _____. ... Paddy Carey; or, The boy of Clogheen. An inter-
       lude in one act... New York, Samuel French [n.d.]. 15p.
       (French's American drama, no. xxii).

2264   _____. St. Patrick's eve; or, The order of the day. A drama,
       in three acts. By Tyrone Power, esq. As performed at the
       Theatre Royal, Haymarket. Correctly printed from the
       prompter's copy with remarks... A biographical sketch and
       beautifully engraved portrait, from a painting by Simpson...
       Illustrated with an etching, by Pierce Egan the younger...
       London, Chapman and Hall, 1838. vii, 36p. front. (port.)
       pl. (Added t.-p.: The acting national drama... ed. by
       Benjamin Webster, v. 2 [no. 1]).
          Biographical sketch signed: B. W. [i.e. Benjamin
       Webster].

2265   PRATT, WILLIAM W. ... Ten nights in a bar-room. A drama, in
       five acts... New York, Samuel French [n.d.]. 36p.
       (French's standard drama, no. cccxxxix).

2266   PRESBREY, EUGENE W[ILEY]. A fool's wisdom; a sketch of 1586
       [a drama] by Eugene W. Presbrey. [New York? 1904].
       26 numb. ℓ.

2267   Presentation in the Temple. The presentation in the Temple,
       a pageant, as originally represented by the Corporation
       of weavers in Coventry. Now first printed from the books
       of the company. With a prefatory notice. Edinburgh,
       Printed for the Abbotsford club [by the Edinburgh printing
       company] 1836. 3 p.ℓ., 86p. [Abbotsford club. Publica-
       tions. no. 2].

2268   PRESTON, SARA. Hicks at college, a comedy in three acts. By
       Sara Preston, Amy Oliver and Ralph E. Dyar. Chicago and
       New York, The Dramatic publishing co., 1909. 47p.

2269   Prince Dorus; or, The romance of the nose... London, Thomas
       Hailes Lacy [n.d.]. 35p.

2270   Pub and the baby, a farce-comedy, in one act... Clyde, Ohio,
       Ames' Publishing co., 1889. 13p.

2271   [PUTNAM, MARY LOWELL]. Tragedy of errors. Boston, Ticknor
       and Fields, 1862. 249p.

2272   [_____]. Tragedy of success. Boston, Ticknor and Fields,
       1862. 191p.

2273   Pyne and Harrison opera troupe. Cinderella; or, The fairy and
       little glass slipper; an opera in three acts... music by
       Rossini. Boston, J. H. Eastburn, 1855. 42p.

2274   [RACINE, JEAN BAPTISTE] 1639-1699. Achilles; or, Iphigenia in
       Aulis. A tragedy. As it is acted at the Theatre Royal
       in Drury-lane. Written by Mr. Boyer... London, T. Bennet,
       1700. 4 p.ℓ., 48p.

2275   [_____]. Andromache. A tragedy. As it is acted at the
       Dukes theatre. [Ornament] London, Printed by T. Rat-
       cliffe, and N. Thompson, for Richard Bentley, and sold by
       the booksellers of London and Westminster, 1675. 4 p.ℓ.,
       48p.

2276   _____. ... Athalie; a tragedy by J. Racine; ed. with a com-
       plete commentary for the use of students, by Edward S.
       Joynes... New York, Holt and Williams [etc.]: Boston,
       S. R. Urbino [1871]. 117p.

RACINE, JEAN BAPTISTE

2277   RACINE, JEAN BAPTISTE. Britannicus. A tragedy. Now first
        translated from the French of M. Racine. [London] 1714.
        3 p.ℓ., [11]-57p. front.

2278   [_____]. The distressed mother; a tragedy, in five acts; by
        Ambrose Philips. As performed at the Theatres Royal,
        Drury Lane and Covent-Garden... With remarks by Mrs. Inch-
        bald. London, Longman, Hurst, Rees, Orme, and Brown [n.d.].
        53p. front.

2279   _____. ... Esther, a tragedy by J. Racine; ed. with explana-
        tory notes for the use of students, by Edward S. Joynes...
        New York, H. Holt and co. [etc.]; Boston, C. Schoenhof
        [1883]. vii, 66p. (Students' series of classic French
        plays--v).

2280   _____. Phaedra. A tragedy in five acts. By Racine... New
        York, F. Rullman [1880]. 31p. front.

2281   RACKSTRAW, E. C. "Make-believe," a comedietta, by E. C.
        Rackstraw and W. Muskerry. New York and London, Samuel
        French [c1910]. 23p.

2282   RADLOW, JAMES. The trial of the conspirators. [n.p., n.d.].
        7p. (American Classical League Service Bureau, No. 583).

2283   RANDEGGER, ALBERTO. Esmeralda; an opera, in four acts, by
        Alberto Randegger and Theo. Marzials. The French version
        by Paul Milliet. The music by A. Goring Thomas as repre-
        sented at the Royal Italian Opera, Covent Garden. London,
        Printed and published for the Royal Italian Opera, Covent
        Garden, by J. Miles and co. [n.d.]. 71p. Parallel French
        and English text.

2283A   RANKEN, FREDERIC. ... The chaperons; an original musical
        comedy in three acts. Book and lyrics by Frederic Ranken,
        music by Isidore Witmark... New York, M. Witmark and sons;
        [etc., etc.] 1901. 24p.

2284   RAUPACH, ERNST BENJAMIN SALOMON, 1784-1852. The serf: a
        tragedy, in five acts, altered from the German of Raupach,
        and adapted to the English stage, by R. Talbot, esq. ...
        With remarks, biographical and critical, by D.-G. ...
        London, J. Cumberland [n.d.]. 54p. incl. front. (Cumber-
        land's British theatre. London, ca. 1825-55. v. 19 [no.
        2]).

2285   RAWLEY, BERT C. Andy Freckles, the mischievous boy. Farce
          comedy in one act. Clyde, Ohio, Ames' publishing co.,
          1898. 13p.

2286   _____. Deacon Jones' wife's ghost. A farce in one act. By
          Bert Rawley. To which is added a description of the cos-
          tumes, cast of the characters... Clyde, Ohio, Ames' pub-
          lishing co., 1894. 8p. (On cover: Ames' series of
          standard and minor drama. no. 345).

2287   _____. Lincoln league, a colored oddity in one scene, by
          B. C. Fawley... New York, Dick and Fitzgerald, 1914. 15p.

2288   _____. Our summer boarders; or, The jolly tramp. A farce
          comedy, in two scenes. Clyde, Ohio, Ames' publishing co.,
          1896. 15p.

2289   _____. Pikeville folks. A farce comedy in two acts...
          Clyde, Ohio, Ames' publishing co., 1906. 42p.

2290   _____. Uncle Jed's fidelity; or, The returned cowboy. A
          comedy drama. In three acts, by Bert C. Rawley... To
          which is added a description of the costumes... and the
          whole of the stage business... Clyde, Ohio, Ames' pub-
          lishing co., 1898. 27p. (On cover: Ames' series of
          standard and minor drama, no. 396).

2291   _____. Uncle Zachary of Vermont. A comedy drama, in two
          acts... Clyde, Ohio, Ames' publishing co., 1902. 26p.

2292   RAYMOND, GEORGE LANSING, 1839-1929. The Aztec god and other
          dramas, by George Lansing Raymond, 4th ed., rev. New
          York and London, G. P. Putnam's sons [1916]. [3], 465p.
          CONTENTS. - The Aztec god. - Columbus. - Cecil the seer.

2293   _____. The Aztec god and other dramas... Third ed. New
          York and London, G. P. Putnam's sons, 1908. 446p.

2294   _____. Cecil the seer, a drama of the soul, by Walter Warren
          (pseud.)... Boston, Arena publishing co., 1894. 2 p.ℓ.,
          [iv]-v, 7-151p.

2295   _____. Classes and masses; or, Ned and Nell. A play in five
          acts... Incidentally showing the possibility of writing
          English comedy in a style both natural and metrical...
          Printed not published... Copyright... by George L. Raymond
          ... Washington, D. C. [Press of B. S. Adams] 1901. 82p.

RAYMOND, GEORGE LANSING

2296   RAYMOND, GEORGE LANSING. Columbus, the discoverer; a drama by
Walter Warren [pseud.] Boston, Arena publishing co., 1893.
vi, 164p.

2297   _____. Dante, a drama in two tableaux and six acts. Washington, D. C., Printed, not published by G. L. Raymond [1908].
2 p.ℓ., [7]-141p.

2298   _____. Dante and collected verse. New York and London, G. P.
Putnam's sons, 1909. 329p.

2299   _____. A lady's limitations; a play in three acts and one
scene... Copyrighted... by George L. Raymond... Washington, D. C. [Press of B. S. Adams] 1910. 55p.

2300   _____. A poor woman's fund; a society play in five acts...
Printed not published. Copyright... by George L. Raymond
... Washington, D. C. [Press of B. S. Adams] 1904. 69p.

2301   _____. The ranch girl, a play in four acts... Copyrighted
... by George L. Raymond... Washington, D. C. [Press of
B. S. Adams] 1910. 46p.

2302   _____. The ranch girl. A play in four acts... Incidentally
showing the possibility of writing English comedy in a
style both natural and metrical... Printed not published.
Copyright... by George L. Raymond... Washington, D. C.
[Press of B. S. Adams] 1901. 65p.

2303   _____. Slaves of society, a play in three acts... Copyright
... by George L. Raymond. Washington, D. C. [Press of B.
S. Adams] 1910. 59p.

2304   _____. The suffragettes, a play in three acts... [Washing-
ton, D. C., Press of B. S. Adams] 1908. 53p.

2305   RAYMOND, RICHARD JOHN. Cherry bounce! A farce, in one act...
London, Thomas Hailes Lacy [n.d.]. 18p. front.

2306   _____. ... The emigrant's daughter, a drama in one act...
London, J. Duncombe and co. [n.d.]. 26p. (Duncombe's
edition).

2307   _____. Mr. and Mrs. Peter White, a farce, in one act...
New York, Samuel French [n.d.]. 19p.

REDE, WILLIAM LEMAN

2308 _____. Robert the Devil, Duke of Normandy: a musical romance, in two acts, by R. J. Raymond... Printed from the acting copy, with remarks, biographical and critical, by D.-G. ... As performed at the Theatres Royal... London, J. Cumberland [n.d.]. 35p. incl. front. (Cumberland's British theatre. London, ca. 1825-55. v. 33 [no. 6]).
   Remarks by George Daniel, editor of the series.
   "Mr. Raymond has kept in view the celebrated opera of Don Giovanni, and is indebted little or nothing to the original story." Cf. Remarks, p. 7.
   Without the music (by Barnett).

2309 [_____]. ... The Toodles. A domestic drama, in two acts. As performed at the theatres in New York. New York, S. French [1853?]. 1 p.ℓ., [7]-28p. (The minor drama. Ed. by F. C. Wemyss. [no.] LIV).

2310 REACH, ANGUS B. ... Jenny Lind at last; or, The Swedish nightingale. An apropos operatic bagatelle, in one act... Boston, William V. Spencer, 1856. 16p. (Spencer's Boston theatre, no. xxxiii).

2311 READ, OPIE. The club woman and the hero, a comedietta. Chicago, T. S. Denison [1903]. 20p.

2312 REDE, WILLIAM LEMAN, 1802-1847. The devil and Doctor Faustus: a drama, in three acts, by William Leman Rede... Printed from the acting copy, with remarks, biographical and critical, by D.-G. ... As performed at the Theatres Royal... London, Davidson [n.d.]. 36p. incl. front. (Cumberland's British theatre. London, ca. 1825-55. v. 45 [no. 2]).
   Remarks by George Daniel, editor of the series.

2313 _____. ... The flight to America; or, Ten hours in New York! a drama, in three acts. By William Leman Rede... Correctly printed from the most approved acting copy, with a description of the costume, cast of the characters, entrances and exits, relative positions, and the whole of the stage business; to which are added properties and directions, as now performed in the London and American theatres... Philadelphia, F. Turner; New York, Turner and Fisher [184-?]. 47p. incl. front. (Turner's library of acting plays. v. iv, no. 28).

REDE, WILLIAM LEMAN

2314   REDE, WILLIAM LEMAN. Jack in the water; or, The ladder of
        life. A domestic burletta, in three acts, by Leman Rede...
        Printed from the acting copy, with remarks, biographical
        and critical, by D.-G. ... As performed at the metropolitan
        minor theatres... London, J. Cumberland [n.d.]. 50p.
        incl. front. (Cumberland's Minor theatre. London [ca.
        1830-55]. v. 16 [no. 6]).
            Remarks by George Daniel, editor of the series.
            Reissued in Davidson's shilling volume of Cumberland's
        plays, v. 4 [no. 5].

2315   _____. The rake's progress, a drama in three acts, By
        William Leman Rede... London, T. H. Lacy [186-?]. 48p.
        front. (On cover: Lacy's acting edition. 470).

2316   _____. Sixteen-string Jack, a romantic drama, in three acts,
        by Leman Rede... Printed from the acting copy, with re-
        marks, biographical and critical, by D.-G. ... As per-
        formed at the Theatres Royal... London, G. H. Davidson
        [n.d.]. 57p. incl. front. (Cumberland's Minor theatre.
        London, [ca. 1830-55] v. 16 [no. 10]).
            Remarks by George Daniel, editor of the series.

2317   _____. ... The skeleton witness; or, The murder at the mound.
        A domestic drama, in three acts... New York, Samuel French
        [n.d.]. 44p. (French's standard drama, no. cxcvii).

2318   _____. The two Greens. A farce, in one act, by Leman Rede...
        As performing at the Royal Olympic theatre, correctly
        printed from the prompt copy... London, J. Pattie [n.d.].
        20p. front. (The Universal stage... London, 1840. v. 1
        [no. 8]).

2319   REECE, R. Brown and the Brahmins; or, Captain Pop and the
        Princess Pretty-eyes! An oriental burlesque... London,
        Thomas Hailes Lacy [n.d.]. 35p.

2320   _____. A spelling bee; or, The battle of the dictionaries.
        A new seasonable absurdity... London, E. Rimmel, 1876.
        14p.

2321   REES, ARTHUR DOUGHERTY. Columbus, a drama, with introduction
        and notes, by Arthur Dougherty Rees. Philadelphia, The
        John C. Winston co. [1907]. 129p. incl. col. pl. (coat of
        arms).

REYNARTZ, DOROTHY

2322   _____. Give up your gods; a drama in three acts of pagan and
Christian Russia, by Arthur Dougherty Rees... Philadel-
phia, Press of J. B. Lippincott co., 1908. 118p.

2323   _____. Hogan on the stand. A drama about America. Brooklyn,
N. Y. [n.d.]. 104p.

2324   REES, ROSEMARY. Her dearest friend... London, Thomas Hailes
Lacy [1910]. 24p. (Lacy's acting edition of plays, v. 158).

2325   No Entry.

2326   [REEVE, WILLIAM] 1757-1815. The purse; or, Benevolent tar.
A musical drama in one act, by J. C. Cross [pseud.]. New
York, Published by David Longworth, at the dramatic
repository, Shakspeare-gallery, 1816. 20p.

2327   REEVE, WYBERT. The dead witness; or, Sin and its shadow. A
drama, in three acts, founded on "The widow's story" of
the Seven poor travellers, by Charles Dickens... New York,
Samuel French and son [n.d.]. 35p.

2328   _____. A match for a mother-in-law. An original comedietta,
in one act... New York, Samuel French [n.d.]. 18p.

2329   _____. Not so bad after all; an original comedy in three
acts, by Wybert Reeve. New American ed. correctly reprinted from the original acting edition... New York, H.
Roorbach [c1889]. 41p. (On cover: Roorbach's American
edition of acting plays. no. 10).

2330   _____. Pike O'Callaghan; or, the Irish patriot. An original
drama, in two acts... London, Thomas Hailes Lacy [n.d.].
32p.

2331   REID, JAMES HALLECK. A slave of the mill, a four act melo-
drama, by Hal Reid and Harry Gordon... Perry, Iowa, Chief
printing co., 1905. 1 p.ℓ., 42 numb.ℓ.

2332   The revolt of the bees. An allegory. Boston, Walter H.
Baker and co. [1872]. 67-84p.

2333   REYNARTZ, DOROTHY, tr. ... Carnival; or, Mardi gras in New
Orleans. Comedy in one act. For young ladies. Adapted
from the French by Dorothy Reynartz... New York, The
Roxbury publishing co. [1899]. 16p. (The wizard series).

REYNARTZ, DOROTHY

2334   REYNARTZ, DOROTHY.   ... A cup of coffee. Comedy in one act.
       For young ladies. By Dorothy Reynartz... New York, The
       Roxbury publishing co., 1899. 22p. (The Wizard series).

2335   _____. ... It is never too late to mend; comedy in one act.
       For young ladies. By Dorothy Reynartz... New York, The
       Roxbury publishing co., 1899. 8p. (Wizard series).

2336   REYNOLDS, FREDERIC, 1764-1841. Begone dull care; or, How will
       it end? A comedy, in five acts. As performed at the
       Theatre-Royal, Covent Garden. By Frederick Reynolds.
       Boston, Published by E. Larkin, no. 47, Cornhill, Greenough
       and Stebbins, printers, 1808. 72p.
          Borrowed from George Colman's "Heir at law." Cf. D. E.
       Baker, Biog. dram.

2337   _____. The blind bargain; or, Hear it out: a comedy, in five
       acts, by Frederick Reynolds... Printed from the acting
       copy, with remarks, biographical and critical, by D.-G. ...
       As now performed at the Theatres Royal... London, J.
       Cumberland [n.d.]. 61, [1]p. incl. front. (Cumberland's
       British theatre. London, ca. 1825-55. v. 28 [no. 8]).
          Remarks by George Daniel, editor of the series.

2338   _____. The bridal ring; a melo-drama, in two acts. By
       Frederick Reynolds, esq. ... <from the manuscript> New-
       York, Published by D. Longworth, at the Dramatic repository,
       Shakspeare-gallery, November--1812. 31p. [Dramatic
       pamphlets. v. 29, no. 4].

2339   _____. Delays and blunders: a comedy, in five acts. As per-
       formed at the Theatre-Royal, Covent-Garden. By Frederick
       Reynolds. London, Printed by A. Strahan, for T. N. Long-
       man and O. Rees, 1803. 74, [2]p. Interleaved.

2340   _____. The dramatist; or, Stop him who can. A comedy, in
       five acts; by Frederic Reynolds. As performed at the
       Theatre Royal, Covent-Garden... With remarks by Mrs. Inch-
       bald. London, Longman, Hurst, Rees, Orme, and Brown [n.d.].
       70p. front. (Inchbald, Mrs. Elizabeth. The British
       theatre... London, 1808. v. 20 [no. 1]).

2341   _____. The exile; or, The deserts of Siberia: an operatic
       play, in three acts, by Frederick Reynolds... Printed from
       the acting copy, with remarks, biographical and critical,
       by D.-G. ... As performed at the Theatres Royal... Lon-
       don, J. Cumberland [n.d.]. 54p. incl. front. (Cumber-
       land's British theatre. London, ca. 1825-55. v. 29 [no. 9]).

(REYNOLDS, FREDERIC)
Remarks by George Daniel, editor of the series.
Founded on "Elisabeth, ou Les exiles de Sibérie," by
Sophie Cottin.
Without the music (by Mazzinghi).

2342 _____. The free knights; or, The edict of Charlemagne. A
drama, in three acts, interspersed with music. By Frederick
Reynolds. As performed at the Theatre Royal, Covent Garden.
(From the first London ed. of 1810.) New York, D. Longworth, 1810. 56p.

2343 _____. How to grow rich: a comedy, in five acts, by Frederick
Reynolds... Printed from the acting copy, with remarks,
biographical and critical, by D.-G. ... As performed at
the Theatres Royal... London, J. Cumberland [n.d.]. 58p.
incl. front. (Cumberland's British theatre. London, ca.
1825-55. v. 30 [no. 8]).
Remarks by George Daniel, editor of the series.

2344 _____. Laugh when you can: a comedy, in five acts, by Frederick Reynolds... Printed from the acting copy, with remarks, biographical and critical, by D.-G. ... As now performed at the Theatres Royal... London, J. Cumberland
[n.d.]. 63p. incl. front. (Cumberland's British theatre.
London, ca. 1825-55. v. 23 [no. 4]).
Remarks by George Daniel, editor of the series.

2345 _____. Notoriety: a comedy, in five acts, by Frederick
Reynolds... Printed from the acting copy, with remarks,
biographical and critical, by D.-G. ... As now performed
at the Theatres Royal... London, J. Cumberland [n.d.].
63, [1]p. front. (Cumberland's British theatre. London,
ca. 1825-55. v. 26 [no. 1]).
Remarks by George Daniel, editor of the series.
Memoir and portrait of Quick.

2346 _____. The renegade; a grand historical drama, in three acts.
Interspersed with music. Founded on Dryden's Don Sebastian,
king of Portugal. By Frederic Reynolds. <From the first
London edition, of 1812.> New York, Published by D. Long-
worth, at the Dramatic repository, Shakespeare-gallery.
February--1813. 54p., 1ℓ.
Without the music.
"Yankee naval chronology; being a continuation of Yankee
chronology, woodcut of Decatur's victory on verso.

REYNOLDS, FREDERIC

2347 REYNOLDS, FREDERIC. The will: a comedy, in five acts. By
      Frederic Reynolds... Printed from the acting copy, with
      remarks, biographical and critical, by D.-G. ... As now
      performed at the Theatres Royal... London, J. Cumberland
      [n.d.]. 58p. incl. front. (Cumberland's British theatre.
      London, ca. 1825–55. v. 21 [no. 7]).
            Remarks by George Daniel, editor of the series.

2348 RHAND, TALLY. ... Guttle and Gulpit. A farce, in two acts...
      New York, William Taylor and co. [n.d.]. 36p. (The
      American drama, no. iii).

2349 RHODES, WILLIAM BARNES, 1772–1826. Bombastes furioso: a
      burlesque tragic opera, in one act, by William Barnes
      Rhodes. Printed from the acting copy, with remarks, bio-
      graphical and critical, by D.-G. ... As performed at the
      Theatres Royal... London, Davidson [n.d.]. 24p. incl.
      front. (Cumberland's British theatre. London, ca. 1825–
      55. v. 43 [no. 4]).
            Remarks by George Daniel, editor of the series.
            Without the music.
            Produced also under name: Artaxominous the Great.

2350 RHODES, WILLIAM HENRY, 1822–1876. The Indian gallows, and
      other poems. In two parts. By William H. Rhodes... New
      York, E. Walker, 1846. 6 p.ℓ., 153p. front. CONTENTS. –
      Pt. 1. The Indian gallows. – Pt. 2. Theodosia, the
      pirate's prisoner, a tragedy. Miscellaneous poems, re-
      lating chiefly to scenes in Texas.

2351 RICE, CALE YOUNG, 1872–1943. Charles di Tocca; a tragedy, by
      Cale Young Rice. New York, McClure, Phillips and co.,
      1903. 3 p.ℓ., 140p.

2352 _____. David. New York. The McClure co., 1907. 128p.

2353 _____. David, a tragedy, by Cale Young Rice. New York,
      McClure, Phillips and co., 1904. vi, 116p.

2354 _____. The immortal lure, by Cale Young Rice... Garden
      City, N. Y., Doubleday, Page and co., 1911. 5 p.ℓ., 3-
      92p. CONTENTS. – Giorgione. – Ardiun. – O-umé's gods. –
      The immortal lure.

2355 _____. A night in Avignon. New York, McClure, Phillips and
      co., 1907. 32p.

RITTER, JOHN P., JR.

2356 _____. Porzia. New York, Doubleday, Page and co., 1913. 79p.

2357 RICE, CHARLES, 1819-1880. ... The three guardsmen; or, The queen, the cardinal, and the adventurer. A drama, in three acts. Founded on Dumas' celebrated romance. By Charles Rice... To which are added, a description of the costume ... and the whole of the stage business... New-York, S. French [1850?]. 60p. (French's American drama. The acting edition, no. 46). On cover: French's standard drama, no. 139.
  Acted in London under the title "The Three musketeer" (?).

2358 RICE, ELMER L., 1892-1967. On trial; a dramatic composition in four acts, by Elmer L. Reizenstein... [n.p.] 1914. 108p.

2359 RICE, K. McDOWELL. Dr. Hardhack's prescription, a play for children in four acts. Worthington, Mass., K. McDowell Rice [1908]. 14p.

2360 _____. Good King Wenceslas, a Christmas play for children in two acts. Worthington, Mass., K. McDowell Rice [1907]. 25p.

2361 _____. Mrs. Bagg's bargain day, a comedy in two acts. [Worthington, Mass., K. McDowell Rice, 1904]. 29p.

2362 _____. Uncle Joe's jewel, a comedy in three acts. Worthington, Mass., K. McDowell Rice [1908]. 27p.

2363 RICHARDS, BERT. The spellin' skewl; or, Friday afternoon at Deestrick no. 4. An original burlesque in one scene, by Bert Richards... Clyde, Ohio, Ames publishing co. [1891]. 13p. (Ames' series of standard and minor drama, no. 295).

2364 RISHELL, DYSON, 1858- . Elfrida, a drama. By Dyson Rishell. Philadelphia, J. B. Lippincott and co., 1883. 146p.

2365 RITTER, JOHN P., JR. Book of mock trials: containing fourteen original plays, representing humorous courtroom scenes, adapted to the limits of the parlor, and arranged for public or private performances. By J. P. Ritter, Jr., and William T. Call. New York, Excelsior publishing house [1886]. 160p.

ROBERTON, MARION

2366   ROBERTON, MARION. "Afterwards," a play in one act... London,
        Joseph Williams, 1911. 10p.

2367   ROBERTS, GEORGE. An ample apology. A farce, in one act...
        London, Thomas Hailes Lacy [n.d.]. 16p.

2368   _____. Forty winks, a comedietta, in one act... London,
        Thomas Hailes Lacy [n.d.]. 18p.

2369   _____. Lady Audley's secret. A drama, in two acts. Founded
        on, and in part adapted from, Miss Braddon's novel of that
        name. By George Roberts... [London, Priv. print. by T.
        Scott, 1863?]. 40p. On cover: "The original version."

2370   _____. The three furies. An original comedietta, in one act
        ... London, Thomas Hailes Lacy [n.d.]. 16p.

2371   ROBERTS, LEWIS NILES. Aftermath; a play in three acts, by
        Lewis Niles Roberts... [Dover, England, Grigg and son]
        1914. 104p.

2372   _____. ... Consular assistance; or, Official resistances, a
        farcical divertisement in one act, by Lewis Niles Roberts.
        2d ed., enlarged text. Dover, England, The author, 1914.
        16p.

2373   _____. The lion hunters; or, Modern Dianas; a fantastic
        farce in three acts, by Lewis Niles Roberts. Boston
        [F. H. Gilson co.] 1903. 206p.

2374   ROBERTS, RANDAL. Under a veil. A comedietta in one act. By
        Sir Randal Roberts, Bart., and George M. Baker. Boston,
        George M. Baker and co., 1877. 20p.

2375   ROBERTSON, DONALD. The triumph of youth; or, The white mouse,
        a comedy in three acts from the French of Edoward Pailleron.
        Chicago, The Dramatic publishing co., 1896. 99p.

2376   ROBERTSON, THOMAS WILLIAM, 1829-1871. Birds of prey; or, A
        duel in the dark. A drama, in three acts... London,
        Thomas Hailes Lacy [n.d.]. 42p.

2377   _____. The chevalier de St. George. A drama, in three acts.
        Adapted from the French of Mme. Mélesville and Roger de
        Beauvoir... New York, Robert M. De Witt [n.d.]. 32p.

ROBINSON, HARRIET JANE HANSON

2378 _____. Dreams; or, My Lady Clara. A drama, in five acts. By
T. W. Robertson... As first performed at the Alexandra
theatre, Liverpool, under the management of Mr. R. Baker...
1860... New York, R. M. De Witt, 1875. 38p. (On cover:
De Witt's acting plays. no. 21).

2379 _____. The half caste; or, The poisoned pearl. A drama, in
three acts... New York, Samuel French and son [n.d.]. 36p.

2380 _____. Home; a comedy in three acts, by T. W. Robertson, new
American ed., correctly reprinted from the original
authorized acting ed. ... New York, H. Roorbach, 1890.
40p. (On cover: Roorbach's American edition of acting
plays, no. 38).

2381 _____. Peace at any price! A farce, in one act... New York,
Robert M. De Witt [n.d.]. 10p.

2382 _____. The principal dramatic works of Thomas William
Robertson; with memoir by his son... London, S. Low,
Marston, Searle and Rivington, limited [etc.] 1889. 2 v.
front., ports. Paged continuously. CONTENTS. - v. 1.
Preface. Introduction. Memoir. List of works. Birth.
Breach of promise. Caste. David Garrick. Dreams. Home.
Ladies' battle. M. P. - v. 2. The nightingale. Ours.
Play. Progress. Row in the house. School. Society.
War.

2383 _____. Progress! A comedy, (Founded on "Les ganaches," by
Victorien Sardou). By T. W. Robertson... [London? 1869?].
1 p.ℓ., 56 numb. l. diagr.

2384 _____. "School"; or, The story of Bella Marks. A comedy by
T. W. Robertson... Philadelphia, Ledger job printing
office, 1869. 16p. illus.

2385 _____. Two gay deceivers; or, Black, white, and grey. A
farce, in one act... New York, Robert M. De Witt [n.d.].
10p.

2386 _____. The young collegian [The Cantab] A farce... as first
performed at the Strand Theatre, London... February 14,
1861... New York, Robert M. De Witt [n.d.]. 18p.

2387 ROBINSON, HARRIET JANE HANSON, 1825-1911. Captain Mary
Miller. A drama... Boston, Walter H. Baker and co.
[1887]. 47p.

ROBINSON, J. H.

2388 ROBINSON, J. H. Nick Whiffles. A drama, in three acts...
New York, Samuel French [n.d.]. 35p.

2389 ROBINSON, LENNOX, 1886- . The cross-roads. A play in a
prologue and two acts. By S. L. Robinson. Dublin,
Maunsel and co., limited [1909]. 59, [1]p. (On cover:
Abbey theatre series. vol. XII).

2390 _____. Patriots; a play in three acts, by Lennox Robinson.
Dublin and London, Maunsel and co., ltd., 1912. 4 p.ℓ.,
49p. 1ℓ. (On cover: The Abbey theatre series).

2391 ROBSON, WILLIAM, tr. ... Comedy and tragedy, a comedy. From
the French of M. R. Fournier... New York, Samuel French
[n.d.]. 24p. (The minor drama, no. cxlix).

2392 RODWELL, GEORGE HERBERT BUONAPARTE, 1800-1852. ... The
chimney piece; or, The married maid: a laughable farce.
In one act. By G. Herbert Rodwell... Printed from the
best acting copy, with remarks biographical and critical,
by E. T. W. ... With a fine spirited engraving, by Wood-
side... Philadelphia, Turner and Fisher [1836?]. 26p.
incl. front. (Turner's dramatic library. [vol. I, no. 4]).

2393 No Entry.

2394 No Entry.

2395 _____. My wife's out. A farce, in one act... As first performed at Covent Garden Theatre, London... October 2,
1843... New York, Robert M. De Witt [n.d.]. 16p.

2396 RODWELL, JAMES THOMAS GOODERHAM, d. 1825. A race for a
dinner: a farce, in one act, by J. Thomas G. Rodwell, esq.
Printed from the acting copy, with remarks, biographical
and critical, by D.-G. ... As performed at the Theatres
Royal... London, G. H. Davidson [n.d.]. 78p. incl.
front. (Cumberland's British theatre. London, ca. 1825-
55. v. 19 [no. 6]).
  Remarks by George Daniel, editor of the series.
  Translation and adaption of "Le gastronome sans argent,"
by Scribe and Brulay.

2397 RODWELL, THOMAS G. ... The young widow; or, A lesson for
lovers. A comic piece, in one act... New York, Samuel
French [n.d.]. 25p. (French's American drama, no. lxxx).

2398   [ROGERS, DANIEL] 1780-1839. The knight of the rum bottle &
        co.; or, The speechmakers: a musical farce, in five acts.
        Respectfully dedicated to the managers of the New-York
        theatre, by the editor of the City-hall recorder... New-
        York, Published by David Longworth, At the Dramatic Reposi-
        tory, Shakspeare-Gallery, June--1818. 16p.

2399   ROGERS, MAUD M. When the wheels run down; a play in one act,
        by Maud M. Rogers... New York, London, S. French, c1899.
        15p. (On cover: French's international copyrighted...
        edition of the works of the best authors. no. 27).

2400   ROGERS, WILLIAM. The bandit host; or, The lone hut of the
        swamp. A melodrama in two acts... London, James Pattie
        [n.d.]. 23p. front.

2401   A Roman and an American Christmas compared: a play in two acts,
        by a High School Pupil. [n.p., n.d.]. 4p. (American
        Classical League Service Bureau, No. 466).

2402   A Roman family comes to life, a play written by students of
        the John Adams High School, Cleveland, Ohio. [n.p., n.d.]
        5p. (American Classical League Service Bureau, No. 649).

2403   The romp; a musical entertainment, in two acts... London,
        John Cumberland [n.d.]. 28p. front.

2404   [ROPES, ARTHUR REED] 1859-1933. The messenger boy; a musical
        play in two acts, by James T. Tanner and Alfred Murray.
        Lyrics by Adrian Ross [pseud.] and Percy Greenback; music
        by Ivan Caryll and Lionel Monckton. Lyrics... [New York
        city, Myers and Rosenfeld co., 1900]. 30p.

2405   ROSE, WILLIAM GANSON, 1878-   . Every girl; a humorous
        morality play in two acts, by William Ganson Rose. Phila-
        delphia, The Penn publishing co., 1913. 38p.

2406   The Rose and the ring. Adapted for the private stage from
        Thackeray's Christmas pantomime. Cambridge, Mass., George
        H. Kent, 1880. 43p.

2407   ROSENBERG, JAMES N. The return of mutton. New York, Mitchell
        Kennerley, 1916. 53p.

2408   ROSENFELD, SYDNEY, 1855-1931. Children of destiny; a play in
        four acts by Sydney Rosenfeld. New York, G. W. Dillingham
        co. [1910]. 127p.

ROSENFELD, SYDNEY

2409   ROSENFELD, SYDNEY. The club friend; or, A fashionable physi-
        cian, an original comedy in four acts, by Sydney Rosenfeld
        ... New York, The De Witt publishing house, 1897. 3 p.ℓ.,
        89p.

2410   _____. High C. A comedietta, in one act... New York, Robert
        M. De Witt, 1875. 17p.

2411   _____. Mr. X. A farce, in one act. By Sydney Rosenfeld...
        To which are added, a description of the costumes... and
        the whole of the stage business. New York, R. M. De Witt,
        1875. 17p. On cover: De Witt's acting plays (no. 189).

2412   _____. On bread and water. A musical farce, in one act.
        Imitated from the German. By Sydney Rosenfeld... To
        which are added, a description of the costumes... and the
        whole of the stage business. New York, R. M. De Witt,
        1875. 12p. On cover: De Witt's acting plays. (no. 176).

2413   _____. A pair of shoes. A farce, in one act, by Sydney
        Rosenfeld... Together with a description of the costumes
        ... and the whole of the stage business. New York, De
        Witt, 1882. 12p. On cover: De Witt's acting plays
        (no. 305).

2414   _____. Rosemi Shell; or, My daughter! oh! my daughter... By
        Sydney Rosenfeld... as first performed at the Eagle theatre,
        New York, January, 1876. To which are added, a descrip-
        tion of the costumes... and the whole of the stage business.
        Author's ed. ... New York, R. M. De Witt, 1876. 19p.
        On cover: De Witt's acting plays (no. 195).

2415   ROSKOTEN, ROBERT, 1816-1897. Carlotta; a tragedy in five
        acts. By Robert Roskoten, M.D. Peoria, Illinois [Press
        of J. W. Franks and sons] 1880. 5 p.ℓ., [9]-123p.

2416   ROSS, CHARLES HENRY. The wedding and the twins. A domestic
        drama for home reading, performed by Major Penny, and a
        numerous staff of auxiliaries. With portraits of the
        principal performers, and pictures of the many thrilling
        incidents. The music by the twins themselves... Chicago,
        Rhodes and McClure, 1882. 3 p.ℓ., 15-156p., 1ℓ., 2, 13-
        156p. front., illus.

2417   ROSTAND, EDMOND, 1868-1918. L'aiglon; a play in six acts, by
        Edmond Rostand, tr. by Louis N. Parker. New York, R. H.
        Russell, 1900. 262p. front. ports.

BRITISH AND AMERICAN DRAMA

RUDOLPH, GEORGE E.

2418   _____. Chanticler; a play in four acts, by Edmond Rostand; tr. into English verse by John Strong Newberry. New York, Duffield and co., 1911. xx, 391p.

2419   _____. The fantasticks; a romantic comedy in three acts by Edmond Rostand, freely done into English verse by George Fleming [pseud.] New York, R. H. Russell, 1900. 3 p.ℓ., 146p. front.

2420   _____. La princesse lointaine (The princess far-away) a play in four acts, in verse, by Edmond Rostand; tr. into English verse, with a preface by Charles Renauld. New York, F. A. Stokes co. [1899]. 2 p.ℓ., [iii]-ivp., 1ℓ., 110p. front. (port.).

2421 ROTH, AARON. The wanderers; a play in one act. New York, P. Maisel [c1916]. 31p.

2422 ROVER, WINNIE. The children of to-day. A farce in five acts, by Winnie Rover. New York, The Catholic publication society, 1877. 32p.

2423   _____. The house on the avenue; or, The little mischief-makers. A drama in six scenes. By Winnie Rover. New York, The Catholic publication society, 1877. 62p.

2424   _____. Wealth and wisdom. A drama in six scenes. By Winnie Rover. New York, The Catholic publication society, 1877. 63p.

2425 ROWE, NICHOLAS. ... Jane Shore. A tragedy in five acts... New York, William Taylor and co. [n.d.]. 53p.

2426 ROWLEY, RICHARD. Apollo in mourne, a play in one act. London, Duckworth, 1926. 38p. illus.

2427 ROYLE, EDWIN MILTON, 1862-1942. "The squaw man," a comedy drama in four acts, by Edwin Milton Royle... [New York?] 1906. 90p.

2428 RUBER, EDWIN. The Abbertons, drama in four acts. Philadelphia, Ruber, 1909. 100p.

2429 RUDOLPH, GEORGE E. White Oak Tavern. A melo-drama in four acts. Clyde, Ohio, Ames' publishing co., 1905. 26p.

RUSSELL, LIVINGSTON

2430   RUSSELL, LIVINGSTON. The "coming out" of Miss Cummings;
        humorous monologue for a woman, by Livingston Russell...
        With three poses by Miss Minnie Miller as "Kittie
        Cummings"... New York, E. S. Werner, 1898. 20p. pl.

2431   _____. Engaged; or, Surrendered--hand and heart, a humorous
        monologue for a woman; a companion monologue to "Cupid's
        victim" (monologue for a man published in Werner's maga-
        zine, May, 1891). By Livingston Russell... New York,
        E. S. Werner, 1894. 12p.

2432   RYAN, RICHARD, 1796-1849. Quite at home: a comic entertain-
        ment, in one act, by Richard Ryan... Printed from the
        acting copy, with remarks, biographical and critical, by
        D.-G. ... As performed at the Theatres Royal... London,
        J. Cumberland [n.d.]. 25p. incl. front.

2433   RYAN, SAMUEL E. O'Day, the alderman, a comedy drama in four
        acts. Boston, Walter H. Baker and co., 1901. 64p.

2435   SANFORD, AMELIA. The advertising girls; a masque of very fly
        leaves, in two scenes; by Amelia Sanford. Boston, W. H.
        Baker and co., 1900. 18p.

2436   _____. A corner in strait-jackets, a farce in one act. Bos-
        ton, Walter H. Baker and co., 1904. 17p.

2437   SANTAYANA, GEORGE, 1863-1952. Lucifer; a theological tragedy,
        by George Santayana. Chicago and New York, H. S. Stone
        and co., 1899. 4 p.ℓ., 187p., 1ℓ.

2438   SARDOU, VICTORIEN, 1831-1908. André Fortier, the hero of the
        Calaveras. A drama in 4 acts and 6 tableaux. By Eugene
        Tompkins. A translation and adaptation of "La poudre
        d'or," by Victorien Sardou... Boston, 1879. 85 numb. ℓ.

2439   _____. ... Daniel Rochat. A comedy in five acts. Trans-
        lated from the French of Victorien Sardou, by J. V.
        Prichard... London, S. French; New York, S. French and
        son, 1880. 76p. (French's standard drama. The acting
        edition. No. CCCLXXIX).

2440   _____. Fernanda; or, Forgive and forget. A drama in three
        acts. By Victorien Sardou... Adapted to the English
        stage by Henry L. Williams, Jr. ... New York, R. M. De
        Witt, 1870. 54p. (On cover: De Witt's acting plays,
        no. 101).

SCARBOROUGH, GEORGE

2441   _____. Love and science; a comedy in three acts. Tr. from
        the French of Victorien Sardou. By Henry Bedlow. [Balti-
        more] 1887. 56p.

2442   _____. "Marita." Three act comedy drama from the French of
        Victorien Sardou. Tr. and adapted by Barton Hill... [New
        York] Simmonds and Brown, 1885. 2 p.ℓ., 34, 44, 56ℓ.

2443   [_____]. A scrap of paper. A comic drama, in three acts.
        By J. Palgrave Simpson... London, S. French; New York, S.
        French and son [188-?]. 53p. (On cover: French's acting
        edition. No. 756).

2444   _____. ... The sorceress, a drama in five acts, by Victorien
        Sardou, authorized translation from the French by Charles
        A. Weissert, with an introduction by the translator.
        Boston, R. G. Badger; [etc., etc., 1917]. 136p. (Con-
        temporary dramatists series).

2445   SARGENT, FREDERICK LeROY, 1863-   . Omar and the Rabbi;
        Fitzgerald's translation of the Rubaiyat of Omar Khayyam,
        and Browning's Rabbi Ben Ezra, arranged in dramatic form,
        by Frederick LeRoy Sargent. Cambridge, Harvard coopera-
        tive society, 1909. 28p.

2446   SATTERLEE, CLARENCE, ed. Christmas plays for home and
        parishes. Selected and adapted by Clarence Satterlee.
        New York, De Witt, 1886. 73p.

2447   SAUNDERS, CHARLES H. The pirate's legacy; or, The wrecker's
        fate. A drama in two acts... New York, Samuel French
        [n.d.]. 26p.

2448   SAVILLE, JOHN FAUCIT. The miller's maid; a melo-drama in two
        acts. New York, Samuel French [n.d.]. 30p.

2449   _____. Wapping old stairs. A nautical drama, in three acts
        ... London, John Cumberland [n.d.]. 58p.

2450   SAYERS, DOROTHY LEIGH, 1893-1957. The man born to be king,
        a play-cycle on the life of our lord and saviour Jesus
        Christ. London, Victor Gollancz, ltd., 1943. 343p.

2451   SCARBOROUGH, GEORGE. At bay, a drama in four acts. [New
        Brighton? N. Y., 1913]. 1v. (various pagings).

SCHELL, STANLEY

2452   SCHELL, STANLEY.   ... Boy impersonations, written comp., or
       arranged by Stanley Schell. New York, E. S. Werner and
       co., 1913. 192p. (Werner's readings and recitations
       no. 52).

2453   _____. ... Commencement week, comp., arranged or written, by
       Stanley Schell. New York, E. S. Werner and co., 1915.
       192p., 1 illus. (Werner's readings and recitations, no.
       54).

2454   _____. ... Dramatic selections, comp. and arranged by
       Stanley Schell. New York, E. S. Werner and co., 1915.
       192p. (Werner's readings and recitations, no. 58).

2455   _____. ... Easter celebrations, written, comp., or arranged
       by Stanley Schell. New York, E. S. Werner and co., 1916.
       192p. front. illus. (incl. music) plates. (Werner's
       readings and recitations, no. 57).

2456   _____. ... Girl impersonations, written, compiled, or
       arranged by Stanley Schell. New York, E. S. Werner and
       co., 1912. 192p. illus. (Werner's readings and recita-
       tions, no. 50).

2457   _____. ... Hallowe'en festivities, by Stanley Schell. New
       York, E. S. Werner publishing and supply co. (inc.) 1903.
       166p. illus. (Werner's readings and recitations, no. 31).

2458   _____. ... Lincoln celebrations... comp., arranged and
       written by Stanley Schell. New York, E. S. Werner and
       co., 1910. 2 v. facsim. (Werner's readings and recita-
       tions, no. 45–46).

2459   _____. ... Monologues, comp. and arranged by Stanley Schell.
       New York, E. S. Werner and co., 1904. 160p. (Werner's
       readings and recitations, no. 32).

2460   _____. ... Monologues of today, comp. by Stanley Schell.
       New York, E. S. Werner and co., 1916. 192p. (Werner's
       readings and recitations, no. 58).

2461   _____. An old maid's conference; a humorous entertainment
       in two scenes for any number of males and females, by
       Stanley Schell. New York, E. S. Werner publishing and
       supply co., 1900. 44p. (On cover: The reciter's
       library. v. 3, no. 4).

SCHILLER, JOHANN CHRISTOPH FRIEDRICH VON

2462 _____. ... Platform and all-round recitations, comp. and
arranged by Stanley Schell. New York, E. W. Werner and co.,
1912. 192p. (Werner's readings and recitations, no. 51).

2463 _____. ... Prize contests, comp. and arranged by Stanley
Schell. New York, E. S. Werner and co., 1913. 192p.
(Werner's readings and recitations, no. 53).

2464 _____. Sailors' entertainment; including a carnival, sailors'
drill, and hornpipe for any number of males, by Stanley
Schell... New York, E. S. Werner publishing and supply
co., 1900. 18p.

2465 _____. ... Thanksgiving celebrations, comp. and arranged by
Stanley Schell. New York, E. W. Werner and co., 1907.
192p. (Werner's readings and recitations, no. 40).

2466 _____. ... Washington celebrations, by Stanley Schell. New
York, E. S. Werner and co., 1912. 192p. front., plates,
ports. (Werner's readings and recitations, no. 49).

2467 _____. Werner's Christmas book; comp. and arranged by Stanley
Schell. New York, E. S. Werner publishing and supply co.
(inc.) 1902. 191, [1]p. illus. (incl. music) plates. (On
cover: Werner's readings and recitations, no. 28).

2468 _____. Werner's readings and recitations, no. 17, for children
of primary grades, by Stanley Schell... 3d and illustrated
ed. New York, E. S. Werner publishing and supply co.
(incorporated) 1904. 181p. illus., plates. (Werner's
reading and recitations, no. 17).

2469 SCHILLER, JOHANN CHRISTOPH FRIEDRICH VON, 1759-1805. Cabal
and love, a tragedy. Translated from the German of
Frederich Schiller... London, Printed by J. Bryan, for
T. Boosey, 1795. 3 p.ℓ., 119p., 1ℓ.

2470 _____. The Death of Wallenstein. 1913. (In Kuno Francke, ed.,
The German classics of the nineteenth and twentieth century
[New York, The German publication society, 1913], v. 3,
p. 84-240). Translated by S. T. Coleridge.

2471 _____. ... Early dramas and romances. The robbers, Fiesco,
Love and intrigue, Demetrius, The ghostseer, and The sport
of destiny. Tr. from the German, chiefly by Henry G. Bohn.
London, H. G. Bohn, 1849. xvii, [1]p., 2ℓ., 403, [1]p.
(The works of Frederick Schiller, [vol. IV]).

SCHILLER, JOHANN CHRISTOPH FRIEDRICH VON

2472   SCHILLER, JOHANN CHRISTOPH FRIEDRICH VON. The harper's
        daughter; or, Love and ambition. A tragedy, in five acts.
        Translated from the German of Schiller... By M. G. Lewis
        ... And now published with considerable alterations, as
        performed at the Philadelphia and Baltimore theatres.
        Philadelphia, Published by M. Carey, no. 121, Chestnut
        street. Printed by R. and W. Carr, 1813. 76p. [Dramatic
        pamphlets. v. 33, no. 8].
            Adapted from an earlier adaptation, also by Lewis, of
        Kabale und Liebe, entitled "The minister," 1797.

2473   _____. ... Historical dramas, etc.: Don Carlos. - Mary
        Stuart. - The maid of Orleans. - The bride of Messina.
        Translated from the German. London, H. G. Bohn, 1847.
        516p. front. (port.). (The works of Frederick Schiller.
        [vol. III]).

2474   _____. The Homage of the Arts. 1913. (In Kuno Francke, ed.,
        The German classics of the nineteenth and twentieth century
        [New York, The German publication society, 1913], v. 3,
        p. 266-376). Translated by A. I. du P. Coleman.

2475   _____. The robbers. A tragedy, in five acts. Translated
        from the German of Frederick Schiller. New York, Samuel
        French [n.d.]. 57p.

2476   _____. The robbers, Fiesco, Love and intrigue, by Friedrich
        Schiller; ed. by Nathan Haskell Dole. Boston, F. A.
        Niccolls and co. [1902]. xiv, 423p. front., 4 pl.

2477   _____. Wallenstein's camp. Tr. from the German of Schiller
        by George Moir. With a memoir of Albert Wallenstein, by
        G. Wallis Haven. Boston, J. Munroe and co., 1837. v,
        [7]-142p.

2478   _____. William Tell. 1913. (In Kuno Francke, ed., The
        German classics of the nineteenth and twentieth century
        [New York, The German publication society, 1913], v. 3,
        p. 245-365). Translated by Sir Theodore Martin.

2479   _____. William Tell, a drama, from the German of Schiller;
        tr. by R. Talbot. London, Printed by Plummer and Brewis,
        1829. xii, 180p.

2480   SCHNITZLER, ARTHUR, 1862-1901. The green cockatoo. 1914.
        (In Kuno Francke, ed., The German classics of the nine-
        teenth and twentieth century [New York, The German publica-
        tion society, 1914], v. 20, p. 289-331). Translated by
        Horace Samuel.

SCOTT, CLEMENT WILLIAM

2481 _____. Literature. 1914. (In Kuno Francke, ed., The German
classics of the nineteenth and twentieth century [New York,
The German publication society, 1914], v. 20, p. 332-359).
Translated by A. I. du P. Coleman.

2482 SCHÖNBERG, JAMES. Narcisse the vagrant. A tragedy in five
acts... New York, Samuel French and son [n.d.]. 48p.

2483 SCHÖNHERR, KARL. Faith and fireside. 1914. (In Kuno Francke,
ed., The German classics of the nineteenth and twentieth
century [New York, The German publication society, 1914],
v. 16, p. 417-479). Translated by Edmund von Mach.

2884 SCHOONMAKER, EDWIN DAVIES. The Americans. New York, Mitchell
Kennerley, 1913. 304p.

2485 _____. The Saxons; a drama of Christianity in the North, by
Edwin Davies Schoonmaker. Chicago, Illinois, The Hammers-
mark publishing co., 1905. 214p.

2486 SCHROLL, ELEANOR ALLEN. Why Santa Claus comes in December,
a Christmas play for ten girls and five boys, ages from 10
to 15 years, by Eleanor Allen Schroll. Cincinnati, Ohio,
New York, Fillmore music house, 1909. 15, [1]p.

2487 SCHÜTZE, MARTIN. Hero and Leander, a tragedy. New York,
Henry Holt and co., 1908. 176p.

2488 SCOTT, CLEMENT WILLIAM, 1841-1904, comp. Drawing-room plays
and parlour pantomimes. Collected by Clement Scott from
E. L. Blanchard, W. S. Gilbert, J. Palgrave Simpson [and
others]... London, S. Rivers and co., 1870. xii, 360p.
front.
    Music: p. 359-360.
    CONTENTS. - An induction, by E. L. Blanchard. - Two
gentlemen at Mivart's, by J. P. Simpson. - A medical man,
by W. S. Gilbert. - Harlequin Little Red Riding-Hood, by
Tom Hood. - Fireside diplomacy, by C. S. Cheltnam. -
Ingomar; or, The noble savage, by R. Reece. - Money makes
the man, by Arthur Sketchley. - The happy despatch, by
Alfred Thompson. - An eligible situation, by Thomas Archer
and J. C. Brough. - The pet-lamb, by C. W. Scott. - The
last lily, by C. W. Scott. - The three temptations, by J.
A. Sterry. - His first brief, by Sidney Daryl. - The girls
of the period, by A. B.

SCOTT, W. ATKINS

2489 SCOTT, W. ATKINS. An L. A. W. rest, a farce in one act. New
      York, The Roxbury publishing co. [1899]. 14p.

2490 SCOTT, SIR WALTER, 1771-1832. The poetical works of Sir
      Walter Scott. Complete edition. With illustrations by
      Garrett, Schell, Taylor, Waud and other artists. New York,
      Thomas Y. Crowell and co. [1884]. vi, 659p. illus.
          Includes the following "dramatic pieces": Hallidon
      Hill, Macduff's cross, Auchindrane, The doom of Devorgoil,
      The house of Aspen.

2491 ... The sea of ice; or, A thirst for gold, and the wild
      flower of Mexico. A romantic drama, in five tableaux...
      New York, Samuel French [n.d.]. 40p. (French's American
      drama, no. cxiv).

2492 The secret; or, The hole in the wall. A comic piece, in one
      act. Printed from the acting copy, with remarks, biographi-
      cal and critical, by D.-G. ... As performed at the
      Theatres Royal... London, Davidson [n.d.]. 24p. incl.
      front. (Cumberland's British theatre. London, ca. 1825-
      55. v. 41 [no. 3]).
          Remarks by George Daniel, editor of the series.
          Reissue of Cumberland's earlier edition.
          Attributed to William T. Moncrieff. Cf. Cushing,
      Anonyms.

2493 SEDGEWICK, ALFRED B. ... Circumstances alter cases. Comic
      operetta... New York, Robert M. De Witt, 1876. 33p.

2494 _____. Estranged. An operetta in one act... the music
      selected from... Verdi's "Il Trovatore"... New York,
      Robert M. De Witt, 1876. 30p.

2495 _____. ... A gay old man am I. A musical monologue... New
      York, Happy hours company [n.d.]. 8p.

2496 _____. Leap year. Musical duality... the music selected and
      adapted from Offenbach's celebrated opera, Geneviève de
      Brabant... New York, Robert M. De Witt, 1875. 15p.

2497 _____. My walking photograph. Musical duality, in one act.
      For a lady, a gentleman, and the prompter... the music
      selected and arranged by A. B. Sedgwick from Le Cocq's
      opera, "La fille de Madame Angot." New York, Robert M.
      De Witt, 1876. 26p.

2498   _____. The queerest courtship. Comic operetta in one act... the music selected and arranged by A. B. Sedgewick from Offenbach's celebrated opera, "La Princesse de Trébizonde" ... New York, Robert M. De Witt, 1876. 31p.

2499   _____. Sold again, and got the money. Comic operetta... New York, Robert M. De Witt, 1876. 27p.

2500   _____. ... There's millions in it. A musical and dramatic sketch. New York, Happy Hours Co. [n.d.]. 11p. (The Variety Stage, no. 7).

2501   _____. The twin sisters. Comic operetta, in one act... New York, Robert M. De Witt, 1876. 36p.

2502   SELBY, CHARLES, 1802?-1863. The bonnie fish wife, an original musical interlude in one act... London, Thomas Hailes Lacy [n.d.]. 24p.

2503   _____. ... Boots at the Swan. A farce in one act. By Charles Selby. With the stage business, cast of characters, costumes, relative positions, etc. New York, Baltimore, W. Taylor and co., 1847. 29p. front. (The Minor drama, no. II).

2504   _____. Caught by the ears. A farcical extravaganza, in one act... London, Thomas Hailes Lacy [n.d.]. 21p.

2505   _____. The dancing barber: a farce, in one act... London, The National acting drama office [n.d.]. 21p. front.

2506   _____. A day in Paris. A farce, in one act. London, Thomas Hailes Lacy [n.d.]. 27p.

2507   _____. A fearful tragedy in the seven dials. A farcical interlude, in one act... as first performed at the Theatre Royal Adelphi, May 4, 1857... New York, Robert M. De Witt [n.d.]. 14p.

2508   _____. The fire-eater! A farce in one act... London, Thomas Hailes Lacy [n.d.]. 15p.

2509   _____. ... The guardian sylph! or, The magic rose! a musical fairy interlude, in one act... London, John Duncombe [n.d.]. 24p. front. (Duncombe's edition).

SELBY, CHARLES

2510   SELBY, CHARLES. Harold Hawk; or, The convict's vengeance.
        An original domestic drama in two acts... London, Thomas
        Hailes Lacy [n.d.]. 26p.

2511   _____. ... Hunting a turtle. An original farce, in one act.
        By Charles Selby, comedian... Printed from the best acting
        copy, with remarks biographical and critical... As now per-
        formed in the London and American theatres... Philadelphia,
        F. Turner [etc.]; New York, Turner and Fisher [1836?]. 29p.
        incl. front. (Turner's dramatic library. [no. 12]).
            "First performed in London, Sept. 14, 1835 and... pro-
        duced simultaneously at the American theatre, Philadelphia;
        and Franklin theatre, N. York."

2512   _____. ... The married rake. A farce. In one act. By
        Charles Selby, esq. Printed from the acting copy, with
        costume, cast of characters, and the whole of the stage
        business, as now performed in all the principal theatres.
        Philadelphia, New York, Turner and Fisher [1840?]. 25p.
        (Fisher's edition of standard farces). Cover-title.
        Imperfect? t.-p. wanting?

2513   _____. ... The new footman. A burletta, in one act... New
        York, Samuel French [n.d.]. 22p. (French's American drama,
        no. vii).

2514   _____. Out on the sly; or, A fete at Rosherville! A terpsi-
        chorean burletta, in one act... London, Thomas Hailes
        Lacy [n.d.]. 26p. front.

2515   _____. Peggy Green. A farce. Chicago, The Dramatic publish-
        ing co. [n.d.]. 22p.

2516   _____. Robert Macaire; or, Les [!] auberge des adrets, a melo
        drama in two acts by Charles Selby... London, T. H. Lacy,
        [1850?]. 32p. front.
            Also issued under title: The two murderers.
            Interleaved.

2517   _____. Satan in paradise; or, The mysterious stranger. A
        drama, in two acts. New York, Samuel French [n.d.]. 70p.

2518   _____. The white sergeants. An original drama, in two acts...
        London, National Acting Drama Office [n.d.]. 36p.

SEYMOUR, EDWARD MARTIN

2519   ____. ... The widow's victim. A farce in one act... New York, Samuel French and son [n.d.]. 32p. (The minor drama, no. xxiii).

2520 SENECA, LUCIUS ANNAEUS, ca. 5 or 4 B.C. - 65 A.D. Seneca's tragedies with an English translation by Frank Justus Miller... London, William Heinemann; Cambridge, Mass. Harvard University press, 1938-1939. 2v.

2521 A sequel to Miss Eula M. Young's A day without Latin, by teachers and pupils of Abraham Lincoln High School, New York, N. Y. [n.p., n.d.]. 3p. (American Classical League Service Bureau, No. 480).

2522 ... The sergeant's wife. A drama, in two acts... Boston, William V. Spencer, 1855. 29p. (Spencer's Boston theatre, no. xix).

2523 SERGENT, MARY ELIZABETH. As it really happened; a burlesque of the Aeneas-Dido story [n.p., n.d.]. 5p. (American Classical League Service Bureau, No. 625).

2524 SERLE, THOMAS JAMES. Joan of Arc, the maid of Orleans. A historical romance; in two acts... London, W. Strange, 1837. 38p. front.

2525   ____. ... The yeoman's daughter, a domestic drama, in two acts... London, J. Duncombe and co. [n.d.]. 36p. front. (Duncombe's edition).

2526 SEVERY, MELVIN L. Abandoned farms, comedy drama. Boston, Severy, 1894. 60p.

2527 [SEWALL, JONATHAN] 1728-1796. The Americans roused, in a cure for the spleen; or, Amusement for a winter's evening; being the substance of a conversation on the times over a friendly tankard and pipe. Between Sharp, a country parson. Bumper, a country justice. Fillpot, an innkeeper. Graveairs, a deacon. Trim, a barber. Brim, a Quaker. Puff, a late representative. Taken in shorthand, by Sir Roger de Coverly... New England, printed; New York, Reprinted, by James Rivington [1775].

2528 SEYMOUR, EDWARD MARTIN. Two jolly girl bachelors. Text and stage business edited and revised by Pauline Phelps and Marion Short. New York, Edgar S. Werner and co., 1906. 12p.

SEYMOUR, HARRY

2529   SEYMOUR, HARRY. Aunt Dinah's pledge, a temperance moral
drama, in two acts. Chicago, The Dramatic publishing co.
[n.d.]. 18p.

2530   SHAKESPEARE, WILLIAM, 1564-1616. All's well that ends well;
a comedy, in five acts; by William Shakespeare. Correctly
given, from the text of Johnson and Steevens... London,
Printed by D. S. Maurice [1819?]. 93p. front. [Cabinet
theatre. v. 10, no. 1].

2531   _____. Antony and Cleopatra. A tragedy, in five acts. By
William Shakespeare. Correctly given, from the text of
Johnson and Steevens... London, D. S. Maurice [1819?].
110p. incl. front. [Cabinet theatre, v. 7, no. 1].

2532   _____. Antony and Cleopatra; a historical play, in five acts;
by William Shakespeare. As performed at the Theatres
Royal, Drury Lane... With remarks by Mrs. Inchbald. London, Longman, Hurst, Rees, Orme and Brown [n.d.]. 6 p.ℓ.,
1ℓ., [5]-83p. front. (Inchbald, Mrs. Elizabeth, The
British theatre... London, 1808, v. 4 [no. 5]).

2533   _____. ... As you like it, a comedy; by W. Shakespeare. With
prefatory remarks... The stage business, and stage directions, as it is performed at the Theatres Royal. By W.
Oxberry, comedian. Boston, Wells and Lilly; New York,
A. T. Goodrich and co.; [etc., etc.] 1822. 100p. illus.
(diagr.). (Oxberry, William, The new English drama. Boston [1822?-1824?] v. 20 [no. 2]).

2534   _____. As you like it: a comedy, in five acts; by William
Shakespeare. Correctly given, from the text of Johnson
and Steevens... [London] Printed for the Proprietors, by
D. S. Maurice [1819?]. 83p. front. [Cabinet theatre,
v. 11, no. 1].

2535   _____. As you like it; a comedy, in five acts; by William
Shakespeare. As performed at the Theatres Royal, Drury
Lane and Covent Garden... With remarks by Mrs. Inchbald.
London, Longman, Hurst, Rees, Orme, and Brown [n.d.].
79p. front. (Inchbald, Mrs. Elizabeth. The British
theatre... London, 1808. v. 8 [no. 1]).

2536   _____. The comedy of errors; a comedy, in five acts, by
William Shakespeare. Printed from the acting copy, with
remarks, biographical and critical, by D.-G. ... As now
performed at the Theatres Royal... London, J. Cumberland

(SHAKESPEARE, WILLIAM)
[n.d.]. 52p. incl. front. (Cumberland's British theatre, London, ca. 1825-55. v. 16 [no. 2]).

2537 _____. Comedy of errors. A comedy. In five acts. By William Shakespeare. Correctly given, from the text of Johnson and Steevens... London, D. S. Maurice [1819?]. 62p. incl. front. [Cabinet theatre, v. 5, no. 2].

2538 _____. The comedy of errors; in five acts; by William Shakespeare. As performed at the Theatre Royal, Covent Garden... With remarks by Mrs. Inchbald. London, Longman, Hurst, Rees, Orme, and Brown [n.d.]. 63p. front. (Inchbald, Mrs. Elizabeth. The British theatre... London, 1808. v. 1 [no. 1]).

2539 _____. The tragedy of Coriolanus, by William Shakespeare; ed., with introduction and notes, by H. D. Weiser... New York, The Macmillan co., 1919. xlv p., 1ℓ., 188p. front. (Lettered on cover: Macmillan's pocket classics).

2540 _____. Shakespeare's tragedy of Coriolanus. With introduction, and notes explanatory and critical. For use in schools and families. By the Rev. Henry N. Hudson... Boston, New York [etc.] Ginn and co. [1909]. 221p.

2541 _____. The tragedie of Coriolanus, by William Shakespeare; ed., with notes, introduction, glossary, list of variorum readings, and selected criticism, by Charlotte Porter and Helen A. Clarke. New York, T. Y. Crowell and co. [1908]. 4 p.ℓ., vii-xv, 296p. front.

2542 _____. ... The tragedy of Coriolanus, ed. by Edmund K. Chambers... London [etc.] Blackie and son, ltd., 1898. xvii, [1], 231p.

2543 _____. Shakespeare's Coriolanus. With notes, examination papers, and plan of preparation. (Selected.) By Brainerd Kellogg... New York, E. Maynard and co. [1892]. 5, vi-vii, [2], 8-xxvii, [1], 7-231p. 1 illus. (On cover: English classics).

2544 _____. ... Coriolanus; or, The Roman matron, a tragedy; by W. Shakspeare. With prefatory remarks... faithfully marked with the stage business and stage directions, as it is performed at the Theatres Royal. By W. Oxberry, comedian. London, Pub. for the Proprietors, by W. Simpkin, and R. Marshall [etc.] 1820. 1 p.ℓ., iii, [3]-62p. front. (port.) diagr.

SHAKESPEARE, WILLIAM

2545   SHAKESPEARE, WILLIAM. Coriolanus; or, The Roman matron, a
        historical play, in five acts; by William Shakespeare. As
        performed at the Theatres Royal, Covent Garden... With
        remarks by Mrs. Inchbald. London, Longman, Hurst, Rees,
        Orme, and Brown [n.d.]. 68p. front. (Inchbald, Mrs.
        Elizabeth. The British theatre... London, 1808. v. 5,
        [no. 1]).

2546   _____. Shakespeare's tragedy of Cymbeline; ed., with notes
        by William J. Rolfe... New York, Cincinnati [etc.] Ameri-
        can book co. [1905]. 292p.

2547   _____. Cymbeline; an historical play in five acts, by William
        Shakespeare. Printed from the acting copy, with remarks,
        biographical and critical, by D.-G. ... As performed at
        the Theatres Royal... London, G. H. Davidson [n.d.]. 9,
        [2], 10-73p. incl. front. (Davidson's shilling volume of
        Cumberland's plays. London [ca. 1849-55] v. 7 [no. 2]).

2548   _____. ... Cymbeline, a historical play. In five acts. By
        W. Shakespeare... With notes, critical and explanatory.
        Also, an authentic description of the costume, and the
        general stage business, as performed at the Theatres
        Royal, London. Embellished with a wood engraving... made
        expressly for this work, by Mr. I. R. Cruikshank... Lon-
        don, T. Dolby, 1823. iv, [7]-76p. front. (Dolby's
        British theatre).

2549   _____. ... Cymbeline, a tragedy; by William Shakespeare.
        With prefatory remarks... Faithfully marked with the
        stage business, and stage directions. As it is performed
        at the Theatres Royal. By W. Oxberry, comedian. London,
        Pub. for the Proprietors, by W. Simpkin, and R. Marshall
        [etc.] 1821. 1 pl.ℓ., iii, [3], 79, [1]p. front. (port.)
        diagr. (Oxberry, William. The new English drama. Lon-
        don, 1818-25, v. 12 [no. 2]).

2550   _____. Cymbeline. A tragedy. In five acts. By William
        Shakespeare. Correctly given, from the text of Johnson
        and Steevens... London, D. S. Maurice [1819?]. 112p.
        incl. front. [Cabinet theatre. v. 6, no. 1].

2551   _____. Cymbeline; a historical play, in five acts; by William
        Shakespeare. As performed at the Theatres Royal, Drury
        Lane and Covent Garden... With remarks by Mrs. Inchbald.
        London, Longman, Hurst, Rees, Orme, and Brown [n.d.]. 90p.
        front. (Inchbald, Mrs. Elizabeth. The British theatre...
        London, 1808. v. 4, [no. 2]).

SHAKESPEARE, WILLIAM

2552   _____. Hamlet. A tragedy in five acts. By William Shakespeare... New York. F. Rullman, 1894. 66p. (On cover:
The Mounet-Suily edition).

2553   _____. ... Shakespeare's tragedy of Hamlet, as presented by
Edwin Booth... New-York, F. Hart and co., 1878. 5, [1]p.,
2ℓ., 10-125 numb.ℓ., [127]-136p.

2554   _____. ... Hamlet. A tragedy in five acts. By William
Shakspeare. The stage edition... New York, Philadelphia
[etc.] W. Taylor and co., 1846. vii, [1], [7]-78p.

2555   _____. Hamlet; a tragedy, in five acts. By William Shakespeare. Printed from the acting copy, with remarks, biographical and critical, by D.-G. ... As performed at the
Theatres Royal... London, Davidson [n.d.]. 12, [2], [9]-
78p. incl. front. (Cumberland's British theatre. London
[ca. 1825-55] v. 4 [no. 4]).

2556   _____. ... Hamlet, a tragedy, in five acts. By W. Shakespeare... With notes, critical and explanatory. Also, an
authentic description of the costume, and the general stage
business, as performed at the Theatres Royal, London. Embellished with a wood engraving... Made expressly for this
work, by Mr. I. R. Cruikshank... London, T. Dolby, 1823.
iv, [2], [7]-77, [1]p. front., illus. (plans). (Dolby's
British theatre).

2557   _____. ... Hamlet, a tragedy; by William Shakespeare...
faithfully marked with the stage business, and stage
directions, as it is performed at the Theatres Royal.
London, Pub. for the Proprietors, by W. Simpkin and R.
Marshall [etc.] 1818. 1 p.ℓ., xxviii, [2] 84p. front.
(port.) diagr.

2558   _____. Hamlet, prince of Denmark; a tragedy, in five acts;
by William Shakespeare. As performed at the Theatres
Royal, Drury Lane and Covent Garden... With remarks by
Mrs. Inchbald. London, Longman, Hurst, Rees, Orme, and
Brown [n.d.]. 93p. front. (Inchbald, Mrs. Elizabeth.
The British theatre... London, 1808. v. 1 [no. 3]).

2559   _____. ... The tragedy of Julius Caesar... with an appendix
containing suggestions for its study, by Franklin Thomas
Baker... New York, etc., American book co. [1898]. 125p.

SHAKESPEARE, WILLIAM

2560   SHAKESPEARE, WILLIAM. Julius Caesar: a tragedy, in five acts.
       By William Shakespeare. Printed from the acting copy,
       with remarks, biographical and critical, by D.-G. ... As
       performed at the Theatres Royal... London, G. H. Davidson
       [n.d.]. 63p. incl. front. (Cumberland's British theatre.
       London, ca. 1825-55. v. 5 [no. 7]).

2561   _____. ... Julius Caesar, a tragedy, in five acts, by William
       Shakespeare... With notes, critical and explanatory.
       Also, an authentic description of the costume, and the
       general stage business, as performed at the Theatres Royal,
       London. Embellished with a wood engraving... Made express-
       ly for this work, by Mr. I. R. Cruikshank... London,
       T. Dolby, 1824. iv, [5]-64p. front. (Dolby's British
       theatre).

2562   _____. ... Julius Caesar, a tragedy; by William Shakespeare.
       With prefatory remarks... Faithfully marked with the stage
       business, and stage directions, as it is performed at the
       Theatres Royal. By W. Oxberry, comedian. London, Pub.
       for the Proprietors, by W. Simpkin, and R. Marshall [etc.]
       1822. vi, 7-80p. front. (port.) diagr. (Oxberry, William.
       The new English drama. London, 1818-25. v. 16 [no. 3]).

2563   _____. Julius Caesar: a tragedy, in five acts; by William
       Shakespeare. As performed at the Theatres Royal, Covent-
       Garden... With remarks by Mrs. Inchbald. London, Long-
       man, Hurst, Rees, Orme, and Brown [n.d.]. 78p. front.
       (Inchbald, Mrs. Elizabeth. The British theatre... London,
       1808. v. 4 [no. 4]).

2564   _____. ... King Henry IV. Part I. A tragedy, in five acts.
       By W. Shakespeare... With notes, critical and explanatory.
       Also an authentic description of the costume, and the
       general stage business. As performed at the Theatres
       Royal, London. Embellished with a wood engraving... made
       expressly for this work, by Mr. I. R. Cruikshank... Lon-
       don, T. Dolby [1823?]. iv, [3], 8-67, [1]p. illus.
       (plans.). (Dolby's British theatre).

2565   _____. ... King Henry IV. Part I. A tragedy; by William
       Shakespeare. With prefatory remarks... Faithfully marked
       with the stage business, and stage directions, as it is
       performed at the Theatres Royal. By W. Oxberry, comedian.
       London, Pub. for the Proprietors, by W. Simpkin and R.
       Marshall [etc.] 1822. 1 p.ℓ., ii p., 1ℓ., [2], 82p.
       front. (port.) diagr. (Oxberry, William. The new English
       drama. London, 1818-25, v. 14 [no. 4]).

SHAKESPEARE, WILLIAM

2566 _____. King Henry IV. Part I[-II]... By William Shakespeare.
Correctly given, from the text of Johnson and Steevens.
With remarks. London, D. S. Maurice [1819?]. 2 pt. fronts.
(Cabinet theatre, v. 3, no. 1-2).

2567 _____. King Henry IV. The first [-second] part... in five
acts; by William Shakespeare. As performed at the Theatre
Royal, Covent-Garden... With remarks by Mrs. Inchbald.
London, Longman, Hurst, Rees, Orme, and Brown [n.d.].
2v. fronts. (Inchbald, Mrs. Elizabeth. The British
theatre... London, 1808. v. 2 [no. 1-2]).

2568 _____. King Henry V. An historical play, in five acts, by
William Shakspeare. Printed from the acting copy, with
remarks, biographical and critical, by D.-G. ... As performed at the Theatres Royal... London, J. Cumberland
[n.d.]. 7, [1], [7]-56p. incl. front.

2569 _____. King Henry V. An historical play, in five acts: by
William Shakespeare. Printed from the acting copy, with
remarks to which are added, a description of the costume,
cast of the characters... and the whole of the stage
business, as now performed at the Theatres-Royal, London.
Embellished with a wood engraving... by Mr. I. R. Cruikshank... London, T. Dolby, 1825. iv, [5]-56p. front.
(Dolby's British theatre).

2570 _____. ... King Henry V. An historical play; by W. Shakspeare. With prefatory remarks... Faithfully marked with
the stage business, and stage directions, as it is performed at the Theatres Royal. By W. Oxberry, comedian.
London, Pub. for the Proprietors, by W. Simpkin and R.
Marshall [etc.] 1823. ix, [3], 68p. front. (port.) diagr.

2571 _____. King Henry V. An historical play, in five acts. By
William Shakespeare. Correctly given, from the text of
Johnson and Steevens... London, D. S. Maurice [1819?].
104p. incl. front. [Cabinet theatre. v. 3, no. 3].

2572 _____. King Henry V. A historical play, in five acts; by
William Shakespeare. As performed at the Theatre Royal.
Covent Garden... With remarks by Mrs. Inchbald. London,
Longman, Hurst, Rees, Orme, and Brown [n.d.]. 72p. front.
(Inchbald, Mrs. Elizabeth. The British theatre... Lon-
don, 1808. v. 2 [no. 4]).

SHAKESPEARE, WILLIAM

2573 SHAKESPEARE, WILLIAM. King Henry VI. Part I[-II]... By
William Shakespeare. Correctly given from the text of
Johnson and Steevens... London, D. S. Maurice [1819?].
3 pt. fronts. (Cabinet theatre, v. 2, no. 1-3).

2574 _____. ... Shakespeare's play of Henry the Eighth, as repre-
sented by Edwin Booth. New-York, Printed, for W. Winter,
by F. Hart and co., 1878. 5, [1]p., 2ℓ., 9-60 numb.ℓ.,
[61]-71p.

2575 _____. King Henry VIII: an historical play, in five acts, by
William Shakespeare. Printed from the acting copy, with
remarks, biographical and critical, by D.-G. ... As performed at the Theatres Royal... London, G. H. Davidson
[n.d.]. 60p. incl. front. (Davidson's shilling volume
of Cumberland's plays. London [ca. 1849-55] v. 6 [no. 21]).

2576 _____. King Henry VIII. An historical play, in five acts, by
William Shakespeare. Printed from the acting copy, with
remarks biographical and critical, by D.-G. ... As now
performed at the Theatre Royal... London, J. Cumberland
[n.d.]. 60p. incl. front. (Cumberland's British theatre.
London, ca. 1825-55?, v. 5 [no. 6]).

2577 _____. ... King Henry VIII. An historical play, in five acts,
by William Shakespeare... With notes, critical and explanatory. Also, an authentic description of the costume,
and the general stage business, as performed at the
Theatres-Royal, London. Embellished with a wood engraving
... made expressly for this work, by Mr. I. R. Cruikshank...
London, T. Dolby, 1824. iv, [5]-60p. front. (Dolby's
British theatre).

2578 _____. ... King Henry VIII. A play; by W. Shakspeare. With
prefatory remarks... Faithfully marked with the stage
business, and stage directions, as it is performed at the
Theatres Royal. By W. Oxberry, comedian. London, Pub.
for the Proprietors, by W. Simpkin and R. Marshall [etc.]
1823. xvi, [2], 70p. front. (port.).

2579 _____. King Henry VIII. An historical play, in five acts.
By William Shakespeare. Correctly given, from the text
of Johnson and Steevens... London, D. S. Maurice [1819?].
103, [1]p. incl. front. Cabinet theatre. v. 6, no. 2].

SHAKESPEARE, WILLIAM

2580 _____. Henry the VIIIth. A tragedy. Written by William
Shakespeare. Taken from the manager's book, at the
Theatre Royal, Covent-Garden. London, Printed [by] R.
Butters [180?]. 51p.

2581 _____. King Henry VIII. An historical play, in five acts;
by William Shakespeare. As performed at the Theatre Royal,
Covent Garden... With remarks by Mrs. Inchbald. London,
Longman, Hurst, Rees, Orme, and Brown [n.d.]. 75p. front.
(Inchbald, Mrs. Elizabeth. The British theatre... London,
1808. v. 3 [no. 3]).

2582 _____. King John; a tragedy, in five acts, by William Shakespeare. Printed from the acting copy, with remarks, biographical and critical, by D.-G. ... As performed at the
Theatres Royal... London, G. H. Davidson [n.d.]. 59p.
front. (Davidson's shilling volume of Cumberland's plays.
London [ca. 1849-55] v. 12 [no. 1]).

2583 _____. King John. A tragedy, in five acts; by William Shakespeare. Correctly given, from the text of Johnson and
Steevens... London, Printed by D. S. Maurice [1819?].
84p. incl. front. [Cabinet theatre. v. 4, no. 2].

2584 _____. King John; a historical play, in five acts; by
William Shakespeare. As performed at the Theatre Royal,
Covent Garden... With remarks by Mrs. Inchbald. London,
Longman, Hurst, Rees, Orme, and Brown [n.d.]. 69p. front.
(Inchbald, Mrs. Elizabeth. The British theatre... London,
1808. v. 1 [no. 4]).

2585 _____. ... Shakespeare's tragedy of King Lear, as presented
by Edwin Booth... New-York, Printed, for W. Winter, by
F. Hart and co., 1878. 5, [3]p. 1ℓ., 10-104 numb.ℓ., [105]-
119p.

2586 _____. King Lear: a tragedy, in five acts, by William Shakespeare. Printed from the acting copy, with remarks, biographical and critical by D.-G. ... As performed at the
Theatres Royal... London, G. H. Davidson [n.d.]. 67p.
incl. front. (Davidson's shilling volume of Cumberland's
plays. London [ca. 1849-55] v. 26 [no. 2]).

2587 _____. King Lear. A tragedy, in five acts, by William
Shakespeare. Printed from the acting copy, with remarks,
biographical and critical, by D.-G. ... As performed at
the Theatres Royal... London, J. Cumberland and son [n.d.].
67p. incl. front. (Cumberland's British theatre. London,
ca. 1825-55. v. 6 [no. 6]).

BRITISH AND AMERICAN DRAMA

SHAKESPEARE, WILLIAM

2588   SHAKESPEARE, WILLIAM. ... King Lear, a tragedy; altered from
Shakespeare, by Nahum Tate. With prefatory remarks...
Faithfully marked with the stage business, and stage
directions, as it is performed at the Theatres Royal. By
W. Oxberry, comedian. London, Pub. for the Proprietors,
by W. Simpkin, and R. Marshall [etc.] 1820. x, [2], 71,
[1]p. front. (port.) diagr. (Oxberry, William, The new
English drama. London, 1818-25, v. 10 [no.]).

2589   _____. King Lear. A tragedy, in five acts. By William
Shakespeare. Correctly given, from the text of Johnson and
Steevens... London, D. S. Maurice [1819?]. 111p. incl.
front. [Cabinet theatre. v. 4, no. 1].

2590   _____. King Lear; a tragedy, in five acts; by William Shakespeare. As performed at the Theatres-Royal, Drury-Lane
and Covent-Garden... With remarks by Mrs. Inchbald. London, Longman, Hurst, Rees, Orme, and Brown [n.d.]. 78p.
front. (Inchbald, Mrs. Elizabeth. The British theatre...
London, 1808. v. 4 [no. 1]).

2591   _____. [... Shakespeare's tragedy of King Richard II. As
presented by Edwin Booth... New-York, F. Hart and co.,
1878]. 4, [4]p., 1ℓ., 10-61 numb.ℓ., [63]-72p.

2592   _____. King Richard II. A tragedy, in five acts, by William
Shakespeare. Printed from the acting copy, with remarks,
biographical and critical, by D.-G. ... As performed at
the Theatres Royal... London, J. Cumberland [n.d.]. 54p.
incl. front. (Cumberland's British theatre. London, ca.
1825-55. v. 29 [no. 6]).

2593   _____. King Richard II. A tragedy, in five acts. By William
Shakespeare. Correctly given, from the text of Johnson
and Steevens... London, D. S. Maurice [1819?]. 89p. incl.
front. [Cabinet theatre. v. 9, no. 2].

2594   _____. ... Shakespeare's tragedy of King Richard III. As
presented by Edwin Booth... New-York, F. Hart and co.,
1878. 6 p.ℓ., 2ℓ., 10-102 numb.ℓ., [103]-110p.

2595   _____. King Richard the Third: a tragedy, in five acts, by
William Shakespeare. Printed from the acting copy, with
remarks biographical and critical, by D.-G. ... As performed at the Theatres Royal... London, G. H. Davidson
[n.d.]. 66p. incl. front. (Cumberland's British theatre.
London, ca. 1825-55. v. 1 [no. 5]).

2596 _____. ... King Richard III. A tragedy, in five acts, by W. Shakespeare. Printed from the acting edition, with re-marks. To which are added, a description of the costume, cast of the characters... and the whole of the stage busi-ness, as now performed at the Theatres-Royal, London. Em-bellished with a wood engraving, from an original drawing made expressly for this work, by Mr. I. R. Cruikshank... London, T. Dolby, 1824. iv, [2], [7]-65p. front., illus. (plan). (Dolby's British theatre).

2597 _____. ... Richard the Third, a tragedy; by W. Shakspeare. Adapted to the stage by Colley Cibber... faithfully marked with the stage business and stage directions, as it is per-formed at the Theatres Royal. London, Pub. for the Pro-prietors, by W. Simpkin and R. Marshall [etc.] 1818. iv, [2], 68p. front. (port.) diagr.

2598 _____. King Richard III. A tragedy, in five acts; by William Shakespeare. As performed at the Theatres Royal, Drury Lane and Covent Garden... With remarks by Mrs. Inchbald. London, Longman, Hurst, Rees, Orme, and Brown [n.d.]. 80p. front. (Inchbald, Mrs. Elizabeth. The British theatre... London, 1808. v. 1 [no. 5]).

2599 _____. ... Shakespeare's tragedy of Macbeth, as presented by Edwin Booth... New-York, Printed, for W. Winter, by F. Hart and co., 1878. 5, [3]p., 1ℓ., 10-85 numb.ℓ., [87]-104p.

2600 _____. Macbeth: a tragedy, in five acts, by William Shake-speare. Printed from the acting copy, with remarks, bio-graphical and critical, by D.-G. ... As performed at the Theatres Royal... London, G. H. Davidson [n.d.]. 62p. incl. front. (Cumberland's British theatre. London, ca. 1825-55. v. 1 [no. 3]).

2601 _____. ... Macbeth, a tragedy; in five acts. By W. Shake-speare... With notes, critical and explanatory. Also, an authentic description of the costume, and the general stage business, as performed at the Theatres Royal, London. Embellished with a wood engraving... made expressly for this work, by Mr. I. R. Cruikshank... London, T. Dolby, 1823. iv, [2], [7]-64p. (Dolby's British theatre).

SHAKESPEARE, WILLIAM

2602   SHAKESPEARE, WILLIAM.   ... Macbeth. A tragedy; by William
        Shakespeare. With prefatory remarks... Faithfully marked
        with the stage business, and stage directions, as it is
        performed at the Theatres Royal. By W. Oxberry, comedian.
        London, Pub. for the Proprietors, by W. Simpkin, and R.
        Marshall [etc.] 1821. 1 p.ℓ., iii, [3], 74p. front. (port.)
        diagr. (Oxberry, William. The new English drama. London,
        1818-25. v. 14 [no. 2]).

2603   _____. Macbeth; a tragedy, in five acts; by William Shake-
        speare. At [!] performed at the Theatres Royal, Drury
        Lane and Covent Garden... With remarks by Mrs. Inchbald.
        London, Longman, Hurst, Rees, Orme, and Brown [n.d.].
        72p. front. (Inchbald, Mrs. Elizabeth. The British
        theatre... London, 1808. v. 4 [no. 3]).

2604   _____. ... Measure for measure, a comedy; by W. Shakespeare.
        With prefatory remarks... Faithfully marked with the
        stage business, and stage directions, as it is performed
        at the Theatres Royal. By W. Oxberry, comedian. London,
        Pub. for the Proprietors, by W. Simpkin and R. Marshall
        [etc.] 1822. xi, [3], 69, [1]p. front. (port.) diagr.
        (Oxberry, William. The new English drama. London, 1818-25.
        v. 16 [no. 2]).

2605   _____. Measure for measure. A comedy, in five acts. By
        William Shakespeare... London, D. S. Maurice [1819?].
        91p. incl. front. [Cabinet theatre. v. 8, no. 1].

2606   _____. Measure for measure; a comedy, in five acts; by
        William Shakespeare. As performed at the Theatre Royal,
        Covent Garden... With remarks by Mrs. Inchbald. London,
        Longman, Hurst, Rees, Orme, and Brown [n.d.]. 75, [1], p.
        front. (Inchbald, Mrs. Elizabeth. The British theatre...
        London, 1808. v. 3 [no. 4]).

2607   _____. Merchant of Venice: a play, in five acts, by William
        Shakespeare. Printed from the acting copy, with remarks,
        biographical and critical, by D.-G. ... As performed at
        the Theatres Royal... London, G. H. Davidson [n.d.].
        62p. incl. pl. front.

2608   _____. The merchant of Venice, a comedy, in five acts, by
        William Shakspeare. Printed under the authority of the
        managers, from the prompt book. With notes, critical and
        explanatory... As performed at the Theatres-Royal, London
        ... London, T. Dolby, 1824. vii p., 1[?]ℓ., [9]-61, [1]p.

SHAKESPEARE, WILLIAM

2609 _____. ... The merchant of Venice, a comedy; by William
Shakespeare. With prefatory remarks... Faithfully marked
with the stage business, and stage directions, as it is
performed at the Theatres Royal. By W. Oxberry, comedian.
London, Pub. for the Proprietors, by W. Simpkin and R.
Marshall [etc.] 1820. 1 p.ℓ., ii, [2], 65, [1]p. front.
(port.) diagr. (Oxberry, William. The new English drama.
London, 1818-25. v. 10 [no. 4]).

2610 _____. The merchant of Venice; a comedy, in five acts; by
William Shakespeare. As performed at the Theatre Royal,
Covent Garden... With remarks by Mrs. Inchbald. London,
Longman, Hurst, Rees, Orme, and Brown [n.d.]. 74p. front.
(Inchbald, Mrs. Elizabeth. The British theatre... London,
1808. v. 2 [no. 3]).

2611 [_____]. The Jew of Venice. A comedy. As it is acted at
the theatre in Little-Lincolns-Inn-Fields, by His Majesty's
servants. London, Printed for Ber. Lintott, 1701. 4 p.ℓ.,
46, [1]p.

2612 _____. The merry wives of Windsor. A comedy, in five acts,
by William Shakspeare. Printed from the acting copy, with
remarks, biographical and critical, by D.-G. ... As performed at the Theatres Royal... London, G. H. Davidson
[n.d.]. 62p. incl. front.

2613 _____. The merry wives of Windsor; a comedy, in five acts;
by William Shakespeare. As performed at the Theatres-
Royal, Covent-Garden and Drury-Lane... With remarks by
Mrs. Inchbald. London, Longman, Hurst, Rees, Orme, and
Brown [n.d.]. 82p. front.

2614 _____. The merry wives of Windsor. A comedy, in five acts.
By William Shakspeare. Correctly given, from the text of
Johnson and Steevens... London, Printed by D. S. Maurice
[1819?]. 84p. incl. front.

2615 _____. A midsummer-night's dream: a comedy, in five acts; by
William Shakspeare. Correctly given, from the text of
Johnson and Steevens... London, Printed by D. S. Maurice
[1819?]. 66p. front.

2616 _____. Much ado about nothing: a comedy, in five acts, by
William Shakspeare. Printed from the acting copy, with
remarks, biographical and critical, by D.-G. ... As performed at the Theatres Royal... London, G. H. Davidson
[n.d.]. 1 p.ℓ., [5]-7, [3], [9]-61p. front., pl.

SHAKESPEARE, WILLIAM

2617   SHAKESPEARE, WILLIAM. ... Shakespeare's comedy of Much ado
        about nothing. As presented by Edwin Booth... New-York,
        Printed, for W. Winter, By F. Hart and co., 1878. 4, [2]p.,
        2ℓ., 10-89 numb.ℓ., [91]-94p.

2618   _____. ... Much ado about nothing. A comedy; by W. Shakspeare.
        With prefatory remarks... Faithfully marked with the stage
        business, and stage directions, as it is performed at the
        Theatres Royal. By W. Oxberry, comedian. London, Pub. for
        the Proprietors, by W. Simpkin and R. Marshall [etc.] 1823.
        vii, [3], 72p. front. (port.) diagr.

2619   _____. Much ado about nothing. A comedy, in five acts; by
        William Shakspeare. Correctly given, from the text of
        Johnson and Steevens... London, Printed by D. S. Maurice
        [1818?]. 83p. front.

2620   _____. Othello: a tragedy, in five acts, by William.Shak-
        speare. Printed from the acting copy, with remarks, bio-
        graphical and critical, by D.-G. ... As performed at the
        Theatres Royal... London, G. H. Davidson [n.d.]. 72p.
        front.

2621   _____. Othello, the Moor of Venice; a tragedy, in five acts;
        by William Shakespeare. As performed at the Theatres-
        Royal, Drury-Lane and Covent Garden... With remarks by
        Mrs. Inchbald. London, Longman, Hurst, Rees, Orme, and
        Brown [n.d.]. 89p. front.

2622   _____. ... Shakespeare's tragedy of Othello, as presented by
        Edwin Booth... New-York, Printed, for W. Winter, by F.
        Hart and co., 1878. 5, [3]p. 1ℓ., 10-111 numb.ℓ. [113]-
        125p.

2623   _____. ... Othello, a tragedy; in five acts. By W. Shak-
        speare... with notes, critical and explanatory. Also an
        authentic description of the costume, and the general stage
        business. As performed at the Theatres Royal, London.
        Embellished with a wood engraving... made expressly for
        this work, by Mr. I. R. Cruikshank... also, a portrait of
        Mr. Young, as Iago. London, T. Dolby, 1823. iv, [9]-78p.
        (Dolby's British theatre). No. 9 in a volume of ten plays
        lettered: Plays.
            Imperfect: preliminary matter (including illustration
        and portrait?) following p. iv, wanting.

SHAKESPEARE, WILLIAM

2624 _____. ... Othello. A tragedy, by William Shakespeare. With prefatory remarks... faithfully marked with the stage business, and stage directions, as it is performed at the Theatres Royal. By W. Oxberry, comedian. London, Pub. for the Proprietors, by W. Simpkin, and R. Marshall [etc.] 1819. v, [3], 76p. front. (port.) diagr.

2625 _____. Othello, The Moor of Venice. A tragedy. By William Shakespeare. Collated with the old and modern editions. London, Printed by W. Bowyer and J. Nichols, and sold by W. Owen, 1773. 9 p.ℓ., 182p. front.

2626 _____. Pericles. A tragedy, in five acts. By William Shakspeare. Correctly given, from the text of Johnson and Steevens... London, D. S. Maurice [1819?]. 80p. incl. front.

2627 _____. Rome and Juliet: a tragedy, in five acts, by William Shakspeare. Printed from the acting copy, with remarks, biographical and critical, by D.-G. ... As performed at the Theatres Royal... London, G. H. Davidson [n.d.]. 69p. incl. pl. front.

2628 _____. Romeo and Juliet; a tragedy, in five acts; by William Shakspeare. As performed at the Theatres Royal, Drury Lane and Covent Garden... With remarks by Mrs. Inchbald. London, Longman, Hurst, Rees, Orme, and Brown [n.d.]. 6 p.ℓ., 1ℓ. [5]-78p. front.

2629 _____. ... Romeo and Juliet, a tragedy; by W. Shakespeare, adapted to the stage by David Garrick. With prefatory remarks... Faithfully marked with the stage business, and stage directions, as it is performed at the Theatres Royal. By W. Oxberry, comedian. London, Pub. for the Proprietors, by W. Simpkin and R. Marshall [etc.] 1819. 1 p.ℓ., ii, [2], 67, [1]p. front. (port.) diagr. (Oxberry, William. The new English drama. London, 1818-25. v. 6 [no. 3]).

2630 _____. The Shakespearean plays of Edwin Booth; ed. by William Winter... Philadelphia, The Penn publishing co., 1899. 2 v. fronts. (ports.)

2631 _____. ... Shakespeare's comedy of Katharine and Petruchio, as presented by Edwin Booth... New-York, Printed, for W. Winter, by F. Hart and co., 1878. 4p., 3ℓ., 10-45 numb.ℓ., [47]-49p.

SHAKESPEARE, WILLIAM

2632   SHAKESPEARE, WILLIAM. Taming of the shrew. A comedy, in five acts; by William Shakspeare. Correctly given, from the text of Johnson and Steevens... London, D. S. Maurice [1819?]. 87p. incl. front.

2633   _____. The tempest; or, The enchanted island; a play, in five acts; by William Shakspeare. Adapted to the stage, with additions from Dryden and Davenant, by J. P. Kemble. As performed at the Theatre Royal, Covent Garden... With remarks by Mrs. Inchbald. London, Longman, Hurst, Rees, Orme, and Brown [n.d.]. 71p. front.

2634   _____. ... The tempest, a play; by W. Shakspeare. With prefatory remarks... Faithfully marked with the stage business, and stage directions, as it is performed at the Theatres Royal. By W. Oxberry, comedian. London, Pub. for the Proprietors, by W. Simpkin, and R. Marshall [etc.] 1823. xviii, [2] 56p. front. (port.) diagr.

2635   _____. Timon of Athens: a tragedy, in five acts, by William Shakspeare. Printed from the acting copy, with remarks biographical and critical, by D.-G. ... As performed at the Theatres Royal... London, J. Cumberland [n.d.]. 72p. incl. front.

2636   _____. Timon of Athens: a tragedy, in five acts; by William Shakspeare. Correctly given, from the text of Johnson and Steevens... London, Printed by D. S. Maurice [1819?]. 78p. front.

2637   _____. Titus Andronicus. A tragedy, in five acts. By William Shakspeare. Correctly given, from the text of Johnson and Steevens... London, D. S. Maurice [1819?]. 84p. incl. front.

2638   _____. Twelfth night; or, What you will; a comedy, in five acts, by William Shakspeare. Printed from the acting copy, with remarks, biographical and critical, by D.-G. ... As performed at the Theatres Royal... London, G. H. Davidson [n.d.]. 64p. incl. front.

2639   _____. Twelfth night; or, What you will. A comedy, In five acts; by William Shakspeare. Revised by J. P. Kemble. As now performed at the Theatre Royal, Covent-Garden. London, Longman, Hurst, Rees, Orme, and Brown [n.d.]. 76p. front.

SHAKESPEARE, WILLIAM

2640   _____. Shakespeare's Twelfth night; or, What you will. With
introduction, and notes explanatory and critical. For use
in schools and families. By the Rev. Henry N. Hudson...
Boston, Ginn and Heath, 1880. xxvi, 3-151p. (Lettered on
cover: Annotated English classics).

2641   _____. Shakespeare's comedy of Twelfth night; or, What you
will. Ed., with notes, by William J. Rolfe... New York,
Harper and bros., 1879. vi, [7]-174p.

2642   _____. Twelfth night; or, What you will. A comedy, in five
acts; by William Shakspeare. Printed from the acting copy,
with remarks; to which are added, a description of the
costume, cast of the characters... and the whole of the
stage business, as now performed at the Theatres-Royal,
London. Embellished with a wood engraving... by Mr. T.
Jones... London, T. Dolby, 1825. 1 p.ℓ., [v]-vi, [9]-64p.
front.

2643   _____. ... Twelfth night; or, What you will: a comedy; by
William Shakespeare. With prefatory remarks... Faithfully
marked with the stage business, and stage directions; as it
is performed at the Theatres Royal. By W. Oxberry, comedian. London, Pub. for the Proprietors, by W. Simpkin,
and R. Marshall [etc.] 1821. 1 p.ℓ., ii, [2], 71, [1]p.
front. (port.) diagr. (Oxberry, William. The new English
drama. London, 1818-25. v. 12 [no. 3]).

2644   _____. Twelfth night; or, What you will. A comedy, in five
acts; by William Shakspeare. Correctly given, from the
text of Johnson and Steevens... London, Printed by D. S.
Maurice [1819?]. 78p. incl. front.

2645   _____. ... The two gentlemen of Verona. A comedy; by
William Shakspeare. With prefatory remarks... Faithfully
marked with the stage business, and stage directions, as it
is performed at the Theatres Royal. By W. Oxberry,
comedian. London, Pub. for the Proprietors, by W. Simpkin,
and R. Marshall [etc.] 1823. viii, [2], 69, [1]p. front.
(port.) diagr.

2646   _____. Two gentlemen of Verona. A comedy, in five acts.
By William Shakspeare. Correctly given, from the text of
Johnson and Steevens... London, D. S. Maurice [1819?].
72p. incl. front.

SHAKESPEARE, WILLIAM

2647   SHAKESPEARE, WILLIAM. The winter's tale; a play, in five
        acts, by William Shakspeare. Printed from the acting copy,
        with remarks, biographical and critical, by D.-G. ... As
        performed at the Theatres Royal... London, Davidson [n.d.].
        1 p.ℓ., [5]-8, [2], [9]-71p. front.

2648   _____. The winter's tale. A play, in five acts, by William
        Shakspeare. Printed from the acting copy, with remarks,
        biographical and critical, by D.-G. ... As performed at
        the Theatres Royal... London, J. Cumberland [n.d.].
        1 p.ℓ., [5]-8, [2], [9]-71p. front., pl.

2649   _____. The winter's tale; a play, in five acts; by William
        Shakspeare. As performed at the Theatre Royal, Drury Lane
        ... With remarks by Mrs. Inchbald. London, Longman,
        Hurst, Rees, Orme, and Brown [n.d.]. 90p. front.

2650   _____. ... The winter's tale, a play, in five acts. By W.
        Shakspeare... With notes, critical and explanatory. Also,
        an authentic description of the costume, and the general
        stage business, as performed at the Theatres-Royal, London.
        Embellished with a wood engraving... made expressly for
        this work, by Mr. I. R. Cruikshank... London, T. Dolby,
        1828. 1 p.ℓ., [7]-72p.

2651   _____. ... The winter's tale. A play; by W. Shakspeare.
        With prefatory remarks... Faithfully marked with the stage
        business, and stage directions, as it is performed at the
        Theatres Royal. By W. Oxberry, comedian. London, Pub. for
        the Proprietors, by W. Simpkin and R. Marshall [etc.] 1823.
        xi, [3], 87, [1]p. front. (port.) diagr.

2652   _____. Winter's tale. A play, in five acts. By William
        Shakspeare. Correctly given, from the text of Johnson and
        Steevens... London, Printed by D. S. Maurice [1819?].
        100p. incl. front.

2653   SHAW, ALEXANDER WILSON. The girl in the picture; a play in
        two acts. Boston, The Gorham Press; Toronto, The Copp
        Clark co., ltd., 1914. 87p.

2654   SHEARER, EDITH MAY. Paris of Troy; a classical pageant-play.
        New York, Teachers College, Columbia University, 1927.
        16p. (Service Bureau for Classical Teachers, Bulletin IX,
        December 1927).

SHERIDAN, RICHARD BRINSLEY BUTLER

2655 [SHEARS, MRS. L. D.]. The wife's appeal: a temperance drama.
In six acts... New York, 1878. 48p.

2656 SHEIL, RICHARD LALOR, 1791-1851. The apostate, a tragedy, in
five acts; as performed at the Theatre Royal, Covent-Garden.
By Richard Sheil, esq. London, J. Murray, 1817. x, 83,
[2]p.

2657 _____. Bellamira; or, The fall of Tunis. A tragedy, in five
acts; as performed at the Theatre Royal, Covent-Garden.
By Richard Sheil, esq. 3d ed. London, J. Murray, 1818.
1 p.ℓ., [v]-xii, 76 (i.e. 78)p.

2658 _____. Evadne; or, The statue: a tragedy, in five acts...
By Richard Sheil, esq. London, Printed by W. Clowes, and
sold by J. Murray, 1819. 3 p.ℓ., [v]-vi p., 2ℓ., 86, [2]p.
"The author has employed a part of the fable of
Shirley's 'Traytor,' in the construction of his plot."--
Pref.

2659 SHELDON, EDWARD BREWSTER, 1886-1946. Egypt, a play in four
acts, by Edward Sheldon. New York, Tower bros. stationery
co. [1912]. Cover-title, 52p.

2660 _____. "The garden of paradise," a play in nine scenes, by
Edward Sheldon based on a story of Hans Andersen [n.p.,
1914]. 192p.

2661 _____. "The Nigger," an American play in three acts. New
York, The Macmillan co., 1910. 269p.

2662 _____. Romance, a play in three acts with a prologue and an
epilogue, by Edward Sheldon. New York, Press of Tower
bros. stationery co. [1913]. Cover-title, 73p.

2663 SHERIDAN, RICHARD BRINSLEY BUTLER, 1751-1816. The critic; or,
A tragedy rehearsed. A dramatic piece, in three acts.
By R. B. Sheridan... London, Printed by D. S. Maurice
[1819?]. 43p. incl. front. [Cabinet theatre. v. 5, no. 5].

2664 _____. The critic; or, A tragedy rehearsed. As performed at
the Theatre Royal in Drury-Lane. By R. B. Sheridan...
New ed. Dublin, Printed for C. Macwilliam, 1806. 53p.

SHERIDAN, RICHARD BRINSLEY BUTLER

2665   SHERIDAN, RICHARD BRINSLEY BUTLER. The duenna; a comic opera,
        in three acts; by Richard Brinsley Sheridan, esq. As per-
        formed at the Theatres Royal, Drury Lane and Convent Gar-
        den... With remarks by Mrs. Inchbald. London, Longman,
        Hurst, Rees, Orme, and Brown [n.d.]. 74p. front.

2666   _____. Pizarro: a tragic play, in five acts... London, G. H.
        Davidson [n.d.]. 60p. front.

2667   _____. The rivals; a comedy, in five acts; by Richard
        Brinsley Sheridan, esq. As performed at the Theatres
        Royal, Drury Lane and Covent Garden... With remarks by
        Mrs. Inchbald. London, Longman, Hurst, Rees, Orme, and
        Brown [n.d.]. 90p. front. (Inchbald, Mrs. Elizabeth.
        The British theatre... London. 1803. v. 19 [no. 2]).

2668   _____. St. Patrick's day; or, The scheming lieutenant: a
        comic piece, in one act, by Richard Brinsley Sheridan...
        Printed from the acting copy, with remarks, biographical
        and critical, by D.-G. ... As performed at the Theatres
        Royal... London, J. Cumberland [n.d.]. 32p. incl. front.
        (Cumberland's British theatre. London, ca. 1825-55.
        v. 28 [no. 7]).

2669   No Entry.

2670   No Entry.

2671   No Entry.

2672   No Entry.

2673   No Entry.

2674   No Entry.

2675   No Entry.

2676   No Entry.

2677   No Entry.

2678   No Entry.

2679   SHIELDS, CHARLES WOODRUFF, 1825-1904. The reformer of Geneva;
        an historical drama. New York and London, G. P. Putnam's
        sons, 1898. 125p.

2680 SHIPP, J. A. Abyssinia, a musical comedy in six scenes, book
      and lyrics by J. A. Shipp and Alex Rogers. New York, 1905.
      Various pagings.

2681 SHIRLEY, ARTHUR. Miss Cleopatra. A farce. In three acts.
      (Adapted from "Les amours de Cléopatre")... London and
      New York, Samuel French, 1898. 40p.

2682 _____. Saved; or, A wife's peril, comedy-drama in four acts
      adapted from "La maison du Mari." Chicago, The Dramatic
      publishing co. [n.d.]. 42p.

2683 A book of short plays. XV-XX centuries. London, Published
      for the English Association by the Oxford University Press,
      1940. 299p. CONTENTS: Abraham and Isaac from the Brome MS.
      - Everyman. - The play of the wether [by] John Heywood. -
      A Yorkshire tragedy. - The Inner Temple masque [by] William
      Browne of Tavistock. - St. Patrick's day [by] R. B. Sheri-
      dan. - The falcon [by] Tennyson. - Riders to the sea [by]
      J. M. Synge. - Catherine Parr [by] Maurice Baring. - Royal
      favour [by] Laurence Housman. - Shall we join the ladies?
      [by] J. M. Barrie. - Silly Willy [by] Clifford Bax. - Nix-
      nought-nothing [by] Naomi Mitchison.

2684 SIEGFRIED, W. A. Phyllis, the beggar girl. A romantic melo-
      drama in three acts. Clyde, Ohio, Ames' publishing co.,
      1890. 11p.

2685 SIGURJÓNSSON, JÓHANN. Modern Icelandic plays. Eyvind of the
      hills. The Hraun farm... Translated by Henninge Krohn
      Schanche... New York, The American-Scandinavian Founda-
      tion, 1916. xii, 131p. pl. (music).

2686 SIMKINS, W., JR. The pirates lair; or, Gorgonzago's revenge.
      London, R. A. Everett and son [n.d.]. 123p. illus.

2687 SIMMS, EVELYN. The conspirators, a comedy in two acts for
      girls only, by Evelyn Simms... New York, Dick and Fitz-
      gerald, 1910. 22p.

2688 SIMMS, GEORGE A. Pheelim O'Rooke's curse. An Irish drama in
      four acts... Clyde, Ohio, Ames' publishing co., 1890. 25p.

2689 SIMMS, WILLIAM GILMORE. Norman Maurice; or, The man of the
      people; an American drama. Philadelphia, Lippincott,
      Grambo and co., 1853 [c1851]. 169p. CONTENTS. - Norman
      Maurice. - Caius Marius; an historical legend. - Bertram;
      an Italian sketch. - The death of Cleopatra.

SIMPSON, JOHN PALGRAVE

2690   SIMPSON, JOHN PALGRAVE, 1807-1887. Broken ties. Domestic
        drama, in two acts. By J. Palgrave Simpson... London and
        New York, S. French [1873?]. 41p. (On cover: Lacy's
        acting edition. no. 1439).
            "As performed... June the 8th, 1872."
            Based on "La Flammina," by Mario Uchard.

2691   _____. A cloud in the honeymoon. A comic sketch, in one act.
        By J. Palgrave Simpson. Together with a description of
        the costumes... and the whole of the stage business. New
        York, De Witt, c1884. 12p. (On cover: De Witt's acting
        plays. no. 326).

2692   _____. Court cards. A comic drama, in two acts. London,
        Thomas Hailes Lacy [n.d.]. 44p.

2693   _____. Dreams of delusion. A drama, in one act. Adapted
        from the French drama, "Elle est folle"... New York,
        Samuel French [n.d.]. 38p.

2694   _____. Haunted hearts. By J. Palgrave Simpson. New York,
        J. W. Lovell co. [1883]. 1 p.ℓ., 86p. (On cover: Lovell's
        library, v. 3, no. 125).

2695   _____. ... Marco Spada. A drama, in three acts. By J. Pal-
        grave Simpson, esq. ... New-York, W. Taylor and co.; Bal-
        timore, Maryland, W. and H. Taylor [1854?]. 1 p.ℓ., [v]-
        vi p., 2ℓ., [9]-51p. (Modern standard drama. Edited by
        F. C. Wemyss. no. 99).
            Adapted from Scribe's libretto of Auber's opera of the
        same name.
            "Remarks" signed: F. C. W., i.e. Francis Courtney Wemyss.

2696   _____. A scrap of paper; or, The adventures of a love letter.
        A comic drama, in three acts... New York, Harold Roorbach
        [n.d.]. 53p.

2697   _____. Shadows of the past. A comedy drama, in two acts...
        New York, Samuel French [n.d.]. 36p.

2698   SITES, WILL C. A lady servant; or, Mistress for an hour. An
        original sketch in one act... Clyde, Ohio, Ames' publish-
        ing co., 1903. 8p.

SMITH, HARRY BACHE

2699   Six plays. The green pastures [by] Marc Connelly. Street
        scene [by] Elmer Rice. Badger's green [by] R. C. Sheriff.
        Down our street [by] Ernest George. Socrates [by] Clifford
        Bax. Alison's house [by] Susan Glaspell. London, Victor
        Gollancz, 1931. 672p.

2700   Sixteen thousand years ago! An Ethiopian act... New York,
        Dick and Fitzgerald [n.d.]. 8p.

2701   SKETCHLEY, ARTHUR. Quite at home. A comedietta, in one act.
        New York, Robert M. De Witt [n.d.]. 10p.

2702   SKIFF, FRANK D. Cuchilanca; or, The rancher's fate. A play
        in three acts... Cincinnati, T. J. Smith, 1864. 65p.

2703   SLATER, RUTH W. The sound of Latin. 5p. (American Classical
        League Service Bureau, No. 728).

2704   SLOANE, GEORGE. Lilian, the show girl; a romantic drama, in
        two acts... London, Thomas Hailes Lacy [n.d.]. 34p. front.

2705   SMITH, ALBERT RICHARD, 1816-1860. The Alhambra; or, The three
        beautiful princesses. A new and original burlesque extrava-
        ganza... London, Thomas Hailes Lacy [n.d.]. 25p.

2706   _____. Hop-o'-my-thumb; or, The seven league boots, a romance
        of nursery history. In two acts. Written expressly for
        General Tom Thumb, by Albert Smith... London, T. Brettell,
        1846. 24p.

2707   SMITH, BEULAH. Christmas shopping, comedy for children. New
        York, Edgar S. Werner and co., 1904. 16p.

2708   No Entry.

2709   SMITH, GEORGE TOTTEN. Her hero, a vaudeville sketch. Chicago,
        T. S. Denison and co. [1906]. 11p.

2710   SMITH, HARRY BACHE, 1860-1936. Verses of The belle of
        Bohemia, a musical comedy in two acts. Libretto by Harry
        B. Smith. Music by Ludwig Englander... [New York?] 1900.
        30p.

2711   _____. A pleasant comedie of the life of Will Shakespeare,
        player of the Globe theatre on the Bankside, wherein may
        be found sundrie variable and diverting humours, together
        with a setting fourthe of the many follies of stage players
        in generall, and also certaine songs set to airs newly

SMITH, HARRY BACHE

      (SMITH, HARRY BACHE)
         invented, as it hath not been divers times enacted by the
         Righte Honourable the lord chamberlayne his servants, nor
         yet by any others, to the present regret of the author,
         Harry B. Smith. Chicago, Presse of the Dial journal, 1893.
         xxviii, 116p.

2712   _____. Richard Wagner, his life and adventures related in his
         own words with music and scenes from his music dramas. A
         picture play by Harry B. Smith. [New York, Press of the
         Chauncey Holt co., 1921]. 3 p.ℓ., 72p.

2713   SMITH, HYACINTH STODDART. Cordia (a drama in three acts).
         By Hyacinth Stoddart Smith. (In Poet lore. Boston, 1908.
         vol. XIX, no. II, p. 165-192).

2714   SMITH, JONATHAN S. The siege of Algiers; or, The downfall of
         Hagdi-Ali-Bashaw. A political, historical and sentimental
         tragi-comedy, in five acts. By Jonathan S. Smith, of Phil-
         adelphia... Philadelphia, Printed for the author, by J.
         Maxwell, 1823. 140p., 1ℓ.

2715   SMITH, LAURA ROUNTREE. Harvest time, a play for Thanksgiving.
         Dansville, New York, F. A. Owen publishing co., 1905. 16p.

2716   SMITH, RICHARD PENN, 1799-1854. The deformed; or, Woman's
         trial, a play, in five acts. By Richard Penn Smith...
         Philadelphia, C. Alexander, pr., 1830. Cover-title, 87p.

2717   _____. The disowned; or, The prodigals, a play, in three
         acts. By Richard Penn Smith... Philadelphia, C. Alexander,
         pr., 1830. Cover-title, 67p.

2718   _____. The eighth of January, a drama, in three acts. By
         Richard Penn Smith... As performed at the theatres,
         Chestnut street, Philadelphia, Baltimore, and Washington.
         Philadelphia, Neal and Mackenzie, 1829. iv, [5]-54p.

2719   SMITH, S. JENNIE. A free knowledge-ist; or, Too much for one
         head, a comedy in two acts. Chicago, T. S. Denison [1893].
         12p.

2720   SMITH, SPENSER THEYRE. A case for eviction, a comedietta
         in one act... New York, Harold Roorbach, 1890. 20p.

2721   _____. Cut off with a shilling, a comedietta in one act...
         New York, Harold Roorbach, 1890. 24p.

SOANE, GEORGE

2722   ____. A happy pair, a comedietta in one act... New York, Harold Roorbach, 1890. 19p.

2723   [____]. His own enemy. A farce, in one act. By the author of "A Happy Pair."... New York, Robert M. De Witt [c1875]. 20p.

2724   ____. Mrs. Hilary regrets. Comedietta... London, J. Williams; New York, E. Schuberth and co., 1896. 24p.

2725   ____. My lord in livery. A farce in one act. London, T. H. Lacy [1888] 28p. (Lacy acting edition of plays, no. 1920).

2726   ____. Old cronies, a comedietta in one act for two male characters... New York, Harold Roorbach, 1890. 17p.

2727   ____. Uncle's will, an original comedietta in one act... Philadelphia, The Penn publishing co., 1899. 22p.

2728   ____. Which is which? A comedietta in one act... New York, Harold Roorbach, 1889. 24p.

2729   SMITH, W. H. The drunkard; or, The fallen saved. A moral domestic drama, in five acts... New York, William Taylor and co. [n.d.]. 64p.

2730   ____. Six charade plays. In prose and verse... London, Thomas Hailes Lacy [n.d.]. 95p.

2731   [SMITH, WILLIAM RUSSELL, 1815-1896]. The royal ape: a dramatic poem. Richmond, West and Johnston, 1863. 85p.

2732   SMYTHE, SMILEY. "The man with the hod." An Irish comedy sketch... Chicago, Will Rossiter, 1907. 14p.

2733   Snow-bound. A musical and dramatic entertainment... Boston, Lee and Shepard [n.d.]. 46p.

2734   SOANE, GEORGE, 1790-1860. The dwarf of Naples. A tragi-comedy, in five acts. First performed at the Theatre royal, Drury lane, on Saturday, March 13, 1819. By George Soane... London, Printed by and for T. Fodwell, 1819. 4 p.ℓ., 52p.

2735   ____. The Falls of Clyde. A melo-drama, in two acts, by George Soane... Printed from the acting copy, with remarks, biographical and critical, by D.-G. ... As performed at the Theatres Royal ... London, J. Cumberland [n.d.].

SOANE, GEORGE

(SOANE, GEORGE)
40p. incl. front. (Cumberland's British theatre. London,
ca. 1825-55. v. 31, no. 7).
Remarks by George Daniel, editor of the series.

2736 _____. Faustus: a romantic drama, in three acts, by George
Soane... Printed from the acting copy, with remarks, biographical and critical, by D.-G. ... As performed at the
Theatres Royal... London, J. Cumberland [n.d.]. 8, [2],
[13]-58p. front. (Cumberland's British theatre. London,
ca. 1825-55. v. 33 [no. 3]).
Remarks by George Daniel, editor of the series.
Reissued in Davidson's shilling volume of Cumberland's
plays, v. 28 [no. 2].

2737 _____. The innkeeper's daughter; a melo-drama, in two acts.
Now performing at the Theatre Royal, Drury-Lane. By George
Soane, A. B. The music by Mr. T. Cooke... London, W.
Simpkin and R. Marshall, 1817. iv p., 2ℓ., [9]-67p.
Founded on Southey's poem "Mary, the maid of the inn."
Without the music.

2738 _____. Masaniello, the fisherman of Naples: an historical
play, in five acts. London, J. Miller, 1825. 4 p.ℓ.,
61p.
Adapted from Auber's "La muette de Portici."
Ascribed to Soane. Cf. Genest, v. 9, p. 290-291;
Theatrical observer, Feb. 17, 1825.
Without the music (by Bishop).

2739 [_____], supposed author. Pride shall have a fall; a comedy:
in five acts - with songs. Dedicated by permission to the
Right Hon. George Canning, &c. &c. &c. First performed at
the Theatre Royal, Covent Garden, March 11, 1824. London,
Printed for Hurst, Robinson and co., 1824. 4 p.ℓ., 115p.
First edition.
Attributed also to G. Croly.

2740 _____. Rob Roy: a romantic drama, in three acts, by George
Soane... Printed from the acting copy, with remarks, bio-
graphical and critical, by D.-G. ... As performed at the
Theatres Royal... London, G. H. Davidson [n.d.]. 45p.
incl. front. (Cumberland's British theatre. London, ca.
1825-55. v. 36 [no. 10]).
Based on Scott's "Rob Roy."
Remarks by George Daniel, editor of the series.
Without the music.
Reissue of Cumberland's earlier edition.

SOMERSET, CHARLES A.

2741 _____. Zarah. A romantic drama, in two acts, by George Soane
... Printed from the acting copy, with remarks, biographical and critical, by D.-G. ... As performed at the metropolitan minor theatres... London, J. Cumberland and son
[1836?]. 31p. front. (port.). (Cumberland's British
theatre. London, ca. 1825-55. v. 35 [no. 1]).
Remarks by George Daniel, editor of the series.
"Memoir of Mrs. Nisbett": p. [8].

2742 SOMERSET, CHARLES A. Crazy Jane. A romantic play, in three
acts. By C. A. Somerset... Printed from the acting copy,
with remarks, biographical and critical, by D.-G. ... As
performed at the metropolitan minor theatres... London,
C. Cumberland [n.d.]. 57p. incl. front. (Cumberland's
Minor theatre. London [ca. 1830-55] v. 2 [no. 4]).
Remarks by George Daniel, editor of the series.

2743 _____. ... Day after the fair. A burletta... New York,
Samuel French [n.d.]. 33p. (The minor drama, no. cxxiii).

2744 [_____]. A day after the fair. A burletta, in one act, as
performed at the Covent Garden theatre, London. New York,
Elton's dramatic repository, 1828. 24p.

2745 _____. The mistletoe bough; or, Young Lovel's bride: a
legendary drama, in two acts, by C. A. Somerset... Printed
from the acting copy, with remarks, biographical and critical, by D.-G. ... As performed at the Theatres Royal...
London, Davidson [n.d.]. 36p. incl. front. (Cumberland's
Minor theatre. London [ca, 1830-55] v. 12 [no. 9]).
Remarks by George Daniel, editor of the series.

2746 _____. Shakspeare's early days: a historical play, in two
acts, by C. A. Somerset... Printed from the acting copy,
with remarks, biographical and critical by D.-G. ... As
performed at the Theatres Royal... London, J. Cumberland
[n.d.]. 48p. incl. front. (Cumberland's British theatre.
London, ca. 1825-55. v. 28 [no. 3]).
Remarks by George Daniel, editor of the series.

2747 _____. The tower of London; or, The rival queens; a grand
historical spectacle, in two acts; founded in part on
Mr. Harrison Ainsworth's popular work, so called, and
adapted for representation, by C. A. Somerset... As performed nightly at Astley's Royal amphitheatre, correctly
printed from the prompt book... London, J. Pattie [n.d.].
38p. incl. front. (The Universal stage... London, 1840.
v. 2 [no. 5]).

SOMERSET, CHARLES A.

2748   SOMERSET, CHARLES A. "Yes!" An operatic interlude, in one
        act, by C. A. Somerset... Printed from the acting copy,
        with remarks, biographical and critical, by D.-G. ... As
        now performed at the metropolitan minor theatres... Lon-
        don, J. Cumberland [n.d.]. 24p. incl. front. (Cumber-
        land's Minor theatre. London [ca. 1830-55] v. 2 [no. 6]).
            Remarks by George Daniel, editor of the series.
            Without the music.
            Reissued in Davidson's shilling volume of Cumberland's
        plays, v. 18 [no. 3].

2749   SONNEBERG, WALTER. Social eccentricities; more than three
        hundred epigrams--each one inspiration for a sermon, an
        essay or a play, by Walter Sonneberg; illustrated by Wm. L.
        Hudson. New York, Broadway publishing co. [1900]. 2 p.ℓ.,
        54p. front. (port.) 4 pl.

2750   SOPHOCLES, ca. 496-406 B.C. ... The seven plays, in English
        verse by Lewis Campbell... New edition, revised. London,
        New York, and Toronto, Henry Frowde, Oxford University
        Press [1906]. xxvii, 316p. front. (port.).

2751   _____. The tragedies... a new translation, with a biographi-
        cal essay, and an appendix of rhymed choral odes and
        lyrical dialogues. By the late E. H. Plumptre... Boston,
        D. C. Heath, 1894. xcv, 502p.

2752   _____. The tragedies of Sophocles: In English prose, The
        Oxford translation. New ed., revised according to the
        text of Dindorf, London, H. G. Bohn, 1849. xvi, 339p.

2753   _____. The wife of Heracles, translated by Gilbert Murray.
        London, George Allen and Unwin, ltd. [n.d.]. 89p.

2754   [SOUBRON, OTTO] d. 1917. Asa Groot; or, The judge of Swanzey,
        a drama of Puritan days, in five acts (by Barba Rossa)
        [pseud.] Milwaukee, Wisconsin, The International literary
        bureau [1901]. 3 p.ℓ., 40p.

2755   SOUTHERNE, THOMAS, 1660-1746. Isabella. A tragedy in five
        acts; by Thomas Southerne. As performed at the Theatre
        Royal, Covent Garden... With remarks, by Mrs. Inchbald.
        London, Longman, Hurst, Reese, Orme, and Brown [n.d.].
        56p. front. (Inchbald, Mrs. Elizabeth. The British
        theatre... London, 1808. v. 7 [no. 1]).

2756   SOUTHEY, ROBERT, 1774-1843. ... Wat Tyler, a dramatic poem,
       by Robert Southey... [Sherwin's ed.] London, Printed by
       W. T. Sherwin [1817]. 15p.

2757   SOWERBY, GITHA. Rutherford and Son, a play in three acts,
       New York, Goerge H. Doran co. [1912]. 123p.

2758   SPANGLER, W. H., JR. New Years in New York; or, The German
       baron, an original comedy... Clyde, Ohio, A. D. Ames,
       1883. 27p.

2759   SPEEGLE, KATHLEEN. Inflictus Caesar; a tragedy of ancient
       Rome [n.p., n.d.]. 4p. (American Classical League
       Service Bureau, No. 709).

2760   SPENCER, GEORGE. A return ticket. An original farce, in one
       act, by George Spencer and James Walter... London, Thomas
       Hailes Lacy [n.d.]. 18p.

2761   SPICER, HENRY, d. 1891. Honesty: a drama, in five acts. By
       Henry Spicer... London, G. W. Nickisson, 1842. vi p.,
       1ℓ., 98p.

2762   The spirit of seventy-six; or, The coming woman, a prophetic
       drama, followed by A change of base, and Cotor Mondschein.
       Boston, Little, Brown, and co., 1896. 141p.

2763   The spoiled child: a farce, in two acts, printed from the
       acting copy, with remarks, biographical and critical by
       D.-G. ... As performed at the Theatres Royal... London,
       G. H. Davidson [n.d.]. 33p. incl. front. (Cumberland's
       British theatre. London, ca. 1825-55. v. 14 [no. 5]).
           Remarks by George Daniel, editor of the series.
           Reissue of Cumberland's earlier edition.
           Ascribed variously to Mrs. Jordan, Richard Ford and
       Isaac Bickerstaffe. Cf. Dict. nat. biog.; Baker; Oxberry's
       New English drama, v. 15 [no. 4] p. ii.

2764   STANFORD, FREDERIC. Noughtology or nothing. Conceit. A
       serio-comic drama in four acts. London, Printed by W.
       Mitchell, 1889. 53p.

2764A STANGÉ, STANISLAUS, d. 1917. ... Dolly Varden; comic opera
       in two acts. Books and lyrics by Stanislaus Stangé, music
       by Julian Edwards... New York, M. Witmark and sons; [etc.,
       etc.] 1901. 24p.
           Vocal excerpts.

STANGÉ, STANISLAUS

2764B   STANGÉ, STANISLAUS. ... Love's lottery; comic opera in two
        acts. Book by Stanislaus Stangé, music by Julian Edwards...
        New York, Chicago, London [etc.] M. Witmark and sons; [etc.,
        etc.] 1904. 251p.
        Publisher's plate no: 6844.

2764C   _____. ... When Johnny comes marching home, three act mili-
        tary spectacular comic opera; book and lyrics by Stanislaus
        Stangé, music by Julian Edwards... New York, London [etc.]
        M. Witmark and sons, [c1902]. 232p.
        Publisher's plate no. 4943.

2765   STAPLES, FRANK. Absent treatment, comedy in one act. Pasadena,
        1910. 14p.

2766   State secrets: or, The tailor of Tamworth. A popular farce,
        in one act. New York, Samuel French [n.d.]. 18p.

2767   STEDMAN, W. ELSWORTH. The confidential clerk; a stirring
        play in four acts, by W. Elsworth Stedman... New York,
        T. H. French; [etc., etc.] 1892. 51p. (On cover:
        French's standard drama, the acting edition, no. 414).

2768   _____. The yankee detective, a drama in three acts. Chicago,
        T. S. Denison, 1886. 32p.

2769   STEELE, ASA MANCHESTER. A sire of battles; a drama in four
        acts. By Asa M. Steele. Philadelphia, For the author,
        International printing co. [1900]. 82p.

2770   STENMAN, C. A. Our Jack. A drama, in three acts... Clyde,
        Ohio, Ames' publishing co., 1900. 28p.

2771   STEPHENS, GEORGE. Dramas for the stage, by George Stephens...
        London, Ineditus, 1846. 2v.

2772   STERLING, SARA HAWKS. Hamlet's brides; a Shakespearean
        burlesque in one act, by Sara Hawks Sterling. Boston,
        W. H. Baker and co., 1900. 19p. (On cover: Baker's
        edition of plays).

2773   STEVENS, DANA J. Old Acre folk; a rustic drama in two acts,
        by Dana J. Stevens. Boston, W. H. Baker and co., 1903. 36p.
        (On cover: Baker's edition of plays.)

2774   STEVENS, THOMAS WOOD, 1880-   . Ryland, a comedy [by] Thomas
        Wood Stevens and Kenneth Sawyer Goodman. Chicago, The
        Stage guild [1912]. 29p.

292

2775 STEVENSON, AUGUSTA. The puppet princess; or, The heart that squeaked; a Christmas play for children, by Augusta Stevenson... Boston and New York, Houghton Mifflin co. [1915]. 4 p.ℓ., [3]-58p. front., plates.

2776 STEWART, ANNA BIRD. Belles of Canterbury; a Chaucer tale out of school. A play in one act for eleven girls, by Anna Bird Stewart. New York and London, Samuel French, c1912. Cover-title, 20p.

2777 STEWART, FREDERICK. A Roman executive election; a play in one act [n.p., n.d.]. 4p. (American Classical League Service Bureau, No. 464).

2778 STEWART, J. C. The baby elephant. A negro sketch, in two scenes. Chicago. The Dramatic publishing co., 1875. 9p.

2779 _____. Eh? What is it? An Ethiopian sketch. New York, The De Witt publishing house, 1871. 7p.

2780 _____. Hemmed in. An Ethiopian sketch. New York, Robert M. De Witt, 1871. 6p.

2781 _____. The last of the Mohicans. An Ethiopian sketch... as first produced at the Théâtre Comique, New York, May, 1870 ... New York, Robert M. De Witt [n.d.]. 6p.

2782 _____. The two black roses. An Ethiopian sketch. New York, Robert M. De Witt, 1871. 7p.

2783 STILWELL, LAURA JEAN LIBBEY. The abandoned bride, a drama in four acts. Brooklyn, 1908. 97p.

2784 [STIMSON, FREDERIC JESUP] 1855-1943. The light of Provence, a dramatic poem, by "J. S. of Dale." New York and London, G. P. Putnam's sons, 1917. vi, 1ℓ., 115p.

2785 STIRLING, EDWARD, 1807-1894. ... Aline; or, The rose of Killarney. A drama, in three acts... New York, Samuel French [n.d.]. 35p. (French's American drama, no. lviii).

2786 _____. A cheap excursion. An original farce, in one act... London, Thomas Hailes Lacy [n.d.]. 14p.

2787 _____. ... Clarence Clevedon; his struggles for life or death. An original drama, in three acts... London, Thomas Hailes Lacy [n.d.]. 50p. front. (Cumberland's British theatre).

STIRLING, EDWARD

2788   STIRLING, EDWARD. The dragon knight; or, The queen of beauty!
       A drama, in two acts... London, J. Duncombe and co. [n.d.].
       30p. front. (Duncombe's edition).

2789   _____. ... The hand of cards; game, life--stakes, death!
       An original drama, in three acts... London, Thomas Hailes
       Lacy [n.d.]. 43p. front. (Cumberland's British theatre).

2790   _____. ... Industry and indolence; or, The orphan's legacy!
       A drama, in three acts... London, Duncombe and Moon
       [n.d.]. 46p. front.

2791   _____. ... Lilly Dawson; or, A poor girl's story! A domestic
       drama, in three acts... London, John Duncombe [n.d.].
       42p. front.

2792   _____. ... Margaret Catchpole, the heroine of Suffolk! or,
       The vicissitudes of real life! A drama, in three acts...
       London, John Duncombe [n.d.]. 48p. front. (Duncombe's
       edition).

2793   _____. Norah Creina. A drama in one act... New York,
       Samuel French [n.d.]. 14p.

2794   _____. Out of luck; or, His grace the duke. A farce, in one
       act, by E. Stirling... As performed at the Royal Sadler's
       Wells theatre; correctly marked from the prompt copy...
       London, J. Pattie [n.d.]. 23p. front. (The Universal
       stage... London, 1840. v. 1 [no. 7]).

2795   _____. ... The rag-picker of Paris, and the dressmaker of
       St. Antoine. A drama in three acts and a prologue... New
       York, Samuel French [n.d.]. 35p. (French's American drama,
       no. xi).

2796   _____. ... The sealed sentence! An original drama, in two
       acts... London, John Duncombe [n.d.]. 28p. front.
       (Duncombe's edition).

2797   _____. Teddy Roe: a farce. -- In one act. New York, Samuel
       French [n.d.]. 15p.

2798   _____. Wild ducks. A farce, in one act... First performed
       at the Theatre Royal, Marylebone, Monday, January 7, 1850.
       London, S. G. Fairbrother [n.d.]. 18p.

2799   STOBART, MRS. ST. CLAIR. Meringues. A drawing-room duologue. London and New York, Samuel French [n.d.]. 8p.

2800   Stocks up! Stocks down! A duologue. In one scene. Chicago, The Dramatic publishing co. [n.d.]. 6p.

2801   STOCQUELLER, J. H. An object of interest. A farce, in one act. New York, Clinton T. De Witt [n.d.]. 18p.

2802   STONE, ABBIE ANNA. A. D. 1813; or, America's triumph, a historical spectacular naval melodrama in five acts. Milwaukee, 1893. 42p.

2803   STONE, PHYLLIS. The singing shepherd, a nativity play in four scenes. London, Samuel French, ltd. [n.d.]. 18p.

2804   STRINDBERG, AUGUST, i.e. JOHAN AUGUST, 1849-1912. ... Advent; a play in five acts [by] August Strindberg; translated by Claud Field. Boston, R. G. Badger; [etc., etc.] 1914. 110p. (Contemporary dramatists series).

2805   _____. The creditor, a tragi-comedy, by August Strindberg. Tr. by Mary Harned. (In Poet lore. Boston, 1911. vol. XXII, no. II, p. 81-116).

2806   _____. The creditor, a tragic comedy, by August Strindberg... tr. from the Swedish by Francis J. Ziegler. Philadelphia, Brown bros., 1910. 118p.

2807   _____. Easter (a play in three acts) and stories from the Swedish of August Strindberg... tr. by Velma Swanston Howard. Cincinnati, Stewart and Kidd co., 1912. 4 p.ℓ., 3-269p. front (port.) facsim.

2808   _____. Facing death, a drama in one act by August Strindberg ... [Easton, Pennsylvania, 1911]. [16]p.

2809   _____. The father (a tragedy) by August Strindberg; tr. by N. Erichsen. Boston, J. W. Luce and co., 1907. 1 p.ℓ., v-x, 99p.

2810   _____. Julie, a tragedy, by August Strindberg. Tr. from the Swedish by Arthur Swan. (In Poet lore. Boston, 1911. vol. XXII, no. III, p. 161-194).

STRINDBERG, AUGUST

2811   STRINDBERG, AUGUST. Lucky Pehr (a drama in five acts) from
        the Swedish of August Strindberg... tr. by Velma Swanston
        Howard. Cincinnati, Stewart and Kidd co., 1912. 4 p.ℓ.,
        3-181p. front. (port.) facsim.

2812   _____. Master Olof; a drama in five acts, by August Strind-
        berg; tr. from the Swedish, with an introduction by Edwin
        Björkman, from the prose version of 1872. New York, The
        American-Scandinavian foundation; [etc., etc.] 1915.
        3 p.ℓ., [v]-xxiii, 125p. (Half-title: Scandinavian
        classics. v. XV).

2813   _____. ... Motherlove (Moderskärlek) an act, by August Strind-
        berg... English version by Francis J. Ziegler. Philadel-
        phia, Brown bros., 1910. 41p. (Modern authors' series).

2814   _____. The stronger, a play in one act, by August Strindberg.
        Tr. by F. I. Ziegler. (In Poet lore. Boston, 1906. v.
        XVII, no. I, p. 47-50).

2815   STRONG, J. EARL. Absinthe, a drama. New Castle, Kentucky,
        1906. 13p.

2816   STUART, CHARLES, fl. 1780-1800. The stone eater, an inter-
        lude. As it was acted at the Theatre-Royal, Drury-Lane,
        with universal applause. By C. Stuart. London, Printed
        for H. D. Symonds, 1788. 19p.

2817   The studio. An Ethiopian farce, in one act. Clyde, Ohio,
        A. D. Ames, 1870. 9p.

2818   STURGIS, JULIAN, 1848-1904. Count Julian; a Spanish tragedy,
        by Julian Sturgis. Boston, Little, Brown, and co., 1893.
        122p.

2819   _____. Little comedies... New York, D. Appleton and co.,
        1880. 180p. CONTENTS. Apples; Fireflies; Picking up
        the pieces; Half way to Arcady; Mabel's holy day; Heather.

2820   SUDERMANN, HERMANN, 1857-1928. Honor; a play in four acts,
        by Hermann Sudermann, tr. by Hilmar R. Baukhage with a
        preface by Barrett H. Clark... New York, S. French;
        [etc., etc.] 1915. 104p.

2821   _____. John the Baptist; a play, by Hermann Sudermann, tr.
        by Beatrice Marshall. London, J. Lane; New York, John
        Lane co., 1909 [1908]. vi p., 1ℓ., 201, [1]p.

SUTER, WILLIAM E.

2822 _____. The joy of living (Es lebe das Leben). A play in
five acts, by Hermann Sudermann, tr. from the German by
Edith Wharton. New York, C. Scribner's sons, 1902. vii,
185p.

2823 _____. ... Magda; a play in four acts, by Hermann Sudermann,
tr. from the German by Charles Edward Amory Winslow. Boston and New York, Lamson, Wolffe and co., 1896. iv p.,
1ℓ., [7]-161p.

2824 _____. Argument of Magda. Drama by H. Sudermann. English
argument by E. Beall Ginty... New York, F. Rullman, 1896.
29p.

2825 _____. Roses, four one-act plays; Streaks of light--The last
visit--Margot--The far-away princess, by Hermann Sudermann;
tr. from the German by Grace Frank. New York, C. Scribner's
sons, 1909. 3 p.ℓ., 183p.

2826 _____. The vale of content. Das Glück im Winkel; a drama in
three acts, by Hermann Sudermann; tr. by William Ellery
Leonard. [Boston? 1915]. 2 p.ℓ., p. [443]-469.

2827 SULLIVAN, TIMOTHY PAUL. "Ole Virginny"; historical drama in
four acts, by T. P. Sullivan. Chicago, M. A. Donohue and
co., 1907. 76p.

2828 SULLIVAN, VINCENT PHILAMON, 1887- . The siren and the
Roman (Cleopatra and Anthonius); or, Luxury, love and the
lost. A new tragedy in five acts, by "Lucyl" (Vincent P.
Sullivan)... Brooklyn, 1911. 2 p.ℓ., 57p.

2829 SUMMERS, JOHN. Oliver Cromwell, an historical drama in five
acts. By John Summers. The famous history of the common-
wealth of England. London, The International copyright
bureau, ltd. [1906]. 88p.

2830 SUMMERS, KNIGHT. Not at home! Monologue. London and New
York, Samuel French [n.d.]. 8p.

2831 SUTER, WILLIAM E., 1811-1882. Catherine Howard; or, The
throne, the tomb, and the scaffold. An historical play,
in three acts. From the celebrated play of that name by
Alexandre Dumas. Adapted by W. D. Suter... As first performed at the Surrey theatre, London... 1858. To which is
added a description of the costumes, cast of the characters
... New York, R. M. De Witt [187-]. 40p. (On cover: De
Witt's acting plays. no. 55).

SUTER, WILLIAM E.

2832   SUTER, WILLIAM E. ... Dick Turpin and Tom King. A serio
        comic drama, in two acts... New York, Samuel French [n.d.].
        24p. (French's minor drama, no. cclxxxiii).

2833   _____. The highwayman's holiday. A farce, in one act...
        London, Thomas Hailes Lacy [n.d.]. 22p.

2834   _____. Holly Bush Hall; or, The track in the snow. A drama,
        in two acts... London, Thomas Hailes Lacy [n.d.]. 43p.

2835   _____. The idiot of the mountain. A drama, in three acts...
        London, Thomas Hailes Lacy [n.d.]. 54p.

2836   _____. Incompatibility of temper. A farce, in one act...
        New York, Samuel French and son [n.d.]. 13p.

2837   _____. John Wopps; or, From information I received. A farce,
        in one act. Boston, Charles H. Spencer [n.d.]. 14p.

2838   _____. A life's revenge; or, Two loves for one heart. A
        drama, in three acts... Clyde, Ohio, Ames' publishing co.
        [n.d.]. 39p.

2839   _____. ... The lost child; or, Jones's baby. An original
        farce, in one act... New York, Samuel French [n.d.]. 15p.
        (French's minor drama, no. cccxxii).

2840   _____. The pirates of the savannah; or, The tiger hunter of
        the prairies. A romantic drama, in three acts. London,
        Thomas Hailes Lacy [n.d.]. 44p.

2841   _____. A quiet family. An original farce... New York,
        Samuel French [n.d.]. 19p.

2842   _____. The robbers of the Pyrenees. A drama, in two acts,
        and a prologue... London, Thomas Hailes Lacy [n.d.]. 47p.

2843   _____. ... Two gentlemen in a fix; or, How to lose the train.
        An interlude... Boston, Charles H. Spencer [n.d.]. 12p.
        (Spencer's universal stage, no. viii).

2844   _____. ... A very pleasant evening. A farce, in one act...
        Boston, Charles H. Spencer [n.d.]. 13p. (Spencer's
        universal stage, no. xxxix).

2845   SUTHERLAND, OLIVE. The schoolboy's dream. [n.p., n.d.].
        3p. (American Classical League Service Bureau, No. 272).

2846   SUTRO, ALFRED, 1863-1933. Five little plays, by Alfred Sutro.
        London, Duckworth [1925]. 131p. CONTENTS. - The man in
        the stall. - A marriage has been arranged. - The man on the
        Kerb. - The open door. - The bracelet.

2847   _____. Freedom; a play in three acts, by Alfred Sutro. New
        York, Brentano's, 1916. 3 p.ℓ., 106p.

2848   _____. Mollentrave on women, a comedy in three acts. London,
        Samuel French, ltd.; New York, Samuel French, 1905. 86p.

2849   _____. The open door. A duologue. London and New York,
        Samuel French [n.d.]. 15p.

2850   _____. The price of money, a play in four acts. New York,
        Samuel French, 1906. 106p.

2851   _____. The walls of Jericho, a play in four acts. New York,
        Samuel French, 1906. 95p.

2852   SWAN, MARK ELBERT, 1871-   . Brown's in town, a farcical
        comedy in three acts, by Mark E. Swan... New York, S.
        French; [etc., etc.] 1915. 95p. diagr.

2853   SWARTOUT, NORMAN LEE. Close to nature; a farcical episode
        in the life of an American family, in four acts, by Norman
        Lee Swartout... Boston, W. H. Baker and co., 1915. 180p.

2854   SWAYZE, MRS. J. C. ... Ossawattomie Brown; or, The insurrec-
        tion at Harper's Ferry. A drama, in three acts... New
        York, Samuel French, 1859. 27p. (The standard drama,
        no. ccxxvi).

2855   SWINBURNE, ALGERNON CHARLES, 1837-1909. The Duke of Gandia.
        New York and London, Harper and bros., 1908. 58p.

2856   _____. Mary Stuart, by Algernon Charles Swinburne; ed. by
        William Morton Payne... Boston and London, D. C. Heath
        and co., 1906. xlii, 264p. front. (port.).

2857   _____. Rosamund, queen of the Lombards; a tragedy, by
        Algernon Charles Swinburne. 2d ed. London, Chatto and
        Windus, 1900. 88p.

2858   _____. Swinburne's drama, selected and ed. by Arthur Beatty
        ... New York, T. Y. Crowell and co., c1909. xxii, 384p.
        front. (port.). CONTENTS. - Dramas: Atalanta in Calydon,

SWINBURNE, ALGERNON CHARLES

    (SWINBURNE, ALGERNON CHARLES)
      Erechtheus, Mary Stuart. - Chronological list of Swin-
      burne's writings. - Bibliographies. - Lives. - Criticisms.
      - Notes.

2859   SWITZER, MARVIN D. Nip and tuck. Farce in one act. Clyde,
        Ohio, Ames' publishing co., 1898. 8p.

2860   SYMONS, ARTHUR, 1865-1945. The toy cart, a play in five acts,
        by Arthur Symons. Dublin and London, Maunsel and co., ltd.,
        1919. 4 p.ℓ., 114p.

2861   _____. Tragedies, by Arthur Symons. New York, The John Lane
        co.; London, W. Heinemann, 1916. 4 p.ℓ., 151p. CONTENTS.
        - The harvesters. - The death of Agrippina. - Cleopatra,
        in Judea.

2862   SYNGE, JOHN MILLINGTON, 1871-1909. The shadow of the glen
        and Riders to the sea; by J. M. Synge. London, E.
        Mathews, 1910. 63 [1]p. (On cover: Vigo cabinet series).

2863   _____. The tinker's wedding, a comedy in two acts, by J. M.
        Synge, Dublin, Maunsel and co., ltd., 1907. vii [1], 52p.

2864   TAGORE, SIR RABINDRANATH, 1861-1941. The king of the dark
        chamber... New York, Macmillan, 1916. 206p.

2865   _____. The king of the dark chamber, by Rabindranath Tagore,
        tr. into English by the author. New York, The Macmillan
        co., 1914. 206p.

2866   _____. The post office... Tr. by Devabrata Mukerjea.
        Indian ed. London, Macmillan and co., 1961. 88p.

2867   _____. The post office, by Rabindranath Tagore. New York,
        The Macmillan co., 1914. 95p.

2868   The tailors; or, A tragedy for warm weather: a burlesque
        tragedy, in three acts. (In The London stage. London
        [1824-27]. v. 4 [no. 5] [7]-16p., 1 illus.).
           Caption title.
           Ascribed to Samuel Foote, apparently without justifica-
        tion. Cf. Baker, Biog. dram., and Genest.

2869   TALBOT, R. The serf, a tragedy, in five acts, altered from
        the German of Raupach... Clyde, Ohio, A. D. Ames [n.d.].
        36p.

2870 TALFOURD, FRANCIS. Abon Hassan; or, The hunt after happiness.
      A semi-original fairy extravaganza, in rhyme, in one act...
      London, Thomas Hailes Lacy [n.d.]. 38p.

2871 _____. Alcestis, the original strong-minded woman; a classi-
      cal burlesque, in one act, being a most shameless misinter-
      pretation of the Greek drama of Euripides... London,
      Thomas Hailes Lacy [n.d.]. 26p.

2872 _____. Atalanta; or, The three golden apples. An original
      classical extravaganza in one act... London, Thomas
      Hailes Lacy [n.d.]. 44p.

2873 _____. A household fairy. A domestic sketch, in one act...
      as first performed... Dec. 24, 1859... New York, Robert M.
      De Witt [n.d.]. 12p.

2874 _____. Shylock; or, The merchant of Venice preserved. An
      entirely new reading of Shakespeare... New York, Samuel
      French [n.d.]. 30p.

2875 TALFOURD, SIR THOMAS NOON, 1795-1854. ... Ion. A tragedy,
      in five acts... New York, Samuel French [n.d.]. 80p.
      (French's standard drama, no. i).

2876 TALLADAY, JENNIE. Uncle Sam's relation. New York, Edgar S.
      Werner and co. [1904]. 35p.

2877 Taming a tiger. A farce in one act. Adapted from the
      French... New York, Robert M. De Witt [n.d.]. 13p.

2878 TANNER, MINNIE H. Cinderella; a drama, by Minnie H. Tanner.
      New York, Hastings and Habberton [1872]. Cover-title, 12p.

2879 TARKINGTON, BOOTH, 1869-1946. Beauty and the Jacobin; an
      interlude of the French revolution, by Booth Tarkington;
      with illustrations by C. D. Williams. New York and London,
      Harper and bros., 1912. 4 p.ℓ., 99, [1]p. front., plates.

2880 _____. The ghost story; a one-act play for persons of no
      great age, by Booth Tarkington. Cincinnati, Stewart Kidd
      co. [c1922]. 42p.

2881 TASSIN, ALGERNON. Rust; a play in four acts. New York,
      Broadway Publishing co., 1911. 172p.

TAYLEURE, CLIFTON W.

2882   TAYLEURE, CLIFTON W. ... The boy martyrs of Sept. 12, 1814.
        A local historical drama, in three acts... Boston, William
        V. Spencer, 1859. 30p. (Spencer's Boston theatre, no. cci).

2883   _____. ... Horseshoe Robinson; or, The battle of King's
        Mountain. A legendary patriotic drama, in three acts...
        New York, Samuel French, 1858. 40p. (French's standard
        drama, no. ccxiii).

2884   TAYLOR, CHARLES E. Weary Willie. A farce in one act. Clyde,
        Ohio, Ames' publishing co., 1906. 10p.

2885   TAYLOR, C. W. The drunkard's warning. A temperance drama,
        in three acts. Chicago, The Dramatic publishing co. [n.d.].
        38p.

2886   TAYLOR, SIR HENRY, 1800-1886. Philip Van Artevelde, a
        dramatic romance in two parts. Boston, Fields, Osgood and
        co., 1870. 456p.

2887   TAYLOR, MALCOLM STUART. Aar-u-ag-oos; or, An East Indian
        drug. An entirely original farce, in one act, by Malcolm
        S. Taylor... With cast of characters, description of
        costumes... and the whole of the stage business carefully
        marked from the author's original manuscript... Clyde,
        Ohio, A. D. Ames [1884]. 12p. (On cover: Ames' series
        of standard and minor drama. no. 129).

2888   _____. The afflicted family; or, A doctor without a diploma.
        A farce-comedy, in four acts... Clyde, Ohio, A. D. Ames,
        1883. 46p.

2889   _____. Auld Robin Gray, an emotional drama, in five acts, by
        Malcolm Stuart Taylor... From the famous Scotch ballad of
        the same name by Lady Anne Barnard. Printed from the
        original manuscript, with the stage business carefully
        marked... Clyde, Ohio, A. D. Ames [1881]. 52p. (On
        cover: Ames' series of standard and minor drama. no.
        126).

2890   _____. A honeymoon eclipse; a comedy in one act, by Malcolm
        Stuart Taylor... New York, H. Roorbach, 1900. 18p.

2891   _____. Rags and bottles; or, The two waifs. An original
        comedy, in two acts, by M. Stewart Taylor... Printed from
        the author's original manuscript. To which is added a
        description of the costumes--cast of the characters... and

(TAYLOR, MALCOLM STUART)
the whole of the stage business. Clyde, Ohio, A. D. Ames [1887]. (On cover: Ames' series of standard and minor drama. no. 219).

2892 TAYLOR, REUBEN THORNTON. A pageant to celebrate the founding of La Grange, Oldham County, Kentucky, 1827-1927... [La Grange, Kentucky, The Oldham Era, 1927]. 28p.

2893 TAYLOR, THOMAS PROCLUS. ... The chain of guilt; or, The inn on the heath. A romantic drama, in two acts... London, Thomas Hailes Lacy [n.d.]. 35p. front. (Cumberland's British theatre).

2894 TAYLOR, TOM, 1817-1880. ... The bottle. A drama in two acts. By T. P. Taylor. Founded upon the graphic illustrations of George Cruikshank, esq. With the stage business, cast of chracters, relative positions, etc. New York, J. Douglas, 1847. 57p. incl. front. (The Minor drama. no. 20).

2895 _____. The fool's revenge. A drama, in three acts... London, Thomas Hailes Lacy [n.d.]. 58p.

2896 _____. ... Tom Taylor's tragedy of The fool's revenge, as presented by Edwin Booth... New-York, Printed, for W. Winter, by F. Hart and co., 1878. 4, [2]p., 2ℓ., 10-92 numb.ℓ., [93]-96p. ([Booth, Edwin] The prompt-book. Ed. by William Winter. [v. 9]).
Text of play printed on one side of leaf only.
"This drama is in no sense a translation, and ought not, I think, in fairness, to be called even an adaptation of Victor Hugo's fine play, 'Le roi s'amuse'." --Author's pref.
Issued also as part of The miscellaneous plays of Edwin Booth, ed. by William Winter, 1899.

2897 _____. Tom Taylor's drama of The fool's revenge, as produced by Edwin Booth. Adapted from the text of the author's edition, with introductory remarks, &c., by Henry L. Hinton. New York, Hurd and Houghton [1868]. v. [1], [7]-65p. (On cover: Booth's series of acting plays. no. 4).
"This drama is in no sense a translation, and ought not, I think, in fairness, to be called even an adaptation of Victor Hugo's fine play, 'Le roi s'amuse'."--Introd.

TAYLOR, TOM

2898   TAYLOR, TOM. Henry Dunbar; or, A daughter's trials. A drama
        in four acts. Founded on Miss Braddon's novel of the same
        name. By Tom Taylor... To which is added a description of
        the costume – cast of the characters... and the whole of
        the stage business. New York, R. M. De Witt [187?]. 40p.
        diagrs. (On cover: De Witt's acting plays. (No. 8)).

2899   _____. Historical dramas by Tom Taylor... London, Chatto and
        Windus, 1877. viii, 466p.

2900   _____. Joan of Arc. An original historical play, in five acts.
        Chicago, The Dramatic publishing co. [n.d.]. 41p.

2901   _____. ... The king's rival; or, The court and the stage. A
        drama, in five acts, by Tom Taylor and Charles Reade. New
        York, Samuel French [n.d.]. 50p. (French's American drama,
        no. xxxiii).

2902   _____. Lady Clancarty; or, Wedded and wooed. A tale of the
        assassination plot, 1696. An original drama, in four acts,
        by Tom Taylor. London, S. French; New York, S. French and
        son [187-?]. 68p. (On cover: French's standard drama.
        The acting edition. No. CCCLXVIII).
            "First produced at the Royal Olympic theatre, March 9th,
        1874."

2903   _____. Mary Warner. A domestic drama, in four acts. Chicago,
        The Dramatic publishing co. [n.d.]. 42p.

2904   _____. Masks and faces; or, Before and behind the curtain.
        A comedy. In two acts. By Tom Taylor, and Charles Reade
        ... with editorial remarks, original casts... and all the
        stage business. New York, S. French [186-]. 3 p.ℓ.,
        [7]-60p. (On cover: French's standard drama. The acting
        edition. no. 210).
            "First brought before the public at the Haymarket
        theater, London, under the title of Peg Woffington."--
        Remarks.

2905   _____. New men and old acres. An original comedy, in three
        acts. By Tom Taylor and Augustus W. Dubourg. London and
        New York, Samuel French [n.d.]. 76p.

2906   _____. Nine points of the law. An original comedietta. In
        one act. Boston, Charles H. Spencer [n.d.]. 27p.

TAYLOR, TOM

2907   . Our American cousin, a drama, in 3 acts. By Tom
Taylor. [n.p.] Printed, but not published, 1869. [New
York, S. French, 192-?]. 46p.

2908   . The overland route. A comedy, in three acts. By Tom
Taylor... To which are added, a description of the costumes - cast of the characters... and the whole of the
stage business. New York, R. M. De Witt [187-?]. 51p.
diagrs. (On cover: De Witt's acting plays. (No. 147)).

2909   . Plot and passion. A drama, (founded on the French.)
In three acts. By Tom Taylor... To which is added a
description of the costumes - cast of the characters...
and the whole of the stage business. New York, R. M. De
Witt [187-?]. 39p. diagrs. (On cover: De Witt's acting
plays. (No. 61.)).

2910   . A sheep in wolf's clothing. A domestic drama, in one
act. New York, Robert M. De Witt [n.d.]. 22p.

2911   . Still waters run deep. An original comedy, in three
acts. By Tom Taylor... As first produced at the Royal
Olympic theatre, London, May 14, 1855... New York, C. T.
De Witt [1877]. 37p. (On cover: De Witt's acting plays.
no. 215).

2912   . ... The ticket-of-leave man: a drama, in four acts...
New York, Samuel French [n.d.]. 56p. (French's standard
drama, no. cccxxix).

2913   . ... To oblige Benson: a comedietta in one act... New
York, Samuel French [n.d.]. 24p. (French's minor drama,
no. lxxxvi).

2914   . An unequal match. A comedy, in three acts. By Tom
Taylor... London, S. French and son [188-?]. 66p. (On
cover: French's standard drama. The acting edition, No.
CCCLXXIV).

2915   . ... Victims: an original comedy, in three acts. By
Tom Taylor... To which are added, a description of the
costumes - cast of the characters... and the whole of the
stage business. New York, S. French and son; London, S.
French [188-?]. 44p. (French's standard drama. No.
CLXXXVI).

TEES, LEVIN C.

2916   TEES, LEVIN C. This paper for sale, a farce in one act.
        Philadelphia, The Penn publishing co., 1911. 13p.

2917   TEFFT, NATHAN APPLETON, 1868-   . The gloves. A comedy drama
        in three acts. By Nata A. Tefft. [Bangor, Maine] Bangor
        commercial print., 1895. 2 p.ℓ., 42p.

2918   [TEMPLETON, JON]. The romance of Robert Burns. A pastoral of
        the present and drama of days lang syne. New York, Wright
        and co. [1899]. 326p., 2ℓ. illus., 17 pl., 2 port. (incl.
        front.).

2919   TENNYSON, ALFRED, 1st BARON TENNYSON, 1809-1892. The Foresters,
        Robin Hood and Main Marian. New York, Macmillan and co.,
        1892. 155p.

2920   _____. The poetic and dramatic works of Alfred Lord Tennyson
        ... Boston [etc] Houghton Mifflin co. [1898]. xvii, 887p.
        front. (port.).
            Includes the following dramas: Queen Mary, Harold,
        Becket, The falcon, The cup, The promise of May.

2921   _____. Queen Mary. Boston, James R. Osgood and co., 1875.
        284p.

2922   TERENTIUS AFER, PUBLIUS, ca. 195-159 B.C. The comedies of
        Terence. Literally translated into English prose, with
        notes by Henry Thomas Riley... to which is added the blank
        verse translation of George Colman. New York, Harper and
        bros., 1892. 609p.

2923   [TERRY, DANIEL] 1780?-1829. The antiquary: a musical play,
        in three acts, from Sir Walter Scott, bart. To which is
        prefixed, a memoir of his life. Printed from the acting
        copy, with remarks, biographical and critical, by D.-G. ...
        As performed at the Theatres Royal ... London, G. H.
        Davidson [n.d.]. 77p. front. (Cumberland's British
        theatre. London, ca. 1825-55, v. 31 [no. 3].
            Remarks by George Daniel, editor of the series; also a
        poem on the death of Sir Walter Scott (p. 17-20).
            Without the music (by Bishop).

2924   THAXTER, A. WALLACE. The grotto nymph; or, Fairy favor. A
        fantastico-musical morceau of absurdity. In one consecu-
        tive act and a tableau... New York, Samuel French [n.d.].
        21p.

2925   [THELWALL, JOHN] 1764-1834. The fairy of the lake. A
        dramatic romance. In three acts. (In his Poems...
        Hereford, 1801. p. 1-92).

2926   THOMAS, AUGUSTUS, 1857-1934. Alabama; a drama in four acts.
        Chicago, The Dramatic Publishing co., 1901. 148p. plates.

2927   _____. Arizona; a drama in four acts. New York, R. H. Russell,
        1899. 155p. illus.

2928   _____. As a man thinks, a play in four acts. New York,
        Duffield and co., 1911. 213p. front.

2929   THOMAS, BRANDON. The promise; a play in one act, by Brandon
        Thomas. Printed for private circulation only. New York,
        The De Vinne press, 1886. 40p.

2930   THOMAS, J. F. ... Commercial infidelity; or, Burglary to slow
        music. A play, in three acts. Detroit, Free Press Book
        and Job Printing House, 1873. 31p.

2931   THOMPSON, ALICE C. "Mrs. Alice Meynell." Much too sudden, a
        comedy in one act. Boston, Walter H. Baker and co. [1910].
        12p.

2932   _____. The truth about Jane, a comedy in one act. Boston,
        Walter H. Baker and co. [1909]. 13p.

2933   THOMPSON, AMIRA CARPENTER. The lyre of Tioga. By Mrs. Amira
        Thompson... Geneva, N. Y., Printed for the author by J.
        Rogers, 1829. 180p.
            Contains her A sacred drama on the Book of Esther and A
        pastoral play in one act.

2934   THOMPSON, BENJAMIN, 1776?-1816, tr. The German theatre, tr.
        by Benjamin Thompson, esq. ... London, Vernor and Hood, 1801.
        6v. in 3. plates. CONTENTS: I. Biographical account of
        Baron Augustus von Kotzebue. - The stranger; Rolla, or The
        virgin of the sun; Pizarro, or The death of Rolla. By A.
        von Kotzebue. II. Lovers' vows, or The natural son;
        Adelaide of Wulfingen; Count Benyowsky, or The conspiracy
        of Kamtschatka. By A. von Kotzebue. III. Deaf and dumb,
        or The orphan; The Indian exiles; False delicacy; The happy
        family. By A. von Kotzebue. IV. Otto of Wittelsbach, or
        The choleric count; Dagobert, king of the Franks. By
        J. M. Babo. Conscience, by A. W. Iffland. V. The robbers;
        Don Carlos. By F. Schiller. VI. The ensign, by F. F.
        Schroeder. Count Koenigsmark, by C. von Reitzenstein.
        Stella, by J. W. von Goethe. Emilia Galotti, by G. E.
        Lessing.

THOMPSON, CHARLES

2935   THOMPSON, CHARLES. The gambler's fate; or, A lapse of twenty
        years: a drama, in two acts, founded on the popular French
        play of "La vie d'un joueur," by Charles Thompson, esq.
        Printed from the acting copy, with remarks, biographical
        and critical, by D.-G. ... As performed at the Theatres
        Royal... London, J. Cumberland [n.d.]. 52p. incl. front.
        (Cumberland's British theatre. London, ca. 1825-55. v. 17
        [no. 4]).
            "The French author has borrowed largely from... the
        Gamester." Cf. Remarks by George Daniel, editor of the
        series.
            Reissued in Davidson's shilling volume of Cumberland's
        plays, v. 18 [no. 2].

2936   THOMPSON, ELIZABETH JANE SWEETLAND, 1858-   A double life.
        A drama in five acts. By Mrs. Eliza Thompson ... Toronto,
        Hill and Weir, printers, 1884. 2 p.ℓ., [3]-38p.
            Imprint covered by label: Jamestown, N. Y., Journal
        printing establishment, 1884.

2937   THOMSON, ESTHER. They will gossip [n.p., n.d.]. 5p.
        (American Classical League Service Bureau, No. 604).

2938   Three Australian plays. Introduction by H. C. Kippax. The
        one day of the year [by] Alan Seymour. Ned Kelly [by]
        Douglas Stewart. The tower [by] Hal Porter [n.p.].
        [Harmundsworth] Penguin books [n.d.]. 311p.

2939   The three blacksmiths. An original Ethiopian eccentricity,
        in one scene... New York, Samuel French [n.d.]. 10p.

2940   TIFFANY, ESTHER BROWN, 1858-   Apollo's oracle, an enter-
        tainment in one act, by Esther B. Tiffany... Boston, W. H.
        Baker and co., 1897. 8p. illus. (music). (On cover:
        Baker's novelties).

2941   _____. A tell-tale eyebrow, a comedy in two acts. Boston,
        Walter H. Baker and co. [1897]. 23p.

2942   _____. That Patrick! A comedy in one act. By Esther B.
        Tiffany. Boston, W. H. Baker and co. [1886]. 13p. (On
        cover: Walter H. Baker and co.'s Boston list).

2943   _____. The way to his pocket; a comedy in one act, by Esther
        B. Tiffany... Boston, W. H. Baker and co., 1889. 24p.
        (On cover: Baker's edition of plays).

2944   _____. Young Mr. Pritchard. A comedy in two scenes. By Esther B. Tiffany. Boston, W. H. Baker and co.'s Boston list).

2945   TILDEN, LEN ELLSWORTH. The emigrant's daughter. A border drama, in three acts... Clyde, Ohio, A. D. Ames, 1884. 28p.

2946   _____. The finger of fate; or, The death letter, a melodrama in three acts. Boston, Walter H. Baker and co., 1893. 32p.

2947   TINSLEY, LILY. Cinders, by Lily Tinsley... New York, London, S. French, c1899. 20p. incl. illus. (plan). (On cover: French's international copyrighted... edition of the works of the best authors. no. 24).

2948   TOBIN, JOHN, 1770-1804. The curfew. A play, in five acts, by John Tobin... Printed from the acting copy, with remarks, biographical and critical, by D.-G. ... As performed at the Theatres Royal... London, J. Cumberland [n.d.]. 50p. incl. front. (Cumberland's British theatre. London [ca. 1825-55] v. 43 [no. 9]).
    Remarks by George Daniel, editor of the series.

2949   _____. ... The honey-moon: a play, in five acts. By John Tobin. With the stage business, cast of characters, costumes, relative positions, etc. New York, S. French and son; London, S. French [187-?]. iv, [7]-62, [1]p. (French's standard drama. No. VI).

2950   _____. The honey moon: a comedy, in five acts. By John Tobin, esq. Printed from the acting copy, with remarks, biographical and critical, by D.-G. ... As performed at the Theatres Royal... London, G. H. Davidson [185-]. 63p. incl. front. (Davidson's shilling volume of Cumberland's plays. London [ca. 1849-55] v. 17 [no. 2]).
    Reissue of Cumberland's British theatre, no. 89 (v. 13 [no. 5] wanting in some sets).
    Remarks by George Daniel, editor of the original series.

2951   TOLER, H. M. Thekla, a fairy drama, in three acts... Clyde, Ohio, A. D. Ames, 1884. 14p.

2952   TOLER, SALLIE. Handicapped; or, A racing romance. An original comedy, in two acts. Chicago, The Dramatic publishing co., 1894. 13p.

Too late for the train

2953   Too late for the train. A duologue... Boston, George M.
        Baker and co. [n.d.]. 15p.

2954   TORRENCE, FREDERIC RIDGELY, 1875-1950. Abelard and Heloise,
        by Ridgely Torrence. New York, C. Scribner's sons, 1907.
        4 p.ℓ., 215p.

2955   _____. El Dorado, a tragedy, by Ridgely Torrence... New York
        and London, John Lane, 1903. 132p., 1ℓ.

2956   ... La Tour de Nesle; or, The chamber of death. An historical
        drama, from the French of Victor Hugo. In three acts...
        New York, Samuel French [n.d.]. 39p. (French's American
        drama, no. cxii).

2957   TOWNSEND, CHARLES F., 1857-   Border land. An original
        drama, in three acts. By Charles Townsend... New York,
        The De Witt Publishing house, 1889. 25p. (On cover: De
        Witt's acting plays, no. 352).

2958   _____. ... Broken fetters. An original drama, in five acts.
        By Charles Townsend... Author's ed. New York, The De Witt
        publishing house, 1890. 82p. (On cover: De Witt's
        acting plays, no. 356).

2959   _____. The darkey tragedian. An Ethiopian sketch, in one
        scene. New York, Dick and Fitzgerald [1874?]. 7p.

2960   _____. Deception, an original farce in one act. Chicago,
        T. S. Denison, 1891. 15p.

2961   _____. Down in Dixie, a drama in four acts, by Charles
        Townsend... Author's ed. Chicago, T. S. Denison [1894].
        54p. diagrs. (On cover: Denison's series. vol. IV,
        no. 37).

2962   _____. Early vows, a comedy in two acts. Chicago, T. S.
        Denison [1889]. 28p.

2963   _____. A family affair. A comedy in three acts... Phila-
        delphia, The Penn Publishing co., 1904. 41p.

2964   _____. The golden gulch, an original drama in three acts.
        New York, Dick and Fitzgerald, 1893. 42p.

2965   _____. The iron hand, a drama in four acts, by Charles
        Townsend... Chicago, T. S. Denison [1897]. 39p. diagrs.
        (On cover: Alta series).

TOWNSEND, CHARLES

2966   _____. Isabel, the pearl of Cuba, a melodrama in four acts. New York, Dick and Fitzgerald, 1908. 43p.

2967   _____. A loyal friend, a comedy-drama in four acts, by Charles Townsend... Author's ed. With cast of characters ... and all of the stage business. Philadelphia, The Penn publishing co., 1898. 40p. illus. (plans). (On cover: Dramatic library, v. 1, no. 134).

2968   _____. The Mahoney million, by Charles Townsend; with illustrations by Clare Angell. New York, New Amsterdam book co., 1903. 1 p.ℓ., 5p., 1ℓ., 7-125p. col. front., pl.

2969   _____. The man from Maine; an original drama in five acts, by Charles Townsend... Author's ed. ... New York, H. Roorbach, 1893. 42p. (On cover: Roorbach's American edition of acting plays, no. 60).

2970   _____. Miss Madcap, a comedietta in one act, by Charles Townsend... Author's ed., with the cast of the characters... description of the costumes... and all of the stage business... New York, H. Roorbach [1890]. 12p. diagr. (On cover: Roorbach's American edition of acting plays. no. 28).

2971   _____. The mountain waif, an original drama in four acts. Boston, Walter H. Baker and co. [1892]. 42p.

2972   _____. Uncle Rube; an original drama in four acts... Chicago, The Dramatic publishing co. [1899]. 56p.

2973   _____. Uncle Tom's Cabin. A melodrama, in five acts... New York, Harold Roorbach, 1889. 44p.

2974   _____. Under a cloud, an original comedy drama in two acts, by Charles Townsend. Author's ed., with the cast of the characters... description of the costumes... and all of the stage business... New York, H. Roorbach [1890]. 29p. diagr. (On cover: Roorbach's American edition of acting plays. no. 48).

2975   _____. ... Vacation. An original comedy, in two acts. By Charles Townsend... Together with a description of the costumes – cast of the characters... and the whole of the stage business. Author's ed. New York, The DeWitt publishing house [1893]. 24p. (On cover: De Witt's acting plays. no. 398).

TOWNSEND, GEORGE ALFRED

2976   TOWNSEND, GEORGE ALFRED, 1841-1914. President Cromwell, a
       drama in four acts, by George Alfred Townsend, "Gath."
       New York, E. F. Bonaventure [1884]. 94p.

2977   TOWNSEND, W. THOMPSON. The lost ship; or, The man-of-war's
       man, and the privateer. A nautical drama, in three acts...
       New York, Samuel French [n.d.]. 33p.

2978   _____. Temptation; or, The fatal brand. A drama, in two
       acts... London, Thomas Hailes Lacy [n.d.]. 37p.

2979   _____. Whitefriars; or, The days of Claude du Val. A drama,
       in three acts... London, Thomas Hailes Lacy [n.d.]. 43p.
       front.

2980   TOWSLEE, FRANK. The Summerville bazaar, an entertainment in
       one act. Boston, Walter H. Baker and co., 1911. 26p.

2981   TRASK, KATRINA NICHOLS, 1853-1922. King Alfred's jewel.
       London, John Lane, The Bodley Head; New York, John Lane
       co., 1909. 180p.

2982   [_____]. King Alfred's jewel, by the author of Morset
       Victoria. London, John Lane; New York, John Lane co.,
       1908. vii, 180p. col. front.

2983   _____. Without the walls; a reading play, by Katrina Trask...
       New York, The Macmillan co., 1919. 3 p.ℓ., 3-196p.

2984   A trial of Catiline, written and presented by the Cicero class
       of St. Joseph's Academy, St. Paul, Minnesota [n.p., n.d.].
       9p. (American Classical League Service Bureau, No. 457).

2985   TRIPLET, JAMES. Call at number 1-7. A farce, in one act...
       New York, Samuel French, 1863. 16p.

2986   TROUBETZKOY, AMÉLIE RIVES, 1863-1945. Athelwold. New York,
       Harper and bros., 1893. 118p.

2987   _____. The sea-woman's cloak, and November eve. Two plays
       by Amélie Rives (Princess Troubetzkoy). Cincinnati, Stewart
       Kidd co. [c1923]. 156p.

2988   _____. Seléné. New York and London, Harper and bros., 1905.
       3 p.ℓ., 88, [1]p.

2989   TROWBRIDGE, JOHN TOWNSEND, 1827-1916. Neighbor Jackwood. A
        domestic drama, in five acts. By J. T. Trowbridge...
        Produced at the Boston museum... March 16th, 1857.
        Printed from the acting copy; the stage business, etc.,
        correctly marked... Boston, Phillips, Sampson and co.,
        1857. 72p.

2990   TRUEBA Y COSÍO, JOAQUÍN TELESFORO, 1799?-1835. Mr. and Mrs.
        Pringle: a comic interlude, in one act, by Don T. de Trueba
        Cosío... Printed from the acting copy, with remarks, bio-
        graphical and critical, by D.-G. ... As performed at the
        Theatres Royal... London, J. Cumberland [n.d.]. 27p. incl.
        front. (Cumberland's British theatre. London, ca. 1825-
        55. v. 31 [no. 2]).
            Remarks by George Daniel, editor of the series.
            Based on "La famille Jabutot, ou La veuve sans enfans,
        by Brazier and others.

2991   Truth's advocate and monthly anti-Jackson expositor. By an
        association of individuals. Jan.-Oct. 1828. Cincinnati,
        Lodge, L'Hommedieu, and Hammond, 1828. [4], 400p.
            Contains The Hero of two wars.

2992   TUBBS, ARTHUR LEWIS, 1867-   . The country doctor, a comedy
        in four acts. Boston, Walter H. Baker and co., [1910].
        57p.

2993   _____. Cranberry Corners, a comedy drama in four acts, by
        Arthur Lewis Tubbs... Boston, W. H. Baker and co., 1918.
        67p. (On cover: Baker's edition of plays).

2994   _____. Farm folks, a rural play in four acts, by Arthur
        Lewis Tubbs... Philadelphia, The Penn publishing co.,
        1909. 71p. diagrs.

2995   _____. Home ties, a rural play in four acts, by Arthur Lewis
        Tubbs... Philadelphia, The Penn publishing co., 1910.
        73p.

2996   _____. Not on the bills, a farce in one act, by Arthur Lewis
        Tubbs... Philadelphia, The Penn publishing co., 1912.
        18p.

2997   _____. The village lawyer, a comedy drama in four acts, by
        Arthur Lewis Tubbs... Philadelphia, The Penn publishing
        co., 1914. 84p. diagrs.

TUBBS, ARTHUR LEWIS

2998   TUBBS, ARTHUR LEWIS. The village schoolma'am, a country play
        in three acts, by Arthur Lewis Tubbs... Boston, W. H.
        Baker and co., 1909. 51p. (On cover: Baker's edition of
        plays).

2999   TURNER, GENEVIEVE. Corn Silk, a Mandan legend, adapted for
        school plays, by Genevieve Turner and others. Grand Forks,
        N. D., 1914. 18p.

3000   No Entry.

3001   ... The two Gregories; or, Luck in a name. An operatic farce,
        in one act... New York, Samuel French [n.d.]. 19p.
        (French's American drama, no. lxvii).

3002   TYLER, ROYALL, 1757-1826. The contrast; a comedy, by Royall
        Tyler, with an introduction by Thomas J. McKee. New York,
        The Dunlap society, 1887. 1 p.ℓ., xxxix, [1], 107p. illus.,
        2 p.ℓ. (incl. music). On cover: The publications of the
        Dunlap society. (no. 1).

3003   ULLMAN, BERTHOLD LOUIS, 1882-1965. He talked too much; a
        dramatic version of Horace's ninth satire. [n.p., n.d.].
        4p. (American Classical League Service Bureau, No. 496).

3004   ULRICH, CHARLES. The altar of riches, a comedy of American
        finance in four acts. Chicago, T. S. Denison and co.
        [1909]. 79p.

3005   _____. The dawn of liberty, a colonial comedy-drama in four
        acts. Chicago and New York, The Dramatic publishing co.,
        1905. 73p.

3006   _____. The honor of a cowboy, a comedy drama in four acts.
        Chicago, T. S. Denison and co. [1906]. 76p.

3007   _____. The man from Nevada, a comedy in four acts. Chicago,
        T. S. Denison and co. [1903]. 77p.

3008   _____. Nugget, a western play in four acts. Chicago and New
        York, The Chicago publishing co. [1905]. 51p.

3009   _____. On the Little Big Horn, a comedy drama of the West in
        four acts. Chicago, T. S. Denison and co. [1907]. 82p.

3010   UNDERHILL, JOHN. Damon and Pythias, a drama of Quebec
        liberalism, by John Underhill. [n.p., 1891]. 31p.

Vidocq! The French police spy!

3011 VACHELL, HORACE ANNESLEY. Jelf's, a comedy in four acts, New York, George H. Doren co., 1912. 154p.

3012 Valentine and Orson. A singularly original and touching extravaganza, in two acts... first performed... Dec. 26, 1844. London, R. Hodson [n.d.]. 35p.

3013 VALLENTINE, BENJAMIN BENNATON, 1843-1926. In paradise; a farce in one act; by B. B. Vallentine... [New York, 1899]. 20p.

3014 VANBRUGH, SIR JOHN, 1664-1726. The provoked husband; a comedy, in five acts... by J. Vanbrugh and Colley Cibber. London, John Cumberland [n.d.]. 81p. front.

3015 VAN DERVEER, LETTIE COOK. A day at Happy Hollow school. Lebanon, Ohio, March bros. [1910]. 29p.

3016 VAN ZO POST. The A string, comedy in three acts. New York, 1911. Various pagings.

3017 VATTER, AUGUST. Out of the shadow; a drama in three acts, by August Vatter and John E. Spencer; somewhat altered from the original version... as played... under the title of "A noble sacrifice." Boston, W. H. Baker and co., 1890. 48p. (On cover: Baker's edition of plays).

3018 VEGIARD, J. T. The Dutch recruit; or, The blue and gray. An original allegorical drama of the civil war of 1861-66. In five acts... Clyde, Ohio, A. D. Ames, 1879. 49p.

3019 VENABLE, WILLIAM HENRY, 1836-1920, ed. Dramas and dramatic scenes, ed. by W. H. Venable. Illustrated by Farny. Cincinnati, New York, Wilson, Hinkle and co. [c1874]. vii, 9-336p. illus.

3020 VERCONSIN, EUGÈNE. A drawing-room car. Some incidents of a railway journey. A petite comedy, in one act. Adapted from the French of Eugène Verconsin... New York, Robert M. De Witt, 1876. 12p.

3021 VERDI, GIUSEPPE, 1813-1901. Rigoletto. A lyric drama, in four acts. New York, W. H. Tinson [n.d.]. 23p.

3022 ... Vidocq! The French police spy! A melodrama, in two acts ... London, J. Duncombe [n.d.]. 32p. front.

The village lawyer

3023   The village lawyer; a farce, in two acts. (In The London
        stage. London [1824-27]. v. 4 [no. 43] 5 p.ℓ., illus.).
        Caption title.
            Ascribed to William Macready, the elder.

3024   VOLTAIRE, FRANÇOIS MARIE AROUET DE, 1694-1778. Rome preserv'd;
        a tragedy. Translated from the French of M. de Voltaire...
        London, Printed for J. Curtis, 1760. 2 p.ℓ., 67p.

3025   _____. Saul; a drama, in five acts. Tr. from the French of
        M. de Voltaire. By Oliver Martext, of Arden [pseud.]...
        London, J. Carlile, 1820. 28p.

3026   _____. Zaira. Trans. from the tragedy of Voltaire, and per-
        formed in the Theatre Royal, Liverpool. Music by Federici.
        Liverpool, 1811. 45p.

3027   WAGNER, RICHARD. "Parsifal." The story of this stage conse-
        cration festival play. Containing also the libretto of
        Parsifal. Translated into English from Wagner's authorized
        text. New York, J. S. Ogilvie publishing co., 1903. 96p.

3028   WALDAUER, AUGUST. ... Fanchon, the cricket; a domestic drama,
        in five acts... New York, Samuel French [n.d.]. 48p.
        (French's standard drama, no. cccxxiv).

3029   _____. ... Little barefoot, a domestic drama, in five acts...
        from the German... New York, Samuel French [n.d.]. 42p.
        (French's standard drama, no. cccxxxv).

3030   WALKER, C. E. ... Wallace. A tragedy; by C. E. Walker, esq.
        With prefatory remarks... Faithfully marked with the stage
        business, and stage directions, as it is performed at the
        Theatres Royal. By W. Oxberry, comedian. London, [P]ub.
        for the Proprietors, by W. Simpkin, and R. Marshall [etc.]
        1823. 1 p.ℓ., iii, [3], 58p. front. (port.) diagr.
        (Oxberry, William. The new English drama. London, 1818-25.
        v. 18 [no. 1]).
            At head of title: Oxberry's edition.
            "Remarks" signed: P. P.

3031   _____. The warlock of the glen, a melodrama in two acts.
        London and New York, Samuel French [n.d.]. 21p.

3032   WALKER, JANET EDMONDSON. The new governess, a comedy in one
        act adapted from the German. Chicago, The Dramatic
        publishing co., 1899. 16p.

3033   WALKER, STUART. More portmanteau plays. Edited, and with an
        introduction by Edward Hale Bierstadt. Cincinnati,
        Stewart and Kidd co., 1919. xxx, 209p. (Stewart and
        Kidd Dramatic Series, v. 2). CONTENTS: - The lady of the
        weeping willow tree. - The very naked boy. - Jonathan
        makes a wish.

3034   WALLACE, F. K. Pete and the peddler. A negro and Irish
        sketch, in one scene. By F. K. Wallace. Arranged by
        Charles White... New York, Joseph F. Wagner, 1876. 6p.

3035   WALLACE, J. J. Little Ruby; or, Home jewels. A domestic
        drama, in three acts. By J. J. Wallace... as first per-
        formed at the New Opera House. Ontario, Canada...
        January 6, 1874. Author's ed. ... New York, R. M. De Witt,
        c1872. 38p. On cover: De Witt's acting plays (no. 164).

3036   WALLACK, J. LESTER. ... The veteran; or, France and Algeria.
        A drama, in six tableaux... as performed at Wallack's
        Theatre, January 17, 1859. New York, Samuel French [n.d.].
        63p. (French's standard drama, no. ccxx).

3037   No Entry.

3038   WALTON, J. W. The reporter, a monologue... Cleveland, T. C.
        Schenck and co., 1879. 8p.

3039   The wandering boys. A melo-drama, in three acts, the music by
        Mr. Nicholson. Printed from the acting copy, with remarks,
        biographical and critical, by D.-G. ... As performed at
        the metropolitan minor theatres... London, J. Cumberland
        [n.d.]. 39p. incl. front. (Cumberland's Minor theatre.
        London [ca. 1830-55] v. 3 [no. 7]).
            "As performed at Sadler's Wells, May 24, 1830."
            An opera of the same name, with music by Bishop, was
        produced at Covent Garden, February 24, 1814 (cf. Genest
        and Theat, Inquisitor). A still earlier (?) adaptation
        of M. M. Noah, "Paul and Alexis or The orphans of the Rhine,"
        was acted at Charleston, S. C., in 1812, later altered (?)
        and printed at Boston, 1821, under title "The wandering
        boys; or, The castle of Olival." The Brit. Mus. Catalogue
        ascribes a play of the latter name in Lacy's acting drama
        to John Kerr. (Cf. also L. C. Baker, German drama in Eng.
        on the N. Y. stage, p. 96).
            "The original is 'Le pèlerin blanc,' written by M.
        Pixerécourt, and produced at the Théâtre de l'Ambigucomique,
        Paris, in 1810."--Remarks by George Daniel, editor of the
        series.

WARD, ELIZABETH STUART PHELPS

3040   WARD, ELIZABETH STUART PHELPS, 1844-1911. Within the gates,
        by Elizabeth Stuart Phelps. Boston and New York, Houghton,
        Mifflin and co., 1901, c1900. 150p.

3041   WARE, LEO. Claim ninety-six. A border drama in five acts...
        Clyde, Ohio, Ames' publishing co., 1893. 42p.

3042   _____. My pard; or, The fairy of the tunnel. A western drama
        in four acts... Clyde, Ohio, Ames' publishing co., 1895.
        29p.

3043   _____. Taggs, the waif; or, Uncle Seth. A drama in five acts.
        Clyde, Ohio, Ames' publishing co., 1896. 40p.

3044   WARREN, ERNEST. The nettle. Comedy for 1 male and 1 female...
        Text and stage-business edited and revised by Pauline
        Phelps and Marion Short. New York, Edgar S. Werner and
        co., 1906. 17p.

3045   WARREN, MARIE J. The elopement of Ellen; a farce comedy in
        three acts. Boston, Walter H. Baker co., 1905. 36p.

3046   [WARREN, MERCY OTIS], 1728-1814. The adulateur. A tragedy,
        as it is now acted in Upper Servia... Boston, Printed and
        sold at the New printing-office, near Concert-hall, 1773.
        30p.

3047   [_____]. [... The Group, As lately acted, and to be re-acted
        to the wonder of all superior intelligences, nigh head-
        quarters at Amboyne... Boston, Printed and sold by Edes
        and Gill, in Queen-Street, 1775]. 22p.

3048   Was it really Gaius Julius Caesar? An original drama by the
        pupils of Mrs. Evelyn L. Miller [n.p., n.d.]. 4p.
        (American Classical League Service Bureau, No. 710).

3049   WASHBURN, CLAUDE CARLOS, 1883-   . The baby, a farce in one
        act, by Claude C. Washburn. Duluth, Minnesota, Huntley
        printing co., 1909. 30p.

3050   WATSON, EVELYN. Patsy from Dakota, a comedy in three acts,
        by Evelyn Watson... Franklin, Ohio, Eldridge entertainment
        house, 1914. 36p.

3051   WATSON, MALCOLM, 1873-   . A pretty bequest, a comedietta in
        one act, by Malcolm Watson... London, J. Williams, limited;
        New York, E. Schuberth and co., 1906. 20p. incl. diagr.

3052   WATSON, SIR WILLIAM, 1858-1935. Heralds of the dawn; a play
       in eight scenes by William Watson. New York, John Lane
       co., 1912. 93p. front. (port.).

3053   The way to Wyndham, a humorous dialogue. Lebanon, Ohio, March
       bros. [n.d.]. 7p.

3054   WAYMAN, VIRGINIA. In the ancient days; an assembly program
       [n.p., n.d.]. 11p. (American Classical League Service
       Bureau, No. 435).

3055   No Entry.

3056   WEBSTER, BENJAMIN NOTTINGHAM, 1797-1882. ... The dead heart:
       an historical drama, in three acts, with a prologue... New
       York, Samuel French [n.d.]. 44p. (French's standard drama,
       no. cccxxxviii).

3057   _____. Giralda; or, The miller's wife. A new comic drama,
       in three acts... London, National acting drama office
       [n.d.]. 36p. front.

3058   _____. ... The golden farmer; or, Jemmy Twitcher in England.
       A domestic drama in two acts, by Benjamin Webster, comedian.
       With the stage business, cast of characters, relative
       positions, etc. New York, Berford and co., 1847. 1 p.ℓ.,
       [v]-vii, 38p. front. (Added t.-p.: The minor drama; a
       collection of the most popular petit comedies, vaudevilles,
       burlettas, travesties, etc. ... v. 1 [no. VIII]).
          Series title also at head of t.-p.
          "Memoir of Mr. John Sefton" (signed F. C. W.): p.
       [v]-vii.

3059   _____. High ways and by ways: a farce, in two acts, by
       Benjamin Webster, esq. Printed from the acting copy, with
       remarks, biographical and critical, by D.-G. ... As now
       performed at the Theatres Royal... London, J. Cumberland
       [n.d.]. 35p. incl. front. (Cumberland's British theatre.
       London, ca. 1825-55. v. 28 [no. 5]).
          "Two French pieces have been laid under contribution,
       'Mons. Rigaud, ou Les deux maris', and 'Partie et
       Revanche'."--Remarks by George Daniel, editor of the
       series.

3060   _____. My young wife, and my old umbrella. A farce - in one
       act. Adapted from the French. By Benjamin Webster...
       With original casts, costumes, and all of the stage
       business. As performed at the principal theatres in the

WEBSTER, BENJAMIN NOTTINGHAM

(WEBSTER, BENJAMIN NOTTINGHAM)
United States. Marked and arranged by Mr. J. B. Wright...
New York, S. French [187-?]. 16p. (On cover: French's
minor drama. The acting edition. No. CCXVI).
Adapted from Laurencin's Ma femme et mon parapluie.

3061   _____. ... The old gentleman. A farce, in one act... London,
J. Duncombe and co. [n.d.]. 24p. front. (Duncombe's
edition).

3062   _____. Paul Clifford, the highwayman of 1770: a drama, in
three acts... London, G. H. Davidson [n.d.]. 76p. front.

3063   WEDEKIND, FRANK, 1864-1918. The court singer. 1914. (In
Kuno Francke, ed., The German classics of the nineteenth
and twentieth century [New York, The German publication
society, 1914], v. 20, p. 360-397). Translated by Albert
Wilhelm Boesche.

3064   WEIR, WILLIAM JOHN, 1856-   . A daughter of old Spain, and
other plays, by William J. Weir... San Francisco, John
Kitchen Jr. co., 1923. 248p. front. (port.).

3065   WELLS, ANNA MARIA FOSTER, 1795?-1868. Poems and juvenile
sketches, by Anna Maria Wells... Boston, Carter, Hendee
and Babcock, 1830. 104p.
Contains her The owl and the swallow.

3066   WENDT, FREDERICK W. Ocean sketches, by Frederick W. Wendt;
cover designed by Ethel W. Mumford. New York, The Colonial
book co. [1897]. 2 p.l., 151p., 1l.

3067   WENLANDT, OLIVER. The nigger boarding-house, a screaming
farce in one act and one scene for six male burnt-cork
characters. New York, Fitzgerald publishing corp. [n.d.].
24p.

3068   WENTWORTH, MARION CRAIG. War brides; a play in one act. New
York, The Century co., 1915. 71p.

3069   ... The wept of the Wish-ton-wish. A drama, in two acts.
From J. Fenimore Cooper's... novel of the same name...
New York, Samuel French [n.d.]. 26p.

3070   WESTERVELT, LEONIDAS. The puppet show; a sketch, by Leonidas
Westervelt. 2d ed. New York, The Abbey press [1900].
4 p.l., 11-219p.

3071   _____. The puppet-show. A sketch. By Leonidas Westervelt. New York, F. T. Neely [1898]. 4 p.ℓ., 11-129p.

3072   WESTMACOTT, CHARLES MOLLOY, 1787?-1868. Nettlewig hall; or, Ten to one: a musical farce, in two acts, by C. M. Westmacott, esq.; the music by Alexander Lee. Printed from the acting copy, with remarks, biographical and critical, by D.-G. ... As performed at the Theatres Royal... London, J. Cumberland [n.d.]. 38p. incl. front. (Cumberland's British theatre. London, ca. 1825-55. v. 35 [no. 7]).
     Remarks by George Daniel, editor of the series.
     Without the music.

3073   WHALEN, E. C. From Sumter to Appomattox, a war drama in four acts. Chicago, T. S. Denison and co. [1899]. 59p.

3074   _____. Uncle Dick's mistake, a farce in one act, by E. C. Whalen... Chicago, T. S. Denison, 1889. 13p. (On cover: Amateur series).

3075   _____. Under the spell, a temperance play in four acts. Chicago, T. S. Denison and co. [1890]. 70p.

3076   WHALEY, IRENE GRAFTON. Life with Octavia [n.p., n.d.]. 9p. (American Classical League Service Bureau, No. 644).

3077   What do the Romans do? A glimpse of old Roman foods by the students of Mrs. Ralph Rogers [n.p., n.d.]. 3p. (American Classical League Service Bureau, No. 718).

3078   Whimwhams, by four of us... Boston, S. G. Goodrich, 1828. ixp., 1ℓ., 104(i.e. 204)p.
     Contains Finn's The woolen nightcap; or, ... The mysterious floursack!

3079   WHISTLER, E. J. A trick dollar, a farce in two acts. Chicago, T. S. Denison [1902]. 14p.

3081   WHITE, CHARLES. The black shoemaker, an Ethiopian farce. Arranged by C. White. Cleveland, Ohio, J. R. Holcomb and co. [n.d.]. 10p.

3082   _____. ... The black statue. A negro farce... in one act and one scene... New York, Frederic A. Brady [n.d.]. 27p. (Brady's Ethiopian drama, no. xiii).

WHITE, CHARLES

3083   WHITE, CHARLES. The darkey's stratagem. A negro sketch in
        one act. Arranged by Charles White... Chicago, The
        Dramatic publishing co., 1875. 9p.

3084   _____. De trouble begins at nine, a darkey interlude. New
        York, Fitzgerald publishing corp. [n.d.]. 11p.

3085   _____. Fisherman's luck. An Ethiopian sketch, in one scene...
        Chicago, The Dramatic publishing co., 1875. 5p.

3086   _____. Laughing gas. A Negro burlesque sketch. As arranged
        by Charles White... New York, Robert M. De Witt, 1874.
        5p.

3087   _____. A lucky job. A negro farce. Chicago, The Dramatic
        publishing co., 1874. 12p.

3088   _____. ... The magic penny. A negro farce... in one act and
        three scenes... New York, Frederic A. Brady [n.d.]. 28p.
        (Brady's Ethiopian drama, no. xvii).

3089   _____. The mischievous nigger. A negro farce... in one act
        and one scene... New York, Samuel French [n.d.]. [5]-32p.

3090   _____. ... The mistic spell. A pantomime. In seven scenes...
        New York, Frederic A. Brady [n.d.]. 15p. (Brady's
        Ethiopian drama, no. xii).

3091   _____. Oh! Hush! or, The Virginny cupids! An operatic
        olio... in one act and three scenes... New York, Samuel
        French [n.d.]. 6-21p.

3092   _____. ... The portrait painter. A pantomimic farce... in
        one act and one scene... New York, Frederic A. Brady
        [n.d.]. 25p. (Brady's Ethiopian drama, no. xx).

3093   _____. ... The rival lovers. A negro farce. In one act and
        one scene... New York, Frederick A. Brady [n.d.]. 18p.
        (Brady's Ethiopian drama, no. vii).

3094   _____. The serenade. (Sometimes called "All's well that
        ends well," and "Nip and tuck.") A negro sketch in two
        scenes. Arranged by Charles White... New York, The
        De Witt publishing house, 1876. 5p.

3095   _____. ... The sham doctor. A negro farce. In one act and three scenes... New York, Frederic A. Brady [n.d.]. 17p. front. (Brady's Ethiopian drama, no. VIII).
       With this is bound: Art of self defence [n.p., n.d.; 7-13p.].

3096   _____. Siamese twins. A negro burlesque sketch. Arranged by Charles White... New York, The De Witt publishing house, 1874. 6p.

3097   _____. Vilikens and Dinah, a Negro farce, written and arranged by C. White... Chicago, T. S. Denison [n.d.]. 7p. On cover: The Ethiopian drama.

3098   WHITE, WILLIAM CHARLES, 1777-1818. The clergyman's daughter; a tragedy, in five acts; by William Charles White. As performed at the Boston theatre... Boston, Printed by Joshua Belcher, 1810. 96p.

3099   _____. The poor lodger; a comedy, in five acts; by William Charles White... As performed at the Boston theatre... Boston, Printed by Joshua Belcher, 1811. 90p.

3100   WHITEHEAD, WILLIAM, 1715-1785. The Roman father; a tragedy, in five acts; by William Whitehead, esq. As performed at the Theatre Royal, Covent Garden... With remarks by Mrs. Inchbald. London, Longman, Hurst, Rees, Orme, and Brown [n.d.]. 52p. front. (Inchbald, Mrs. Elizabeth. The British theatre... London, 1808. v. 14 [no. 4]).
       An adaptation, with considerable changes, of Corneille's "Horace."

3101   WHITWORTH, PHYLLIS. John Wesley, a play in three acts. London, The Epworth Press [n.d.]. 101p. illus.

3102   WIDMER, KATE MAYHEW. "The waif of Smith's pocket," a drama in four acts, founded upon F. Bret Harte's sketch M'liss. San Francisco, Francis and Valentine, printers, 1878. 32p.

3103   WIGAN, ALFRED. A model of a wife. A farce, in one act... as first performed at the Theatre Royal, Lyceum... January 27, 1845... New York, Robert M. De Witt [n.d.]. 13p.

3104   WILBRANDT, ADOLF. The Master of Palmyra. 1914. (In Kuno Francke, ed., The German classics of the nineteenth and twentieth century [New York, The German publication society, 1914], v. 16, p. 10-99). Translated by Charles Wharton Stork.

WILDE, OSCAR

3105   WILDE, OSCAR, 1854-1900. The Duchess of Padua, a play; by
        Oscar Wilde. New York, P. R. Reynolds [1907]. 6 p.ℓ.,
        209p. [1]p.

3106   WILEY, SARA KING. The coming of Philibert. New York, The
        Macmillan co., 1907. 163p.

3107   _____. Dante and Beatrice. New York and London, The
        Macmillan co., 1909. 130p.

3108   WILKINS, W. HENRI. The reward of crime; or, The love of gold,
        a drama of Vermont in two acts... Clyde, Ohio, A. D. Ames,
        1880. 20p.

3109   WILKS, THOMAS EDGERTON. ... Ben the boatswain; or, Sailors'
        sweethearts. A nautical drama, in three acts... New York,
        Samuel French [n.d.]. 33p. (French's standard drama,
        no. clxix).

3110   _____. Halvei the unknown. An original drama, in three acts...
        London, Thomas Hailes Lacy [n.d.]. 44p.

3111   _____. Michael Erle: The maniac lover; or, The fayre lass of
        Lichfield. A romantic original drama, in two acts... New
        York, Samuel French [n.d.]. 24p.

3112   _____. ... Raffaelle the reprobate; or, The secret mission
        and the signet ring. A drama, in two acts... Boston,
        William V. Spencer [n.d.]. 32p. (Spencer's Boston
        theatre, no. civ).

3113   _____. ... The roll of the drum; a romantic drama, in three
        acts... London, John Duncombe [n.d.]. 33p. front.
        (Duncombe's edition).

3114   _____. ... The seven clerks; or, The three thieves and the
        denouncer. An original romantic drama, in two acts...
        New York, Samuel French [n.d.]. 27p. (French's American
        drama, no. xv).

3115   _____. ... Wenlock of Wenlock; or, The spirit of the black
        mantle. A melodrama, in three acts... New York, Samuel
        French [n.d.]. 30p. (French's standard drama, no. cxxxi).

3116   WILLIAMS, BARNEY. ... Irish assurance and yankee modesty, an
        original farce in two acts... New York, Samuel French
        [n.d.]. 24p. (French's American drama, no. lxiv).

3117 WILLIAMS, CHARLES. Gonzalvo; or, The corsair's doom; a
tragedy in five acts, The elopement; a petit comedy in two
acts, Neoma, in three cantos, and other poems. Philadelphia,
T. K. and P. G. Collins, Printers, 1848. 163p.

3118 WILLIAMS, ESPY WILLIAM HENDRICKS, 1852-1908. Espy Williams'
Parrhasius; a southerner returns to the classics. Edited
with an introduction by Paul T. Nolan. Lexington, 1958.
x, 22p.

3119 _____. Selected works of Espy Williams, southern playwright.
Edited with an introduction by Paul T. Nolan. Lexington,
1960. xvi, [2], 295p. music.

3120 _____. ... Witchcraft; or, The witch of Salem. A legend of
old New England. In five acts. By Espy W. H. Williams...
New Orleans, E. A. Brandao and co., 1886. 53p.

3121 WILLIAMS, FRANCIS HOWARD, 1844-1922. The Princess Elizabeth.
A lyric drama. By Francis H. Williams. Philadelphia,
Claxton, Remsen and Haffelfinger, 1880. 212p.

3122 _____. A reformer in ruffles, a comedy in three acts...
[Philadelphia] The author [1883]. 56p.

3123 _____. Theodora; a Christmas pastoral. By Francis Howard
Williams. Philadelphia, J. B. Lippincott and co. [1882].
30p.

3124 WILLIAMS, GEORGE W. Cleveland's reception party. An original
farce in three scenes... Clyde, Ohio, Ames' publishing co.,
1893. 9p.

3125 WILLIAMS, HENRY LLEWELLYN. The black chap from Whitechapel.
An eccentric Negro piece... New York, Robert M. De Witt
[n.d.]. 14p.

3126 _____. Bobolino, the black bandit. A musical farce. New
York, De Witt, 1880. 8p.

3127 _____. The darkey drama; collection of approved Ethiopian
acts, scenes, interludes, etc.... Part first. London,
Thomas Hailes Lacy [n.d.]. 74p.

3128 _____. Go and get tight! An Ethiopian farce in one scene.
New York, The De Witt publishing house, 1880. 9p.

WILLIAMS, HENRY LLEWELLYN

3129   WILLIAMS, HENRY LLEWELLYN. The Lime-kiln club in an uproar!
        And Ethiopian drollery. In one scene. Chicago, The
        Dramatic publishing co., 1891. 8p.

3130   _____. The moko marionettes. An Ethiopian eccentricity.
        Founded on the laughable absurdity by J. F. McArdle,
        called "The Marionettes." In one act and two scenes.
        New York, De Witt, 1880. 13p.

3131   _____. Sparking. A comedietta, in one act and one scene.
        Founded on L'étincelle of Edouard Pailleron... New York,
        De Witt, Publisher, 1882. 19p.

3132   _____. Wax works at play. Chicago, T. S. Denison [1894].
        12p.

3133   WILLIAMS, MONTAGU. "B. B." An original farce in one act, by
        Montagu Williams and Francis Cowley Burnand. London,
        Thomas Hailes Lacy [n.d.]. 18p.

3134   WILLIAMS, THOMAS JOHN, 1824-1874. Cabman no. 93; or, Found
        in a four wheeler, a farce in one act, by Thomas J.
        Williams. New American ed., correctly reprinted from the
        original authorized acting edition... New York, H.
        Roorbach, c1889. 24p. (On cover: Roorbach's American
        edition of acting plays. no. 4).

3135   _____. A charming pair. A farce, in one act... As first
        produced at the Royal Princess' Theatre, London, on May 27,
        1863... New York, Robert M. De Witt [n.d.]. 18p.

3136   _____. Dandelion's dodges. A farce. Boston, Walter H.
        Baker and co. [n.d.]. 21p.

3137   _____. Ici on parle français; or, The major's mistake; a
        farce in one act by Thomas J. Williams. New American ed.,
        correctly reprinted from the original authorized acting
        edition, with the original casts of the characters,
        synopsis of incidents [etc.]... New York, H. Roorbach,
        c1889. 23p. diagr. (On cover: Roorbach's American
        edition of acting plays, no. 12).

3138   _____. Little Daisy. A comic drama, in one act... London,
        Thomas Hailes Lacy [n.d.]. 22p.

WILLS, ANTHONY E.

3139   _____. ... A terrible tinker! A farce in one act, by Thomas
        J. Williams, esq. ... New York, F. French [187-]. 22p.
        (French's minor drama. no. 320).
            Imperfect: p. 9-10 wanting.

3140   _____. ... Turn him out: A farce in one act... New York,
        Samuel French [n.d.]. 18p. (French's minor drama,
        no. cclxli).

3141   _____. Who is who? or, All in a fog, a farce in one act, by
        Thomas J. Williams. New American edition correctly re-
        printed from the original authorized acting edition...
        New York, H. Roorbach [c1889]. 26p. (On cover: Roorbach's
        American edition of acting plays. no. 21).

3142   WILLIAMS, TICKNOR C. When the Paw-Paw County went dry.
        Lebanon, Ohio, March bros., 1911. 55p.

3143   WILLIAMS, WILLIAM HENRY, 1797?-1846. The wreck; or, The
        buccaneer's bridal: a domestic burletta, in two acts, by
        W. H. Williams, esq. Printed from the acting copy, with
        remarks, biographical and critical, by D.-G. ... As per-
        formed at the Theatres Royal... London, G. H. Davidson
        [n.d.]. 52p. incl. front. (Cumberland's Minor theatre.
        London [ca. 1830-55] v. 4 [no. 6]).
            "Founded on a popular work 'The tales of a voyager'."--
        Remarks.
            "As performed at Sadler's Wells' theatre, Feb. 9, 1830."
        Remarks by George Daniel, editor of the series.

3144   WILLS, ANTHONY E., 1880-   . A count of no account, a farce
        comedy in three acts. New York, Fitzgerald publishing
        corp., 1905. 60p.

3145   _____. Country folks, a comedy drama in three acts, by
        Anthony E. Wills... Boston, W. H. Baker and co., 1911.
        58p. On cover: Baker's edition of plays.

3146   _____. A football romance; a college play in four acts, by
        Anthony E. Wills... New York, Dick and Fitzgerald, 1912.
        74p.

3147   _____. The gypsy, a drama in three acts (adapted from the
        French) by Anthony E. Wills... New York, Dick and
        Fitzgerald, 1911. 55p.

WILLS, ANTHONY E.

3148   WILLS, ANTHONY E. Just plain folks, a comedy drama of rural
        life, in three acts, by Anthony E. Wills... New York,
        Dick and Fitzgerald, 1910. 50p.

3149   _____. Liberty corners, a rural comedy drama in four acts.
        Boston, Walter H. Baker and co. [1905]. 90p.

3150   _____. Never again; a farce in three acts (adapted from the
        German) by Anthony E. Wills... New York, Dick and
        Fitzgerald, 1912. 52p.

3151   _____. Our wives, a farce in three acts, by Anthony E. Wills...
        Boston, W. H. Baker and co., 1910. 49p. On cover:
        Baker's edition of plays.

3152   _____. Too many husbands, a farce in two acts (adapted from
        the French) by Anthony E. Wills... New York, Dick and
        Fitzgerald, 1911. 51p.

3153   WILLS, WILLIAM GORMAN, 1828-1891. Hinko; or, The headsman's
        daughter. A romantic play, in a prologue and five acts.
        Founded on Madame von Birch-Pfeiffer's dramatization of
        Ludwig Storch's novel. New York, Robert M. De Witt [n.d.].
        40p.

3154   _____. A little tramp; or, Landlords and tenants. A comedy
        drama in prologue and three acts. By W. G. Wills...
        London, Printed by A. Andrews, 1884. 61p.
            Produced under title "The young tramp."   The stage
        encycl.; Freeman Wills, "W. G. Wills, dramatist and
        painter."

3155   WILSON, ARTHUR, 1595-1652. ... The Swisser, publié d'après
        un manuscrit inédit avec une introduction et des notes,
        par Albert Feuillerat... Paris, Rischbacher, 1904.
        cxxii, 112p., 1ℓ. CONTENTS: Introduction: 1. ptie.
        Les aventures d'Arthur Wilson. 2. ptie. L'oeuvre
        littéraire de Wilson. Appendices. Bibliographie des
        oevrages cités dans l'introduction (p. [cxix]-cxxii). -
        The Swisser. - Notes.

3156   WILSON, FREDERICK H. Uncle Si; a comedy in four acts;
        originally produced... under the title of "Paradise
        regained." By Frederick H. Wilson. Boston, W. H. Baker
        and co., 1900. 48p. On cover: Baker's edition of plays.

WOODMAN, HANNAH REA

3157 WILSON, J. CRAWFORD. The Gitanilla; or, The children of the Zincali. A drama, in three acts... London, Thomas Hailes Lacy [n.d.]. 50p.

3158 [WILSON, LAWRENCE MAURICE] d. 1964. The hider, a one-act play by L. Decoteau [pseud.] [Montreal, P.Q., The author, n.d.]. [21]p.
    Coteau is the native village of the author.

3159 WILSTACH, PAUL. Thais; "The story of a sinner who became a saint and a saint who sinned"; a play in four acts. Indianapolis, Bobbs-Merrill co., 1911. 150p.

3160 WILTON, M. J. Fun in a cooper's shop. An original Ethiopian sketch. New York, The De Witt publishing house [n.d.]. 9p.

3161 WINBOLT, FREDERICK. Philip of Macedon, a tragedy. London, Alexander Moring, 1904. 98p.

3162 WINKLE, WILLIAM. A great success. A comedy, in three acts. New York, The De Witt publishing house [n.d.]. 46p.

3163 WINSTANLEY, W. The hypocrite unmask'd: a comedy, in five acts. By W. Winstanley... New York, Printed for the author by G. F. Hopkins, 1801. 94p.

3164 WINTERS, ELIZABETH. Columbia, the gem of the ocean, dialogue. Chicago, A. Flanagan [1899]. 12p.

3165 No Entry.

3166 WOOD, ARTHUR. A bilious attack. A farce, in one act... New York, Samuel French and son [n.d.]. 15p.

3167 WOOD, ELLEN (PRICE) "Mrs. Henry Wood", 1814-1887. East Lynne; a drama in five acts, adapted from the famous novel of that name, by Mrs. Henry Wood... Philadelphia, The Penn publishing co., 1894. vii, 5-52p. On cover: Keystone edition of popular plays.

3168 WOODALL, ALLEN E. Lepidus celebrates [n.p., n.d.]. 3p. (American Classical League Service Bureau, No. 554).

3169 WOODMAN, HANNAH REA, 1870-   . Billy Ben's pirate play, a dress rehearsal in one act. By H. Rea Woodman. Franklin, Ohio, Eldridge entertainment house [1912]. 23p.

329

WOODMAN, HANNAH REA

3170   WOODMAN, HANNAH REA. The cinder maid, a romantic comedy for
        little folks, in four scenes. By Rea Woodman... Franklin,
        Ohio, Eldridge entertainment house, 1912. 18p.

3171   _____. The clever doctor. Adapted from Grimm's tale, "The
        clever doctor." A dramatic satire in five acts. By Rea
        Woodman... Franklin, Ohio, Eldridge entertainment house,
        1912. 37p.

3172   _____. Galliger, a high school comedy in three acts. With a
        prologue. By Rea Woodman... Franklin, Ohio, Eldridge
        entertainment house, 1911. 52p.

3173   _____. His uncle John. A play in three acts, with a prologue.
        By H. Rea Woodman... Franklin, Ohio, Eldridge entertainment
        house, 1908. 39p.

3174   _____. The honest shoemaker, a domestic play for little folks,
        in four scenes. Adapted from Grim's [!] fairy tale, "The
        shoemaker and the elves." By Rea Woodman... Franklin,
        Ohio, Eldridge entertainment house, 1912. 16p.

3175   _____. The master's birthday. A play for children, in three
        acts... By H. Rea Woodman... Franklin, Ohio, Eldridge
        entertainment house, 1908. 37p.

3176   _____. The oaten cakes. An historical play for little folks,
        in three scenes. By H. Rea Woodman... Franklin, Ohio,
        Eldridge entertainment house, 1912. 18p.

3177   _____. Preserving a Smith, a burlesque of shadows, in three
        acts, by Rea Woodman... Franklin, Ohio, Eldridge entertain-
        ment house, 1911. 50p.

3178   _____. Prof. Grindem: his commencement. A play in three
        acts, and an epilogue. [By] H. Rea Woodman... Franklin,
        Ohio, Eldridge entertainment house, 1907. 51p.

3179   _____. The rescue of Prince Hal, a comedy of manners, in
        three acts and an epilogue, by Rea Woodman... Franklin,
        Ohio, Eldridge entertainment house, 1911. 51p.

3180   _____. She organized a club. A farce in two acts and a
        prologue. By H. Rea Woodman... Franklin, Ohio, Eldridge
        entertainment house, 1903. 52p.

3181   WOODS, VIRNA, 1864-1903. The Amazons; a lyrical drama, by
       Virna Woods. Meadville, Pennsylvania, Flood and Vincent,
       1891. 73p.

3182   WOODWARD, JOHN A. Madame is abed. Vaudeville, in one act and
       one scene. Translated and adapted by John A. Woodward.
       Boston, Charles H. Spencer, 1871. 16p.

3183   WOODWORTH, SAMUEL, 1785-1842. La Fayette; or, The castle of
       Olmütz. A drama, in three acts, as performed at the New
       York Park theatre, with unbounded applause. By Samuel
       Woodworth... New York, Circulating library and dramatic
       repository, 1824. 50p.

3184   WOOLER, JOHN PRATT, 1824-1878. The haunted mill: an operetta,
       in one act... the music by Mallandaine. London, Thomas
       Hailes Lacy [n.d.]. 15p.

3185   _____. Locked in. A comedietta, in one act... as first per-
       formed... Sept. 17th, 1870... New York, Robert M. De Witt
       [n.d.]. 13p.

3186   _____. Love in livery! A farce, in one act... New York,
       O. A. Roorbach, Jr. [n.d.]. 24p.

3187   _____. Marriage at any price. An original farce, in one act
       ... as first performed at the Royal Strand Theatre, London
       ... July 28, 1862... New York, Robert M. De Witt [n.d.].
       20p.

3188   _____. Old Phil's birthday. A serio-comic drama, in two acts.
       London, Thomas Hailes Lacy [n.d.]. 36p.

3189   _____. ... A winning hazard: an original comedietta, in one
       act. By J. P. Wooler. (In The New York drama. New York,
       c1880. no. 58. p. [26]-32). Caption title.
           Preceded by Dickens' No thoroughfare and Lancaster's
       Manager's daughter.

3190   WRIGHT, A. L. The beggar Venus, a romantic drama in three
       acts. Chicago, T. S. Denison [1888]. 54p.

3191   WYATT, FRANK. Mrs. Temple's telegram, a farce in three acts
       by Frank Wyatt and William Morris. New York and London,
       Samuel French, 1908. 137p.

WYETH, ALBERT LANG

3192   WYETH, ALBERT LANG. Cupid on wheels, a comedy in two acts.
       Philadelphia, The Penn publishing co., 1908. 21p.

3193   WYLIE, JOHN EDWARD. ... Snowed in. A comedy in three acts...
       New York, Samuel French and son [n.d.]. 49p. (French's
       parlor comedies, no. 4).

3194   Xerxes the Great; or, The battle of Thermopyle: a patriotic
       drama. In five acts... Philadelphia, Printed by G.
       Palmer, 1815. 42p.

3195   YANCEY, SHEROD ANNE. The nine Muses; a playlet in verse
       [n.p., n.d.]. 3p. (American Classical League Service
       Bureau, No. 727).

3196   YEATS, WILLIAM BUTLER, 1865-1939. The land of heart's desire.
       Boston, Walter H. Baker and co. [n.d.]. 21p.

3197   YOUNG, CHARLES L. Drifted apart. An original domestic
       sketch, in one act... New York, T. Henry French [n.d.].
       14p.

3198   YOUNG, EULA M. A day without Latin: a playlet in English
       showing the value of Latin. [n.p., n.d.]. 4p. (American
       Classical League Service Bureau, No. 242).

3199   YOUNG, LAURENCE DITTO. The iceman: a farce in one act, by
       Laurence Ditto Young. Philadelphia, The Penn publishing
       co., 1909. 24p.

3200   YOUNG, MARGARET. Kitty. A dramatic sketch. For two female
       characters. Chicago, The Dramatic publishing co. [n.d.].
       11p.

3201   [YOUNG, MARTHA] 1868-   . Plantation songs for my lady's
       banjo, and other Negro lyrics and monologues, by Eli
       Shepperd [pseud.]; with pictures from life by J. W. Otts.
       New York, R. H. Russell, 1901. 150p. incl. plates. front.

3202   YOUNG, RIDA JOHNSON, 1875-   Brown of Harvard, a play in
four acts, by Rida Johnson Young... New York, S. French;
[etc., etc.] 1909. 85p. (On cover: French's standard
library edition).

3203   [YOUNG, WILLIAM H.]. Journal of an excursion, from Troy, N. Y.,
to Gen. Carr's headquarters at Wilson's landing. (Fort
Pocahontas) on the James river, Va., during the month of
May, 1865. By one of the party. Troy, N. Y., Priv.
print., 1871. 59p. Dialogue.

3204   Your past is present, by the students of Sister M. Huberts
[n.p., n.d.]. 3p. (American Classical League Service
Bureau, No. 721).

3205   You're tied to Latin: a playlet or radio sketch, by the
students of Sister M. Concepta, R.S.M. Mount St. Mary's
Academy, Little Rock, Arkansas. [n.p., n.d.]. 5p.
(American Classical League Service Bureau, No. 635).

3206   ZANGWILL, ISRAEL, 1864-1926. The next religion, New York,
The Macmillan co., 1912. 194p.

3207   ZEDIKER, N. Family discipline, a monologue, in one scene
(for a child)... Clyde, Ohio, A. D. Ames, 1886. 5p.

3208   _____. My day and now-a-days, a monologue, in one scene...
(for a child) Clyde, Ohio, A. D. Ames, 1886. 5p.

3209   [ZSCHOKKE, HEINRICH], 1771-1848. Abaellino, the great bandit.
Translated from the German, and adapted to the New-York
theatre. By William Dunlap... New-York, Published by
D. Longworth, at the Shakspeare gallery, near the theatre.
L. Nichols, printer, 1802. 82p. (The New York theatre.
vol. 1 [no. 1]).

Title Index

The A string, 3016.
Aaron and Theodosia; or, The fate of the Burrs, 1633.
Aaron Boggs, freshman, 1102.
Aaron Burr, 1990, 2144.
Aar-u-ag-oos; or, An East Indian drug, 2887.
Abällino der grosse Bandit. See 1553.
Abaellino, the great bandit, 3209.
The abandoned bride, 2783.
Abandoned farms, 2526.
L'abbé de l'epée. See 1198.
Abbé Lawrence, 539.
The Abbertons, 2428.
The abbot's map, 554.
Abduction, 1664.
Abelard and Heloise, 983, 2954.
Abishag the Shulamite, 365.
Abon Hassan; or, The hunt after happiness, 2870.
About four o'clock, 116.
About Thebos, 139.
Above the clouds, 83. See 95.
Abraham and Isaac. See 2683.
Abraham Lincoln, 399, 472, 756, 1983.
Abroad and at home, 1207, 1207A.
The absconder, 796.
Absent treatment, 1210, 2765.
The absent-minded suffragette, 1661.
Absinthe, 2815. See 1720.
The absinthe fiend, 1098.
Absorbing passion, 2240.
Abu Hassan, 1307.
Abyssinia; or, The Negus, 793.
Abyssinia, 2680.
Acacia cottage, 2013.
The academy of stars, 1488.
The Acharnians. See 58.
Achilles. See 284.
Achilles; or, Iphigenia in Aulis, 2274.
Achilles in Scyros, 283.

335

Acting drunk

Acting drunk. See 1626.
The actor; or, A son of Thespis, 1975.
The actor of all work; or, The first and second floor, 526.
Actus Fatis, 5.
Adelaide of Wulfingen. See 2934.
Adhemar. See 1443.
Adolphe et Clara. See 1427.
Adolphus and Clara. See 1427.
The adopted child, 216.
Adrift, 77.
The adulateur, 3076.
Advent, 2804.
The adventure of Lady Ursula, 1217.
The adventures of a college bride. See 156.
The adventures of a love letter. See 1712, 2696.
The adventures of the forefathers of New-England. See 590.
The adventures of Ulysses, 1083.
Adversity. See 868.
The advertising girls, 2435.
Advice to husbands, 1469.
Adzuma; or, The Japanese wife, 61.
Aeneas and Dido. See 1068.
Aeneid. See 1836, 1995.
The afflicted family; or, A doctor without a diploma, 2888.
The affrighted officers. See 229.
The Africans; or, War, love, and duty, 527.
After a storm comes a calm, 1852. See 1860.
After all. See 1820.
After dark, 239.
After Euripides' "Electra." See 125.
After taps, 945.
After the play, 2022.
Aftermath, 2371.
Afterwards, 2366.
Agamemnon, 22. See 547, 1721.
Aglavaine and Selysette. See 1668.
Agnes de Vere; or, The wife's revenge, 368.
The agreeable hours of human life. See 277.
Aida, 961.
L'aiglon, 2417.
The "Alabama," 1853.
Alabama, 2926.
Aladdin; or, The wonderful lamp, 928, 2012.
An alarm of fire, 1024.
The Albany depot, 1245.
The Alcaid; or, The secrets of office, 1418.
The alcalde of Zalamea. See 438.
Alcanor. See 599.

Ames' series of medleys, tableaux, pantomimes, recitations, dialogues, etc.

Ames' series of medleys, tableaux, pantomimes, recitations, dialogues, etc., 800.
Among the lions. See 1760.
Among the moonshiners; or, A drunkard's legacy, 1636.
Amor omnia vincit, 231.
Amoroso, king of Little Britain, 2181.
Les amours de Cléopâtre. See 2681.
Amphitruo. See 2222.
An ample apology, 2367.
Amusement for a winter's evening. See 2527.
Amy Robsart. See 1274.
The ancestress, 1030.
The ancestress! or, The doom of Barostein!, 1523.
André, 786, 1581.
André Fortier, the hero of the Calaveras, 2438.
Andre the Savoyard. See 1443.
Andromache, 1942, 2275.
Andy Blake; or, The Irish diamond, 240.
Andy Freckles, the mischievous boy, 2285.
The angel of the attic, 1896.
Angelo. See 1274.
Angels and ministers, 1220.
Anna Karenina. See 516.
Anne Blake. See 1698.
Anne Boleyn. See 234.
Annie, 364.
The anniversary. See 483.
A. D. 1813; or, America's triumph, 2802.
A. D. 1912, 1837.
A. D. 2000; or, The century plants, 1431.
Another glass, 1897.
Another way out, 1475. See 1476.
Antichrist. See 1695.
Antigone. See 547.
Anti-matrimony, 1645.
Antinoüs, 994.
The antiquary, 2923.
Antony and Cleopatra, 2531, 2532.
Anything for a change, 308.
Apollo in mourne, 2426.
Apollo's oracle, 2940.
The apostate, 2656.
Apples. See 2819.
Apples that glitter like gold may be green. See 1458.
The apprentice, 1935.
An Arabian night in the nineteenth century, 1927.
Arden of Feversham. See 2239.

The avenger of humble life

The avenger of humble life. See 1183.
The awakening, 466.
The awakening of Barbison. See 1007.
Aylmere; or, The bondman of Kent, 536.
The Aztec god, 2292, 2293.
"B. B.", 3133.
Babie, 669.
The baby, 3049.
The baby elephant, 2778.
Bacchides. See 2221, 2222.
A bachelor's baby, 1386.
The bachelor's bedroom; or, Two in the morning. See 1713.
The bachelor's box. See 1738.
Back from Californy; or, Old clothes, 78.
A bad case. See 1722.
A bad job, 1610.
Badger's green. See 2699.
A bailiff's bet. See 2097.
A baker's dozen,
Balboa. See 1663.
Ballads of bravery, 85.
The balloon, 646.
Le Bandit. See 2182.
The bandit host; or, The lone hut of the swamp, 2400.
The banditti; or, Love's labyrinth. See 2000.
Banishing the bitters. See 1626.
The bank cashier, 2055.
The banker's daughter; or, Lilian's last love, 1229.
The banks of the Elbe. See 2180.
The banks of the Hudson; or, The Congress trooper, 716.
Banned by the censor. See 1759.
Bar Haven. See 1727.
Barbara, 1326.
Barbarossa, 354.
The barber of Paris. See 1443.
The barber of Seville. See 1721.
The barber pards. See 967.
The barbers of Bassora, 1857.
Barbesieu; or, The troubadour, 1437.
The bard, the baron, the beauty, the buffer and the bogey. See 55.
Barney the baron, 41.
Barney's resolution. See 1626.
Le baron de Fourchevif. See 1461.
The barrack room, 165.
The Barringtons' "at home", 118.
The bashful man. See 1804.
The basket-maker, 1998.
The Battle of Bothwell Brigg, 852.

Beyond the Rockies

Beyond the Rockies. See 11.
The bicyclers, 117.
The big bonanza. See 626.
A bilious attack, 3166.
Bill Perkins' proposin' day, 2116.
Billy Ben's pirate play, 3169.
Billy's little love affair, 835.
The birds, 56. See 58, 547, 2188.
Birds of a feather, 944.
Birds of prey; or, A duel in the dark, 2376.
Birth. See 2382.
The birth of Galahad, 1224. See 1225.
The birth of Roland, 1169.
The birth place of podgers, 1206.
The birthright. See 1603.
The bittern's swamp. See 36.
Black art, 2052.
The black chap from Whitechapel, 3125.
A black diamond, 2016.
Black 'ell. See 1681.
The Black Maskers, 49.
The black Ole Bull, 1489.
The black phantom. See 44.
The black shoemaker, 3081.
The black statue, 3082.
The black tie. See 1762.
Black, white, and grey. See 2385.
The blackest tragedy of all; or, A peep behind the scenes, 1490.
Black-eyed Susan; or, The little bill that was taken up, 406.
Black-eyed Susan; or, "All in the downs", 1330. See 1334.
The blacksmith of Antwerp, 1999.
Blanchette, 301.
Blennerhassett, 2143.
Blind. See 1669.
The blind bargain; or, Hear it out, 2337.
The blind boy, 1419.
Blinks and Jinks, 1491.
The blockheads; or, The affrighted officers, 229.
The blood red knight! or, The fatal bridge!, 148.
Bloomer girls; or, Courtship in the twentieth century, 910.
Blow for blow, 422.
The blue and gray. See 3018.
Blue Beard; or, The bride, the bogie and the blood, 1317.
Blue Beard; or, Female curiosity. See 527A.
Blue Beard. See 2188.
The blue bird. See 1670.
The blue bird of paradise. See 2188, 2200.
Blue devils, 528.

Breaking the engagement, 2056.
Breezy Point, 1570.
Brian Boroihme; or, The maid of Erin, 1439.
Brian O'Linn, 279.
Bric-a-brac, 280.
The bridal of the borders. See 1597.
The bridal ring, 2338. See 29.
The bridals of Messina. See 1440.
The bride, 80.
The bride of Lammermoor, 435, 520. See 950.
The bride of Ludgate, 1331.
The bride of Messina. See 2473.
Bride roses, 1246.
The bride, the bogie and the blood. See 1317.
The bridge of Tresino. See 447.
The brigand, 2182.
The brigands of Calabria, 302.
Bright Bohemia. See 1977.
Britannicus, 2277.
Broken bonds, 1179.
Broken fetters, 2958.
The broken heart. See 582.
Broken hearts. See 976.
Broken links, 143.
The broken seal, 1517.
The broken sword, 740.
Broken ties, 2690.
Brother Ben, 1858.
Brother Jonathan, 412.
Brother Josiah, 2057.
A brother's love! See 1537.
The brothers of course. See 177.
Brown and the Brahmins; or, Captain Pop and the Princess Pretty-eyes!,
    2319
Brown of Harvard, 3202.
Brown's in town, 2852.
Bruce. See 651.
Brutus; or, The fall of Tarquin, 2074.
Bryan Station, 611.
Bryan's speech with the wind knocked out. See 124.
Bubbles of the day, 1332. See 1333.
The buccaneer's bridal. See 3143.
The building of the ship. See 2040.
The bull-fighter; or, The bridal ring, 29.
A bunch of roses, 656.
The burglar. See 443.
Burglars three. See 659.
The burglar's welcome, 1952.

Captured

Captured; or, The old maid's triumph, 176.
Capuletta, 451.
The card party. See 2188.
Carlmihan; or, The drowned crew!, 875.
Carlotta, 2415. See 643.
Carnac Sahib, 1351.
Carnival; or, Mardi gras in New Orleans, 2333.
The carnival at Naples, 741.
The carnival ball. See 165.
The carpenter of Rouen; or, The massacre of St. Bartholomew, 1372.
The carrier-pigeon. See 2139.
Carroty Nell, 1049.
A case for eviction, 2720.
A case for Sherlock Holmes, 285.
The case of rebellious Susan, 1352.
Caste. See 2382.
Castle adamant. See 977.
The castle of Andalusia, 2000.
The castle of Olival. See 1432.
The castle of Olmütz. See 3183.
The castle of Otranto. See 1323.
The cataract of the Ganges; or, The Rajah's daughter. See 1805.
Catching a governor. See 568.
The catechism, a kindly light, 952.
Catherine Howard; or, The throne, the tomb, and the scaffold, 2831.
Catherine Parr, 125. See 2683.
Catiline. See 1289.
The catspaw. See 1333.
"Caught at last", 1980.
Caught by the cuff, 1136.
Caught by the ears, 2504.
Caught in his own trap. See 1181.
The cave man, 865.
Cecil the seer, 2294. See 2292.
Le célibataire et l'homme marié. See 2247.
A centennial dramatic offering, 1121.
The century plants. See 1431.
Ceres, 594.
Cerisette. See 1443.
The chain of guilt; or, The inn on the heath, 2893.
Chains, 81.
The chamber of death. See 2956.
The champion of her sex, 90.
Chance and change. See 224.
The chancery suit!, 2089.
Chang-Ching-Fou! Cream of Tartar; or, The prince, the princess,
    and the mandarin. See 1700.
A change of base. See 601, 2762.

The Connecticut emigrant

The Cuban patriots, 2145.
Cuchilanca; or, The rancher's fate, 2702.
Cunigunda's vow. See 1792.
The cup. See 2920.
A cup of coffee, 2334.
A cup of tea, 1984.
Cupboard love, 1137.
Cupid, 1004.
Cupid and Psyche, 473.
Cupid on wheels, 3192.
Cupid's joke, 1444.
Cupid's partner, 286.
The curate's daughter. See 1074.
Curculio. See 2221.
A cure for the heartache, 1901, 1902, 1903.
The curfew, 2948.
Curtain raisers, 2139.
Cut off with a shilling, 2721.
A cyclone for a cent, 2117.
Cymbeline, 2546, 2547, 2548, 2549, 2550, 2551.
Cymon and Iphigenia. See 2188.
The cynic. See 1764.
Cyril's success, 423.
'D' company. See 1681.
Daddy Gray, 1086.
Daddy O'Dowd. See 258.
Dagobert, king of the Franks. See 2934.
Daily bread, 968, 969.
Daisy farm, 424.
Damon and Pythias, 3010.
The damsel of three skirts. See 1443.
Dan Wetherby's prize, 394.
The dancing barber, 2505.
The dancing girl, 1355.
Dandelion's dodges, 3136.
Dandy Dick, 2156.
The dandy dolls. See 896.
The danger signal, 671.
Daniel Rochat, 2439.
Daniels. See 1053.
The Danites in the Sierras. See 1768.
Dan'l Druce. See 976.
Dante, 2297, 2298.
Dante and Beatrice, 3107.
Daphne; or, The pipes of Arcadia. See 1745.
Darius Green an' his flyin' machine, 1178.
The darkey drama, 3127.
The darkey tragedian, 644, 2959.

The darkey's stratagem, 3083.
Dark's the hour before the dawn. See 846.
The daughter. See 1440.
A daughter of old Spain, 3064.
The daughter of the regiment. See 749.
A daughter to marry. See 2207.
A daughter's trials. See 2898.
Daulac. See 449.
David, 1485, 2352, 2353.
David Garrick. See 2382.
David of Bethlehem. See 842.
The dawn of liberty; or, Cadunt regum coronae; vicit libertas, 414.
The dawn of liberty, 3005.
Day after the fair, 2743, 2744.
The day after the wedding, 1409.
A day at Happy Hollow school, 3015.
Day in a Roman court, 660.
A day in Paris, 2506.
The day of dupes. See 996.
A day of reckoning, 2187.
A day well spent, 2036.
A day without Latin, 2521, 3198.
The days of Claude du Val. See 2979.
The days of Kirk and Monmouth. See 28.
A day's pleasure. See 1424.
De daughter of de regiment, 838.
De trouble begins at nine, 3084.
The deacon, 615.
The deacon entangled, 2023.
Deacon Jones' wife's ghost, 2286.
Deacon Slocum's presence of mind, 2118.
The dead alive, 1494.
The dead heart, 3056.
Dead reckoning, 545.
The dead shot, 369.
The dead witness; or, Sin and its shadow, 2327.
Deaf and dumb; or, The orphan protected, 1198.
Deaf and dumb; or, The orphan. See 2934.
Deaf as a post, 1495, 2243.
The dear departed. See 1218.
Dearer than life, 425.
The death letter. See 2946.
The death of Agrippina. See 2861.
The death of Alexander, 125.
The death of Cleopatra. See 2689.
The death of General Montgomery, in storming the city of Quebec, 270.
The death of Life in London; or, Tom and Jerry's funeral, 1010.
The death of Rolla. See 2934.

The death of Wallenstein

Don't marry a drunkard to reform him

Don't marry a drunkard to reform him. See 1626.
The doom of Barostein! See 1523.
The doom of Devorgoil. See 2490.
El Dorado, 2955.
Dorothy's fortune. See 1333.
"Dot pooty gompliment", 700.
Douaumont; or, The return of the soldier Ulysses. See 1801.
A double life, 2936.
Double valet. See 1325.
The double-bedded room, 1865.
The Dover road. See 1777.
Doves in a cage. See 1334.
Down East, 10.
Down in Dixie, 2961.
Down our street. See 2699.
The downfall of Hagdi-Ali-Bashaw. See 2714.
The dragon knight; or, The queen of beauty!, 2788.
The drama at home; or, An evening with Puff. See 2188.
The drama of destiny--Karl Hanno, 940, 941.
The drama's levée; or, A peep at the past. See 2188.
The dramatist; or, Stop him who can, 2340.
Le drame de la rue de paix. See 192.
The drawback, 125.
A drawing-room car, 3020.
A dream at home. See 225.
Dreams; or, My Lady Clara, 2378.
Dreams. See 2382.
Dreams of delusion, 2693.
Dred; or, The Dismal Swamp, 325.
A dress rehearsal, 657. See 656.
Drifted apart, 3197.
Driven to the wall; or, True to the last, 41.
The dropping well of Knaresborough. See 30.
Dross; or, The root of evil, 76.
The drowned crew! See 875.
The drummer boy of Shenandoah, 1150.
The drunkard; or, The fallen saved, 2729.
The drunkard's children, 1347.
The drunkard's doom; or, The last nail, 2176.
A drunkard's legacy. See 1636.
The drunkard's warning, 2885.
The Dublin boy. See 240.
The Duchess de la Vallière. See 1599.
The Duchess of Dublin, 89.
The Duchess of Padua, 3105.
A dude in a cyclone. See 683.
Un duel en amour. See 1465.
A duel in the dark. See 2376.

The elevator, 1249. See 1267.
Elfie; or, The Cherrytree inn, 241.
Elfrida, 2364.
Elga, 1128.
An eligible situation. See 2488.
Elisabeth, ou Les exilés de Sibérie. See 2341.
Elizabeth Cooper, 1833.
Elizabeth Prinzessin von England. See 217.
Elizabeth, queen of England, 962.
Ella Rosenberg, 1420.
Elle est folle. See 2693.
Elmwood folks, 218.
Elopement, 1358.
The elopement. See 3117.
The elopement of Ellen, 3045.
The emigrant's daughter, 2306, 2945.
Emilia Galotti, 1545. See 2934.
Emily. See 1792.
Emperor and Galilean. See 1292.
Empire of Talinis, 153.
The enchanted island, 229A.
The enchanted isle; or, "Raising the wind" on the most approved
    principles, 310.
An enemy of the people. See 1290, 1292.
'Enery Brown, 1001.
L'enfant de Geneviève. See 240.
Engaged. See 976.
Engaged; or, Surrendered--hand and heart, 2431.
An engaged girl, 1283.
The English fleet, in 1342, 718.
The English traveller. See 905.
An Englishman's home, 770.
Enlisted for the war; or, The home-guard, 90, 830.
Enoch Arden. See 564.
The ensign. See 2934.
Entertainments for all the year, 701.
Enthusiasm, 80.
L'étincelle. See 3131.
The Epicurean. See 877.
Erechtheus. See 2858.
Ernest Maltravels. See 1735.
Es lebe das Leben. See 2822.
The escape. See 301.
Esmeralda, 2283. See 1274.
La española de Florencia, 436.
Espy Willimas' Parrhasius; a southerner returns to the classics, 3118.
Esther, 2279.
Estranged, 2494.

Faithful unto death

Faithful unto death. See 1097.
The falcon. See 2683, 2920.
The fall of Algiers, 849, 2077.
The fall of British tyranny; or, American triumphant, 1487.
The fall of Jerusalem. See 1774.
The fall of Rome. See 1436.
The fall of Tarquin. See 2074.
The fall of Troy, 850.
The fall of Tunis. See 2657.
The fall of Vicksburg. See 825.
A fallen idol, 1025.
The fallen saved. See 2729.
The Falls of Clyde, 2735.
False alarms; or, My cousin, 1421.
False delicacy. See 2934.
The false Demetrius. See 599.
False pretensions, 932.
False shame, 1452.
A familiar friend, 1526.
La famille Jabutot; ou, La veuve sans enfans. See 2990.
A family affair, 2963.
The family cure. See 907.
Family discipline, 3207.
The family exit. See 1476.
The family reunion, 230.
Family strife in Hapsburg, 1032.
A family strike, 673. See 672.
The family's pride. See 968.
Fanchon, the cricket, 3028.
Fancy free. See 1218.
Fanny and the servant problem, 1327.
Fantasio, 1945.
The fantasticks, 2419.
The far-away princess. See 2825.
The farce of Master Pathelin, 405.
Farm folks, 2994.
The farmer forsworn, 51.
The farmer's sons. See 1438.
The farmer's story, 196, 197.
The fascinators, 1105.
Fashion; or, Life in New York, 1929.
A fashionable physician. See 2409.
The fatal attachment. See 1213.
The fatal blow, 1118.
The fatal brand. See 2978.
The fatal bridge. See 148.
The fatal rubber, 125.
The fatal snow storm, 149.

The fate of the Burrs. See 1633.
The fate of the lily of St. Leonard's. See 2178.
The father; or, American Shandyism. 787.
The father, 2809. See 736.
Father and son; or, The rock of Charbonniere, 878.
Father Junipero Serra. See 1767.
Father Time and his children. See 1746.
A father's will. See 1699.
Faust, 122, 469. See 989, 2312.
Faustus, 2736.
The favourite of fortune. See 1698.
The fawn. See 1792.
The fawn in the forest. See 2188.
The fayre lass of Lichfield. See 3111.
Fazio; or, The Italian wife. See 1775.
A fearful tragedy in the seven dials, 2507.
Feast, 1016.
A feast in the wilderness, 1276.
Feast of Bacchus. See 284.
The feast of lights; or, Chanukon, 213.
Fedia, 801
Feed the brute, 2068.
Female curiosity. See 527A.
Fenris, the wolf, 1647.
Ferguson, of Troy, 1825.
Fernanda; or, Forgive and forget, 2440.
The festival of the Rosiere. See 1809.
A fête at Rosherville! See 2514.
Fettered. See 2133.
The fête at the Hermitage. See 1639.
Fickleness, thy name is man--not woman. See 413.
Fiesco. See 2471, 2476.
Fifteen years of a drunkard's live, 1335.
The fifth commandment. See 1218.
The fight of Sempach! See 1524.
The fighting race, 503.
La figlia del reggimento, 749.
La fille de Madame Angot. See 2497.
The finger of fate; or, The death letter, 2946.
The finger post. See 719.
The fire banner! See 33.
The fire fiend, 769.
The fire-bringer, 1824.
The fire-eater!, 2508.
Fireflies. See 2819.
The fireman, 1343.
Fireside diplomacy. See 2488.
A fireside story, 995.

Firmilian

Firmilian, 75.
The first and second floor. See 526.
The first born. See 968.
First come, first served, 1866. See 1860.
The first night; or, A peep behind the scenes, 869.
A first-class hotel. See 683.
Fish out of water, 1593.
Fisherman's luck, 3085.
Fit and Suitemall: fashions, 821.
Five acts of love, 153.
Five miles off; or, The finger post, 719.
Five o'clock tea, 1251, 1252. See 1260.
Five thousand a year, 720.
La flammina. See 2690.
A flash of lightning, 620.
Flies in the web, 326.
The flight to America; or, Ten hours in New York!, 2313.
The floating beacon, 879.
Flodden Field, 71.
The flower girl. See 1443.
The flower of the family, 91, 95, 898.
The flowers of the forest, 370.
The flowing bowl, 92.
The flutter of the goldleaf, 641.
The follies of a night, 2191.
Folly or saintliness. See 804.
Fontainbleau, 2000A.
A foolish investment, 1847.
A fool's paradise, 1042.
The fool's revenge, 2895, 2896, 2897. See 1274.
The fool's tragedy, 575.
A fool's wisdom, 2266.
A football romance, 3146.
For better or worse. See 1684.
For lack of evidence, 1513.
For love or money, 1026.
For myself alone, 1569.
For rent to-morrow, 1956.
For the red white and blue. See 914.
Forbidden fruit, 242, 243.
The forbidden guests. See 548.
The force of credulity. See 154.
A forced friendship. See 1755.
Foresight; or, My daughter's dowry, 1519.
The forest oracle; or, The bridge of Tresino, 447.
The foresters, Robin Hood and Maid Marian, 2919.
The forging of the ring. See 134.
Forgive and forget. See 2440.

Fulgens and Lucres

Fulgens and Lucres. See 1736.
Fun at Five Point school, 1059.
Fun in a cooper's shop, 3160.
Fun in a post office, 159.
Furianus gets a father, 934.
The furies. See 15.
Gale Breezely; or, The tale of a tar, 1348.
Galliger, 3172.
Galway practice in 1770. See 198.
The gamblers. See 872.
The gambler's fate; or, A lapse of twenty years, 2935.
The gambler's fate; or, Thirty years in a gamester's life. See 1778.
The game called Kiss. See 1412.
The game of life, 328.
The game of love, 329.
The gamester, 1829.
Le gamin de Paris. See 240.
Les ganaches. See 2383.
"The garden of paradise", 2660.
A garland to Sylvia, 1648.
The garroters. See 1260.
Gaspardo, the gondolier; or, The three banished men of Milan!, 32.
Gaston de Blondeville. See 1792.
Le gastronome sans argent. See 2396.
The gay deceivers; or, More laugh than love, 529.
A gay old man am I, 2495.
The gazette extraordinary, 1208.
The Gee Whiz, 46.
Gefährliche nachbarschaft. See 1812.
The geisha's wedding. See 1315.
Geneviève de Brabant. See 2496.
Gengangere. See 807.
The genius, 668. See 1205.
The gentle savage. See 343.
A gentle touch, 1390.
A gentleman from Idaho, 958.
The gentleman in black, 1527.
Gentlemen of the jury, 93.
George Barnwell, 1559.
The German baron. See 2758.
Gertrude Wheeler, M. D., 2050.
Das Gewissen. See 1904.
A ghost in spite of himself. See 1817.
The ghost story, 2880.
Ghosts, 1291. See 1292.
The ghost-seer. See 2471.
The gifted givers, 931.
The gifts of Mother Lingua, 1482.

Gil Blas; or, The boy of Santillane, 1637.
Gil Blas and the robbers of Asturias. See 1637.
Gilderoy; or, The bonnie boy, 150.
Giles Corey of the Salem Farms. See 1577.
Giles Corey, yeoman, 918.
Giorgione. See 2354.
Giovanni in London; or, The libertine reclaimed. See 1807.
The gipsey of Ashburnham Dell! See 446.
The gipsy girl of Paris. See 1087.
Giralda; or, The miller's wife, 3057.
The girl and the outlaw, 1391.
The girl from Klondike; or, Wide awake Nell, 772.
The girl from upper 7, 287.
Girl impersonations, 2456.
The girl in the coffin. See 754.
The girl in the picture, 2653.
The girl miner. See 662.
The girls of the period. See 2488.
The Gitanilla; or, The children of the Zincali, 3157.
Give up your gods, 2322.
The glass of fashion, 1043.
The glory of Columbia; her yeomanry, 788.
The glove, 208.
The gloves, 2717.
Das Glück im Winkel. See 2826.
Go and get tight!, 3128.
Go to bed Tom, 1905.
God. See 650, 652.
The goddess of love, 1957.
The goddess of reason, 1345.
Godfrida, 649.
God's heroes, 140.
God's promises. See 1695.
Goetz von Berlichingen. See 1721.
The Gogo family. See 1443.
The gold mine, 3.
The golden branch. See 2188.
The golden eagle; or, The privateer of '76, 1243.
The golden farmer; or, Jemmy Twitcher in England, 3058.
A golden fetter, 2133.
The golden fleece; or, Jason in Colchis and Medea in Corinth, 2193.
    See 2188.
The golden goblet, 155.
The golden gulch, 2964.
The golden legend. See 1579.
Gonzalvo; or, The corsair's doom, 3117.
The good fairy triumphant over the demon of discord! See 1113.
Good for nothing, 371.

Good King Wenceslas

Haunted hearts

Haunted hearts, 2694.
The haunted house, 955.
The haunted inn, 2092.
The haunted man, 2093.
The haunted mill; or, Con O'Ragen's secret, 1827.
The haunted mill, 3184.
Hazardous ground, 622.
Hazel Kirke, 1656.
He and she, 591.
He stoops to conquer; or, The virgin wife triumphant. See 1785.
He talked too much, 3003.
He would be a soldier, 2153.
The head of Romulus, 1044.
The headsman's daughter. See 3153.
Hear both sides, 1199.
Hear it out. See 2337.
Heart and hand, 1511.
The heart that squeaked. See 2775.
Heather. See 2819.
The heather field. See 1701.
Heaven and earth. See 421.
Hector, 1063.
Hedda Gabler. See 1292.
The heedless ones. See 619.
Heir at law. See 2336.
The heir of Mt. Vernon, 1445.
The heiress hunters, 1106.
Helen's funny babies, 775.
Hemmed in, 2780.
The Henrietta, 1230.
Henriquez, 80.
Henry Dunbar; or, A daughter's trials, 2898.
Henry Granden; or, The unknown heir, 214.
Her Cuban tea, 2119.
Her dearest friend, 2324.
Her first assignment, 288.
Her happiness. See 1205.
Her hero, 2709.
Her last rehearsal. See 1197.
Her Majesty's Ship "Pinafore"; or, The lass that loved a sailor, 973.
H. M. S. Pinafore. See 976.
H. M. S. Plum (His mollified sugar plum), 714.
Her neighbor's creed. See 443.
Her vote, 834.
Herakles, 1576.
Heralds of the dawn, 73, 3052.
The hereditary forester, 1592.
Heredity. See 1722, 2106.

The hermit's prophecy. See 171.
Hernani. See 1274, 1721.
Hernarne, 855.
The hero, 351.
Hero and Leander, 1033, 1312, 2487.
The hero of the gridiron, 540.
The hero of the lake; or, The victory of Commodore Perry, 858.
The hero of two wars. See 2991.
Herod, 2125.
Heroes. See 1310.
He's a lunatic, 613.
Heselrig. See 366.
The Hessian. See 1687.
Hiatus. See 2139.
Hiawatha, 1579.
Hicks at college, 2268.
The hidden spring, 269.
Hide and seek, 1594.
The hider, 3158.
High C, 2410.
High Jack, the heeler, 1497, 1498.
High, low, jack, and the game; or, The card party. See 2188.
High ways and by ways, 3059.
The highland reel, 2001, 2000B.
The highwayman's holiday, 2833.
Hildebrand. See 449.
Hindle wakes, 1219.
Hinko; or, The headsman's daughter, 3153.
Hippolytus. See 547.
His excellency the governor. See 1696.
His father's son, 1270.
His fifty kids, 1958.
His first brief. See 2488.
His Grace the duke. See 2794.
His Highness the Bey, 1239.
His house in order, 2157.
His last legs, 135.
His Lordship. See 656.
His luck. See 1205.
His lucky day, 265.
His Majesty's embassy, 127.
His mollified sugar plum. See 714.
His own enemy, 2723.
His uncle John, 3173.
His uncle's choice. See 2047.
His word of honor, 999.
A hit if you like it. See 2188.
Hit or miss, 2226A, 2227.

The hobby-horse

The hobby-horse, 2158.
Hofer, the Tell of the Tyrol, 880.
Hogan on the stand, 2323.
The hole in the wall, 2245. See 1815, 2492.
Holly Bush Hall; or, The track in the snow, 2834.
The holy city, 306.
The Holy Graal. See 1225.
The Homage of the arts, 2474.
Home, 2380. See 2382.
A home fairy, 6.
Home jewels. See 3035.
Home, sweet home. See 2076.
Home ties, 2995.
The home wreck, 564.
The home-guard. See 90, 830.
Homeopathy; or, The family cure, 907.
The homicides, 80.
L'homme aux trois culottes. See 1443.
L'homme gris. See 1374.
The honest man. See 425.
The honest shoemaker, 3174.
The honest Welshman. See 726.
Honesty, 2761.
Honesty is the best policy, 921, 1529. See 1679.
The honey-moon, 2949, 2950.
A honeymoon eclipse, 2890.
Honor, 2820.
The honor of a cowboy, 3006.
The honor of the Crequy. See 227.
Hop-o'-my-thumb; or, The seven league boots, 2706.
Horace, 552, 553. See 3100.
Horatius. See 553.
Horizon, 623.
Horseshoe Robinson; or, The battle of King's Mountain, 2883.
Hotel; or, Double valet. See 1325.
The hotel; or, The servant with two masters, 1324. See 1325.
Hotel healthy, 1090.
The hour and the man. See 1976.
The hourglass. See 736.
The house. See 1760.
A house divided. See 1078.
The house of Aspen. See 2490.
The house of candles. See 968.
The house of ladies, 1530.
The house of tragedy. See 868.
The house on the avenue; or, The little mischief-makers, 2423.
A household fairy, 2873.
The housekeeper. See 1334.

The illustrious stranger

The innkeeper's daughter, 2737.
An innocent villain. See 1310.
Ins and outs, 1531.
The insurrection at Harper's Ferry. See 2854.
The intelligence office, 1499.
An interview with the poet Horace, 1095.
Interviews; or, Bright Bohemia, 1977.
An intimate acquaintance. See 1310.
Intrigue; or, Married yesterday, 2246.
The intriguing footman; or, The humours of Harry Humbug. See 1665.
The intruder. See 1669.
The invincible prince; or, The island of Tranquil Delights, 2196.
    See also 2188.
The invincible ship. See 1450.
The invincibles, 1906.
Iolanthe. See 975.
Ion, 2875.
Iphigenia in Aulis. See 2274.
Iphigenia in Tauris, 990. See 547.
Iris, 1300, 2160.
Irish assurance and yankee modesty, 3116.
The Irish attorney; or, Galway practice in 1770, 198.
The Irish diamond. See 240.
The Irish emigrant. See 348, 857.
The Irish heiress. See 264.
The Irish linen peddler, 679.
The Irish lion, 376.
The Irish patriot. See 2330.
The Irish tiger, 1869.
The Irishman in London. See 1665.
The iron hand, 2965.
Irrésolu. See 1938.
Is he jealous?, 129.
Is she his wife? or, Something singular, 733.
Is the editor in?, 680, 681.
Isaac of York; or, Saxons and Normans at home, 2224.
Isabel, the pearl of Cuba, 2966.
Isabella, 2755.
The island of Calypso. See 2188.
The island of Jewels, 2197. See 2188.
The island of Tranquil Delights. See 2188, 2196.
The isle of Bong-Bong, 1240.
Israel Bruna, 712.
It is never too late to mend, 2335.
It passes by. See 1820.
The Italian wife. See 1775.
It's all in the pay streak. See 683.
Ivanhoe; or, The knight templar, 170.

Ivanhoe; or, The Jew's daughter

Ivanhoe; or, The Jew's daughter, 722.
Ivanhoe. See 2226.
Jack in the water; or, The ladder of life,   2314.
Jack Long; or, The shot in the eye,   1349.
Jack Sheppard,   377, 1073.
Jack Sheppard and Joe Blueskin; or, Amateur road agents,   777.
The Jack Trust. See 936.
Jack's the Lad,   1018.
The Jacobite,   2198.
James and John. See
James the First of Scotland. See 366.
Jane Eyre,   332.
Jane Shore,   2425.
Japan. See 1315.
The Japanese wife. See 61.
Jason and Medea,   125.
Jason in Colchis and Medea in Corinth.   See 2188, 2193.
Je dîne chez ma mère. See 1660.
Jean. See 1443.
Jean la Poste,   247.
Jean Valjean; or, The shadow of the law,   933.
Jeanne d'Arc,   123, 1649.
Jedediah Judkins, J. P.,   299.
Jedermann. See 843.
Jelf's,   3011.
Jemmy Twitcher in England. See 3058.
Jenny Lind at last; or, The Swedish nightingale,   2310.
Jessie Brown; or, The relief of Lucknow,   248.
Jessy Vere; or, The return of the wanderer,   1145.
Jesus,   816.
Le jeune mari. See 2257.
La jeunesse de Henri V. See 2075.
The Jew and the doctor,   723.
The Jew of Mogadore,   598.
The Jew of Venice,   2611.
The Jewess; or, The council of Constance. See 1808.
The Jewess,   2199.
The Jewess of Toledo,   1034.
The Jewish maiden's wrong. See 488.
The Jew's daughter. See 722.
Jimmie Jones; or, Our hopeful son,   1305.
Jim's beast. See 1760.
Joan of Arc; or, The maid of Orleans,   883, 2524, 2900.
Joconde; ou, Les coureurs d'aventures. See 1809.
Joconde; or, The festival of the Rosiere. See 1809.
Joe,   132.
Joe Ruggles; or, The girl miner,   662.
John Bull; or, The comedy of 1854,   1340.

John Buzzby; or, A day's pleasure, 1424.
John Delmer's daughters, 665.
John Dobbs, 1870.
John Endicott. See 1577.
John Jones; or, I'm haunted by a fiend!, 378.
John of Paris, 2228.
John of Procida; or, The bridals of Messina. See 1440.
John the Baptist, 2821.
John Wesley, 3101.
John Wopps; or, From information I received, 2837.
Joining the timpanites; or, Paddy Mcflings' experience, 1182.
Joint owners in Spain, 351.
The jolly bachelors, 395.
The jolly tramp. See 2288.
Jonathan Bradford; or, The murder at the road-side inn, 884.
Jonathan Dobson, the Congress trooper. See 716.
Jonathan makes a wish. See 3033.
Jones's baby. See 2839.
Joseph entangled, 1359.
Josephine, the child of the regiment; or, The fortune of war, 379.
Joseph's jealousy. See 1695.
The journalists, 926.
The joy of living, 2822.
Joyzelle. See 1671.
The jubilee, 482.
Judah, 1360.
The judge of Swanzey. See 2754.
The judgment of Paris, 988.
Judith. See 1412.
Juditium. See 1695.
La juive. See 1808, 2199.
Julian. See 1792.
Julie, 2810.
Julius Caesar, 1376, 2559, 2560, 2561, 2562, 2563.
Jumbo-jum!, 1377.
The jumpkins jumble, 1954.
June and after, 127.
The junior, 1842.
Juno tries to change the decrees of fate, 1836.
Just my luck. See 1682.
Just plain Dot, 2043.
Just plain folks, 3148.
Justice, 947. See 949.
Justice Whisker's trial, 46.
Justitia Omnibus, 1378.
Kabale und Liebe. See 2472.
The Kansas immigrants; or, The great exodus, 682.
Karl and Anna, 908

Karl Hanno

Karl Hanno. See 940, 941.
Kate, 1231.
Kathleen Mavourneen; or, St. Patrick's eve, 1385.
Katrina's little game, 352.
Katty O'Sheal, 2149.
Kenilworth, 1413.
A Kentucky belle, 468.
Kill or cure, 635.
The killing of the children of Israel. See 1695.
Kind to a fault, 317.
King Alfred and the neat-herd, 125.
King Alfred's jewel, 2981, 2982.
The king and deserter. See 1667.
King Charles the Second's merry days. See 1813.
King Charming; or, The blue bird of paradise, 2200. See 2188.
King Christmas. See 2188.
King Edward the Third. See 222.
King Foxy of Muir Glacier, 46.
King Hal, 1994.
King Henry IV, 2564, 2565, 2566, 2567.
King Henry V, 2568, 2569, 2570, 2571, 2572.
King Henry VI, 2573.
King Henry VIII, 2574, 2575, 2576, 2577, 2578, 2579, 2580, 2581.
A king in disguise, 7.
King John, 2582, 2583, 2584.
King Lear, 2585, 2586, 2587, 2588, 2589, 2590.
King Lear's wife, 237.
The king of the dark chamber, 2864, 2865.
The king of the peacocks. See 2201, 2188.
King Ottocar, his rise and fall, 1035.
King Philip, 459. See 457.
King, queen and knave. See 1876.
King Richard II, 2591, 2592, 2593.
King Richard III, 2594, 2595, 2596, 2597, 2598.
King Stephen. See 1400.
King Victor and King Charles. See 362.
The King's bench. See 1207.
The king's march. See 1794.
The king's rival; or, The court and the stage, 2901.
Kitty, 3200.
Kitty Clive, 1831.
The kleptomaniac. See 443.
The knickerbockers at school, 1446.
The knight and wood demon. See 1552.
The knight of Arva, 249.
The knight of the burning pestle, 168.
The knight of the rum bottle and co.; or, The speechmakers, 2398.
The knight templar. See 170.

The last judgement.

The last judgement, 153.
The last lily. See 2488.
The last loaf, 1478.
The last nail. See 2176.
The last night of a nation, 460. See 457.
The last of the English, 576.
The last of the family. See 599.
The last of the Mohicans, 2781.
The last of the Pollywogs. See 337.
The last visit. See 2825.
A late delivery, 184.
Latin is practical. See 1711.
Laugh when you can, 2344.
Laughing gas, 3086. See 754.
The laughter of the gods. See 792.
Launcelot and Guenevere, 1225.
Launched but not anchored. See 2040.
The lawyer's clerk. See 172, 380.
The league of youth. See 1292, 1299.
Leap year, 2496.
Leave it to me, 1147.
Leave it to Polly, 289.
Led astray, 250.
The "left-handed" sleeve, 702.
A legend of Lisbon! See 199.
Legend of Montrose. See 2231.
A legend of "Norwood"; or, Village life in New England, 624.
The legend of the Christmas tree, 1399.
Lend me five shillings, 1871.
Leonor de Guzman. See 234.
Lepidus Celebrates, 3168.
The lesser evil. See 227.
A lesson for lovers. See 2397.
Lestocq; or, The fete at the Hermitage, 1639.
A letter of introduction, 1255, 1256. See 872.
The liar, 900.
The liars, 1361.
The libertine reclaimed. See 1807.
Liberty corners, 3149.
Licensed. See 1476.
Life as it is; or, The convict's child, 221.
Life at Salt Lake City. See 829.
A life chase, 192.
Life for life. See 1698.
Life in London. See 1010, 1818.
Life in Louisiana. See 257.
Life in New York; or, Tom and Jerry on a visit, 333.
Life in New York. See 1929.

Life in the clouds; or, Olympus in an uproar, 334.
Life is a dream. See 1721.
The life of an actress. See 245.
The life of man, 49.
The life of woman; or, The curate's daughter, 1074.
Life with Octavia, 3076.
A life's ransom. See 1698.
A life's revenge; or, Two loves for one heart, 2838.
The light, 768.
The light in the window. See 754.
The light of Provence, 2784.
Light weights, 1000.
Like falling leaves. See 965.
A likely story, 1257, 1258. See 1260.
Lilian, the show girl, 2704.
Lilian's last love. See 1229.
Lilies that fester, 2239.
Lilly Dawson; or, A poor girl's story!, 2791.
A limb o' the law, 2018.
The Lime-kiln club in an uproar!, 3129.
Lincoln celebrations, 2458.
Lincoln league, 2287.
The lion and the lady. See 542.
A lion at bay, 2134.
The lion hunters; or, Modern Dianas, 2373.
Little barefoot, 3029.
The little bill that was taken up. See 406.
The little brown jug, 95, 96, 1565.
Little Daisy, 3138.
The little devil's share. See 52.
Little Doubt, 46.
The little dream. See 949.
The little fairy at the bottom of the sea. See 316.
Little Lise. See 1443.
Little Madcap's journay, 46.
The little mischief-makers. See 2423.
Little orphan of the family of Tchao. See 1939.
The little pilgrims and the book beloved, 1191.
The little rebel, 565.
Little Ruby; or, Home jewels, 3035.
A little tramp; or, Landlords and tenants, 3154.
The little treasure, 1116.
The little wife, 494.
A little world, 959.
A live woman in the mines; or, Pike county ahead!, 663.
A lively legacy, 1433.
The living corpse. See 801.
The loan of a lover, 2202, 2203.

Lock and key

Lock and key, 1188A.
Locked in, 3185.
Locked in with a lady, 12.
The locket. See 1708.
Lodgers and dodgers, 1139.
Logan, 746.
Die Logenbrüder. See 737, 738.
Lola, 658.
Lola Montes; or, A countess for an hour. See 568.
London assurance, 251, 252, 253, 254.
London Bridge; or, The mysteries of the old mint, 1943.
London forty years ago. See 1849.
London frolics in 1638. See 2206.
The London merchant. See 1559.
The lone hut of the swamp. See 2400.
The long and the short and the tall, 1084.
The long strike, 255.
Look before you leap; or, Wooings and weddings, 1584.
The lord of the manor. See 1747.
Lost and found. See 902.
The lost child; or, Jones's baby, 2839.
Lost in London, 1582, 2135.
The lost mine. See 101.
The lost New Year, 574.
The lost ship; or, The man-of-war's man, and the privateer, 2977.
The lottery of life, 335.
The lottery ticket; or, The lawyer's clerk, 172, 380.
Louva, the pauper, 684.
Love. See 1440.
Love à la mode, 1659.
Love and ambition. See 2472.
Love and fortune. See 2188, 2204.
Love and friendship; or, Yankee notions, 1561.
Love and intrigue. See 2471, 2476.
Love and laugh. See 1803.
Love and law, 1978.
Love and lottery! See 524.
Love and murder, 336.
Love and pride. See 1599, 1600.
Love and science, 2441.
Love at the academy. See 339.
Love behind the scenes, 2053.
Love by induction, 1155, 1156.
Love in a flue; or, The sweep and the magistrate, 1986.
Love in a village, 211.
Love in all corners, 778.
Love in danger, 820.
Love in humble life, 2079, 2080.

Lucullus' dinner-party

La maison du Mari. See 2682.
La maison en loterie. See 172.
The major's mistake. See 3137.
Make your wills. See 1729, 1730.
Make-believe, 2281.
Making Bill an elk. See 1788.
Mâlmôrda, 506.
Malvina, 1640.
Mammon. See 650, 652.
Mammon and his message, 650.
Man and wife, 626.
The man born to be king, 2450.
The man from Maine, 2969.
The man from Nevada, 3007.
The man hating Palatine. See 403.
The man in the stall. See 2846.
The man of fortitude; or, The Knight's adventure, 1192.
The man of the people. See 2689.
The man of the times; or, A scarcity of cash, 183.
The man of two lives!, 200.
The man on the Kerb. See 2846.
The man who stole the castle, 946.
The man with the hod, 2732.
The manager's daughter, 1470.
Man-fish. See 1501.
Manfred. See 421.
Manfroy, Duke of Athens, 127.
Manners and modes. See 542.
The manoeuvres of Jane, 1362.
The man-of-war's man, and the privateer. See 2977.
Manuel. See 1726.
Many sides to a character. See 1599, 1601.
The march of intellect, 1641.
A March wind, 351.
Marco Spada, 2695.
Mardi gras in New Orleans. See 2333.
Margaret Catchpole, the heroine of Suffolk! or, The vicissitudes of real life!, 2792.
Margot. See 2825.
Maris and Magdalena, 1204.
Maria Magdalena, 1152.
Mariana, 806.
Marie Antoinette, 963.
Marie de Méranie. See 1698.
Marino Faliero.
Marion. See 1690.
Marion de Lorme. See 1274.
The marionettes. See 3130.

Marita

Marita, 2442.
Marjorie's lovers. See 1481.
Marlow, 2083.
Marmion; or, The battle of Flodden Field, 129.
Marriage a lottery, 636.
Marriage at any price, 3187.
A marriage has been arranged. See 2846.
The marriage of Bacchus. See 2188.
The marriage of Guenevere. See 1225.
The marriage of Sobeide, 1195.
The marriage question, 519.
Marriageables, 802.
Married and buried. See 1423.
Married and settled. See 560.
Married and single, 2247.
The married bachelor; or, Master and man, 1992.
Married daughters and young husbands, 632.
Married life, 382.
Married lovers, 2262.
The married maid. See 2392.
The married rake, 2512.
Married yesterday. See 2246.
The marrying of Ann Leette, 128.
Martin Chuzzlewit. See 735.
The martyr, 80.
The martyr of Antioch. See 1776.
A martyr romance, 696.
Mary Magdalen. See 842.
Mary of Magdala, 1173.
Mary Stuart, 2856. See 2473, 2858.
Mary, the maid of the inn. See 2737.
Mary Tudor. See 1274.
Mary Warner, 2903.
Mary's birthday; or, The cynic. See 1764.
Mary's wedding. See 450.
Masaniello; or, The dumb girl of Portici. See 1780, 1677A.
Masaniello, the fisherman of Naples, 2738.
Masaniello. See 1677.
The mashers mashed, 608.
The masked ball. See 1779.
Masks. See 1760.
The masonic ring; or, The adventures of a college bride, 156.
The masque of the seasons. See 1792.
Masques of Cupid, 227.
The massacre of St. Bartholomew. See 1372.
The master, 79.
Master and man, 1970.
The master builder, 1293. See 1290.

Master George Washington, 1447.
The master of Palmyra, 3104.
The master of the house. See 1218.
Master Olaf, 2812.
The master's birthday, 3175.
Mat of the iron hand. See 892.
The match, 80.
Match at midnight. See 2206.
A match for a mother-in-law, 2328.
Match-breaking; or, The prince's present, 1426.
Matchmakers, 797.
Mater, 1650.
Maternity. See 872.
Matinata. See 1476.
Matrimonial masquerading. See 390.
Matrimony, 1427.
Maud's command; or, Yielding to temptation. See 1626.
Maud's peril, 2136.
Maximilian. See 1709.
Mayflower '76, 160.
Mazeppa. See 1781.
Measure for measure, 2604, 2605, 2606.
Medea, 840, 1036, 1520. See 547, 1721.
A medical man. See 2488.
A meeting of liquor dealers. See 1626.
Meg's diversion, 578.
The melting pot; or, The Americanization of the strangers within our
    gates, 206.
The member for literature, 125.
The memoirs of Charles Paul de Kock. See 1443.
Men of the day. See 847.
Menaechmi. See 2221.
Menschenhass und Reue. See 1456.
Le menteur. See 900.
Mercedes, 21.
Merchant of Venice, 236, 2607, 2608, 2609, 2610. See 2611.
The merchant of Venice preserved. See 2874.
The merchant's wedding; or, London frolics in 1638, 2206.
Meringues, 2799.
The merry Christmas of the old woman who lived in a shoe, 90.
The merry cobbler, 912.
Merry Jerry, 46.
The merry monarch. See 2075.
The merry mourners. See 2002.
The merry outlaws of Sherwood. See 890.
A merry widow hat, 1028.
The merry wives of Windsor, 2612, 2613, 2614.
The merry-go-round. See 181.

Messalina

Messalina, 1577.
The messenger boy, 2404.
Messrs. Grin and Barrett, 1959.
Messmates, 97.
Metamore; or, The last of the Pollywogs, 337.
'Methinks I see my father!' or, 'Who's my father?', 1907.
Mettius Curtius, 508.
Miatonimo, 461. See 457.
Michael and his lost angel, 1363. See 736.
Michael Erle: The maniac lover; or, The fayre lass of Lichfield, 3111.
Michael Kramer, 1129.
Michel et Christine. See 2079.
Michel Perrin. See 2218.
Midas, 1996.
The middy ashore, 201.
The midnight intruder, 779.
A midnight mistake, 1932.
The midnight watch!, 1872.
Midsummer eve, 237.
A midsummer-night's dream, 2615.
The mikado, 974.
Miles Dison. See 450.
Miles gloriosus. See 2221.
Milkmaid of Montfermeil. See 1443.
Milky white, 579, 580.
The mill of the gods, 1161.
The miller and his men, 2230.
The miller of Derwent water, 885.
The miller of New Jersey; or, The prison-hulk, 338.
The miller's maid, 2448.
The miller's wife. See 3057.
Milly dear, 351.
Mind your own business, 1533.
The minerali; or, The dying gift, 2226.
Minette's birthday, 48.
The minister. See 2472.
A minister pro tem, 1392.
Minna von Barnhelm. See 1721.
Minnie at the movies, 266.
The miracle of good St. Valentine. See 1746.
The miracle of Saint Anthony. See 1672.
Miriam's crime, 581.
The mischievous nigger, 3089.
The miser. See 1795, 1796.
Les miserables. See 933.
Miserrimus; or, The broken heart, 582.
The miser's troubles. See 781.
The misleading lady, 984.

Le monde renversé

The mysteries of the old mint

The mysteries of the old mint. See 1943.
A mysterious disappearance, 95, 99.
The mysterious floursack! See 3078.
The mysterious stranger. See 2517.
The mystery of Ardennes, 23.
The mystery of the charity of Joan of Arc, 2099.
The mystic charm; or, A wonderful cure, 1947.
The mystic spell, 3090.
Naboth's vineyard, 66.
Nancy and company, 627.
Naomie; or, The peasant girl's dream, 2020.
Narcisse the vagrant, 2482.
Narcissus, 1948.
A narrow escape, 1164.
Nathan Hale, 871.
Nathan Hale of '73, 604.
Nathan the wise, 1546.
The natural son. See 2934.
Nature. See 1737.
Nature and philosophy, 1949.
Nature's nobleman, 2049.
Naval engagements, 639.
The necessary evil, 1414.
Ned and Nell. See 2295.
Ned Kelly. See 2938.
Needles and pins. See 626.
Negro dialect recitations, 100.
The Negus. See 793.
Neighbor Jackwood, 2989.
Nell Gwynne; or, The prologue. See 1334.
Neoma. See 3117.
Neptune's defeat; or, The seizure of the seas, 340.
Nero, 2126. See 284.
Nero; or, The fall of Rome, 1436.
The nervous man and the man of nerve, 203.
The nettle, 3044.
Nettlewig hall; or, Ten to one, 3072.
Nevada; or, The lost mine, 101.
Never again, 3150.
Never say die, 90.
The new Aladdin and the same old lamp, 1318.
The new boy, 1480.
New Canterbury tales, 1170.
The new cook, 1961.
The new footman, 2513.
The new governess, 3032.
New hay at the old market. See 532.
The new Haymarket spring meeting. See 2188.

Not guilty

Not guilty, 2138.
Not on the bills, 2996.
Not so bad after all, 2329.
Not so bad as we seem; or, Many sides to a character, 1601.
    See 1599.
Not such a fool as he looks, 429.
Notoriety, 2345.
The notorious Mrs. Ebbsmith, 2164.
Notre Dame; or, The gipsy girl of Paris, 1087.
Noughtology or nothing, 2764.
Noureddin, and the fair Persian, 812.
Nowadays. See 1761.
Nugget, 3008.
No. six Duke Street. See 174.
No. 3 Fig Tree Court, Temple. See 2031.
O Gemini! or, The brothers of course, 177.
The oaten cakes, 3176.
Oath bound; or, Faithful unto death, 1097.
Oberon, 2210, 2211.
Oberon; or, The charmed horn, 1985.
An object lesson in history, 518.
An object of interest, 2801.
The obstinate family, 1991.
Obtaining a promise. See 1626.
The ocean of life; or, "Every inch a sailor!", 1076.
Ocean sketches, 3066.
The octoroon; or, Life in Louisiana, 257.
O'Day, the alderman, 2433.
Odds with the enemy, 685, 686. See 672.
The O'Dowd, 258.
Oedipus. See 547.
Oedipus at Colonos. See 547.
Oedipus the king. See 1721.
Of arms and the man, we sing!, 1995.
Official resistances. See 2372.
Oh! Hush! or, The Virginny cupids!, 3091.
Oh, that property man!, 1064.
Les oiseaux de proie. See 239.
Olaf Liljekrans. See 1289.
Old Acre folk, 2773.
Old and young, 2007.
Old Andy, the moonshiner, 970.
The old chateau; or, A night of peril, 567.
Old clothes. See 78.
The (old clothes) merchant of Venice; or, The young judge and ole
    jewry, 2008.
Old colony days, 207.
Old cronies, 2726.

One summer's day

One summer's day,   835.
One, two, three, four, five,   2010.
O'Neal, the great; or, Cogger na caillie,   509.
Only cold tea.   See 683.
An only daughter,   687.
The onward march to freedom.   See 417.
The open door,   2849.
Open house; or, The twin sisters,   383.
An open secret,   448.
The opera.   See 872.
Opposite neighbors,   2070.
The orange girl,   1541.
The order of the day.   See 2264.
Order of the fan,   2014.
Orestes,   1515.
Oriana,   20.
An original idea,   2015.
The orphan.   See 2934.
The orphan of China,   1939.
The orphan of Geneva.   See 764.
The orphan protected.   See 1198.
The orphan's legacy!   See 2790.
L'orphelin et le meurtrier.   See 740.
Orpheus and Eurydice.   See 2188.
Orpheus in the Haymarket,   2212.   See 2188.
Osorio,   522.
Ossawattomie Brown; or, The insurrection at Harper's Ferry,   2854.
The ostler and the robber.   See 882.
"Othello",   2024.
Othello,   2620, 2621, 2622, 2623, 2624, 2625.
Othello travestie,   752.
Otho the Great.   See 1400.
O'Toole's battle of ante-up,   1962.
Otto of Wittelsbach.   See 1792.
Otto of Wittelsbach; or, The choleric count.   See 2934.
O-umé's gods.   See 2354.
Our American cousin,   2907.
"Our boys",   430.
Our boys of 1776.   See 103.
Our clerks; or, No. 3 Fig Tree Court, Temple,   2031.
Our country aunt; or, Aunt Jerusha's visit,   2032.
Our daughters,   1009.
Our domestics,   1140.
Our English friend,   628.
Our folks,   104.
Our hopeful son.   See 1305.
Our Jack,   2770.
Our Jeminy; or, Connecticut courtship,   538.

Parlor dramas

The physician

The physician, 1366.
Physiognomy. See 905.
The picaroons, 401.
The Piccolomini; or, The first part of Wallenstein. See 521.
Picking up the pieces. See 2819.
"Pickwick", 1089.
Pickwick papers. See 1814.
The Pickwickians. See 1814.
The picture of a London play-house. See 526.
Pictures. See 1205.
Pie. See 1476.
La pie voleuse; ou, La servante de Palaiseau. See 1678.
The pie-dish. See 896.
Pierrette; or, The village rival, 887.
The pigeon. See 948.
Pigeons and spiders. See 1675.
Pike County ahead! See 663.
Pike O'Callaghan; or, The Irish patriot, 2330.
The Pikeville centennial, 396.
Pikeville folks, 2289.
Pilkerton's Peerage, 1134.
The pillars of society. See 1292.
The pilot, 888.
The pioneer's daughter. See 1096.
Pious Aeneas, 125.
A pipe of peace, 445. See 443.
The piper, 2084, 2085.
The pipes of Arcadia. See 1745.
Pippa passes. See 362.
Pique. See 626.
The pirate, 2213.
The pirates lare; or, Gorgonzago's revenge, 2686.
The pirate's legacy; or, The wrecker's fate, 2447.
The pirates of Penzance. See 976.
The pirates of the Savannah; or, The tiger hunter of the prairies, 2840.
Pistols for seven. See 1234, 1235.
Pizarro, 1455.
Pizarro; or, The death of Rolla. See 2934.
The plaintiff. See 972.
Plantation songs for my lady's banjo, 3201.
Play. See 2382.
The play of the wether. See 2683.
Played and lost, 1625.
Playing with fire, 342.
Plays in the market-place, 409.
Plays of gods and men, 792.
A pleasant comedie of the life of Will Shakespeare, 2711.

The raft

The raft, 1563.
The rag-picker of Paris, and the dressmaker of St. Antoine, 2795.
Rags and bottles; or, The two waifs, 2891.
Rahab, 411.
Rahna's triumph, 153.
The railroad to ruin. See 244.
Rain. See 1205.
"Raising the wind" on the most approved principles. See 310.
Raising the wind, 1428.
The Rajah's daughter. See 1805.
The rake's progress, 2315.
Raleigh, the shepherd of the ocean, 1442.
Ralph Coleman's reformation. See 1626.
Rameses of Mummy Row. See 223.
The ranch girl, 2301, 2302.
The rancher's fate. See 2702.
Randall's thumb, 978.
Rasmus Montanus. See 1721.
The raven, 1143.
Ravenswood, 950.
Read-aloud plays, 1205.
A ready-made suit, 477.
The real Lady Hilda, 589.
The real thing, 118.
The realm of time, 2102.
The reason. See 1760.
Rebecca's triumph, 107,
The rebellion. See 1983.
The reclaimed husband. See 1622.
The reconciliation, 1130.
Reconciliation. See 1450.
The recovered ring. See 1383.
The rector, 592.
The red mask; or, The wolf of Bohemia. See 345.
The red mask; or, The wolf of Lithuania, 345.
The red robe. See 736.
The red rover; or, The mutiny of the dolphin, 889.
The redemption of Bill Gunther; or, Making Bill an elk. See 1787.
Reflected glory, 1029.
Reform. See 542.
A reformer in ruffles, 3122.
The reformer of Geneva, 2679.
The regicides, 462. See 457.
The register. See 1267.
A regular rah! rah! boy, 293.
A regular scream, 294.
The rehearsal, 125.
Rejected. See 683.

Relations and friends. See 2208.
The relief of Lucknow. See 248.
Remorse, 523. See 521, 868.
The renegade, 2346.
The rent day. See 1334.
The reporter, 3038.
The republicans of Brest. See 1350.
Reputation; or, The state secret, 2216.
The rescue; or, The villain unmasked, 664.
The rescue of Prince Hal, 3179.
Retired from business. See 1333.
The return of Christmas, 118.
The return of mutton, 2407.
The return of the soldier Ulysses. See 1801.
The return of the wanderer. See 1145.
A return ticket, 2760.
The returned cowboy. See 2290.
Reverses, 863.
The review; or, The wags of Windsor, 531.
Reviewing for examination, 1631.
The revolt, 418.
The revolt of the bees, 108, 2332.
The revolution. See 25.
The revolutionary pensioner. See 905.
The reward of crime; or, The love of gold, 3108.
Richard Coeur de Lion, 1609.
Richard Wagner, 2712.
Richelieu. See 1602.
Richelieu; or, The conspiracy. See 1599.
Riders to the sea. See 736, 2683, 2862.
The riding to Lithend, 237.
Rienzi. See 1792.
The rifle and how to use it, 282.
Rightful heir. See 1282.
The rightful heir to Rochdale castle. See 1558.
Rigoletto, 3021.
Ring-around-a-rosie, 295.
Rip Van Winkle, 1316.
Riquet with the tuft. See 2188.
The rising of the moon. See 736.
The rival lovers, 3093.
The rival merchants. See 1585.
The rival queens. See 2747.
The rival sergeants; or, Love and lottery!, 524.
The rivals, 2667.
Roamersholm. See 1292.
Rob Roy, 2234, 2740.
Rob Roy Macgregor; or, Auld lang syne, 2235. See 2234.

The robber of the Rhine

The robber of the Rhine, 35.
The robbers, 2475, 2476. See 2471, 2934.
The robbers of the Pyrenees, 2842.
The robber's wife, 2236.
Robert Burns, 759.
Robert E. Lee, 760.
Robert Emmet, a tragedy of Irish history, 507.
Robert Emmet, the martyr of Irish liberty, 2151.
Robert Macaire; or, Les [!] auberge des adrets, 2516.
Robert the Devil, Duke of Normandy, 2308.
Robin Hood; or, The merry outlaws of Sherwood, 890.
Robin Hood; or, Sherwood forest. See 1192.
Robin of Sherwood, 585.
Robinson Crusoe, 1572.
Robinson Crusoe; or, The bold buccaneers, 2237.
Rochester; or, King Charles the Second's merry days, 1813.
The rock of Charbonniere. See 878.
The rocket, 2166.
The Rocky Ridge vaudeville show, 397.
Rodolph the wolf; or, Columbine Red Riding-Hood, 2217.
The rogue's comedy, 1367.
Le Roi s'amuse. See 1274.
The roll of the drum, 3113.
Rolla; or, The virgin of the sun. See 2934.
Rolla's tod. See 1455.
A Roman and an American Christmas compared, 2401.
Le Roman d'une pupille. See 1722.
A Roman executive election, 2777.
A Roman family comes to life, 2402.
The Roman father, 3100.
Romance, 2662.
Romance and reality; or, The young Virginian, 346.
The romance of a day. See 725.
The romance of a poor young man, 861.
The romance of George Rogers Clark and Thèrése de Leyba, 157.
The romance of Robert Burns, 2918.
The romance of the nose. See 2269.
Romancie, 856.
A romantic farce. See 651.
Rome and the modern world, 147.
Rome preserv'd, 3024.
Romeo and Juliet, 2627, 2628, 2629.
Romiero, 80.
The romp, 2403.
Room forty-five, 1265.
The root of evil. See 76.
Rory O'Moore, 1590.
Rosa, 1284.

St. Patrick's eve; or, The order of the day

St. Patrick's eve; or, The order of the day, 2264.
Saint Robert's cave. See 1806.
Saint Ronan of Brittany. See 1008.
Saints and sinners, 1368.
The saloon must go, 1277.
Sam Weller; or, The Pickwickians, 1814.
Sanctuary, a bird masque, 1651.
Sans-cravate. See 1443.
Santa Claus, 1631.
Santa's rescue, 1000.
Santiago; or, For the red, white and blue, 914.
Sappho, 1037.
Sappho and Phaon, 1652.
Saratoga; or, "Pistols for seven", 1234, 1235.
Sardanapalus. See 421.
Satan in paradise; or, The mysterious stranger, 2517.
"Saul", 465.
Saul, 3025.
A sausage from Bologna, 474.
Saved; or, A wife's peril, 2682.
Savourneen dhellish. See 848.
The saw-mill; or, A Yankee trick, 1135.
The Saxons, 2485.
Saxons and Normans at home. See 2224.
A scale with sharps and flats, 610.
The scamps of London; or, The cross roads of life! See 1802.
The scape-goat, 2249, 2250.
Scaramouch in Naxos. See 651.
A scarcity of cash. See 183.
The scarecrow. See 736.
The scarlet letter, 50. See 1121.
Scenes and songs of ye olden time, 2066.
Scenes in a sanctum, 514.
Scenes of Parisian life. See 1443.
The scheming lieutenant. See 2668.
School, 864. See 2382.
"School"; or, The story of Bella Marks, 2384.
School and parlor comedies, 1023.
School drama. For titles beginning with "school" see the subject
   index under "College and school drama."
The school for critics. See 2021.
The school for prodigals, 1281.
The school of reform; or, How to rule a wife, 1909.
The school of reform; or, How to rule a husband, 1910, 1911.
The schoolboy's dream, 2845.
The schoolfellows. See 1334.
The schoolmistress, 2167.
A scrap of paper, 2443.

The seven champions of Christendom

The siege of Rochelle, 891.
Siegfried's death, 1153.
The signet-ring. See 2073.
The silent man. See 1770, 1771.
A silent woman, 1464.
Silly Willy. See 2683.
The silver age, 1516.
The silver shield, 1046.
Simple Silar; or, The detective from Plunketsville, 480.
Simpson and co., 2251, 2252.
Sin and its shadow. See 2327.
The sin and sorrow, 1542.
The sin of David, 2131.
Sinatra takes a bow, 453.
The singing shepherd, 2803.
Single life, 388.
Sink or swim!, 1913.
A sire of battles, 2769.
The siren and the Roman (Cleopatra and Anthonius); or, Luxury, love
   and the lost, 2828.
Sister Angela, 2045.
Sister Anne. See 1443.
The six degrees of crime; or, Wine, women, gambling, theft, murder
   and the scaffold, 1184.
Six months ago, 614.
Six times nine, 296.
The six years' tragedy. See 1171.
Sixteen thousand years ago!, 2700.
Sixteen-string Jack, 2316.
Sixty years since. See 893.
The sixty-third letter, 2028.
The skeleton witness; or, The murder at the mound, 2317.
The skirts of the camp. See 2097A.
The slave, 1914.
The slave girl, 1473.
A slave of the mill, 2331.
Slaves of society, 2303.
The sleepers awakened, 8.
The sleeping beauty in the wood. See 2188.
The sleeping princess; or, The beauty and the bicycle, 1319.
The sleeping-car, 1267.
The sleeping-draught, 2105.
The sleep-walker; or, Which is the lady?, 2029, 2030.
Slick and Skinner; or, The barber pards, 967.
The smart set; correspondence and conversations, 872.
The smile of Mona Lisa, 193.
Smith. See 651.
The Smiths, 186.

The smoking car

The smoking car, 1268.
Snakes in the grass, 389.
The snapping turtles; or, Matrimonial masquerading, 390.
The snow storm; or, Lowina of Tobolskow, 151.
Snow-bound, 2733.
Snowed in, 3193.
A snug little kingdom, 38.
A social crisis; or, Almost a tragedy of tongues, 2048.
Social eccentricities, 2749.
Society. See 2382.
Socrates. See 2699.
Socrates asks why. See 1563.
Sold again, and got the money, 2499.
A soldier of fortune, 300.
The soldier's daughter, 490.
Solomon's song. See 1412.
Solon Shingle; or, The people's lawyer, 1373.
Somebody's coat, 1503.
Something singular. See 733.
La somnambule. See 1816.
The somnambulist; or, The phantom of the village, 1816.
The son of Don Juan, 807.
The son of the night, 957.
A son of the soil. See 1749.
A son of Thespis. See 1975.
The son-in-law of M. Poirier. See 1721.
The sophomore, 1844.
The sorcerer. See 976.
The sorceress, 2444.
Sorosis; or, The onward march to freedom, 417.
Sorrow. See 872.
Sorry for Billy, 708.
The sound of Latin, 2703.
A southern Cinderella, 1110.
The Southern cross, 612.
A southern rose, 353.
Sowing the wind, 1047.
Die Spanier in Peru; oder Rolla's tod. See 1455.
Sparking, 3131.
The sparkling cup, 690. See 672.
Special performances, 1122.
The spectre bridegroom; or, A ghost in spite of himself, 1817.
The spectre of the Nile. See 877.
A spectre on horseback. See 717.
The speechmakers. See 2398.
Speed the plough, 1915, 1916, 1917.
The spellin' skewl; or, Friday afternoon at Deestrick no. 4, 2363.
A spelling bee; or, The battle of the dictionaries, 2320.

The Sphinx: a "touch from the ancients", 312.
The spirit of ancient Rome, 901.
The spirit of seventy six; or, The coming woman, 601, 2762.
The spirit of the black mantle. See 3115.
The spitfire, 1886.
The spoil'd child, 1187.
The spoiled child, 2763.
The sport of destiny. See 2471.
Sports on a lark, 1020.
The sprightly widow. See 1783.
Spring gardens, 2219.
The spring recital. See 754.
The spy, 208.
"The squaw man", 2427.
The squire, 2168.
Squire for a day, 1504.
Squire Judkins' apple bee, 1404.
The staff of diamonds, 1149.
Stage struck; or, The loves of Augustus Portarlington and Celestina
   Beverley, 744.
Star bright, 2046.
The star of Bethlehem. See 1007.
The star of Seville. See 1721.
Stars in their eyes, 1082.
A state of things. See 1933.
The state secret. See 2216.
State secrets; or, The tailor of Tamworth, 2766.
The statue. See 2658.
Stella. See 2934.
Stichus. See 2221.
Still waters run deep, 2911.
Stocks up! Stocks down!, 2800.
The stoic's daughter, 125.
The stone eater, 2816.
The stooping lady, 1172.
Stop him who can. See 2340.
The storm, 761.
A stormy night, 1395.
The story of Bella Marks. See 2384.
Strafford. See 362, 363.
A strange book, 1401.
A strange marriage. See 1510.
The stranger, 1456. See 2934.
Strathmore. See 1698.
Streaks of light. See 2825.
Street scene. See 2699.
Streets of London. See 262.
The streets of New York, 263.

Strife

Strife. See 736.
The stripling, 80.
The stronger, 965, 2814.
The sublime tragedy of the lost cause, 2140.
Success. See 542.
Success; or, A hit if you like it. See 2188.
Such stuff as dreams. See 1794.
Such things are, 1301.
The suffragettes, 2304.
The sugar house, 351.
Suil Dhuv, the coiner, 727.
Suite B, 1474.
The summer. See 872.
The Summerville bazaar, 2981.
Sundown to dawn; or, London forty years ago, 1849.
The sunken bell, 1131, 1132.
Sunlight; or, The diamond king, 1091.
Sunshine through the clouds, 1486.
Supper for two; or, The wolf and the lamb, 972.
A surprise party. See 227.
Surrendered--hand and heart. See 2431.
Survival. See 1205.
The Swedish nightingale. See 2310.
The sweep and the magistrate. See 1986.
The sweet girl-graduate, 2122.
The sweet girl graduate's dream. See 1448.
Sweet Lavender, 2169.
Sweethearts, 979. See 976.
Sweethearts and wives, 1430.
The Swiss cottage; or, Why don't she marry?, 166.
The Swisser, 3155.
Sword and queue, 1038.
The sybil; or, The elder Brutus. See 599, 2074.
Sydney Carton; a tale of two cities, 1112.
Sylvester Daggerwood, 532.
Sympathetic souls, 1048.
Der Tag, 146.
Taggs, the waif; or, Uncle Seth, 3043.
The tailor of Tamworth. See 2766.
The tailors; or, A tragedy for warm weather, 2868.
Take care of little Charley, 347.
Taken from the French. See 1860.
The tale of a tar. See 1348.
A tale of blood. See 1072.
A tale of mystery, 1200.
A tale of two cities. See 1112.
The tales of a voyager. See 3143.
Tales of the Munster festivals. See 2236.

Their day

Their day. See 1412.
Their first meeting. See 1753.
Their godfather from Paris, 2223.
Their wife. See 1763.
Thekla, 2951.
Theodora, 3123.
Theodosia, the pirate's prisoner. See 2350.
Théophile. See 1008.
There'll come a day. See 1082.
There's millions in it, 2500.
Theresa's vow. See 997.
Thérèse; or, The orphan of Geneva, 764, 764A, 765.
Theseus, 596.
Theseus and Ariadne; or, The marriage of Bacchus. See 2188.
The Thesmophorizausae. See 58.
They the crucified, 1209.
They will gossip, 2937.
They're both to blame. See 2257.
The thing that's right. See 905.
A thirst for gold, and the wild flower of Mexico. See 2491.
Thirty years in a gamester's life. See 1778.
Thirty-three next birthday, 1887.
This fine-pretty world, 1653.
This paper for sale, 2916.
This picture and that. See 1724.
This way to the tomb, 785.
A thorn among the roses, 90.
Those dreadful twins, 2060.
Those landladies, 455.
Those red envelopes, 2061.
Thou shalt not lie, 1039.
The three banished men of Milan! See 32.
The three beautiful princesses. See 2705.
The three blacksmiths, 2939.
Three blind mice; or, Marjorie's lovers, 1481.
Three blind mice, 1944.
The three furies, 2370.
The three glass distaffs. See 2188.
The three golden apples. See 2872.
The three graces, 1002.
The three guardsmen; or, The queen, the cardinal, and the
    adventurer, 2357.
The three musketeers. See 2357.
The three secrets, 1538.
The three sisters, 487. See 483.
The three temptations. See 2488.
The three thieves and the denouncer. See 3114.
Thrice married, 2071.

The tournament of Idylcourt

The tournament of Idylcourt, 90.
The tower. See 2938.
The tower of Lochlain; or, The idiot son!, 1336.
The Tower of London; or, The death omen and the fate of Lady Jane
    Grey, 1176.
The tower of London; or, The rival queens, 2747.
Town and country, 1918, 1919, 1920, 1921, 1922.
Towneley miracle plays. See 1695.
The toy cart, 2860.
Toynbee in Elysium, 419.
The toy-shop, 747.
The track in the snow. See 2834.
Tradition. See 1763.
A tragedian in spite of himself. See 483.
A tragedy for warm weather. See 2868.
Tragedy of errors, 2271.
The tragedy of Nan. See 1703.
The tragedy of Pompey the Great. See 1704.
Tragedy of success, 2272.
The tragedy of superstition, 130.
A tragedy rehearsed. See 2663, 2664.
The tragic Mary, 866.
Trail of the torch, 1168.
The traitor. See 2658.
The trances of Nourjahad. See 1406.
Transmogrifications. See 587.
Travellers in America. See 790.
The travelling man, 1014.
The treason and death of Benedict Arnold, 475.
Treason, strategems, and spoils. See 274.
The treasure of Hidden valley. See 1788.
Trelawny of the "Wells", 2172.
The trend. See 1000.
Trente ans; ou, La vie d'un joueur. See 2935.
Trial by jury. See 975.
The trial of Cain, 351.
A trial of Catiline, 2984.
The trial of Latin Language, 1092.
The trial of Mary and Joseph. See 1695.
The trial of the conspirators, 2282.
Trials for the truth. See 120.
The trials of a country editor, 47.
Tribulation; or, Unwelcome visitors, 2253, 2254.
A trick dollar, 3079.
The trifler. See 1710.
Trinummus. See 2221.
Le triomphe des fées, 517.
A trip to Niagara; or, Travellers in America, 790.

A trip to Paris, 1506.
The triple wedding, 133.
The triple wedding; or, The forging of the ring, 134.
T'riss; or, Beyond the Rockies, 11.
Tristram the jester, 1099.
The Triumph of Mammon, 652.
The triumph of the Philistines and how Mr. Jorgan preserved the
   morals of Market Pewbury under very trying circumstances, 1370.
The triumph of youth; or, The white mouse, 2375.
The triumphs of Britannia. See 2192.
The troubadour. See 1437.
Il trovatore. See 2494.
True!, 1467.
A true lover's knot, 114.
True to the core. See 1679.
True to the last. See 41.
A trumped suit. See 1722.
The trust, 276.
The trustee, 360.
The truth. See 736.
The truth about Jane, 2932.
Truth's advocate and monthly anti-Jackson expositor, 2991.
Tulu. See 936.
Turn him out, 3140.
The turn in the road, 297.
Turning the tables, 2255.
The turnpike gate. See 1438A.
Twelfth night; or, What you will, 2638, 2639, 2640, 2641, 2642,
   2643, 2644.
Twenty minutes under an umbrella, 763.
Twenty per cent; or, My father, 728.
Twice killed, 2037.
The twilight of the gods, 1560.
The twin brothers. See 1274.
The twin sisters, 2501. See 383.
'Twixt axe and crown, 217.
Twixt midnight and morn, 1967.
The two black roses, 2782.
The two Bonnycastles, 1888.
The two buzzards; or, Whitebait at Greenwich, 1889.
The two Caesars. See 1835.
Two can play at that game, 2147.
Two drams of brandy, 1627.
The two drovers, 991.
Two faces under a hood, 729.
The two Figaros, 2220.
The two Foscari. See 421.
The two galley slaves, 2082.

Two gay deceivers; or, Black, white, and grey, 2385.
Two gentlemen at Mivart's. See 2488.
Two gentlemen in a fix; or, How to lose the train, 2843.
The two gentlemen of Verona, 2645, 2646.
Two ghosts in white, 691. See 672.
The two Greens, 2318.
The two Gregories; or, Luck in a name, 3001.
The two Gregories; or, Where did the money come from?, 730.
Two houses under one roof. See 1595.
Two in a garden. See 1166.
Two in the morning. See 1713.
Two jolly girl bachelors, 2528.
Two loves for one heart. See 2838.
Two men of Sandy Bar, 1123.
The two murderers. See 2516.
Two negatives make an affirmative, 1158. See 1156.
The two orphans, 697, 2038.
The two Pompeys, 1507.
The two puddifoots, 1890.
Two roses, 18.
Two strikes, 1052.
Two strings to your bow, 1325.
The two thorns, 19.
Two veterans, 1067.
The two waifs. See 2891.
Two's company. See 1000.
'Twould puzzle a conjurer, 2256.
Tyranny of tears, 467.
Ulysses, 2132. See 284.
The unborn. See 1762.
Uncle, 433.
Uncle Dick's mistake, 3074.
Uncle Jed's fidelity; or, The returned cowboy, 2290.
Uncle Joe's jewel, 2362.
Uncle John, 391.
Uncle Oliver; or, A house divided, 1078.
Uncle Rip, 2096.
Uncle Robert; or, Love's labor saved, 603.
Uncle Rube, 2972.
Uncle Sam's relation, 2876.
Uncle Seth. See 3043.
Uncle Si, 3156.
Uncle Tom's Cabin, 2973.
Uncle Zachary of Vermont, 2291.
Uncle's will, 2727.
Under a cloud, 2974.
Under a spell, 1462.
Under a veil, 2374.

Under blue skies, 1396.
Under the curse, 1628.
Under the gaslight, 629.
Under the laurels, 692.
Under the spell, 3075.
An unequal match, 2914.
The unexpected guest, 1269.
Unexpected guests. See 443.
An unhappy pair, 1021.
An unhistorical pastoral. See 651.
The universal exchange, 510.
The unknown heir. See 214.
The unseen empire, 361.
The unveiling, 268.
The unwelcome visitor. See 868.
Unwelcome visitors. See 2253, 2254.
Up for the cattle show, 1522.
Up to date America; or, The sweet girl graduate's dream, 1448.
Up Vermont way, 2051.
The upholsterer; or, What news!, 1940.
The upper ten thousand, 1508.
Used up. See 1714.
Vacation, 2975.
The vale of content, 2826. See 736.
Valentine and Orson, 3012.
A valet's mistake, 541.
La vallée du torrent. See 740.
A valuable fish, 456.
Vandyke Brown, 930.
A variety contest, 2067.
Velasquez and the "Venus", 125.
The veneered savage. See 936.
Venice preserved, 2026.
Venus and Adonis. See 2188.
Venus and the shepherdess. See 1315.
The very naked boy. See 3033.
A very pleasant evening, 2844.
"Very tragical mirth", 1068.
The veteran; or, The farmer's sons, 1438.
The veteran; or, France and Algeria, 3036.
Viae ad sapientiam. See 1054.
The vicissitudes of real life! See 2792.
A victim of woman's rights, 1574.
Victims, 2915.
The victorious duchess. See 1663.
The victory of Commodore Perry. See 858.
La vida es sueño, 437.
Vidocq! The French police spy!, 3022.

La vie d'un joueur

La vie d'un joueur. See 2935.
Le vieux garçon et la petite fille. See 2007.
The vikings at Helgeland. See 1292.
Vilikens and Dinah, 3097.
The village lawyer, 2997, 3023.
Village life in New England. See 624.
The village postmaster, 1311.
The village rival. See 887.
The village school ma'am, 2998.
The villain unmasked. See 664.
Vim; or, A visit to Puffy farm. See 402.
The virgin of the sun. See 2934.
The virgin wife triumphant. See 1784.
The Virginia veteran, 2260.
Virginius, 1441. See 1440.
The visions of freedom, 90.
Visions of the future. See 1525.
A visit from Fra Diavolo. See 180.
A visit to Puffy farm. See 402.
The voice of love, 208.
Vor sonnenaufgang. See 1127.
The Voysly inheritance, 128.
The vultures, 181.
Wagner, 1897. See 872.
The wags of Windsor. See 531.
Wah-na-ton; or, 'Way out West, 916.
The waif of Smith's pocket, 3102.
The waif's Thanksgiving, 1061.
Waiting. See 1763.
Waiting for Oscar, 709.
Wakefield, a folk-masque of America, 1655.
Walk for a wager; or, A bailiff's bet, 2097.
Wallace: the hero of Scotland, 152.
Wallace, 3030. See 366.
Wallenstein. See 521.
Wallenstein's camp, 2477.
The Walloons. See 599.
The walls of Jericho, 2851.
Walpole; or, Every man has his price, 1604.
The wanderers, 2421.
The wandering boys; or, The castle of Olival, 1432.
The wandering boys, 3039.
The wandering minstrel. See 1732.
Wanted a brigand; or, A visit from Fra Diavolo, 180.
Wanted, a correspondent, 693. See 672.
Wanted: a housekeeper, 2011.
Wanted--a wife, 923.
Wanted a wife; or, A checque on my banker, 1819.

"A wet blanket"

"A wet blanket", 502.
What do the Romans do?, 3077.
What every woman thinks she knows, 1968.
What happened to Jones, 305.
What next?, 731.
What news? See 1940.
What shall I take?, 782.
What's the use of Latin?, 471.
The Wheatville candidates, 1607.
When a woman loves, 1981.
When Buckingham met the queen, 1159.
When Johnny comes marching home, 2764C.
When love is young. See 542.
When the Paw-Paw County went dry, 3142.
When the wheels run down, 2399.
When the worm turned, 1398.
When we dead awaken, 1298.
When we were twenty-one, 836.
Where are those men!, 960.
Where did the money come from? See 730.
Which is the lady? See 2029, 2030.
Which is which?, 2728.
Which of the two?, 1891.
Whigs and democrats; or, Love of no politics, 1151.
While life shall last, 593.
Whimwhams, 3078.
The whistler! or, The fate of the lily of St. Leonard's, 2178.
The white cat. See 2188.
The white hawk. See 1412.
The white horse, 1928.
The white mouse. See 2375.
White Oak Tavern, 2429.
The white pilgrim. See 1750.
The white sergeants, 2518.
Whitebait at Greenwich. See 1889.
Whitefriars; or, The days of Claude du Val, 2979.
Who is who? or, All in a fog, 3141.
Who killed Cock Robin? See 1715.
Who stole the chickens?, 1509.
Who stole the pocket-book? or, A dinner for six, 1892.
Who's been here since I've been gone. See 1505.
Who's my father? See 1907.
Who's the heir? See 1688.
Why did you die? See 1716.
Why don't she marry? See 166.
Why elect Latin?, 1449.
Why Santa Claus comes in December, 2486.
The wicked world. See 975.

The Wicklow mountains, 2005A.
Wide awake Nell. See 772.
Wide enough for two, 694.
The widow. See 1742.
A widow hunt, 571.
The widow's marriage. See 234.
The widow's story. See 2327.
The widow's victim, 2519.
The wife: A tale of a Mantua maker!, 1005.
The wife: a tale of Mantua. See 1440.
The wife of Heracles, 2753.
The wife of Marobius, 817.
A wife without a smile, 2174.
The wife's appeal, 2655.
The wife's confession, 208.
A wife's peril. See 2682.
The wife's portrait. See 1698.
The wife's revenge. See 368.
The wife's secret, 1586.
The wild duck, 1299. See 1287, 1292.
Wild ducks, 2798.
The wild huntsman, 1308.
The wilderness, 837.
The wiles of the widow, 1564.
Wilful murder; or, Deeds of dreadful note, 762.
Wilhelm Meister. See 1747.
The will, 2347. See 905.
The will for the deed, 732.
Will Watch; or, The black phantom, 44.
"William", 2062.
William Shakespeare, pedagogue and poacher, 951.
William Tell, 1022, 2478, 2479. See 1440, 1721.
The windmill, 1851.
Wine, women, gambling, theft, murder and the scaffold. See 1184.
Winning a wife, 1828.
A winning hazard, 3189.
The winterfeast, 1417.
The winter's tale, 2647, 2648, 2649, 2650, 2651, 2652.
The wisdom of the wise, 573.
The witch of Salem. See 3120.
The witch of the woods, 46.
Witchcraft, 80. See 1718.
Witchcraft; or, The witch of Salem, 3120.
The witching hour. See 736.
The witch's mirror, 1321.
With trumpet and drum. See 1689.
Within the gates, 1993, 3040.
Without the walls, 2983.

Wives as they were, and maids as they are, 1303.
Wives by advertisement; or, Courting in the newspapers, 1337.
The wizard, 162.
The wizard of the sea. See 1371.
The wizard of the wave; or, The ship of the avenger, 1079.
Woffington, 630, 631.
The wolf and the lamb. See 972.
The wolf of Bohemia. See 345.
The wolf of Gubbio, 2086.
The wolf of Lithuania. See 345.
The woman. See 1450.
The woman in the case, 873.
The woman of Paris, 181.
Woman of spirit. See 481.
Woman's constancy. See 695.
Woman's trial. See 2716.
Woman's trials. See 2063.
Woman's vows and mason's oaths, 766.
Women's wit; or, Love's disguises. See 1440.
The wonder, a woman keeps a secret, 464.
The wonderful Christmas telescope, 818.
A wonderful cure. See 1947.
The wonderful lamp. See 928, 2012.
The wonderful telephone, 783.
The wood daemon; or, The clock has struck. See 1552.
Woodbarrow farm, 1328.
Woodcock's little game, 1893.
The woodman, 765A.
The wooer, the waitress and the villain. See 54.
Wooings and weddings. See 1584.
The woolen nightcap; or, The mysterious floursack! See 3078.
A world discovered. See 1900.
The World's fair drama, Christopher Columbus, 1124.
The world's own, 1244.
The worsted man, 119.
The wounded hussar; or, Rightful heir, 1282.
The wraith of the lake, 1080.
The wreck; or, The buccaneer's bridal, 3143.
The wreck ashore, 392.
The wrecker's fate. See 2447.
The writing on the wall, 1925.
Xantippe and Socrates, 125.
Xerxes the Great; or, The battle of Thermopyle, 3194.
Xilona. See 1663.
Yankee chronology; or, Huzza for the Constitution!, 791.
The yankee detective, 2768.
Yankee notions. See 1561.
The yankee peddler; or, Old times in Virginia, 138.

Subject Index

Moving picture plays

Mysteries and miracle plays, 1695, 1848.
Mythology, Classical, 237, 850, 988, 1041, 1068, 1083, 1458, 1560,
     1660, 2188, 2523, 2654, 3195.
New England, 624, 3120.
Niagara Falls, N. Y., 790.
Oxford University. College of St. John the Baptist, 1948.
Operas, 62, 68, 69, 115, 121, 122, 154, 211, 212, 306A, 373, 384,
     493, 512A, 527A, 715A, 718, 724A, 725, 729, 743, 744A, 749, 750,
     765A, 793, 849, 891, 961, 1188A, 1192, 1207, 1207A, 1216, 1300,
     1317, 1318, 1319, 1320, 1406, 1418, 1421, 1427, 1431, 1433A, 1438,
     1511, 1540, 1594, 1639, 1640, 1677A, 1785, 1857, 1898, 1914, 1930,
     1994, 2000, 2000A, 2000B, 2001, 2004A, 2005A, 2076, 2077, 2097A,
     2199, 2205, 2209, 2210, 2211, 2212, 2226A, 2228, 2273, 2283, 2349,
     2665, 2764A, 2764B, 2764C, 3021.
Pageants, 1642.
Pantomimes, 544.
Parr, Catherine, queen, consort of Henry VIII, king of England,
     1512-1548, 125, 2683.
Passion plays, 816.
Pennsylvania Dutch, 353.
Perry, Oliver Hazard, 1785-1819, 858.
Pompeius Magnus, Gnaeus, 106-48 B.C., 1704.
Puppet plays, 549, 550.
Quebec (Province)--Hist., 270, 3010.
Readings and recitations, 100, 182, 395, 607, 699, 703, 800, 905,
     1339, 2462, 2463, 2467, 2468.
Religious drama, 952.
Richelieu, Armand Jean du Plessis, cardinal, duc de, 1585-1642,
     1599, 1602.
Robert le Diable, 2308.
Robin Hood, 585, 2205, 2919.
Rome, 147, 901.
Rome--Hist., 1040, 1436.
Rome--Hist.--Kings, 753-510 B.C., 2074.
Rome--Politics and government, 2777.
Rome--Social life and customs, 470, 660, 934, 1473, 2401, 2402, 3077.
Russia--Hist., 2322.
Secret societies, 1182.
Sedgemoor, Battle of, 1685, 28.
Serbo-Croatian plays, 1450.
Serra Junípero, Miguel José, 1713-1784, 1767.
Shakespeare, William, 1564-1616, 951, 2711, 1521.
Sheppard, Jack, 1702-1724, 1073.
Slave-trade, 527.
Sorrento, Italy, 1974.
Sothern, Edward H., 1630.
Stratton, Charles Sherwood, 1838-1883, 2706.
Suffrage, 1088.

Temperance plays, 26, 77, 676, 690, 1277, 1335, 1347, 1620, 1622, 1623, 1626, 1627, 1628, 1636, 2176, 2265, 2529, 2655, 2729, 2885, 2894, 3075.
Tennessee, 1177.
Thanksgiving Day, 1061, 2017, 2715.
Turpin, Richard, 1706-1739, 2832.
U. S.--Hist.--Colonial period, 120, 207, 457, 461, 590, 1403, 1442, 1445, 1941, 3005.
U. S.--Hist.--Revolution, 25, 103, 158, 270, 338, 441, 457, 475, 716, 786, 871, 1056, 1243, 1273, 1487, 1544, 1687, 2883.
U. S.--Hist.--War of 1812, 791, 858, 2802, 2882.
U. S.--Hist.--War with the Barbary pirates, 2714.
U. S.--Hist.--Civil War, 9, 825, 982, 1150, 1549, 1983, 2140, 2854, 3018, 3073.
U. S.--Politics and government, 1151.
Utah, 829.
Vermont, 2051, 3108.
Virgilius Maro, Publius, 70-19 B.C., 5, 1483, 1836.
Virginia, 138, 2827.
Wagner, Richard, 1813-1883, 2712.
Wallace, Sir William, d. 1305, 152.
Washington, George, pres. U. S., 1732-1799, 25, 398, 499, 799, 1447, 1655.
Waterloo, Battle of, 1815, 43.
Wesley, John, 1703-1791, 3101.
The West, 11, 101, 194, 623, 682, 773, 829, 916, 1091, 1096, 1768, 1769, 2301, 2302, 2350, 2491, 3006, 3007, 3008, 3009, 3041, 3042.
Woffington, Margaret, 1714-1760, 630, 631, 2904, 584.
Woman, 226.
Woman--Rights of women, 1574, 2762.
Woman--Suffrage, 356, 922, 1114, 1661, 1968, 2304.
Wyoming, 1789.

Index of Editors

Addis, J.B., 1585.
Alden, Henry Mills, 1836-1919, 1248.
Archer, William, 1292.
Baker, Franklin Thomas, 2559.
Bierstadt, Edward Hale, 3033.
Booth, Edwin Thomas, 1833-1893, 1602, 2553, 2574, 2585, 2594, 2599,
    2617, 2622, 2630, 2631, 2896.
Buchanan, Milton A., 437.
Chambers, Sir Edmund Kerchever, 1866-1954, 2542.
Christy, E. Byron, 267.
Clark, Barrett H., 661.
Clarke, Helen A., 2541.
Cloak, F. Theodore, 242.
Coleridge, Derwent, 521.
Cook, Thomas R., 501.
Croker, Thomas Francis Dillon, 1831-1912, 2188.
Cumberland, Richard, 1732-1811, 304.
Daniel, George, 1789-1864, 35, 36, 62, 63, 171, 204, 211, 216, 233,
    373, 374, 375, 383, 389, 520, 531, 695, 715A, 716, 717, 718, 719,
    722, 723, 724A, 726, 727, 730, 740, 744A, 877, 878, 879, 881, 882,
    888, 1076, 1198, 1331, 1341, 1405, 1411, 1418, 1423, 1425, 1427,
    1428, 1433A, 1438A, 1453, 1456, 1529, 1552, 1553, 1554, 1567,
    1594, 1595, 1637, 1639, 1640, 1641, 1665, 1725, 1729, 1780, 1781,
    1803, 1805, 1806, 1807, 1809, 1810, 1816, 1817, 1818, 1855, 1901,
    1904, 1906, 1907, 1909, 1912, 1914, 1915, 1918, 1923, 1936, 1985,
    1992, 2002, 2003, 2005, 2006, 2007, 2010, 2076, 2077, 2078, 2079,
    2082, 2088, 2090, 2091, 2093, 2094, 2096, 2105, 2181, 2194, 2207,
    2226A, 2228, 2230, 2236, 2237, 2251, 2253, 2282, 2284, 2308, 2312,
    2314, 2316, 2337, 2340, 2343, 2344, 2345, 2347, 2349, 2396, 2432,
    2492, 2536, 2547, 2555, 2568, 2575, 2582, 2586, 2587, 2592, 2595,
    2600, 2607, 2612, 2616, 2620, 2627, 2635, 2638, 2647, 2648, 2671,
    2672, 2673, 2674, 2675, 2735, 2736, 2740, 2741, 2742, 2745, 2746,
    2748, 2763, 2923, 2935, 2948, 2950, 2990, 3059, 3072, 3143.
Dibdin, Thomas John, 1771-1841, 1939, 2227.
Dole, Nathan Haskell, 2476.
Dunn, Allan, 1994.
Edmonston, C.M., 168.
Farrar, Thomas J., 1518.

433

Feuillerat, Albert

Feuillerat, Albert, 3155.
Forman, H. Buxton, 1400.
Francke, Kuno,   51, 926, 989, 990, 1034, 1036, 1038, 1081, 1099, 1129,
    1131, 1133, 1152, 1153, 1195, 1592, 2470, 2474, 2478, 2480, 2481,
    2483, 3063, 3104.
George, Hereford B., 363.
Ginty, Elizabeth Beall, 1288.
Hellman, George S.,   1307, 1308.
Henderson, W.J.,   961.
Hinton, Henry L., 2897.
Hovey, Mrs. Richard, 1225.
Hudson, Henry N., 2540, 2640.
Hughes, Glenn, 697.
Humboldt, Archibald,
Inchbald, Elizabeth Simpson, 1753-1821,   1797, 1902, 1924, 1934,
    1937, 1938, 2000, 2000A, 2278, 2532, 2535, 2538, 2545, 2551, 2558,
    2563, 2567, 2572, 2581, 2584, 2590, 2598, 2603, 2606, 2610, 2613,
    2621, 2628, 2633, 2649, 2667, 2755, 3100.
Jansen, Frances Marianne Cumberland, 599.
Johnson, Samuel, 1709-1784,   2530, 2531, 2534, 2537, 2550, 2566, 2571,
    2573, 2579, 2583, 2589, 2593, 2605, 2614, 2615, 2619, 2620, 2632,
    2636, 2637, 2644, 2646, 2652.
Joynes, Edward S.,   551, 2276, 2279,
Kellogg, Brainerd, 2543.
Kemble, J.P.,   2633, 2639.
Kippax, H.C.,   2938.
Lee, Margaret L., 1948.
Lodge, George Cabot, 1873-1909, 1577.
Lopez, Mathias, d. 1845, 130, 1430, 1910.
Mackail, J.W.,   1668.
Mencken, Henry Louis, 1880-1956, 301.
Moore, F.E., 1580.
Neilson, William Allen, 306.
Nicoll, Allardyce, 242.
Nolan, Paul T., 213, 1379, 3118, 3119.
Nordmann, Rudolf, 69.
Oxberry, William, 1784-1824,   2533, 2544, 2549, 2562, 2565, 2570,
    2578, 2588, 2602, 2604, 2609, 2618, 2624, 2629, 2634, 2643, 2645,
    2651, 3030.
P., P.,   532.
Payne, William Morton, 2856.
Phelps, Pauline, 2528, 3044.
Phelps, William Lyon, 253, 1297.
Porter, Charlotte, 2541.
Ricci, Seymour De, 1736.
Robertson, Thomas William Shafto, 1857-1895, 2382.
Rolfe, William J.,   2546, 2541.
Rosenberg, S.L. Millard, 436.

Sargent, Epes, 1903.
Sedgwick, Alfred B., 254.
Shepherd, Richard Herne, 222.
Short, Marion, 2528, 3044.
Steevens, George, 1736-1800, 2530, 2531, 2534, 2537, 2550, 2566, 2571, 2573, 2579, 2583, 2589, 2593, 2605, 2614, 2615, 2619, 2626, 2632, 2636, 2637, 2644, 2646, 2652.
Stratton, Clarence, 1290.
Sturtevant, Catherine, 626.
Sumichrast, Frederick C., 552.
Tucker, Stephen Isaacson, 1835-1887, 2188.
Vocht, Henry de, 162.
Weiser, H.D., 2539.
Wemyss, Francis Courtney, 1797-1859, 377, 2309, 2695.
Williams, H.I., 1862.
Winter, William, 1836-1917, 236, 2896.
Young, A.B., 2987.

Index of Authors and Joint Authors

INDEX OF AUTHORS, JOINT AUTHORS, AND OTHERS
WHO MIGHT BE CONSIDERED AS RESPONSIBLE
FOR THE WORKS, BUT WHO ARE NOT
THE MAIN ENTRY

Bocage, 625.
Boccaccio, Giovanni, 1313-1375, 2105.
Bouilly, Jean Nicolas, 1763-1842, 1198.
Braughn, George H., joint author, 950.
Brazier, Nicolas, 1783-1838, 2990.
Bridgers, Ann Preston, joint author, 2.
Brieux, Eugène, 1858-1932, 736.
Brisbarre, Édouard, Louis Alexandre, 1818-1871, 262.
Brockett, O.G., 840.
Brough, J.C., joint author, 2488.
Brougham, John, 1810-1880, joint author, 1525.
Brown, Marian Katherine, joint author, 410.
Browne, William, of Tavistock, 2683.
Browning, Robert, 1812-1889, 2445.
Brulay, 2396.
Bulwer, Sir Henry, 1801-1872, 341.
Bunner, Henry Cuyler, 1855-1896, 1722.
Burnand, Francis Cowley, joint author, 3133.
Burton, John, joint author, 593.
Bury, Joseph Désiré Fulgence de, d. 1845, 2253, 2259.
Byron, George Gordon Noël Byron, 6th baron, 1788-1824, 1781.
Caigniez, Louis Charles, 1762-1842, 1419, 1678, 2229.
Calderón de la Barca, Pedro, 1600-1681, 1721.
Call, William T., joint author, 2365.
Carmouche, Pierre François Adlophe, 1797-1868?, 374.
Carré, M., joint author, 122.
Chaucer, Geoffrey, 1345?-1400, 2776.
Chekhov, Anton Pavlovich, 1860-1904, 736.
Cheltnam, Charles Smith, 2488.
Chivot, Henry, 463.
Cibber, Colley, 1671-1757, joint author, 3014.
Cibber, Theophilus, 1703-1758, 1659.
Cobb, Sylvanus, 1823-1887, 331.
Collins, William Wilkie, 1824-1889, joint author, 735.
Colman, George, 1762-1836, 2336.
Connelly, Marc, 1890-   , 2699.
Constanduros, Mabel, 1794.
Cooper, James Fenimore, 1789-1851, 888, 3069.
Cormon, Eugene, joint author, 697.
Corneille, Pierre, 1606-1684, 900, 1721, 3100.
Cottin, Marie Risteau, called Sophie, 1770-1807, 2341.
Courcy, de, joint author, 625.
Coyne, J. Denis, joint author, 564.
Croly, George, 1780-1860, supposed author, 2739.
Cumberland, Richard, 1732-1811, 2074.
Daryl, Disney, 2488.
D'Avenant, Sir William, 1608-1668, 2633.
De Bornier, H., 1722.

Index of Translators

Danton, Annina Periam

Danton, Annina Periam, 1034.
Danton, George Henry, 1034.
Da Ponte, Lorenzo, 1188.
Day, W.G., 1300.
Delafield, John H., 1519, 1739.
Duddington, J.N., 1450.
Dukes, Ashley, 1382.
Dunlap, William, 3209.
Edgren, A. Hjalmar, 1383.
Edwards, Pierrepont, 861.
Eisemann, Frederick, 301, 485.
Erichsen, N., 2809, 736.
Fell, Marina, 484.
Field, Claud, 2804.
Fielding, Henry, 1707-1754, 1797.
Fitzball, Edward, 1792-1873, 68.
Fleming. George, pseud., 2419.
Frank, Grace, 2825.
Freeman-Tilden, 181.
Frere, J. Hookham, 1721.
Gillpatrick, Wallace, 1053.
Ginty, E. Beall, 2824.
Glazier, B.F., 79.
Gosse, Edmund, 1293.
Graham, James, 806, 807.
Green, Julian, 2099.
Grummann, Paul H., 1081.
Guthrie, William Norman, 1296.
Harned, Mary, 1128, 2805.
Haughton, John A., 1168.
Hayden, Philip M., 1721.
Heard, John, 1099.
Henderson, Ernest F., 926.
Herford, C.H., 1285.
Herman, John Armstrong, 193.
Hickie, William James, 57, 58.
Hill, Barton, 2442.
Holcroft, Fanny, 1545.
Hollander, Lee M., 736.
House, Roy Temple, 1130, 1193.
Hovey, Richard, 736, 1676.
Howard, Velma Swanston, 2807, 2811.
Inchbald, Elizabeth Simpson, 1753-1821, 1453.
Irving, Lawrence, 998.
Jackson, N. Hart, 697.
Jebb, Sir Richard Claverhouse, 1841-1905, 1721.
Kaathoven, Alive Van, 600.
Klingenfeld, Emma, 1295.

Langner, Ruth, 908, 805.
Leonard, William Ellery, 736, 2826.
Lewis, Matthew Gregory, 1775-1818, 2472.
Lewisohn, Ludwig, 1129.
Logan, W. McGregor, 1433A.
Lord, Henrietta Frances, 1291, 1294.
Lynch, Hannah, 804.
Lyons, Joseph A., 1796, 1784.
Lyster, Frederic, 123.
MacCarthy, Denis Florence, 1721.
Mach, Edmund von, 2483.
McLaren, Malcolm, 987.
MacLeod, Melba I., 840.
Marshall, Beatrice, 2821.
Martext, Oliver, of Arden, pseud., 3025.
Martin, Sir Theodore, 1721, 2478.
Marx-Aveling, Mrs. F., 1287, 1292.
Mathews, Charles, 900.
Meader, Clarence L., 49.
Medbourne, M., 1800.
Meltzer, Charles Henry, 1131, 1132.
Mial, Bernard, 1675.
Middleton, Edda, 1037.
Miller, Frank Justus, 2520.
Miller, Theodore A., 1036.
Milliet, Paul, 2283.
Moir, George, 2477.
Montanelli, Joseph, 1520.
Morgan, Bayard Quincy, 1195.
Morgan, Morris H., 1721.
Morrison, Mary, 736, 1133.
Morshead, E.D.A., 1721.
Murphy, Olive Frances, 482.
Murray, George Gilbert Aimé, 1866-1957, 15, 59, 547, 839, 1721, 2753.
Myrick, Arthur B., 1721.
Newberry, John Strong, 2418.
Orbeck, Anders, 1289.
Otway, Thomas, 1795.
Oxenford, John, 1812-1877, 192.
Page, Curtis Hidden, 1721.
Parker, Louis N., 2417.
Payne, John Howard, 1791-1852, 764A, 765.
Phillips, Henry, 469.
Pierra, Adolfo, 438.
Pierson, Merle, 1721.
Plumptre, E.H., 2751.
Pogue, Arrah na, 247.
Pray, Isaac C., 963.

Prichard, J.V.

Wiemken, Helmut, 843.
Wigan, Horace, 192.
Wilkinson, Sarah S., 764.
Williams, Henry L., 1738, 2440.
Williams, Thomas, 962, 1520.
Winslow, Charles Edward Amory, 2823.
Winter, William, 1173.
Young, Stark, 487.
Ziegler, Francis J., 2806, 2813, 2814.

Index of Pseudonyms

Index of Illustrators

Angell, Clare, 2968.
Blashfield, Edwin Howland, 227.
Cruikshank, George, 1792-1878, 2894.
Cruikshank, Isaac R., 2548, 2556, 2561, 2564, 2569, 2577, 2596, 2601, 2623, 2658.
Cruikshank, R., 1433A.
Egan, Pierce, the younger, 2215, 2220, 2264.
Falls, Charles B., 1673.
Ferris, Stephan J., 1463.
Findlay, 875.
Fisher, Harrison, 443.
Genthe, Arnold, 1144, 1651.
Herford, Oliver, 1165.
Hogarth, William, 1697-1764, 1074.
Hudson, William L., 2749.
Jones, T., 1872, 2642.
MacKaye, Arvia, 1655.
McPharlin, Paul, 661.
Merritt, Hal, 586.
Mumford, Ethel W., 3066.
Nendick, Buckton, 1960.
Otts, J.W., 3202.
Rackham, Arthur, 500.
Smith, Orrin, 2220.
Speed, Lancelot, 185.
Stanley, Emma, 226.
Wall, J.P., 1533.
Webster, F.W., 2225.

Index of Composers

Mallandaine